PLATO'S REASONS

SUNY series in Ancient Greek Philosophy

Anthony Preus, editor

PLATO'S REASONS
Logician, Rhetorician, Dialectician

Christopher W. Tindale

Published by State University of New York Press, Albany

© 2023 State University of New York

All rights reserved

Printed in the United States of America

No part of this book may be used or reproduced in any manner whatsoever without written permission. No part of this book may be stored in a retrieval system or transmitted in any form or by any means including electronic, electrostatic, magnetic tape, mechanical, photocopying, recording, or otherwise without the prior permission in writing of the publisher.

For information, contact State University of New York Press, Albany, NY
www.sunypress.edu

Library of Congress Cataloging-in-Publication Data

Name: Tindale, Christopher W. (Christopher William), author.
Title: Plato's reasons : logician, rhetorician, dialectician / Christopher W. Tindale.
Other titles: Reasons
Description: Albany : State University of New York Press, [2023] | Series: SUNY series in ancient Greek philosophy | Includes bibliographical references and index.
Identifiers: LCCN 2023009050 | ISBN 9781438495538 (hardcover : alk. paper) | ISBN 9781438495552 (ebook) | ISBN 9781438495545 (pbk. : alk. paper)
Subjects: LCSH: Plato. | Reasoning. | Logic. | Dialectic.
Classification: LCC B398.L85 T56 2023 | DDC 128—dc23/eng/20230801
LC record available at https://lccn.loc.gov/2023009050

10 9 8 7 6 5 4 3 2 1

In Memoriam,
Klaus Grötsch and Andreas Welzel,
Es ist nicht die Länge der Reise,
sondern die Freunde die man unterwegs findet.

Contents

Acknowledgments — ix

Abbreviations and Translations — xi

General Introduction: Inside the City of Reason — 1

Part I: The Logician

Introduction to Part I: Plato and the Intricacies of Logic — 15

Chapter 1   Socratic Arguments — 25

Chapter 2   Refutation: The Logic of the Early Dialogues — 47

Chapter 3   Contentious Arguments: Preconditions for Aristotle's Theory of "Fallacy" in the Dialogues of Plato — 63

Chapter 4   Strong Arguments — 89

Part II: The Rhetorician

Introduction to Part II: Plato's Style — 109

Chapter 5   Plato's Attack on Rhetoric: Fractures in the Standard Narrative — 115

Chapter 6	The *Atopic* Philosopher	135
Chapter 7	Platonic Devices	155
Chapter 8	Back in Plato's Labyrinth: The Rhetorical Challenges of the *Republic*	179
Chapter 9	Rhetoric in the Middle Plato and Beyond	201

Part III: The Dialectician

Introduction to Part III: A New Dialectic		223
Chapter 10	Tracing Dialectic	229
Chapter 11	The Song that Dialectic Sings: Methods in the Middle Dialogues	251
Chapter 12	The Dialectician	271
References		293
Index		309

Acknowledgments

I began this project sometime during 2005, although it experienced several false starts. The desire to isolate and study distinct aspects of Plato's argumentative practice and character has been particularly challenging and led to repeated reorganizations of the material until something workable eventually emerged. Along the way I have accrued debts to many people, particularly to classes of students in senior seminars at Trent University and the University of Windsor. They are too numerous to mention here, but I thank them all for their enthusiasm and interest as, talking together, we found our way through the maze-like dialogues of our subject.
Several of the arguments from parts I and III and almost all the chapters in part II had some exposure at conferences over the years, particularly the annual meetings of the Classical Association of Canada, and at talks at my current institution. I am grateful for the patience and constructive suggestions of many audiences of the CAC, as well as to my colleagues in Philosophy and Classics at the University of Windsor.

Several people deserve special mention. Patricia Fagan generously checked and corrected my transliterations of the Greek. Jianfeng Wang pulled the bibliography into shape, correcting a number of errors in the process. Others have been supportive of the project in different ways, among these I must mention Brad Levett, Daniel Mejia Saldarriaga, Philip Rose, Christopher Roser, and Antonio Rossini.

I have been fortunate to see several book projects find the light of day, but with none of them have I received the kind of meticulously detailed reviews that were provided by the three readers for the press. Beyond much welcomed encouragement, they directed me away from errors and toward sources that I might not otherwise have found, and they helped the development of a number of ideas. I am extremely grateful to all three for taking so seriously the often onerous task of manuscript review, and to my editor at SUNY press, Michael Rinella, for his support of the project, including the enlisting of such strong readers. Also at SUNY, my gratitude goes to Diane Ganeles and all involved in the production of the volume.

Given the length of time that it has taken to complete this project, it is perhaps unsurprising that some with whom I had discussed ideas are no longer present to judge the result. They include Klaus Grötsch and Andreas Welzel, to whom the book is dedicated and who were engaged in the project at the early and later stages, respectively. Their influence is present in the conversations behind this book.

Abbreviations and Translations

Platonic (and Pseudo-Platonic) Texts

Alc.	*Alcibiades*
Alc2.	*Second Alcibiades*
Ap.	*Apology*
Chrm.	*Charmides*
Cl.	*Cleitophon*
Cra.	*Cratylus*
Crito.	*Crito*
Def.	*Definitions*
Euthd.	*Euthydemus*
Euthphr.	*Euthyphro*
Grg.	*Gorgias*
H.Ma.	*Hippias Major*
H.Mi.	*Hippias Minor*
Lch.	*Laches*
Laws.	*Laws*
Ltr.	*Letters*
Lys.	*Lysis*
Menex.	*Menexenus*
Meno.	*Meno*
Phd.	*Phaedo*
Phdr.	*Phaedrus*
Phil.	*Philebus*
Prm.	*Parmenides*
Prt.	*Protagoras*
Rep.	*Republic*

Sph.   *Sophist*
Stm.   *Statesman*
Symp.   *Symposium*
Tht.   *Theaetetus*
Ti.   *Timaeus*

Aristotle's Texts

Apr.   *Prior Analytics*
Metaph.   *Metaphysics*
NE.   *Nicomachean Ethics*
PA.   *Parts of Animals*
Poet.   *Poetics*
Pol.   *Politics*
Rhet.   *Rhetoric*
Top.   *Topics*

Other Sources

DK.   Diels, Hermann, and Walter Kranz. 1952. *Die Fragmente der Vorsokratiker.* Berlin: Weidmannsche Verlagbuchhandlung. (Diels, Hermann, and Walter Franz. *The Older Sophists.* Edited by Rosamund Kent Sprague. Columbia: University of South Carolina Press, 1972.)

DL.   *Diogenes Laertius: The Lives and Opinions of Eminent Philosophers.*

General Introduction

Inside the City of Reason

Plato was an Athenian designer of labyrinths who lived in the fifth century before the common era. The labyrinths he built, he built from words, reflecting the ways language leads us into confusion. And the paths of escape he indicated, through a complex mixture of individual words and conversation—through *dialegesthai*—have offered readers over the centuries the possibility of understanding the meanings that matter to them. Through the medium of the dialogue form, Plato drew on all his resources as a logician, rhetorician, and dialectician, valuing each of these as integral parts of his project. How they manifest themselves and operate together in Plato's work is the subject of this book.

While it is clear that on many points we think like Plato, negotiating the footnotes of our tradition, or at least owe the contours of our thinking to his insights, it is far less clear that he thought like us. This makes the task of clarifying his ideas on logic, rhetoric, and dialectic that much more challenging. On the one hand, Plato's thought is so inflected with the conditions that produced it that it can never be totally "freed" from itself and cast into contemporary meaning. On the other hand, he is so encased in our own traditions of thought that unbroken threads of meaning across the centuries are assumed and sometimes asserted. Why we would be interested in illuminating Plato's conceptions of logic, rhetoric, and dialectic is simply because these three tools or methods, or however we conceive them, represent important perspectives of contemporary argumentation theory. Insofar as a history of this interdisciplinary field is to be gathered, Plato's place in it has yet to be established. To contribute to such a history is another goal of this book.

For most scholars working in the late twentieth century and early twenty-first century, the roots of argumentation theory can be traced to Aristotle and the attention he gives to three types of argument: the logical, the dialectical, and the rhetorical (Wenzel 2006). While Aristotle treats dialectic and rhetoric as complementary (*antistrophic: Rhet.* 1345a), each of the two is conceptually distinct, as is his treatment of logic. While there is recognition of an interest in argumentation in earlier thinkers, the orthodoxy of an Aristotelian origin has remained largely uncontested. Several features of the current study will correct, or at least challenge, that narrative. Pre-Aristotelian investigations bring to light an implicit set of ideas in Plato that indicate a rich engagement with argumentation in its logical, rhetorical, and dialectical aspects. This is not to propose that we would find a fully-formed logic in Plato similar to that which appears in Aristotle, nor that Plato understands rhetoric and dialectic in ways with which Aristotle would fully agree. It is to suggest that Aristotle's treatments do not arise in a vacuum but emerge instead from activities in the Academy with which he would have been fully acquainted. On these terms, the logic that appears is distinct from the abstract logic of the tradition, even as Plato's later dialectic lays its foundation. Instead, we find promoted in the early and middle dialogues logical relations that concern the contexts of argumentative situations and the agents operating in those contexts. In similar ways, the rhetoric that Plato comes to endorse and rely upon values the communicative power of argumentation and the central role that audiences play in its progress. Related to this, the evolving dialectic, transformed from earlier Socratic practice, depends for its expression and application on an array of strategies and methods related to different dialogic goals. All of these points will be familiar to contemporary theorists who have worked on Aristotle's argumentation theory.

In questioning the Aristotelian orthodoxy, discussions will arise in response to several important questions. Can we say, for example, that Socratic argument consists of no more than the *elenchus*? That Plato's attitude toward rhetoric was one of general dismissal such that it has no role to play in the development of his thought? That Plato's dialectic is the same method that we see Socrates using in the early dialogues? I have already suggested negative responses to these questions, and on a certain level I think that is appreciated, and yet ideas persist that suggest otherwise. That resistance to revision is a further point to consider in the pages ahead.

Each section of this work has its own introduction wherein I situate the discussions of those chapters in the context of the tradition and the principal ideas that tend to dominate the discussions of the concept involved, whether it be logic, rhetoric, or dialectic. In this general introduction I propose to explain the project as a whole and set it into a slightly different context.

Plato's Logic

Much of the now standard story on Plato's logic involves modern and contemporary logicians assuming that what they find in Plato is evidence of abstract logical thought. Just as much of the standard story on Socratic argument limits us to the *elenchus*. The grounds for both of these claims are explored and found wanting in the chapters of part I.

While there is indeed a sense of abstractness to the logic we associate with Plato's later dialectic, there is something far more interesting happening in the earlier stages of his work. Abstractness, Richard Robinson ([1941] 1953) insists, is something that contemporary logicians read into Plato's dialogues, falling victim to the common ailment of finding what one had set out to look for in the first place. The arguments of Robinson and others that counter this perspective are detailed in the early chapters, but we might anticipate them here by considering just how unavoidable it is for translations to follow the general interpretations of the translators.[1] As my bibliography makes clear, when it comes to editions of Plato's works, I have availed myself of a number of translations, from different generations of translators, and often used multiple translations of a single dialogue. In this way, I have drawn on different readings of the underlying ideas and monitored some of the debates that emerge over choices of translation. In addition, I have offered modifications of my own where I deemed it appropriate. Translating Plato or deciding on the "best" translation of a dialogue is not a straightforward matter.

Each translator strives for accuracy on her or his own terms. There are exceptions to this rule, of course. Alain Badiou's (2012) "hyper-translation" of the *Republic* tells us more about how Badiou might have written the work

---

1. A case in point that concerns Aristotle rather than Plato is the appearance in 2018 of three new translations of the *Rhetoric*, one by a political theorist (Aristotle 2019—it appeared in 2018), another by a philosopher (Aristotle 2018a), and a third by a classicist (Aristotle 2018b). Unsurprisingly, significant choices of words and phrases reflect the disciplinary perspectives of the translators and the ways in which they interpret discussions according to the larger background understanding of what they judge to be important.

himself than it expresses any real concern to capture Plato's intentions. So, he provides additions and corrections to the political philosophy, along with some interpretative interventions (Badiou challenges the received view of Plato's dualism, for example—362n3), and there is a marked anti-rhetorical thrust to the translation that characterizes Badiou's work in general. On a different track is I. A. Richards's (1942) insightful but notably sparse "literal" translation of the *Republic* that reflects Richards's decades-long work in what he called Basic English and his efforts to promote it.[2] Badiou and Richards reflect some of the different ways a translator might approach Plato and the kinds of license they feel authorized to adopt.

Within such larger decisions are the "smaller" worries over the correct way of rendering a term in English—decisions that turn out to have considerable bearing on larger questions of Plato's meaning. With regard to his status as a logician recognizable to contemporary readers, for example, is the reading of *sumphonein* in the *Phaedo*. In chapter 11, I will review some of the different possible translations attached to this term and the very different conceptions of Plato's view of hypothesis that follow from the various choices. Such variety in translation encourages interpretations ranging from a strong entailment (as in "following logically from") to a weaker agreement (as in "in harmony with"). At stake is the kind of dialectician (and logician) we judge Plato to have been.[3]

If this book fits with any earlier effort, it would be that of Richard Robinson and his *Plato's Earlier Dialectic*, first published in 1941, and in my view a seminal text for the subjects addressed. The initial edition was widely reviewed and many of those reviews challenged some of Robinson's translation choices. The unavailability of the first edition after the war created an opportunity for Robinson to publish a revision, one that allowed him to make corrections where he thought they were warranted and respond to criticisms where he thought such a response was also warranted. The principal focus of his defense concerns what he calls evolutionist and creationist views. Robinson promotes the first, which holds that human thinking has evolved with specific elements emerging at various points in our history. This includes the development of logical thought. The oppos-

---

2. By any standard that measures reception, this translation should be judged a success. The US government printed two million copies for its overseas armed forces.

3. In a similar vein, *dialegesthai* invites a comparable range of choices across an array of dialogues as its meaning seems to vary from the casual conversation to the focused scrutiny of a company investigating a term's definition (Timmerman and Schiappa 2010).

ing—creationist—view holds that principles of logic are self-evident and have been present in human thought since the outset, always available to the right kind of mind. Hence, they judge the logic of Plato against modern insights. Paul Friedländer's (1945) ambivalent review is a case in point. Although generally sympathetic to Robinson's promotion of Plato's "loose way" of expressing himself logically, he questions several of his translations as misleading (when Friedländer believes Plato is pursuing a strictly defined logical process, for example).

Subsequently, the thrust of some of the reviews of the second edition of Robinson's study still focus mainly, or even solely (Kerferd 1955), on the disputed details of the logic. Robinson's interpretations of Plato's understanding of the early *elenchus* and of hypotheses are both challenged. With respect to the *elenchus*, he holds that Plato believed an interlocutor was refuted by his own argument without any additional premises. He allows that there are places where additional premises are used, but he judges that Plato was simply unaware of this. Robinson's position on Plato's early logic is thus largely unchanged between the two editions (while his position on hypotheses was revised in light of earlier criticisms). Plato's status as a logician and the kind of logic he endorsed remain matters of contention. While this book has no ambitions toward resolving these matters, I hope to advance a coherent picture of Plato as logician that shows a progressive treatment from the early Socratic dialogues through to the later engagement with a developed sense of dialectic.

Then there are the matters of how we should view Socratic argument itself and whether it should be restricted to what we understand as the *elenchus*. I would note here that whether argument types attributed to Socrates in Plato's dialogues were employed by the historical figure is largely beside the point. I am principally interested in Plato's engagement with argument and the way he negotiates the use of the different types that are employed. But this said, some distinction between Plato's ideas and the practices of the historical Socrates are relevant to my study. In pursuing the emergence of Platonic dialectical argumentation from its Socratic predecessor, I adopt the distinction Gregory Vlastos (1994) makes between $Socrates_E$, the historical figure, and $Socrates_M$, the Platonic invention. But whether the distinction comes down solely to Plato's creative imagination is again beyond our ability to decide. Still, I think there are more reasons to be confident about our knowledge of the historical Socrates than commentators like Robin Waterfield (2009) suggest. Waterfield finds the evidence for what Socrates actually did and believed to rely too heavily on Plato's account and so he looks outside the dialogues for further evidence with which to compile an image of an anti-democratic provocateur (Waterfield 2009, 29). But we know more than this. Insofar, I will argue, as these Greeks were committed to a strong relationship between identity and action, we can construct an interesting image of the *philosophy* of the historical Socrates by focusing on practices that are distinct from Plato's own philosophical practices. Yes, they were both ethical thinkers who focused on the virtues. But on the negative side, unlike Plato, Socrates did not write, teach, or actively engage in politics. They present quite contrasting views of philosophy in action, and therefore of philosophy itself. Along these lines, any tendency to equate Socratic argument with the *elenchus* alone may come down to a failure to appreciate the distinctions at work in the arguments Plato had Socrates advance.

In part I, I explore a wider sense of Socratic dialectic that includes at least three separate types of argument, each with a different goal. While the *elenchus* aims at refutation of those who claim to know (largely more established figures of Athenian society), the hortatory (protreptic) argument and the maieutic argument both exhibit different goals and engage a different, younger audience. The hortatory argument presents reasons for why someone should turn to a specific action, principally to take up philosophy, while the maieutic arguments draw ideas from the interlocutors in a way that advances the understanding of a concept for all concerned (something missing from the results of the *elenchus*). It is the last of these, the maieutic, that finds its place in the later dialectic of Plato and so will be revisited in part III. But each of these three types of argument indicates an engaged logic that we can describe as ethotic.

Plato's *Dialogues* conjures an atmosphere of intimacy that belies any insistence that the logic that drives his discussions, especially in the early drama-infused texts of the Socratic period, is in any way abstract. Indeed, we can, at our convenience and to the degree that we are so disposed, extract arguments from the dialectic and treat them to the kind of scrutiny that characterizes the contemporary logic classroom, just as we can do this with any discourses from any period of our history, whether or not such analyses were intended by the producers of those discourses or are even an appropriate way to approach them. Without question, Plato's sense of logic becomes more complex in the later dialogues, but it still retains its roots in the lives of those engaged in any inquiry; it still retains the character of an ethotic logic.

By an ethotic logic I mean one personalized and rooted in human character, or what will come to be called *ethos*. Contemporary readers may be perplexed at Aristotle's admission in his *Rhetoric* that audiences are often not persuaded by good arguments. Additional "proofs" are required, and one of those lies with the character of the arguer. "Persuasion is through character," insists Aristotle, "whenever the speech is stated so that it makes the speaker worthy of trust" (*Rhet.* 1356a4–5). He then goes on to add the surprising observation that *ethos* "is pretty much (one might almost say) the most controlling factor in persuasion" (Aristotle 2018b).

From where did such stress on the importance of character arise? In part, the answer lies in Greek society itself, but it would also have been reinforced by a particular reading of Plato's dialogues. Consider how the "logical" examination of Euthyphro that provides one illustration of the *elenchus* is a deep examination of Euthyphro's beliefs that has serious consequences for the rightness or wrongness of his actions. As explained early in that dialogue, Socrates is on his way to the court to defend himself against a charge of impiety, and it would be enormously valuable to him if Euthyphro could provide a definition of "piety" that Socrates could use in his defense. But it is just as important that Euthyphro should be able to give an account that justifies his actions in bringing charges against his own father because of that man's supposed wrongdoing. As Euthyphro first explains the concern, "it is impious, they say, for a son to prosecute his father for murder" (*Euth.* 4d–e); whereas Euthyphro is convinced it would be impious for him *not* to do so. There's no middle ground here, no room for inaction. So Euthyphro *must* have the knowledge that justifies his action and the ideas to which he is committed if he is to maintain his self-worth. The investigation is not into an abstract concept (piety), as some commentators would have it, but into the life of the interlocutor. Character is on display here and is found wanting by the logic of the *elenchus*, but this is an ethotic logic.

The ethotic character is prevalent throughout extant texts that come down to us and reflects the important connection between action and argument. Consider what is conveyed by Antisthenes when he writes in the *Ajax*: "Do not examine words when you are judging virtue, but rather actions. For a battle too is decided not by word but by action" (Boys-Stones and Rowe 2013, 23). Virtue is to be discerned not in the words that people put forward but in the actions they perform. Another way of casting this is to consider the way actions can be used to justify positions and thus operate argumentatively. That is what we see clearly expressed by the Socrates of the *Apology*, who offers his judges "substantial evidence . . . not words but what [they] value more, deeds" (*Apol.* 32a). Like words, actions are public expressions of character, and perhaps the thinking here is that they are less susceptible to misinterpretation. Whatever the explanation, a consequence of this position can be seen in attempts to draw character into the light of day through words that express it, and on this front the *elenchus* qualifies. That it can also be cast in terms of later logical systems is neither here nor there; its power lies in its ethotic probing and the consequences such exercises have for the lives of those involved.

Plato's Rhetoric

There is a tendency in the literature to place Plato at the head of a long history of negative reactions to rhetoric. But the reality is more ambiguous.[4] Consider, for example, the very different reactions of two later writers, Aristides (c. 117–c. 177 AD) and Quintilian (c. 35–c. 100 AD). Aristides's (2017; 2021) orations include extensive replies to Plato challenging the negative view of rhetoric on display in his work, particularly the *Gorgias*, and finding in Plato's own accounts an appreciation of the "real form of oratory" (2017, 653). Aristides thus believes he is drawing from Plato what is present but unconscious. Quintilian (2015), by contrast, finds in Plato a champion of rhetoric. Of the *Gorgias*, he writes, "most writers, satisfied with reading a few passages from Plato's *Gorgias*, unskillfully extracted by their predecessors (for they neither consult the whole of that dialogue, nor any of the other writings of Plato), have fallen into a very grave error, supposing that the philosopher entertained such an opinion as to think that oratory was not an art" (Quintilian *Institutio Oratoria*, bk. 2, 15.24–5). Quintilian thus believes he is drawing from Plato what is consciously present.

Of all the ways in which Plato has been misjudged by the tradition, labeling him as a despiser of rhetoric is the most egregious. In the five chapters of part II, I work to reinforce Quintilian's observation and extend it far beyond the *Gorgias*. Not only did Plato recognize the need to harness the power of rhetoric for his own political goals, but he also stands out as an accomplished rhetor in his own right.

I discuss exactly what it is about rhetoric that concerns Plato in the *Gorgias* (387–85), concluding that his target there is a political rhetoric that we might associate with Periclean Athens. This was a rhetoric that

---

4. While we might trace the current disdain toward rhetoric to the work of Ramus and his critiques of Aristotle, Cicero, and Quintilian, the ambivalences toward rhetoric were active long before the 1500s (see Ong 1958).

dominated the Athenian responses in the Melian debate reported by Thucydides and the subsequent subjugation of Melos. On this darkest moment in then-recent Athenian history, Plato, unlike almost every other writer of his period, appears strangely silent given his anti-democratic propensities. But allowing also that Plato will often use silence as a rhetorical strategy to draw attention to an idea, the absence of a direct reference to Melos no longer appears so unusual.

In rejecting the political rhetoric that had proved popular in the city in which he was raised, Plato advocates a rhetoric that must promote justice over injustice. This prefigures the argument of the *Phaedrus* (the events of which take place *outside* of the political sphere) for a true rhetoric that contrasts the *eikotic*. Here, the question of whether rhetoric is an art with a corresponding knowledge is settled in the affirmative, and the philosopher can now return to the polis better equipped to engage friend and foe while crafting an environment in which all can flourish.

In general, Plato is a rhetorical force. Rhetoricians theorize about rhetoric; rhetors produce and deliver it. Plato is both. Theorizing about rhetoric begins in the *Gorgias*, reaches a firm account in the *Phaedrus*, and receives supplementary details thereafter in dialogues as far ranging as the *Statesman* and *Philebus*. Plato's adoption of rhetorical strategies is clear throughout his work, and I explore several of them, like the silence alluded to above and the adoption of mythic discourse to address specific audiences. In many ways such strategies confirm the choice of the dialogue form to communicate ideas. This is a mode of discourse that most efficiently captures the range of Plato's stylistic achievements.

Nowhere is all this more apparent than in the *Republic*, where two important questions come to the fore: (1) What discourse best allows the promotion of justice in the state, which is to ask, How can the polis be rhetorically addressed in ways that promote the general interests? (2) How are novice philosophers addressed with protreptic arguments in their education? The use of rhetoric in the *Republic* and the centrality of its importance to the project that emerges there sets the groundwork for the promotion of rhetoric in subsequent dialogues. In later dialogues like the *Sophist*, the *Statesman*, and *Philebus*, rhetoric is far from absent, as the silence of the literature on Plato might suggest. In fact, its value as a necessary aid to dialectic is clarified.

This means that the presence of a positive conception of civic rhetoric in Aristotle is far from original, and the importance of rhetorical argumentation is not without precedence in Aristotle's immediate influences. With more apparent organization, due to the different type of texts involved, Aristotle was able to build on the ideas that Plato had advanced, offering a model of rhetorical reason already suggested by his mentor.

Plato's Dialectic

In a number of respects, chapter 9 could find its place in either part II or III since in discussing the role of rhetoric in Plato's later works it is impossible to avoid detailed accounts of some of his dialectical tools and strategies. And as the forgoing will suggest, disentangling any of the three subjects of study from Plato's treatments can be challenging. In the later dialogues, the logic that had receded into the background is reasserted in the methods of dialectic, just as the value of rhetoric finds further emphasis. But by the time we emerge from the *Republic*, there is without doubt a dialectic in force that differs markedly from its Socratic predecessor.

As we turn to consider Plato's mature account of dialectic, there is a complexity that confounds us, especially if we take late dialogues like *Sophist* and *Statesman* to be genuine investigations of those concepts (the Sophist and the Statesman) intent on discovering the agreed definition in each case. Commentators are quick to point out that on this front the investigations fail and the use of dialectic is often confused. But on what terms might they be judged successful? What is actually going on in those illustrative cases of Platonic dialectic? Answers to these questions are offered in the chapters of part III.

Part of the story of dialectic as it appears and evolves across the works of Plato is the range accorded to the spectrum term *dialegesthai* (Timmerman and Schiappa 2010). How this term is translated in various dialogues can be an eye-opener in part because of the ways by which Plato so often hides the serious idea in the casual remark. I made reference to this variety of meanings for *dialegesthai* in note 3. Its possible senses accommodate the casual conversation as well as the cooperative investigation into a term's definition, something that occupies the dialecticians of Plato's late dialogues.

Two specific things come to the fore in part III. One is an emphasis on the late pedagogy captured in the dialogues, reflective of what happens in the Academy, and the second is the way (partly in the course of this pedagogy) "dialectic" becomes an umbrella term for a variety of methods matched to the minds that learn to employ them.

The dialogues reveal an evolution of Plato's methodology, abandoning the Socratic dialogue for the hypothetical method and then the hypothetical method for the method of Collection and Division. These best capture the dialogical nature of Plato's dialectic, but we also see at work the use of examples, images, and myth. Plato employs what works, and what works for him changes, just as the audiences he is addressing vary. One can imagine in the background the ways in which the curricula of the Academy would be modified to reflect the emerging methods of the day, particularly from the hypothetical method to the method of Collection and Division. There would have been a period, then, during which the students focused on developing a hypothesis to test ideas and develop definitions.[5] In fact, this focus on definitions, a vestige of the Socratic practice, finds its apotheosis in the late dialogues. Whatever the provenance of the book *Definitions*, variously attributed to Speusippus and other members of the Academy, it certainly reflects an abiding interest of the scholars and students working there. In this sense, the pedagogical aspect of the dialectic is given prominence in the closing sections of the book.

Plato's co-constructing of knowledge through dialectic uses what in today's terms would be called an inquiry dialogue (Walton 2006a). Participants start with the need to acquire proof about some matter, conduct a search for evidence, and achieve the goal of proving (or disproving) a hypothesis (Walton 2006a, 183). That this process resonates with the activity of the science laboratory simply indicates the distance between early and contemporary instantiations of inquiry. I. A. Richards (1942) captured this well in his general advice on the subject of reading: "What should guide the reader's mind? Our answer was 'Our awareness of interdependence of how things hang together, which makes us able to give and audit an account of what may be meant in a discussion—that highest activity of REASON which Plato named Dialectic'" (240). Indeed, this highest achievement of a discussion (*dialegesthai* again) is the goal of the dialectic of the late dialogues, and the specter of the Academy in which such discussions were pursued haunts those works.

---

5. Such a stage may be reflected in some of Aristotle's works, if these illustrate the teaching he did at the Academy (see Kennedy's introduction in Aristotle 2007, 4–5). His "definition" of rhetoric, for example, is posed hypothetically as a working definition to be explored: "Let rhetoric be . . ." (*estō dē*). Here, there is no commitment to a definition, just an interest in exploring the possibilities of a direction of inquiry (*Rhet.* 1355b25; Aristotle 2007).

So, a vestige (or development) of the maieutic argument that was a crucial part of the argumentative practice of Socrates is apparent in the pedagogical exercises of the later dialogues. The examining (and refuting) of experts has been left aside after the *Republic*. But the drawing of ideas out of the young, although modified in these late dialogues, has its roots in Socrates's midwifery. Socrates may have been moved to the sidelines of most late dialogues, or even dismissed, but the influence is ever-present, a lesson learned perhaps in Plato's youth and dwelt upon over a lifetime of thought and practice.

Philosophy is a dispositional discipline with a deeply constructive rhetorical nature. It modifies the mind, creating attitudes of critical attention and insight. The Platonic student leaves the lists better equipped to illuminate the shadows in which meanings and arguments vie for adherence, better equipped to sift through the complexity of ideas and so bring clarity and judgment to the issues that divide us, better equipped to escape the labyrinth of confused meanings in which the untrained mind becomes lost.

Anthropological considerations of how humans have used and developed argumentation push us back further into the shadows of a pre-Aristotelian moment, before the initiatives we associate with Aristotle begin to emerge. Outside of the Greek tradition, non-Aristotelian logics are promised by Indigenous knowledge systems, the other*wise* to our own ways of knowing (Tindale 2021a). These systems were largely assimilated with or eliminated by Western colonial impulses. Like these others, Plato somehow occupies a place outside of the Aristotelian tradition, even as we identify him as a precursor to what develops. But is this a faithful lineage? In what ways does the argumentation Plato sees and employs approximate what we understand and see today? These are questions I leave the reader to ponder while considering the arguments of this book.

Part I
The Logician

Introduction to Part I
Plato and the Intricacies of Logic

> He revived again by all possible means [the whole of philosophy] and also for this reason he gained in addition . . . this gracefulness in his arguments and, on the other hand, he himself introduced for the first time many ideas of his own.
>
> —Philodemus (I, 1–6)

Nothing can diminish Aristotle's foundational role as *the* superior logician of the early Western tradition, one who develops a systematic approach to reasoning and argument. The shadow is cast so widely, however, that it is so easy to overlook any contributions made by others, including those of Plato. In the late nineteenth century, Wincenty Lutoslawski (1897), who judged Plato the first logician in the history of human thought (3) could write with surprise that "Plato's logic remains almost unknown, as may easily be seen from a short survey of the chief opinions expressed on this subject" (7). Since then, a number of important studies have emerged (Robinson [1941] 1953; Ritter 1933), although what counts as logic in Plato's work remains a matter on which there tends to be debate. In his examination of ancient formal logic, Bocheński (1951, 16) suggests that, with some notable exceptions associated with the analytic syllogism, "nearly everything in Aristotle's logic . . . is probably a reflex elaboration and development of procedures used already, at least in a rudimentary way, by Plato." But corroborating this demands considerable powers of interpretation.

For Lutoslawski, Plato's logic first emerges in the *Meno* with an interest in hypothetical reasoning that will characterize the middle dialogues as an appreciation of classification grows, culminating in the dialectic expressed in the *Sophist* and other later dialogues. In fact, when he speaks of logic here, he seems to have in mind the patterns of reasoning that will hint at, and then issue in, the full-fledged dialectic of the late dialogues. Much of the argument for this "growth" depends on the chronology of the dialogues, and so the bulk of Lutoslawski's book sees him drawing on the then-recent trend in stylistics to identify the course of Plato's writings and hence the development of his logical interests within them.

The lack of any kind of systematized approach to logic in Plato arises in part from the very different kinds of texts that have come down to us.[1] Were we to try to extract Aristotle's skills as a logician from his dialogues alone, we likely would face the same difficulties as we do with Plato. Nor should we assume a disinterest on Plato's part. Every indication is given that he is attracted to the array of techniques available to express in language the insights he extracts from the intelligible world and the move toward an accomplished conception of dialectic (no matter how rudimentary or controversial this might be judged) cannot be achieved without a serious engagement with the processes of reasoning and argument. That dialectic, emerging in the middle dialogues and developing thereafter, is built upon an earlier appreciation of the power that logical reasoning exhibits.[2] There are suggestions, moreover, that Plato's work was influenced by the logical interests of other Socratics. Eucleides, for example, known to us as the narrator of the *Theaetetus*, raised concerns about the argument from analogy that appear to be echoed in some of Plato's treatment (Kahn 1996, 14).[3]

---

1. Of course, other readings of the development of Plato's thought and writings will draw different conclusions about his contributions to the systematization of argument. Ryle's (1966) story that sees progress away from "eristic" dialogues that reflect the method of refutation finds "the notion of a valid argument is just beginning to separate itself off from the notion of an unrebutted argument" (206). In insisting further that after Zeno it was Plato who introduced systematized argument in the form of dialectic, Ryle further complains that "we have uninquisitively failed to ask what trained his dialectical powers" (207). My answer to such a challenge is developed in part III.

2. This dialectic will be explored in detail in the later chapters of this book. For now, it suffices to note that it develops from the Socratic variety of the early dialogues, through the method of hypothesizing in the middle dialogues, to reach an array of types like the method of collection and division of the late dialogues. But, as will be shown, this path is not as smooth and clear as suggested here.

3. Phaedo lists him among the foreigners present at Socrates's death (59c); Boys-Stones and Rowe identify him as the founder of a school in Megara whose members excelled

Of course, none of these Socratics springs fully formed from a vacuum; successful modes of argumentation were actively employed in the works of earlier Greek thinkers.

Friedrich Solmsen (1975) discusses the pre-Platonic life of argumentation in terms of two strands of the "*in utramque partem disputare*," or assertions "supported by argumentation moving both ways" (1975, 11). The first we see in Gorgias's text on non-being (*DK* 82, B3), arguing first that nothing exists and then that the nonexistent does not exist. The second strand develops from this and considers alternatives: "This is one variety of the *in utramque partem disputare*. Both alternatives are disproved, and therefore the proposition that could be true in the one way or the other is definitely refuted" (17).[4] The strategy arises in other extant texts: Antiphon's *Tetralogies* (*DK* 87, BII–IV), for example, provide arguments first on one side of a legal case, then on the other. One person—Antiphon—constructs opposing arguments. And of course, Diogenes Laertius attributed to the Sophist Protagoras the claim that on every issue there are two opposing arguments (*DL* 1853, 397). Here, we have both the strategies of arguing on both sides of an issue and of collecting opposing arguments, if they can be considered two strategies.

Nola Heidlebaugh notes the interest expressed by the Sophists in contradiction, contraries, and oppositions (2001, 35), and G. B. Kerferd judges that at the heart of the sophistic movement is antilogic: the practice of "opposing one *logos* to another *logos*" (1981, 63).[5] Less clear among contemporary scholars is a sense of what was at stake in such "opposition," and this is what we must first clarify.[6]

---

in logic (2013, 309–10).

4. In his study of the history of rhetoric, Richard Enos argues that "the persuasiveness in Gorgias' epideictic oratory derives from his ability to elevate the proper course of action by stylistically illustrating the antithetical, cowardly behavior rejected by heroic warriors who died in battle. Through the portrayal of the diametrically opposed choices confronting the warriors, the listeners might gain an insight into the implications of valor" (Enos 1993, 76).

5. This in part, says Kerferd, distinguishes antilogic from eristics.

6. Kerferd reads Plato as ambivalent toward antilogic. It stands between eristics and dialectic, being weak or strong depending for which end it is used. The definition proceeds: "Or in discovering or drawing attention to the presence of such an opposition in an argument or in a state of affairs" (1981, 63). If this is part of antilogic, then it will be reflected in Socratic practice. But this also seems quite distinct from the issuing of two opposing arguments that is attributed to Protagoras.

Another text in which we might expect to see an opposing argument strategy is the *Dissoi Logoi*. The authorship is disputed. Guthrie judges it to be the notes of a pupil or teacher reflecting Protagoras's methods (1971, 316).[7] At the same time, there is a case to be made for seeing a strong Hippian influence. T. M. Robinson, however, tries to resolve the question with compromise, settling on a Sophist authorship that combines Protagoras, Hippias, and Gorgias, with the major influence coming from Protagoras (1984, 51, 72). But he does this reluctantly, as if to fulfill the reader's expectation, since his insistence is that the author is "unequivocally" unknown.[8]

The text provides relativistic insights such as "The same thing is good for some but bad for others, or at one time good and at another time bad for the same person" (*DK* 90, 1, 1).[9] But if we are looking for instances of one person arguing on both sides of an issue, we will search in vain. Technically, it is the single author of the *Dissoi Logoi* who marshals opposing arguments. This author does not *assert* both sides, instead reporting what "some" say against what "others" say.

Suffice it to say, we have in the strategy of opposing arguments a distinctive feature of pre-Platonic argumentation. It is sufficiently established for Phaedrus to express surprise when Socrates does *not* use it. This follows his first speech, after which Phaedrus says: "I thought you were about to speak at the same length about the non-lover, to list his good points and argue that it's better to give one's favors to him" (*Phdr.* 241d).[10] Socrates

---

7. Untersteiner (1954) argues that it is not a sophistical work at all, but an attack upon Gorgias by a Pythagorean of the ethical tradition (308). The association that Guthrie makes with Protagoras gets some support from Ryle's speculative reading of the debate over the teaching of virtue that is referenced in *Dissoi Logoi* 6, where arguments are given pro and contra the thesis. Noting that Plato puts one of the pro arguments into the mouth of Protagoras in the *Protagoras*, Ryle suggests "it may be that Plato knew that Protagoras was the original author of this *pro* argument and perhaps of the thesis itself" (Ryle 1966, 197).

8. The text is found as an appendix to the works of Sextus Empiricus, and Robinson argues for its composition around 403–395 BCE (1984, 34–41).

9. Reference to the *Dissoi Logoi* is to Robinson's edition.

10. The standard way of quoting Plato refers to the Renaissance edition of his works published in Geneva in 1578 by Henri Estienne (1528–1598), more usually known by the Latinized version of his name: Stephanus. This three-volume complete edition of Plato had pages numbered continuously from the beginning to the end of each volume. Thus, a quotation from Plato includes the name of the dialogue and the page number in the Stephanus edition followed by the letter of the section that includes the first word of the quotation.

counters with fear that should he praise the opposite side, the Nymphs that occupy the area in which they are resting would take complete possession of him. It is only after he has invoked his own opposing (divine) sign, which prevents him from leaving, that Socrates can proceed with the second speech. While this is not obviously a case of what Solmsen takes to be "argument-and-counterargument" (1975, 46), it does fit with the general dismissals in the *Phaedrus* of the practices laid out in the handbook tradition, practices that captured common rhetorical moves.

Plato also opposes another strategy that Solmsen finds connected to the *in utramque partem disputare* but that should be given separate consideration. This is the appeal to what is likely (*tò eikós*—Solmsen 1975, 21). Elsewhere, he calls *eikós* one of the kinds of evidence popular in earlier argumentation that will be given a more logical foundation by Aristotle (Solmsen 1968, 317).[11] Again, we see regular use of this in Antiphon's *Tetralogies*, where one set of likelihoods is countered with another. In this countering, we can see why Solmsen would identify *eikós* reasoning with opposing arguments, but there is a larger issue at stake. Particularly in legal judgments, jurists do not have firsthand access to the events of the case. Thus, arguers would have to present the facts in terms of what was likely to have happened and counter with further likelihoods (or unlikelihoods) as the trials proceeded. In doing this, the appeal was made to the jurists' experiences, of what they judged to be likely. Here, the arguments were measured against the standard of human experience (to which each person had immediate recourse) rather than to any access to what "actually" occurred.

Still, in referring to this aspect of the common handbooks, Plato is less than enthusiastic. He has Socrates clearly link what is *eikós* to what is accepted by the crowd, regardless of its truth. The complaint is raised that "sometimes, in fact, whether you are prosecuting or defending a case, you must not even say what actually happened, if it was not likely to have happened—you must say something that is likely instead. Whatever you say, you should pursue what is likely and leave the truth aside" (*Phdr.* 272e). While the earlier users may have championed this strategy *because* the truth was not accessible, for Plato this is never a route to take. Arguments that rely on likelihoods will not be part of Plato's repertoire.

---

11. In fact, Solmsen will refer to "probability" rather than "likelihood," but given the potential confusions that could arise with more modern notions of probability, it is preferable to retain the term "likelihood" (Tindale 2010).

The Standard Story on Plato and Reason

Much of the standard story on Plato's logic involves logicians assuming that what they find in Plato, even the early Plato, and particularly the *elenchus* or refutation, is evidence of abstract logical thought. While Plato lacked the tools that Aristotle would develop, it is believed that the thinking must necessarily have been there because it is present in all humans and certainly in all intelligent humans.

Robinson ([1941] 1953) explores the merits of this narrative, giving credence to little of it. His view of the *elenchus* is itself fairly standard, seeing it as the method of refutation of an individual's thesis and noting its prevalence in the early dialogues, after which it diminishes until it eventually "incorporates into the larger whole of dialectic, which somewhat changes its character" (19). Indeed, as we will see in part III, by the time Plato's own dialectic has replaced it, it will have lost its character altogether!

Robinson considers the presence of the syllogism in the *elenchus* using the following understanding of argument:

> If a writer says "A is B and therefore C is D," that is an argument. But if he says "A is B and that is why C is D," it is not an argument; for he is assuming that we already believe that C is D, and merely inviting us to realize that it follows from A's being B. When the conclusion is stated before the premises, then, other things being equal, we more definitely have an argument than when the premises are stated before the conclusion. The more explicit arguments, as those of geometry, always tell you first what they are proposing to prove. This state of affairs prevents us from discovering any propositions true of all the arguments of the early dialogues as such (1953, 20).

The last point is an important qualification, affecting as it does our understanding of logic in the early dialogues. Likewise, the sense of "syllogism" assumed to be at work is Aristotelian, not in the strong modern sense that involves class inclusion but rather of the weaker variety involving any "argument in which, certain things being laid down, something other than these necessarily comes about through them" (*Top.* I.1, 100a25).[12] In fact, the sense of syllogism employed in the early dialogues (where the term is

---

12. From the Pickard-Cambridge translation, edited by Barnes (Aristotle 1984).

largely absent) is "adding up the facts," only in the middle and later dialogues does the notion of inference emerge.[13]

This weaker sense of the syllogism is important for a distinction between direct and indirect refutations. Of thirty-nine arguments in the early dialogues, thirty-one are judged to be of the indirect variety, where a falsehood is deduced from a thesis. Moreover, Robinson suggests that we have no reason to believe Plato is even aware of the distinction and what it holds for modern readers: "We have not been saying, and must not say, that he himself was aware of these variations in the abstract way in which we have described them" (Robinson [1941] 1953, 27). Even the insistence that the logic is obvious and so must have been recognized by Plato must be resisted. To say that anything must have been obvious to Plato because it is obvious to us is a belief "destructive of any true history of human thought, and ought to be abandoned. Evidently, there must have been a time when the human race, or its immediate ancestor, possessed no logical propositions at all, true or false" (28–29).

Communication theorist Marshall McLuhan (1962) observes the growing doubt "about the *a* priori character of logical categories" (25) on the part of scholars studying nonliterate societies. And Plato, as we will see, marks the transition from the oral to the literate with all the suspicion that is conveyed in the *Phaedrus*. In a similar vein, Robinson believes logical propositions of an abstract nature arose only with the late Plato and Aristotle.[14] This is a thesis we will explore further in part III. For now, it is worth noting that Robinson gives something of an echo to John Locke's ([1689]

---

13. On this point, Robinson is at odds with Lutoslawski (1897) whose detailed investigation of Plato's logic includes a claim that Plato makes use of "a correct syllogism" in the *Charmides* (160d), introduced by the word "syllogism" (*sullogismos*), although Lutoslawski allows that it has not yet the meaning of a logical term (1897, 203). Indeed, in addressing Charmides, Socrates is inviting him to "collect his thoughts" on what they have been discussing before proceeding further. There is no sense here of the technical meaning the term will acquire under Aristotle. See also Kahn (1996) who warns of the difficulties that can arise from imposing our notion of deduction on Plato. The latter's conception of inference, he insists, "does not have the formal precision of Aristotle's syllogistic" (315–16).

14. On this point, Robinson differs markedly from many of his critics who challenged the view in reviews of the 1941 edition. In his introduction to the second edition (1953), Robinson identifies such critics as "creationists" (vi) who believe, contrary to Robinson's evolutionary position, that logic was a self-evident science immediately available to earlier thinkers like Plato. On his rejection of this view, the Robinson of 1953 remains fixed, and rightly so.

1996) similar warning: "There are many men that reason exceeding clear and rightly, who do not know how to make a syllogism. He that will look into many parts of *Asia* and *America*, will find men reason there, perhaps, as acutely as himself, who yet never heard of a syllogism, nor can reduce any one argument to those forms." He goes on to observe that should we insist otherwise, it would follow that before Aristotle "there was not one man that did or could know anything by reason" (Locke [1689] 1996, bk. IV, chap. XVII, sec. 4). The point being observed by Locke, and by Robinson in Plato, is that reasoning ability registers itself in many ways and should not be limited or reduced to abstract thought.

Thus, a passage in the *Phaedo* attracts controversy, to the degree that some would eliminate the passage altogether as being unlikely for Plato to have authored (Robinson [1941] 1953, 30). At 101d Socrates says to Cebes that a hypothesis should not be discussed "until you had examined whether the consequences that follow from it agree with one another or contradict one another." The worry is that the passage seems to assume that the consequences of a single thesis may contradict each other, thereby disproving the thesis, and "that the consequences of a single thesis may contradict each other without the aid of any extra premiss" (30). Again, the concern arises from the assumption that Plato's logical views were like our own.[15]

The larger lesson may issue from the warnings with which Robinson prefaces his study, namely that there are varieties of misinterpretation and the efforts of translation naturally encourage these to be made. We might be selective in our choice of passage, for example (Robinson calls this the "mosaic misinterpretation"). But the most pertinent variety of misinterpretation for the current discussion is "misinterpretation by abstraction," where it is inferred that because an author mentions something that we relate to something else, then the author was aware of the same relationship. Such readings all insinuate the future, that is, read "into your author doctrines that did not become explicit until later" ([1941] 1953, 2). Even under the advice of his own caution, Robinson treads close to the line at times. But those who criticize Plato for not reasoning as they (now) do have clearly crossed it.

Still, what Robinson's study shows is the grounds for a view of Plato's logic, and particularly the *elenchus*, that favors abstractions. He essentially

---

15. And that we should overlook the hypothetical manner in which the point is put. We assume, again, that any position taken in the dialogues can find its way back to Plato himself. This passage will be explored in more detail in chapter 11.

provides the grounds for believing in the standard narrative at the same time as he breaks from it. The treatment of definitions furthers that tendency. But there is, beneath this, a recognition made by Robinson that I will want to develop in chapter 2. That is, "the Socratic elenchus is a very personal affair" (15). What Robinson means here is that with each example of the *elenchus* it is the interlocutor who is to be convinced by the argument, and no one else. It matters that the interlocutor is committed to the opening statements and then recognizes the power of the logical progression, which leads to a conclusion that he must accept. It is this personalizing tendency that creates a tension with the desire to see abstractness in the logic, to lift the lesson out of the life for which it is relevant and universalize it in some way. We will return to the ethotic nature of the *elenchus* in the discussions ahead.

Aristotle insists that the historical Socrates had no belief in Platonic Forms but was interested in what a thing is, which led him to inquire after definitions (*Metaph.* 987b2–3; 1078b17–31). There is a self-serving ring in the way Aristotle phrases the matter; like other post-Platonic movements, Socrates is enlisted by Aristotle as a crucial progenitor, thereby lifting the authority of the new ideas. But it also gives pause to any hasty endorsement of some translators' decision to propose that Socrates sought not a standard or measure by which to judge a thing, but the form itself.[16] "What is holy (or pious)?" is an example of what Robinson calls a "What is X?" question (50).[17] An alternative question—"Is X Y?"—receives nothing like the same space or attention.[18]

Again, Robinson's caution is one I would echo: we can indeed choose to describe the inquiries by adopting terms like "definition" and "example," but "if we extract from it explicit rules and principles of definition, we

---

16. Hence, as one illustrative instance, after being given examples of what is holy (and unholy) by Euthyphro, Socrates reminds him that what had been asked for was the *eidos*, duly rendered "form" by Reeve (2002) and "the essential aspect" by the more Aristotelian-minded Fowler (Plato 1914).

17. There are actually fewer instances of "What is X?" questions in the early dialogues than might be thought. Besides the *Euthyphro*, we see the *Laches*, the *Charmides*, and the *Hippias Major* primarily concerned with pursuing such questions. Perhaps the "What is Knowledge" of the *Theaetetus* and the first half of the *Meno*, if they are judged early, would count. With some qualifications, we might include the *Lysis*. But the investigations in many of the dialogues that are judged early are not characterized this way (*Ion, Lesser Hippias, Crito,* and *Protagoras*).

18. On Socrates's definitional questions, see also Benson (1990), who is responding to Nehamas (1975).

pass to a stage of abstraction higher than the dialogues themselves display" (52). We can reframe Socrates's instructions in terms of the rules in modern textbooks, but in doing so we may well be reading back onto Plato ideas that are modern. "The actual picture in the dialogues is not more but less abstract than the picture here given; for Socrates does not use the letter X; he never gives the function but always one of its arguments" (52).[19] Suffice it to say that an exploration of Socratic definition, on modern terms, moves us further away from the personalized arguments of the Socratic dialogues and reinforces the belief in the abstractness of Plato's early logic.

In the forgoing discussion, while ostensibly introducing chapters that will explore Plato's logic, I have, in turn, made frequent reference to dialectic and argumentation. This indicates the difficulties involved in distinguishing concepts when approaching Plato's use of "reasons." In terms of a developed logic, the connections with his view of dialectic will ultimately be unavoidable, and we will explore these in part III. But argumentation will occupy us throughout and it will reappear in the studies of part I. Modern argumentation theory finds its roots in Plato (van Eemeren et al. 2014, 53–61) and as the above discussion of pre-Platonic strategies indicates, argumentation was pervasive in Greek society, and a facility in it, a necessity. Effective citizenship demanded an ability to argue well in the law courts and legislative assemblies. It was no accident that the Sophists, who professed to teach such abilities, attracted the number of students that they did.

Taking Robinson's cautions to heart, the following chapters explore the "logic" of the early dialogues and some of the features (like false reasoning) that lead us into later dialogues. Particular attention is paid to Socratic dialectic, with a defense of the thesis that it cannot be reduced to the *elenchus* alone. Plato has Socrates employ types of argument with goals other than refutation. Against the background of this dialectic, we will see that Plato endorses a conception of strong argument that corroborates Robinson's recognition of the importance of personalized argumentative encounters.

---

19. In spite of his own advice, Robinson proceeds to "make use of modern terms and higher abstractions in order to criticize the What-is-X question" ([1941] 1953, 53).

Chapter 1

Socratic Arguments

> [Socrates] restrained many of them from such vices, leading them to love virtue, and giving them hopes that if they would take care of themselves, they would become honourable and worthy characters
>
> —Xenophon (*Memorabilia* I, II, 2)

Varieties of Argument

Confusions over how we should understand the Socratic method and, in particular, the *elenchus* stem in part from a failure to adequately distinguish the different types of argument that Socrates adopts across the dialogues. There are three that will be of specific interest here: the Socratic refutation or elenctic arguments,[1] hortatory (or protreptic) arguments, and the maieutic arguments associated with Socrates's role as midwife. These three are of interest because of the attitude that Plato takes toward them, dropping it in one case and developing and adapting in the cases of the other two.[2]

---

1. The *elenchus* is often taken to include more than one of these types of argument, usually the maieutic. I will restrict it to refutation arguments, as discussed below.

2. In restricting the *elenchus* in this way, I agree with Tarrant (2002) and not with Vlastos (1983). Tarrant writes: "It is my contention that the real solution is that *elenchus* was never a term, either in Plato or in his later interpreters, for *all* Socrates' investigations through question and answer but that this noun and its corresponding verbs were applied to those examples of interrogation whose *purpose* was refutation" (2002, 63). See also, Tarrant 2000, 115–18. We will return to this, and the seminal work of Vlastos on the *elenchus*, in the next chapter.

Socratic refutations are the arguments most readily associated with a Socratic *method*, and I will explore them in more detail in the next chapter. There, we will identify a series of steps by which an interlocutor's statements are examined, leading to the contradiction of that individual's initial statement and the subsequent confusion of the individual involved. This is very much a method that, while ostensibly designed to discover some truth, results only in the realization that a person did not know what he claimed to have the expertise to know (and often to be able to teach). This captures the role of Socrates as the nay-saying philosopher and is reflected in a range of metaphors like the gadfly of the *Apology* and the numbing stingray of the *Meno*.

Hortatory arguments are essentially persuasive in nature. They involve giving reasons for a particular course of action that an interlocutor (usually a youth) is being urged to follow. This type of argument is noteworthy because of the association with rhetoric, toward which Plato is thought to be at least ambivalent. This is why it is important to distinguish hortatory arguments from other kinds of persuasive arguments.[3]

The third type, the maieutic argument, provides one of the metaphors most associated with Socrates, although it is a matter of dispute whether the historical figure actually employed it (Burnyeat [1977] 1992). Here, Socrates, being barren of ideas himself, acts as an intellectual midwife in assisting young men in the birth of their ideas then testing them for quality and destroying the "wind-eggs" that don't match up. We see the midwife arguments demonstrated in the *Theaetetus* and to a certain degree in the *Symposium*.

All three of these types of argument are dialectical. That is, all involve conversations between Socrates and one or more interlocutors. And thus they all create difficulties for the reader who wants to be clear about the positions that are being endorsed. But there is a further sense of "dia" that it appropriate here, where it means "through," with individuals reasoning through a question together, seeing where the inquiry takes them. This sense is characterized by the metaphor of a *path* of inquiry that Socrates often adopts.

So, it is correct to say that collectively these three argument types define "Socratic dialectic." But the three are distinct in the goals they aim to achieve: the recognition of a person's unknowing or ignorance; the taking

---

3. There is a wider sense to "hortatory" that simply means giving advice. Thus, several of Isocrates's letters are hortatory in character (see Jebb 2016, 67–74).

up of an action that involves some kind of self-care; and the emergence of a person's ideas in a constructive fashion. It is also to be noted that while elenctic arguments involve experts who tend to be older men, the other two types are designed for the young.

One of the positions for which I argue in this book is that Plato reacts differently to these three types of argument. The ways in which Plato is identifiable as a logician, rhetorician, and dialectician involve his developments and occasional adoptions of the different types of Socratic argument. As we will see in the next chapter, Plato essentially drops the argument of refutation as a method for achieving the ends that he comes to value. This is not to say that it disappears—it makes an important appearance in the *Philebus*, for example, for illustrative purposes—but it is not a method of argument that Plato finds adequate to his task of bringing ideas from the invisible realm into the visible. This is made clear in *Republic* VI (487b), where the method of refutation is identified as particularly unpopular. On the other hand, the hortatory and midwife arguments are embraced by Plato. In the former, we see his ongoing engagement with the power of constructive rhetorical persuasion. And in the latter, we find the kernel out of which a distinctive Platonic dialectic will emerge along with a model of argumentation that will prove important to the curricula of the Academy. In fact, insofar as the midwife metaphor is an invention of Plato's own, we can see him developing his own sense of dialectic out of and beyond the Socratic limits and issuing in the full-fledged treatments of the late dialogues.

Hortatory Arguments

Because so much attention tends to be invested in the *elenchus*, I will first devote the remainder of this chapter to exploring the second and third types of argument, beginning with the hortatory, and showing some sense of what Plato makes of them. To this end, I will draw on the *Euthydemus* and the *Republic*, where arguments that urge interlocutors to pursue specific actions are clearly persuasive in nature.

The *Euthydemus* provides one of the clearest examples, although commentators also see hortatory arguments implicit in the *Theaetetus* (Magrini 2017) and assumed in the *Menexenus* (Barney 2001).

Among the many things accomplished in the *Euthydemus* is the drawing of sharp distinctions between two dialectical methods: the eristics of the Sophist brothers Euthydemus and Dionysodorus, and the method of Socrates, in this case through hortatory arguments. A crucial exchange takes place at 274d–e. The brothers have claimed many things, among them that they can teach virtue better and faster than anyone else (*Euthd.* 273d). Greatly impressed by this and eager for a demonstration, Socrates asks for clarification about the kind of persuasion involved: Are the brothers "able to make only that man good who is already persuaded that he ought to take lessons from you, or can you also make the man good who is not yet persuaded on this point"? (274d–e).[4] Persuasion is here identified as central to the acquisition of virtue, although in the first case, where there is a predisposition as a result of prior persuasion, the task would seem easier. Socrates further asks whether these two kinds of persuading belong to the same art, to which Dionysodorus replies that it is the same art (274e).

This identifies the Sophist brothers as those best positioned to provide a hortatory argument that would lead a person to philosophy and the practice of virtue. To this end, Socrates suggests that their demonstration should involve the persuading of the young man Cleinias "that he ought to love wisdom and have a care for virtue" (275a). That this is an invitation to provide a hortatory argument could not be clearer, nor could it be clearer what Socrates understands such an argument involves. Cleinias is to be moved dialectically through persuasive discourse to a specific action.

Thus, the disappointment is evident when all Euthydemus and Dionysodorus provide is an eristical display designed to confuse and confute the boy. They batter him with questions, rooted in various equivocations, in order to solicit refutations that he cannot avoid if he is to answer the questions within the parameters that they allow.[5] The result is the boy's confusion, Socrates's frustration, and the gathered crowd's elation, as they laugh at and applaud the eristical displays. Socrates's reaction is significant. He interjects with the suggestion that the brothers are introducing Cleinias to the rituals of some kind of sophistic mysteries, making fun of him before the serious work begins. He proceeds:

> They said they would give a demonstration of hortatory skill, but now it seems to me that they must have thought it nec-

---

4. I draw here from the Rosamond Kent Sprague translation (Plato 1965).

5. We will explore these Sophistical refutations when we examine refutation arguments generally in the next chapter and these early indications of fallacious reasoning in chapter 3.

essary to make fun of you before beginning.⁶ So, Euthydemus and Dionysodorus, put an end to this joking: I think we have had enough of it. The next thing is to give an exhibition of persuading the young man that he ought to devote himself to wisdom and virtue. (278c–d)

As if he is suspicious of what the brothers will do, Socrates explains that he will first give his own demonstration of how he understands hortatory arguments, and thus the first Socratic episode of the dialogue begins, providing a contrast with the eristical performance that had preceded it.

The pattern of Socrates's questioning is important here. He offers a suggestion from the start ("Do all men wish to do well?") rather than working with something initiated by the interlocutor, although he is still soliciting agreements on the basis of which he proceeds. Still, it is Socrates who is leading the inquiry rather than conducting an independent investigation of another person's beliefs. And, moreover, Socrates seems to be clear about where he is going, what points he wants the discussion to arrive at. Thus, the sense of a real and equal co-investigator that is important to the *elenchus*, whether this is a conceit or not, is absent here. Point by point, Cleinias agrees that we wish to do well through having many good things and that such good things include money, health, and good looks as well as noble birth, power, and honor and then self-control, justice, and courage. Here we have marshaled three distinct sets of goods, all essential for doing well. With the inclusion of a further good—wisdom—Cleinias thinks that the list is complete. But Socrates then recalls the greatest good of all—good fortune. Again, Cleinias agrees. But once again Socrates reconsiders and points out that they have made a mistake, since by including wisdom they had already included good fortune. "Wisdom is surely good fortune, I said—this is something even a child would know" (279d). At this, Cleinias (like the reader) is surprised. Wisdom and good fortune do not seem synonymous. So, Socrates must instruct the boy further, offering examples of successful performances (flute playing, writing and reading, navigating, campaigning, and medical practice) where the success depends on better luck through being wise. After a series of agreements, Socrates can ask: "Then it is your

---

6. It is possible that the suggestion here is that just as Socratic dialectic can humiliate an interlocutor before the serious business of exploring ideas can begin, so Sophistic dialectic has a similar preliminary stage.

opinion that it is luckier to do things in the company of wise men than ignorant ones?" (280a). With Cleinias's agreement to this, Socrates claims to have shown that wisdom will make men fortunate such that with wisdom present there is no need for any further good fortune.

They have reached the agreement that having many good things should make them happy and able to do well. But this would only follow if there were some advantage involved, but there is no advantage possible without also using such good things. That is, some kind of practice is called for. What comes next, logically, is a consideration of whether the use is correct, since the outcome would be harm if it is not.

Socrates's reference here (281a) to "what comes next" clearly suggests there is a pattern to these hortatory arguments, one that should be followed to acquire the insights involved. Socrates indicates the same thing when, on completing his hortatory argument, he invites Euthydemus and Dionysodorus to pick up the demonstration with its next step.

Prior to this next stage, Cleinias and Socrates consider the uses of things that are wrong against uses that are correct and reach the conclusion that if ignorance controls the use, then greater evils will ensue than if wisdom does. The following argument is then expounded: "Since we all wish to be happy, and since we appear to become so by using things and using them rightly, and since knowledge was the source of rightness and good fortune, it seems to be necessary that every man should prepare himself by every means to become as wise as possible" (282a). Here, three premises, each of which serves as a subclaim from the previous argumentation, lead to the conclusion that they have been seeking, the correctness of which Cleinias sees, that everyone should devote themselves to becoming wise. Of course, it also matters that such wisdom can be taught. But Cleinias believes it can (282c). And so, Socrates concludes and Cleinias replies as follows:

> Soc.: Since you believe both that [wisdom] can be taught and that it is the only existing thing which makes a man happy and fortunate, surely you would agree it is necessary to love wisdom and you mean to do this yourself.
>
> Clen.: This is just what I mean to do, Socrates, as well as ever I can. (282c–d)

The result of this hortatory argument, which is built from extended argumentation, is the successful persuasion of Cleinias to adopt a particular action, that is, to love wisdom by turning to philosophy. Here we see illustrated Socrates's example of what he wanted a hortatory argument to be, as he announces to Euthydemus and Dionysodorus (282d). The Sophist brothers are then invited to either give a demonstration of the same thing (presumably present an argument to lead the boy to the same action) or show Cleinias what comes next, that is, "whether he ought to acquire every sort of knowledge, or whether there is one sort that he ought to get in order to be a happy man and a good one, and what it is" (282e).

Plato stresses the importance of this move by having Socrates reiterate his concern to Crito, noting that he "paid particular attention" to what should come next. In general, the bookend conversations between Socrates and Crito that frame the dialogue along with these interludes involving him, sandwiched between the Sophistic and Socratic segments, are a device to draw attention to what Plato deems important in the dialogue. Too often, the *Euthydemus* is valued solely for its examples of eristics, and while this is indeed *an* important feature of the text, there are other valuable things going on. We will return to the role of Crito later.

The Sophist brothers, of course, fail to deliver on their promise to provide anything remotely like the hortatory argument that has been demonstrated. They present another series of eristic exchanges, this time drawing in Ctesippus. Undoubtedly, there are some important issues advanced in this segment: the possibility of false speaking, the nature of contradiction, and whether speakers should be held to what they had said earlier (287b). But from the point of view of what interests us here, the segment's real significance lies in what it does *not* do, which is add to our understanding of hortatory arguments.

For this, we turn to the next Socratic segment (288d–290e), the hortatory part of which is quite short but draws considerably more insight from Cleinias. They had left off with the agreement that it was necessary to love wisdom and turn to philosophy. Now, they inquire about the nature of the knowledge involved. They agree, through reviewing examples, that what they need "is a kind of knowledge which combines making and knowing how to use the thing it makes" (289b). Socrates asks whether the art of writing speeches would qualify, to which Cleinias responds that he does not think so. The following exchange then ensues:

Soc.: On what ground do you say this?

Clen.: Well, I notice that certain speech writers have no idea of how to use the particular speeches they themselves have written, in the same way that lyre makers have no idea of how to use their lyres. And in the former case too, there are other people who are capable of using what the speech writers have composed but are themselves unable to write. So it is clear that in regard to speeches too, there is one art of making and another of using. (289d)

This exchange is interesting on several fronts. Euthydemus and Dionysodorus have, after all, been presented earlier as speech writers. And the closing section of the dialogue would appear to involve the interjection of the ideas of, and a commentary on, another speech writer, namely Isocrates. So this is an implicit rejection of these figures as people who have and practice the best kind of knowledge.

But of more immediate significance is the change in Cleinias and the corresponding development of the dialectical exchanges with Socrates. If we look back over the first Socratic segment, we see that Cleinias's responses had been short and perfunctory ("Certainly," "Yes," "he agreed"). Now we see Cleinias both offer an opinion of his own (speech writing is not the art that combines making and knowing how to use what is made) and then give support of his claim in an expansive passage. Socrates's request that Cleinias defend his claim with reasons is a new development, showing an advance in Cleinias's education and the expectations Socrates has of him. The ability (or failure) to give an account of oneself is a perennial Platonic issue, and Cleinias's performance here suggests a crucial elevation in his status.

Some might judge that, strictly speaking, this second Socratic episode is not a hortatory argument because there is no clear action that results from it or that could result from it. But there again, Socrates treats it as an extension of the argumentative process that he and Cleinias engaged in earlier. Moreover, his comments prior to the segment suggest that this argument could well be intended for the Sophist brothers themselves: "I think I ought once again to take the lead and give an indication of what sort of persons I pray they will show themselves to be. Beginning where I left off earlier, I shall do my best to go through what comes next so as to *spur them to action*" (288c–d, italics are mine). The action he wants from them is to provide a serious argument, rather than the "conjuring tricks" on evidence so far. But if we can extend this type of argument to include its impact on an audience, these secondary participants (and the *Republic* will encourage us to think in such terms), then we are still dealing with hortatory argument, even if the dialectical nature is being revised. Regardless of this, it remains the case that Cleinias's current performance can be seen as an immediate product of his turn to philosophy, where he now begins to give an account of himself rather than just responding pro forma. His answers *are* the action that was at stake earlier and serve to confirm the success of Socrates's argumentation. Cleinias will give two more expansive responses on the art of hunting and on generalship. That we are expected to note these impressive interventions is marked by the side response of Crito to Socrates: "Did that boy utter all this?" (290e). Socrates expresses sudden absentmindedness. Perhaps it was someone else, he muses. But only if we take the demonstration at face value does the full worth of the hortatory art come through.

This remains lost on Crito. As a final lesson from the *Euthydemus* before we leave it for a while, we should note Crito's closing quandary. He worries what to do with his sons. One is still quite small, but Critobulus is at an age where he needs someone who can improve him. But when he looks around at the men who set up to educate the young, all of them strike him as unsuitable. He laments in conclusion "that I cannot see how I am to persuade the boy to take up philosophy" (307a). This is an amazing confession given all that has gone before. Yes, the Sophist brothers, who claim to educate, are vivid examples of the unsuitable kind. But in the exchange between Socrates and young Cleinias, Crito has been provided with a compelling example of how to persuade a boy to take up philosophy. Plato stresses Crito's failure to see what should have been apparent to him in order to make that even more apparent to the reader: hortatory arguments, when properly conducted, are a vital form of persuasion.

Details of the Account

What, then, have we learned about hortatory arguments as they are illustrated in the *Euthydemus*?

In his seminal paper on the *elenchus*, Gregory Vlastos (1983) situates the *Euthydemus* among a group belonging to the end of the early dialogues in which adversary arguments are abandoned as a method of philosophical investigation (Vlastos 1994, 30). As we have seen, such a judgment may overlook what is achieved philosophically in the tension *between* styles of argument that are demonstrated by the Sophists and Socrates. Certainly, Vlastos's further view that the only theses investigated are treated by Socrates in the didactic style of the middle dialogues "where the interlocutor is a yes-man, who may ask questions and occasionally raise objections, but never puts up a sustained resistance to a Socratic thesis" (1994, 30) cannot be sustained in light of the emergence of Cleinias as an active philosophical novice with supported opinions of his own. To call Cleinias "docility itself" (30) is to perhaps fall prey to the oversight that hampered Crito.

It is through the participation and responses of Cleinias that we are able to assemble the crucial features of hortatory argument. Our examination has uncovered the following:

- Goal: The outcome of the persuasive argument involves a specific action on the part of the interlocutor or audience.

- Medium: The interlocutor or audience is moved to this point through dialectic, exploring ideas by means of the posing and answering of questions.

- Stimulus: The questioning begins with a statement from Socrates, rather than a belief to which the interlocutor is committed.

- Procedure: The progress (as in other dialectical argument types) is rooted in agreements. Each point follows from what went before, not according to some necessary logic, but along the lines of practical inferences with an experiential plausibility (e.g., good things will make us happy if there is some advantage involved, and there is no advantage without use, but then the use must be correct).

- Outcome: Success is demonstrated through the ability of the interlocutor to give an account of ideas put forward, to defend claims with reasons. These "real" arguments serve as evidence that the action has been performed and suggest completeness to the hortatory argument.[7]

As we will see in further discussions, some of these features are common to other types of Socratic argument. What stands out as unique to the hortatory form is the goal and perhaps the specific outcome.

Hortatory Argument beyond the *Euthydemus*

Vlastos's reading does direct us to the development of Socratic dialectic beyond the early dialogues into the middle dialogues. And this development

---

7. Below, I consider what counts as failed accounts in the examples of Alcibiades and Cleitophon.

is applicable to the hortatory form of the dialectic. The *Republic* is a fitting place to look for this, given the central interest in a persuasive argument that will turn people to the just life and away from the unjust life (*Rep.* 357b). We will explore this dialogue in more depth later. But for now, it should suffice if we consider the two prongs of persuasive argument that are called for in the *Republic*. Potential philosophers need to be persuaded to turn to philosophy. This should involve the kind of process demonstrated between Cleinias and Socrates in the *Euthydemus*. But there is also the more difficult persuasion required to get others to accept these philosophers as legitimate governors of the state.

This second task will be particularly challenging because, on one level, people distrust Socratic dialectic! Adeimantus offers this criticism in Book VI. People react to Socrates in a specific way when they hear him speaking: "They think that because they are inexperienced in asking and answering questions, they are led astray a little bit by the argument at every question, and that when these little bits are added together at the end of the discussion, a great false step appears that is the opposite of what they said at the outset" (487b).[8] Several issues are apparent here. First, the kind of dialectic that is found problematic is that which we have already associated in a preliminary way with the *elenchus*: questions and answers that explore someone's statements but result in the refutation of their original assertion. Secondly, Adeimantus proceeds to add to this complaint that of those who do take up philosophy, the majority are bad, while the remainder are useless to the city. Socrates responds, ambiguously, that they seem to be telling the truth, so it is not clear whether the appearances involved refer to the appearance/reality distinction. But more to the point, Socrates's subsequent discussion explains the attitudes toward the philosophers and says nothing about the concern regarding the dialectical method.

There are numerous places in Plato's middle dialogues where commentators have suggested direct or indirect breaks between Plato and Socrates,[9] and this passage should be added to the list. As a method of refutation, the *elenchus* takes an individual to the point of confronting their own ignorance, but to proceed beyond that point, other dialectical resources are needed. As the analyses of Plato's use of argument types have already suggested, Plato has a number of goals in his works and adopts different argument types

---

8. From C. D. C. Reeve's Hackett translation (2014).

9. See Vlastos 1991 for an account of the shift in methods. I will explore this in detail in chapter 10.

to achieve those goals. The acquisition of truth that is so important to the Platonic philosopher (unlike the Socratic predecessor) cannot be achieved by means of the *elenchus* as this was employed in the early dialogues. *Republic* VI associated that method with a problematic view of philosophers, and this is a view that must be revised. Philosophers, going forward, will need different logical and persuasive tools. Here, I am interested in the persuasive tools exhibited through the use of hortatory arguments. I will return to consider this passage further in chapter 8.

The need exists (perhaps more urgently so) to turn the young to philosophy. But this task is more difficult in the wider context of the city environment. Even when the young are "turned around and drawn toward philosophy," people who depend on that individual will try "to prevent him from being persuaded," even to the extent of impeding the persuader (494d–e). And there is also the internal difficulty of the subject itself that leads many of those suited for philosophy to abandon it: the difficulty "concerned with arguments" (498a).[10] This introduces the prospect of failed hortatory arguments, whether for internal or external reasons. Alcibiades's revealing speech in the *Symposium* suggests that even the personal influence of Socrates may not have been sufficient to avoid this failure. At one point Alcibiades laments that he is ashamed that he is doing nothing about his way of life, "though I have already agreed with [Socrates] that I should" (*Symp.* 216b–c). The implication is that he had been persuaded by a hortatory argument but had been unable to translate it into action. Of course, it was part of the neutral definition of a hortatory argument that it had the goal of a specific action on the part of the interlocutor or audience. But it must be a measure of the success of the argument that the goal is forthcoming. In Alcibiades's case, the suggestion is, the failure is due to the individual involved.[11]

---

10. Later (*Rep.* 539b) we learn that young people tend to misuse argument when they first encounter it, using it for disputation (*antilogos*) and imitating those who have refuted them by refuting others. This leads not only to the discrediting of philosophy but also to the confusion of the young. On the face of it, this would seem a further indictment of the *elenchus*.

11. Arguably, the *Symposium* gives us examples of the product of hortatory arguments in the principal participants. This is suggested when Alcibiades addresses the "jury" that is to judge Socrates and identifies that the common characteristic binding them as a group is their all having been struck and bitten by philosophy as a result of their contact with Socrates (218a).

In addition to the case of Alcibiades, the suggestion that failure is due to the nature of the candidate is apparent in the *Cleitophon*, allowing that it is authentic.[12] Cleitophon criticizes Socrates on a number of points about his notion of justice and the way he presents it, suggesting the dialogue is related to the analyses of the *Republic*. But Cleitophon's closing criticism bears very much on Socrates's apparent refusal to provide him with a hortatory (protreptic) argument to lead him to justice: "Either you do not possess the knowledge or else you refuse to let me share it" (*Cl.* 410c).[13] He will turn, instead, to Thrasymachus, since Socrates seems "really willing to refrain at last from addressing to me these hortatory discourses" (410d). There may be clues in what Cleitophon says in this short dialogue and the way he seems to have misinterpreted the nature of justice as Socrates presents it that support his exclusion from the appropriate discourse. Indeed, he does not fare well in the *Republic* itself, where he attempts an interjection (*Rep.* 340b–c). But his interaction there is actually with Polemarchus (although he is commenting on the exchange between Socrates and Thrasymachus) and it is Polemarchus who corrects him, after which he falls silent and we hear no more. So, it seems that hortatory arguments are not suited for everyone. Or more to the point, not everyone is suited for them. In the *Cleitophon* and *Republic* I, Cleitophon is presented as such an unsuitable character along with the reasons for his unsuitability.

The contrast discussed in *Republic* VI between those who are drawn to philosophy and those who are led astray by external influences is a contrast we often find in Platonic dialogues, if only in the background, between the interests of the philosophers and those of the Sophists. People in general are more easily persuaded by the Sophists (and against philosophers) because Sophists speak to them in their terms, knowing what they believe. The Sophist then calls this wisdom and starts to teach it. But on Plato's terms, the Sophist in fact knows nothing about the reality of things taught (*Rep.* 493b–c). It is then no surprise that the majority cannot be philosophic.

The populism on display here might more charitably be cast as a humanism because that more readily describes the interests of the various Sophists operating in the state, including the still-present Thrasymachus who listens passively to this argument without complaint. In fact, Socrates

---

12. Its authenticity did not seem in dispute in antiquity, with doubts arising with Ficino (Slings 1999, 11).

13. Quotes from the *Cleitophon* are from Bury's translation (Plato 1929a).

emphasizes such a division in explaining that while the Sophists direct their attentions to human affairs, philosophers have no such leisure and look rather toward things that are orderly and the same (500b). This is a division of interests that draws Plato again and again. The Sophistic humanism being offered is a perennial threat to his own project. This is something we will return to in the chapters ahead.

Plato also uses the *Republic* to demonstrate different rhetorical devices that can be employed in hortatory argumentation. The beneficiaries of these arguments are the philosophically inclined Glaucon and Adeimantus. Like Cleinias, they are brought to philosophical insight through dialectical exchanges with Socrates. We will take up their examples in chapter 8.

Maieutic Arguments

Like the hortatory argument, the maieutic also bears a similarity to the *elenchus*, again due to its dialectical nature. But in this case the effort is directed to drawing out what the interlocutor knows. It is, then, methodologically subsequent to any elenctic result, which only discloses ignorance and cannot involve knowledge.

Maieutic arguments are most readily associated with the figure of the midwife and find their expression in two central dialogues, the *Symposium* and *Theaetetus*.[14] Ironically, one performance of the maieutic may be suggested in the reported conversation between Diotima and Socrates where Socrates does not take the midwife role. The discussion is dialectical, but it differs from other forms of Socratic argument in that Socrates, the respondent, knows things, and Diotima, conducting the investigation, knows he knows. This apparent play at autobiography on the part of Plato's character, with Socrates in the role of student providing one of the key reversals in the dialogue, does more than allow Socrates to avoid constructing a speech of his own (he is barren of ideas, after all). In addition, it sheds light on the presence of the philosophical midwife and, thereby, paves the way for the example of the *Theaetetus*.[15]

---

14. Diogenes Laertius (1853) casts the net far wider: "Of the midwife description we have the two *Alcibiades*'s, the *Theages*, the *Lysis*, the *Laches*" (*DL.* [Plato] XXXII).

15. Both dialogues belong to the middle to late period of Plato's life. The *Symposium* is dated between 385 and 370 BCE, and the *Theaetetus* around 369.

Diotima, Socrates tells us, taught him the "art of love," which in the context of the dialogue in which it occurs figuratively invites thoughts on the art of philosophical engagement. Having insisted that the purpose of love is "giving birth in beauty," at *Symposium* 206c–e,[16] Diotima explains that all are pregnant both in body and soul, proceeding to detail the pain of giving birth. This insertion "of a female bodily process into a text" (Hobbes 2007, 253) brings issues of reproduction to the fore, and it is to this context that the midwife image belongs. But it is not explicitly referenced here. The pregnant young of whom Diotima speaks seek out others of a like quality: "If he also has the luck to find a soul that is beautiful and noble and well-formed, he is even more drawn to this combination" (*Symp.* 209b). Out of this relationship ideas are conceived and given birth, and the two together then nurture the newborn (209c). The suggestion here is the newborn will also be well-formed (thus not in need of one aspect of the midwife's skills that will be noted below). Plato clearly creates a parallel between the Eros of Diotima's speech and the "Socrates" of Alcibiades's later speech (a speech given by a character who was not present during the delivery of the first part of the parallel). Both are a combination of poverty and plenty, both geniuses with "enchantments, potions, and clever pleadings" (203d). Both are caught in the divide between the mortal and immortal (and so notably asexual), and both are neither wise nor ignorant. Those limited to this middle realm, identified earlier as spirits (*daimons*), have the function of acting as messengers between gods and humans (202e), and we might allow that the midwife is a kind of intermediate of this type.

If this is indeed the renowned midwife of Plato's invention, then it is a description, not an illustration. For the latter, we must turn to the *Theaetetus*. And we might also further wonder about the type of argument that Diotima is presenting. While some of the young Socrates's statements are dismissed, none is examined over the course of a refutation. And nothing is drawn out of the young Socrates, so Diotima's discourse is not obviously maieutic in that sense. But Socrates does confess to having been persuaded by her argument and to thus try to persuade others (212b). So, he has been moved to action, and his subsequent behavior (as testified to by the other encomiasts) is indicative of Diotima's success. On these terms, we can assign her argument at least to the category of the hortatory.

---

16. I draw here from the Nehamas and Woodruff (1989) translation.

Myles Burnyeat begins his seminal paper on Socratic midwifery by observing that some passages in literature are so well known they paradoxically become very difficult to read (Burnyeat [1977] 1992, 53). Those of the *Theaetetus*, in which the nature and role of the intellectual midwife are apparently explicated, count among such passages. The image of Socrates as midwife, assisting others in bringing ideas to birth, is such a fixture of our textual history that its nature is assumed as unproblematic and it rarely becomes the topic of investigation. Burnyeat's analysis addresses the questions of whether the midwife image was associated with the historical Socrates or was a product of Plato's creativity and, having decided for the latter, the role that it serves Plato.

Principal evidence against the historical authenticity of the image, in Burnyeat's mind, is the ignorance that Theaetetus displays about the simile in the dialogue. Theaetetus is aware that Socrates employs the method of posing questions, that he is the son of a midwife (which Burnyeat and others accept), that he reduces people to a state of perplexity, and that the midwife role is fulfilled by women beyond the age of having children. But he has not heard that the questioning and perplexity are part of Socrates's having adopted his mother's role (*Tht.* 149a). Nor has he heard that midwives are the best matchmakers. In stressing these things, Plato "can have no other motive" (Burnyeat [1977] 1992, 54) than to divide fact from fiction, placing Socratic midwifery in the imaginary realm.

While this reading and division has been challenged (by Tomin [1987], for example, who sees the "parallel" allusion in the "earlier" *Clouds* as evidence for the historical fact of the association), Burnyeat's reading seems the more widely accepted interpretation. Tarrant (1988), for example, argues that the dating of both the *Theaetetus* and *Clouds* is ambiguous enough to obscure any claim of influence from one to the other and that, moreover, the "parallel" discussion in *Clouds* simply does not provide the required allusion since no intellectual midwifery is entailed there.

On the other hand, the argument for an association with the historical Socrates is strengthened by the discussion of Aristides in his *Reply to Plato* (2017). In the course of his disagreement over Plato's treatment of rhetoric, Aristides quotes several passages from the Socratic writer Aeschines of Sphettus, including the following from his lost dialogue *Alcibiades*. Socrates is speaking: "Thanks to the love I happened to feel for Alcibiades I had experienced exactly what happens to the Bacchants. When the Bacchants are inspired by their god, they draw honey and milk from places from which others cannot even draw water. I too, although I possess no learning that I might teach to someone and so do him good, nevertheless believed that by keeping company with Alcibiades I could make him better through my love" (Aeschines, cited in Aristides 2.74). On one reading, the phrase "although I possess no learning that I might teach to someone" may just be a remark of another Socratic reinforcing the argument that Socrates was not a teacher. But it can equally be a reference to the professed barrenness that is central to the midwife image. And of course, the first idea follows from the second anyway, so they are not in conflict. Moreover, the boast that, like the Bacchants, he can draw honey and milk from, we presume, young men like Alcibiades adds to the picture of someone devoid of ideas himself drawing them from others. If this reading is plausible, as I believe it is, it sets the invention of the barren Socrates outside of Plato's control alone and finds it shared by other writers of Socratic dialogues. Whatever the origin, we are left with a powerful image to add to Plato's inventory of stylistic devices. But of more relevance here, it is an image that captures the practices of maieutic argument.

It is the *Theaetetus* that gives us the fullest portrait of this form of argument and the situations that encourage it. In an investigation of the candidacy of sense experience as knowledge between 149a and 210b, three definitions are drawn from Theaetetus and examined.

In the dialogue, Socrates associates himself with female midwives, taking on their use of drugs and incantations to rouse the pangs of labor, their role as a matchmaker, and their status of sterility. But his role is judged more important than theirs because the female midwives do not assist in the birth of both children and images of them (*Tht.* 150b). The intellectual midwife by contrast, is different insofar as the art involved is "practiced upon men, not women, and in tending their souls in labour, not their bodies" (150c).[17] Moreover, Socrates's art includes the testing of the ideas that have been given birth and the judgment of whether to keep them and allow them to grow or to destroy them. Thus, the intellectual midwife's art involves the birth, testing, and assessment of ideas.

The first idea drawn from Theaetetus is his statement that knowledge is nothing other than perception or sense experience (151e). Socrates takes this definition and proposes that they examine it together to determine if it is real offspring or a wind-egg. This is the most examined definition in the dialogue, involving detours into associated ideas like Protagoras's measure maxim,[18] which Socrates judges to be tantamount to Theaetetus's

---

17. Translations of the text are taken from Fowler's Loeb edition (Plato 1921).

18. That the human being is the measure of all things, of things that are, that they are, and of things that are not, that they are not (*Tht.* 152a).

definition. However, indications within the text suggest that what we are actually witnessing here is the process of the idea coming to birth, which is not completed until 160e. At 157d, for example, after canvassing ideas related to the measure maxim, Socrates reminds Theaetetus that he is "merely acting as a midwife" to him: "Uttering incantations and giving you a taste of each of the philosophical theories, until I may help to bring your own opinion to light. And when it is brought to light, I will examine it and see whether it is a mere wind-egg or a real offspring." This indicates, then, that the birthing process is ongoing, as they search to verify the full nature of Theaetetus's idea. And, indeed, they finally confirm that on the terms explored, perception is knowledge and there is complete identity between the doctrine of Homer and Heraclitus, the doctrine of Protagoras, and "the doctrine of Theaetetus" (160d):

Soc.: Shall we say that this is, so to speak, your new-born child and the result of my midwifery? Or what shall we say?

Theat.: We must say that, Socrates. (160e)

The full extraction of the idea is not complete until 160d. It is then that the real testing begins, as the midwife must "perform the rite of running around with it in a circle—the circle of our argument" (160e) to see if it is worth rearing. Like a newborn child is carried around the family hearth and explored in that light to determine the presence of imperfections, the newborn idea will be similarly explored via the light of Socratic questioning.[19] Plato then provides another long stretch of the dialogue in which Protagoras's maxim is rigorously critiqued and found lacking, a critique that includes calling forth Protagoras from his grave to offer his own defense (166a, ff). During this process the third partner in the dialogue, the mathematician Theodorus, helps defend the doctrine because he had been a friend of Protagoras. What is noteworthy about this is that the testing of the newborn idea does not just involve the midwife, but others may be called to participate as the "family hearth" is extended to include friends and associates.

The examination ends with the recognition by Theaetetus that knowledge is not in the sensations but in the process of reasoning about them (186d), and Theaetetus is invited to offer a further definition to continue

---

19. The image of light/fire/sun that we associate with Platonic revelation is in operation here, extending this family of ideas.

the central exploration of the dialogue on the nature of knowledge. This definition and the third, which follows it, will be found like the first to be a wind-egg not worth raising. These refuted ideas are rejected, "exposed" and left to die. No one among the participants is prepared to defend them further or live with them. In the context of the society involved, the unwanted child is exposed to the elements and perishes.

Having discussed the phases of the midwife's activity (if not the details of the arguments involved), we turn now to the question of how this fits Plato's ends and belongs with the presentation of Socrates's behavior generally. Commentators have viewed the activity of the midwife in the *Theaetetus* as an extension of the elenctic examinations that characterize earlier dialogues, and some have also judged this to be a further reflection of the destructive ways Socrates proceeds. But both judgments need to be qualified, as my previous discussion of the hortatory arguments and future discussion of refutation arguments should indicate.

I. M. Crombie stresses that "no account of Plato is satisfactory if it fails to stress the midwife's ruthlessness" (1964, 17). But the ruthless activities Crombie is referring to are those on display in the *Apology*, where Socrates details his practice of examining the experts and reducing them to a position of being unable to say what they claim to know and where Crombie also wants to see the midwife at work. Indeed, it is because of his earlier "destructive" behavior that Tarrant judges we should not expect Socrates to be practicing midwifery on Euthydemus or Euthyphro (Tarrant 1988, 116). This does explain why we see the image only appearing after the early dialogues. But it overlooks what consideration of the full midwife analogy reveals: that the midwife is a product of Plato's *pharmakon*, with both positive and negative effects. Success is welcome around the hearth. But failure leads to the discarding of ideas, just as Athenian midwives would have "discarded" infants that failed to meet certain conditions. This darker aspect of Socrates lurks in the margins of the dialogue, just as what Plato has discarded has been moved to the margins of history, waiting to be tested again and perhaps rehabilitated by later generations.[20]

There are indeed allusions to the *Apology* in the *Theaetetus*. Socrates tells Theaetetus that the god compels him to act as a midwife (150c), just as the god had compelled him in the *Apology* to explore the claims of the experts. And there is a further reference to his "inner voice" (151a), acting as a negative

---

20. I have in mind the rehabilitation of Sophistic ideas like Protagoras's "measure maxim" by scholars such as Guthrie (1971) and Kerferd (1981).

restraint, forbidding him to associate with some men. Both elements link the two dialogues. But, more generally, the practices of the *Apology* (along with the examination of experts in dialogues like the *Euthyphro*) and the *Theaetetus* are noteworthy for their differences more than their similarities.

The principal difference lies, as Tarrant has observed (1988, 116), in the nature of the interlocutor. On the one hand (the *Apology*) we have experts, variously displayed, confident in their knowledge and arrogant in their (initial) exchanges. On the other hand (*Theaetetus*), we have young men who have yet to give birth and need assistance in the process, having no sense of the quality of the ideas they eventually produce. This suggests Theaetetus is one of many, among whom we might count the encomiasts of the *Symposium* and young companions of Socrates like Hippocrates in the *Protagoras* and Cleinias in the *Euthydemus*.

Hence, we should contrast (rather than compare) the maieutic process in the *Theaetetus*, where a candidate idea, born from the mind of a young man, is explored using the full resources of those present, including Theodorus and the (imagined) Protagoras, with the examination of an expert like Euthyphro, in which we see the full measure of the *elenchus*. Euthyphro comes forward confident in a prior knowledge that has supposedly informed his practice (and now the prosecution of his father) and willing to act as Socrates's teacher, as other experts will. By exploring his statements, or statements to which he is committed, Socrates leads him through a labyrinth of arguments (indeed like the circle of argument that characterizes the test of the *Theaetetus*) to a point where he is brought to perplexity, and hence given the opportunity to confront his own ignorance, to experience firsthand what he does not in fact know (rather than being told that he does not know it). Without doubt the early dialectic can be seen as a precursor of the midwife's maieutic activity, but it is not simply an early instantiation of it.

Details of the Account

Like hortatory arguments, those that are maieutic are distinct in their character and the conditions that govern them. The principal difference lies in the goal, but they also differ in structure and the ways they develop. And as noted earlier, there will be overlaps between them. Still, we can identify the following aspects with respect to the maieutic argument:

- Goal: The outcome of the maieutic argument involves not an action but a specific idea drawn from and belonging to the interlocutor.

- Medium: The interlocutor or audience is moved to this point through dialectic, exploring ideas by means of the posing and answering of questions.

- Stimulus: The questioning begins with an initial statement from the interlocutor.

- Procedure: The progress (as in other dialectical argument types) is rooted in agreements. Each point follows from what went before, not according to some necessary logic but along the lines of practical inferences with an experiential plausibility.

- Outcome: Success is demonstrated in the ability of the new idea to withstand examination by inquiry. Held to the light of reason, it is studied for flaws and pronounced fit should it be found free of flaws.

The Contrasts Made Clear

Hortatory arguments end, that is, the interlocutor either is or is not persuaded to take up the particular action (often, to turn to philosophy). And as we will see in the next chapter, the same holds for elenctic arguments: once a refutation has been given, the interlocutors go back to the beginning and start again, or they leave off the exchange altogether. But *maieutic* arguments can continue; there is no necessary end to the giving birth of ideas. Of course, one could insist that once one idea has arrived and been tested, then any continuation of the process would involve a new idea and in this sense it would resemble the *elenchus*. But the point is that with *maieutic* argument we see something on which Plato could build. Once a young mind has been turned toward philosophy—persuaded of its value—it becomes fertile ground for new ideas and a conduit for bringing such ideas from the intelligible realm into the visible. Thus, hortatory arguments are an important step in the progress of argument types in Plato's work. As will be seen in part III, to function dialectically, young men must first have been led in this way to an appreciation of philosophy. As such, argumentation can become a vehicle for the Platonic interest in moving beyond ignorance and opinion to the unfolding of permanent truths.

Chapter 2

Refutation

The Logic of the Early Dialogues

> When he himself went through any subject in argument, he proceeded upon propositions of which the truth was generally acknowledged, thinking that a sure foundation was thus formed for his reasoning
>
> —Xenophon (*Memorabilia* IV, VI, 15)

Introducing Socrates: The Structure of the *Laches*

The Socratic *elenchus* is one of the most closely and frequently scrutinized features of Greek philosophy, including the recent attention paid to it by Robinson ([1941] 1953) and Vlastos (1983). Yet its nature and meaning remain the subject of serious dispute (Scott 2002). It is agreed that it involves an examination, of either a person or a person's statements (Kahn 1996, 111). And it is further agreed that it ends in some kind of refutation (the choice of translation favored for *elenchus* by Liddell and Scott in their *Greek-English Lexicon* [1843]) of an assertion that has been "tested" by asking questions about it. Such a refutation invariably involves the uncovering of an inconsistency between a person's expressed statement and other things they believe (Young 2009, 59). What interests us here is the degree to which a "logic"[1] can be identified with this practice.

---

1. At this point, I will retain the broadest meaning for such a concept. Clearly, there was logic involved in the hortatory and maieutic arguments of chapter 1. But as we will see in this chapter, there is a more rigorous sense of "following from" than we have seen so far.

Examples of the *elenchus* are said to be repeatedly on display in the "early" Socratic dialogues, those that ostensibly show the practices and beliefs of the historical philosopher. Among these, the *Laches* is particularly useful for understanding what is involved, since this is a dialogue that seems explicitly designed to introduce both Socrates and his method.

The principal participants are the generals Laches and Nicias, along with Socrates. But the initiators of the discussion are Lysimachus and Melesias, who had been acquainted with Socrates's father, Sophroniscus, and are interested in finding teachers for their sons, Aristides and Thucydides, who are also present. As with other dialogues interested in the nature of virtues, father and son relationships are important here, with a concern for the characters of the younger men being particularly prevalent. This was the concern that drove Crito's interest in the *Euthydemus*. But there, the interlocutor of interest was a young man being directed toward philosophy; in the *Laches*, our interlocutors are mature purveyors of ideas associated with the principal concept of the inquiry—courage.

The characters of the *Laches* have different levels of acquaintance with Socrates, with that of Lysimachus and Melesias being the weakest. They had known him as a youth but seem unfamiliar with his current activities. It is the sons, Aristides and Thucydides, who identify him when called upon (*Lch.* 181a), reminding us of Socrates's fame among the youth. But the stronger acquaintance is held by Nicias and Laches. Socrates had served with Laches at Delium, fighting against the Boeotians, and had given a commendable account of himself during the retreat. If the rest of the soldiers had been prepared to act like Socrates, asserts Laches, then the disaster would have been averted (181b). We will see this association to be directly relevant to the ensuing conversation.

Nicias's acquaintance is of a different kind but perhaps even more significant because the activity he identifies is the one with which we should be most interested. While the issue seems to be about the boys and their education, Nicias warns that it will quickly shift once the discussion gets going. It appears to him that Lysimachus is not aware that

> whoever comes into close contact with Socrates and has any talk with him face to face, is bound to be drawn round and round by him in the course of the argument[2]—though it may have

---

2. Rosamond Kent Sprague gives "being led about by the man's arguments," but this introduces a suggestion that seems out of sync with Socrates's actual practice. Since, he will

started at first on a quite different theme—and cannot stop until he is led into giving an account of himself, of the manner in which he now spends his days, and the kind of life he has lived hitherto; and when once he has been led into that, Socrates will never let him go until he has thoroughly and properly put all his ways to the test. (187e–188a)

To enter into a conversation with Socrates is to become ensnared in a deeply personal investigation of one's life and actions. This is a point to which I will return at the end of the chapter.

That a harmony between the private and public self is held in high value is indicated by Laches in one of his early confessions. Sometimes he is a discussion-lover (*philologos*) and at others, a discussion-hater (*misologos*). When he hears someone discussing virtue or some other kind of wisdom, then his worthiness is measured in the harmony existing between the speaker's words and deeds (188d). Such a man achieves the greatest of harmonies, "fitting his deeds to his words in a truly Dorian mode." The person who acts in the opposite manner distresses Laches, making him look like a discussion-hater. It is such a harmony that Socrates exhibits in the *Apology* and that he expects in those he tests. It is such a harmony that characterizes the just person of *Republic* IV (443d–e), who must harmonize both the three parts of the self and the internal nature with the external role to which that person is best suited.

In fact, what we are being presented with in the opening half of the *Laches* is a compendium of central tenets that will characterize many other dialogues, emphasizing the introductory nature of this particular dialogue. It is, after all, not until virtually the midway point at 190e that any actual Socratic inquiry begins. Before that we learn not just of Socrates's propensity for interrogating the lives of those with whom he speaks, and of the importance of a harmony between words and actions, but also of the importance of valuing the knowledge of experts over the opinion of a majority (184e), along with the high value that is placed on being able to say what it is a person knows (190c). In such ways the long prologue of the *Laches* serves as a primer on Socratic behavior and themes, preparing the reader for what is to be illustrated here and in other companion dialogues.

---

insist elsewhere, it is never *his* arguments that do the leading but simply the statements themselves, once they have been drawn from the interlocutor. Moreover, the mention of "round and round" in Lamb's Loeb translation, which I draw from here, evokes the labyrinthine tangle of statements in which Euthyphro finds himself lost (*Euthphr.* 11c–d).

The second half of the dialogue presents a full account of Socratic refutation through a pattern of three definitions that are provided by interlocutors, then examined and subsequently found wanting. In other early dialogues, the first such definition is routinely presented in a casual way—as if the question is not difficult and can easily be handled—and using a practical illustration. This is the case in the *Laches*. The issue has developed from whether fighting in armor is a useful subject for the young to learn to who is expert in the care of the soul to what is meant by a particular part of virtue, namely courage. Laches sees nothing difficult in this, offering that courage is remaining at one's post to face the enemy and not running away (190e).

This is not what Socrates is looking for, and he is quick to share the blame for the mistake, not having asked the question correctly.[3] What Socrates does not do is draw attention to the dissonance between Laches's definition and his earlier praise of Socrates's behavior in the retreat at Delium, where we must suppose he was courageous while retreating.[4] This would immediately reveal a disharmony between action and speech. But on this point Plato remains silent.[5] Instead, Socrates is made to list a number of other examples that would seem equally to be cases where courage is apparent, before he points out that what he is looking for is not such an array of examples but what all of these cases have in common (191e). This quest for the universal standard by which acts can be measured and thus judged courageous or cowardly is a fixed opening feature of the kind of Socratic argument that interests us—the *elenchus*. The first definitions fail before they begin because they are misconceived.

So far, we have not directly seen refutation in the dialogue. The treatment of Laches's second definition remedies this. In an effort to identify what is the same in all cases of courage, Laches offers that "it is a certain endurance of the soul" (192b). It is quickly observed that some endurance is simply foolish, whereas they agree that courage is a fine (*kalon*) thing. So, there is a slight qualification and courage is offered as "wise endurance"

---

3. In other dialogues, like the *Euthyphro* or *Meno*, Socrates takes pains to first elicit the agreement of his interlocutor that what they are after is the standard by which acts can be judged (as pious or virtuous).

4. What we suppose here is confirmed by Alcibiades in the *Symposium* (221a–b), who judges that Socrates was more composed than Laches.

5. Plato's use of silence as an argumentative strategy is explored in chapter 7.

of the soul (192d). This definition is on the right track insofar as it is the kind of definition that Socrates was expecting. It can be tested in the way that becomes common in the "Socratic" dialogues.

Socrates begins by asking whether all kinds of wisdom are involved here and providing the example of someone who endures in spending money wisely. This is not the kind of thing Laches intends. Nor does he mean the kind of endurance shown by a doctor who refuses food and drink to a son whose lungs are inflamed. More apt to the setting is the next example, of a man in battle who endures because he calculates help is on the way, the enemy has inferior numbers, and his position is strong. Who is courageous, this man or the one in the opposite camp who holds out against such odds? For Laches, it is the one in the opposite camp. And yet, observes Socrates, such a man's endurance is more foolish than that of the first man. Further examples are offered, pitting people who know against those who take risks, and in each case Laches sees courage in the behavior of the one without knowledge or skill. Socrates draws this examination to a close by recalling their agreement that foolish endurance was disgraceful and harmful, while courage was fine. "But now," he concludes, "on the contrary, we are saying that this base thing—foolish endurance—is courage" (193d). Laches agrees that they are not talking sense.

By investigating the statements drawn from Laches, they move from an assertion that courage is wise endurance (*A*) to the recognition that courage is not wise endurance (*not-A*). The second definition has led to a contradiction and has thereby been refuted, and this serves as an example of Socratic refutation. It is part, but not all, of the Socratic method or practice because this involves a pattern of investigation that includes the interlocutor's responses to the experience of being tested, as they move from a position of certainty (claiming they know what is at stake) to one of confusion and perplexity where they are no longer confident and cannot speak. Laches, for example, had conveyed confidence that he knew what courage was in the casual way in which he approached the first definition. And even the second definition is offered with a measure of reluctance: "[Courage is] a certain endurance of the soul, *if I am to speak of the natural quality that appears in them all*" (192b–c, my italics). This is a common reaction on the part of such interlocutors, as Socrates insists that it is indeed necessary to say this, since it is only such "sayings" that can be examined. Likewise, Laches's next reaction is part of the pattern of the experience, as he realizes that he cannot say what courage is:

> For my part I am ready, Socrates, to continue without faltering; and yet I am unaccustomed to discussions of this sort. But a certain ambitious ardor has got hold of me at hearing what has been said, and I am truly vexed at finding myself unable to express offhand what I think. For I feel that I conceive in thought what courage is, but somehow or other she has given me the slip for the moment, so that I fail to lay hold of her in speech and state what she is. (194a–b)

The confession here is important: he is "unable to express" what he thinks and cannot "lay hold of her in speech and state what she is." An interlocutor's failure to say what he thought he knew and his confrontation with his own ignorance is a further fixed stage in the procedure. Later, we will consider how other interlocutors express themselves at this point. In the *Laches*, it is particularly painful given the earlier agreement that "of that which we know . . . we can also say what it is" (190c). The implication is clear: if you cannot state it, you did not know it.

In other dialogues, an interlocutor is given another chance to offer a third definition. But in the *Laches*, it is Nicias who takes up the challenge, with Laches joining Socrates and sharing the important role of examining what is being said (197e). Nicias defines courage as "the knowledge of what is to be dreaded or dared, either in war or in anything else" (195a).

The long examination of this definition need not delay us, given that we have already looked in detail at the previous one. Suffice it to note that the investigation proceeds on the establishment of certain agreements: that they are not looking for all of virtue, but that courage is a part of virtue, and that fearful things are future evils, while those involved with hope are future non-evils or goods. It then transpires that the same knowledge has an understanding of the same things, whether future, present, or past. So, courage cannot be knowledge of the dreaded and dared "for it comprehends goods and evils not merely in the future, but also in the present and the past and in any stage" (199c). Moreover, Nicias is talking about all virtue after all, since this is the case with all kinds of knowledge (199e). Nicias's original definition (*A*) has led to its opposite (*not-A*).

What we have in the *Laches* is a logical analysis nestled within a pattern of encounters that focuses on the experience the interlocutor has of seeing his own ideas scrutinized, moving him from a position of confidence to one of perplexity and confusion and the resulting realization that he does not know what he thought he knew, or at least cannot say what it is. Elsewhere, we might find examples of both the specific logical investigation and the wider experiential pattern.

The Power of Refutation

In the *Apology*, for example, the larger discourse is a trial speech, but it contains examples of the *elenchus* in the exchanges between Socrates and Meletus. Each of the two specific charges brought against Socrates—that of corrupting the youth and that of not believing in the gods in whom the city believes but in other spiritual entities (*Ap.* 24b–c)—is addressed in this way. In the second instance, for example, Socrates asserts that Meletus appears to contradict himself (*Ap.* 27b). But the appearance, of course, would not be sufficient to establish the case. Socrates invites the jury to "examine" with him the apparent contradiction. Socrates's approach is to offer comparable situations to the one that seems expressed by Meletus's indictment: that Socrates does not believe in gods but does believe in spiritual or divine matters. No one believes in human activities who does not believe in humans, or horsemen's activities who does not believe in horses, or flute-playing activities who does not believe in flute-players. Meletus finally answers in agreement to the proposition that no one believes in spiritual activities who does not believe in spirits. He allows that Socrates believes in spiritual things and teaches about them. Spiritual things require spirits, and these are either gods or children of gods. In which case, Meletus is contradicting himself, since he says that Socrates does "not believe in gods and then again that [he does], since [he does] believe in spirits" (*Ap.* 27c–d). As a logical exercise, this is a simple case of seeing what must follow if something else is the case. More particularly, it shows an inconsistency in Meletus's belief set, especially if the second charge has been expressed in this contradictory way (as first stated, it was simply that Socrates believed other spiritual things than the city's gods). It illustrates the core of elenctic inquiry: taking an expressed belief and showing that it leads to a contradiction.[6] As Socrates aptly observes: "You cannot be believed, Meletus, not even by yourself" (*Ap.* 26e).

As a trial speech, the *Apology* is not a Platonic dialogue per se. It was important to illustrate the kind of dialectical activity that has supposedly led

---

6. Brickhouse and Smith (1991) argue that the cross-examination of Meletus provides other results beyond just the refutation of the charges.

to Socrates being on trial, and that is what these exchanges with Meletus accomplish, but the larger discourse of the text fits into a different genre. Other dialogues do serve as clearer vehicles for Socrates's practice, and without the detailed preliminaries of the *Laches*. The *Euthyphro*, for example, gives us the full treatment: three definitions, the first of which is misstated and the other two of which lead to contradictions once tested; the shifts in confidence experienced by Euthyphro; the arrival at a state of complexity; and an aporetic conclusion.

Unlike the conversation of the *Laches*, in the *Euthyphro* Socrates firsts elicits his interlocutor's agreement that what they are in search of is the standard by which piety can be judged. He asks, "Isn't the pious itself the same as itself in every action?" (*Euthphr.* 5d),[7] to which Euthyphro readily agrees. The importance of this agreement registers later when it is clear that Euthyphro would like to take it back, but he cannot do so. The success of Socratic dialectic depends on the participants' commitments to the statements they assert.[8] To the extent that this is present, there may be little difference between the testing of persons and the testing of statements. These statements are an extension of the person, an act they perform like other actions. As Socrates looks for that harmony between speech and action that Laches had identified as important, so he holds his interlocutors to what they have said. As he explains this to Euthyphro: "For you agreed that all impious actions are impious and all pious actions pious through one form, or don't you remember?" (*Euthphr.* 6d). Euthyphro does remember, and he cannot take it back.

This charge from Socrates is in response to Euthyphro's first definition. As with the example in the *Laches*, the interlocutor begins with examples of what is close at hand, failing to recognize that it is the common feature of these cases that needs to be identified. Likewise, Euthyphro exhibits a faith in his statements such that he believes they really require no investigation. But that is the thrust of the method on show here. After Euthyphro's revision of his second definition (piety is what *all* the gods love [*Euthphr.* 9e]), Socrates asks, "Then aren't we going to examine that in turn, Euthyphro,

---

7. Citations to the *Euthyprho* are to the Reeve translation (Reeve 2002).

8. In contrast to the eristic method of the Sophists that we saw in the *Euthydemus*, which required no such commitment. At one point there, Dionysodorus complains that no one should care what was said earlier: "Are you such an old Cronus as to bring up what was said in the beginning?' (*Euthd.* 287b). But consistency across the discussion is exactly the point.

to see whether what we said is true? Or are we going to let it alone and accept it from ourselves and from others just as it stands?" The task is to follow the statements and see where they lead. Because these statements issue from the belief set of the interlocutor, they are public expressions of the private life. And in examining them, that life itself is examined, and so the examination takes on an acutely personal value.

As the dialogue proceeds, the dynamic in the relationship between Socrates and Euthyphro begins to shift. Euthyphro had presented himself in the role of teacher, fully in control of knowledge that will inform the lives of both of them, since Socrates is charged with impiety and Euthyphro has issued a similar charge against his own father. These are the very real consequences of the discussion that is unfolding. Socrates, genuinely or otherwise, has welcomed Euthyphro's expertise and readily placed himself in the role of student. But after a crucial point in the dialogue, when Euthyphro allows that the pious is loved by the gods because it is pious and is not pious because it is loved by the gods, the relationship abruptly changes (*Euthphr.* 10d). In this admission, Euthyphro has effectively placed the inquiry into piety outside of his domain of expertise. After all, he is an expert on the gods and religious affairs. If piety derives its nature from the gods, then Euthyphro's expertise is relevant. But if, as he now agrees, the existence of piety is not dependent on the gods but separate from them, then Euthyphro has no more authority to pronounce on its nature than, well, Socrates. Suddenly, the teacher/student roles dissolve and the pair find themselves on level pegging. What might have appeared as a dry exercise in contradiction (Euthyphro's second definition, *A*, has led to another *not-A*) is so much more: the ground beneath Euthyphro's feet is giving way, everything he has believed up to this point is now in question, and his status in Athenian society is in danger of being disrupted. This is the fate that expert after expert receives as they encounter examples of the *elenchus*. It is, of course, very different from what was experienced by the young recipients of hortatory and maieutic arguments in the previous chapter.

If what we see in early dialogues like the *Laches* and the *Euthyphro* is reflective of the practices of the historical Socrates, then from the start of his philosophical life Plato was acquainted with a logic rooted in personal experience. Here is an interest in "what follows from what" not in terms of an academic exercise, but in terms of the beliefs that inform the lives of real people. This is why the moments of perplexity that result from the specific elenctic episodes are so disturbing for those who experience them. They involve disconnections between what they believe and what they can defend. Thus the alarm Euthyphro conveys when he says: "I have no way of telling you what I have in mind, for whatever proposition we put forward goes around and refuses to stay put where we establish it" (*Euthphr.* 11b). This logical labyrinth in which they have become lost, an idea reinforced by the reference to Socrates's "ancestor" Daedalus and his construction of statues so lifelike they could move, is a fitting metaphor for the method itself. The challenge is always to find statements that "stay put" and do not move around. Language is a fluid medium that does not work well as a repository for the fixed ideas of Plato's metaphysics. Yet it is the only tool at hand. It must be organized into statements that act as ballasts, weighing down the truth in the visible world of flux: a world of examples, of courage and piety, that is underlain by something permanent about which these examples report. On Platonic terms, the suggestion is that no fixed point will be found until they escape the labyrinth in a movement upward, as Daedalus and Icarus did. This is one of the earliest allusions to a metaphor that will act as a unifying argumentative device in the middle dialogues—the sun.

The disorienting experience provided by the *elenchus* is felt by friend and foe alike. Crito, a friend if not a philosophical equal, confesses that puzzlement felt in common by many Socratic interlocutors when, having confidently bribed his way into the jail with the intent of freeing Socrates, he is reduced to confusion when his argument that such an escape would be just is contradicted. "I cannot answer your question, Socrates" (*Crito* 50a). But the literal "for there is nothing in my mind" better conveys the pain of confusion involved, because this conclusion also has consequences for the participants.

Crito's discomfiture comes at the end of a series of rehearsed arguments because here the investigation is not being conducted for the first time. Socrates invites Crito to recall what they have found on an earlier occasion to see if their conclusions about just actions "are still the same." Hence, the repeated refrain from Crito: "Yes, it still stands. . . . It still stands" (*Crito* 48b). The "expert" here, deemed so because of past insight, allows affection to dim his reason. But just as importantly, it indicates that Socratic inquiry has achieved success in the past.[9] In his gentle rebuke of Crito, Socrates appeals to the fixedness of past insights and a stability that underlies the sudden exigencies of the moment. Socrates is not, he reminds Crito, "the sort of person who's just now for the first time persuaded by nothing within

---

9. Suggesting, to my mind, that the *Crito* belongs later in the corpus, since it offers a post-*aporia* approach to arguments.

me except the argument that on rational reflection seems best to me . . . I can't now reject *arguments I have stated before* just because this misfortune has befallen me" (*Crito* 46b, my italics).[10] Once left, it seems the labyrinth can be revisited. But at least now the statues are no longer Daedalian, and there's a Theseus who knows the way out.

Details of the Account

Having discussed and illustrated the *method* of the *elenchus*, it will be useful in summary to set out its features in the same manner as was done for the hortatory and maieutic arguments of chapter 1:

- Goal: The outcome of the refutation argument ostensibly is to see whether a person who claims to know X (courage, piety, etc.) is able to give an account of X. While it may involve an insight into the said person's ignorance (which the testing of statements has exposed), this is more a consequence than a professed goal.

- Medium: Once again, the interlocutor is moved to this point through dialectic, exploring ideas by means of the posing and answering of questions. This is characteristic of all Socratic arguments.

- Stimulus: The questioning begins with an assertion (definition), A, from the interlocutor that expresses his belief about X. But the deeper source is some event or events from the lives of the interlocutors; they have personal stakes in the outcome of the investigations because of the way their lives are externalized in the statements examined.

- Procedure: Here, the steps involved are easier to identify, in part because they are replicated in different dialogues. (1) The interlocutor is *committed* to the statements put forward and cannot retract that commitment. (2) The various statements are *examined* to see where they lead. Here, an argument has a serial nature, set out in a path to be followed. (3) The

---

10. Citations to the *Crito* are from the Reeve translation (Reeve 2002).

argument leads from *A* to a *contradiction, not-A*. This readily captures the refutation that defines the argument-type. (4) The contradiction elicits *confusion* in the interlocutor, which, from a positive viewpoint, can produce the insight that he does not know what he thought he knew.[11]

- Evidence: Success of the refutation is seen in the logical demonstration as the argument develops from *A* to *not-A*. Here, Plato's Socrates reveals himself as a careful reasoner of some acuity.

Relationships between the Account of the *Elenchus* and Other Types of Argument

There are intrinsic connections between the three types of argument that have been canvassed, which accounts for why they are often folded together in common accounts of "Socratic dialectic" or reduced to the *elenchus*, as if that covers all the reasoning of the Socrates of Plato's dialogues. In the first, evidence of a common connection lies in the source for the material (statements) of the arguments. The hortatory argument illustrated in the *Euthydemus* transforms in the second Socratic segment in ways that begin to suggest ideas are being drawn from Cleinias (that he is giving birth to them) as he is asked, and is able, to give an account of what he believes. Once the young man has been turned to philosophy, having been persuaded by the hortatory argument, then he becomes a candidate for original thought, albeit with the assistance of the midwife. And, as we will explore further in the next section, the refutation of arguments that characterizes the *elenchus* amounts to a refutation of those who profess those arguments. They involve the public exposure of private beliefs now tested under a device of logical inquiry. All three types of Socratic argument delve deeply into, and draw their impetus from, the interlocutors.

A second and related point is the firsthand experience available to those interlocutors. They are invited to see things for themselves, rather

---

11. There is often an ambiguity in the text as to the existence of this insight. Perhaps it is an insight more intended for the audience (readers) than the interlocutor. A figure like Euthyphro seems never to fully understand the ignorance that is revealed to him, and it is unclear where he is going when he hurries off at the end of the dialogue (to withdraw the charge against his father, or to continue to pursue it). A figure like Meno, on the other hand, readily grasps the import of the contradiction and the consequences that follow (leading to his expression of the paradox associated with his name [*Meno* 80d]).

than simply being shown. The reader will repeatedly grasp that Socrates has "thought ahead" in the argument and seen where it is going. He could simply call a halt to a thread of inquiry when he realizes it will fail. But he allows it to continue because there is value in the other participants experiencing this failure for themselves.[12] This practice highlights the role that argumentation of this type plays in Platonic pedagogy. We may recall the claims of the *Apology* that Socrates was not a teacher.[13] On the face of the matter, there were political reasons for Plato saying this. Several of Socrates's so-called students (like Alcibiades and Critias) were complicit in the downfall and treatment of Athens at the end of the Peloponnesian War. And while a general amnesty had been issued regarding the actions of Athenians during the rule of the tyranny that Sparta had imposed after victory, that "forgetting" does not seem to have extended to Socrates's alleged influence. But this aside, there are genuine pedagogical reasons for the claims Plato makes about Socrates. The *Meno* provides a vivid contrast between the paid education that Meno has received from Gorgias, where he has been told many things but is unable to replicate what he has been told when called upon (73c–76d), and the painstaking approach of Socrates to both Meno and the boy from Meno's household as he invites them into a firsthand encounter with ideas from which, we assume, they will emerge with a firmer grasp of what they have encountered.[14]

We also see similarities in the failures that arise with respect to each kind of argument. As Socrates explains to Crito in the *Euthydemus*, his attempt together with Cleinias to find the one knowledge that combines its nature with its use fails. They were caught in a type of labyrinth of words, and however they tried to advance, they kept finding themselves back again at the beginning: "We twisted around again and found ourselves practically at the beginning of our search" (*Euthd.* 291b–c). This cannot fail to evoke the similar description from the *Euthyphro*, where Euthyphro finds that he is caught in such a labyrinth because none of their statements stays where they have put them but keep moving around. While these failures issue only in frustration rather than the harsher treatment of the failed "wind-eggs"

---

12. This is vividly illustrated in the *Lysis* where Lysis himself learns to allow his friend to experience the failure of his reasoning. I will consider this in part II.

13. This point is one of the major variants between Plato's account of the trial and that of Xenophon (2013).

14. I give more attention to these events of the *Meno* in the discussion of Plato's dialectic in chapter 11.

of the *Theaetetus*, they reinforce the fact that we are being given plausible strategies of argument that are prone to error rather than guarantees of success requiring only the application of a simple and trite formula. Again, the onus falls on the abilities of the interlocutors to think for themselves and strive for improvements in their reasoning and understanding.

The Ethotic Element in Socratic Arguments

We are used to thinking of arguments as detached, static things. This is a consequence of people encountering arguments in the logic classroom, where they have been detached from their sources and can then be laid out, rather like lifeless specimens, and tested for cogency. But the hortatory, maieutic, and elenctic arguments of Socratic practice reveal a different side (or depth) to such "products" of the argumentative experience. As has been repeatedly observed in this chapter, Socratic arguments are characterized by their involvement with the lives of the participants. It is the dialogic nature of the discourse that brings this to light. In saying this, I refer not just to the medium through which the examples come down to us—the Platonic *Dialogues*—although there is a necessary relationship here, but more precisely to the *activities* that are being illustrated.

In these argument types we witness reason in action when argumentation is used to investigate beliefs and the lives that issue from those beliefs. Through these processes we glimpse the intimacy between character and action on which the Greeks relied. A good person will do good things, and vice versa. We see this implied in part of Socrates's defense in the *Apology*: that a good person will harm no one, not even themselves. This is a feature that may well distinguish the varieties of Socratic dialectic from later Platonic dialectic. The introduction of Socrates and his ways in the *Laches* make clear how the worthiness of an individual is measured in the harmony between actions and words, as he strives to fit "his deeds to his words in a truly Dorian mode" (*Lch.* 188d).

Later, in the *Rhetoric*, Aristotle[15] will draw attention to the importance of character (ethos), arguing that "it is hardly an exaggeration to say that there is no more authoritative proof than character" (1356a13).[16] This judg-

---

15. Or if not Aristotle himself, given the debates over authorship (McAdon 2004), an associate who is thoroughly Aristotelian in understanding and voice.
16. From the 2018 Waterfield translation (Aristotle 2018b).

ment derives from the claim that we are more ready to trust good people, and so speakers should aim to convey credibility through their choices of words (and from this derives a whole tradition of ethotic argument,[17] where character becomes a central consideration in the evaluation of reasoning). But a more varied and complex appreciation of ethos is already operating in Plato's texts, where what is said cannot be divorced from who says it, where the commitments of speakers track them through their subsequent statements, and where actions and beliefs are intimately woven together.

Aristotle's concern for credibility is already apparent in the human drama of Plato's *Apology*. What is at stake there is Socrates's attempt to protect the harmony of character that he has brought into balance over the course of his life and the court's attempt to disrupt that harmony. At one point, in countering the belief that he set allegiance with one political system over another, Socrates resorts to a particular kind of "substantial evidence" in providing the jury with "not words, but what you value, deeds" (*Ap.* 32a). And he proceeds to narrate two events from his autobiography that reveal him defying both the tyranny and the democracy on different occasions when each was in power in Athens because in each case authorities were demanding he do something unjust. In repeating the strategy of his argument—"again not by words but by deeds" (*Ap.* 32d)—Socrates demonstrates a consistency of character (along with a clear knowledge of the right virtuous choice). Likewise, having been found guilty and required to suggest a punishment (and with the closeness of the vote against him one would have appreciated a sympathetic response to a proposal of exile), Socrates proposes free meals for life in the Prytaneum, thus reinforcing his belief that he is a benefactor of the state. In proposing this, there is a sense that Socrates cannot speak otherwise; exile would be a harm and, as noted above, he is incapable of harming anyone, even himself. The consistency of character and argument thus dominates the argumentation of the trial once it is viewed from the perspective of the principal life involved.

This, then, is the common feature that Plato captures in the three kinds of Socratic argument—the interrelation of life and reason.[18] And this is not an atypical feature particular to Plato and Socrates, it reflects the beliefs of the cognitive environment of Athens at that time. In his *Defense of Palamedes*, Gorgias draws attention to the character of Palamedes, stressing the shameful

---

17. For discussions of this tradition see Tindale (1999, 74–75; Walton 2006b).

18. On this reading, Kahn (1996, 97) is unwise to insist on a distinction between an *elenchus* that tests persons and one that tests propositions.

actions he avoided doing because "it is impossible for one applying himself to the latter to apply himself to this sort of thing" (*DK* 82, B1, 1a 31). The claim here is that there is a strong (causal even) relationship between the public actions performed by a person and the internal character behind them. Actions become a window into the character. Moreover, a wicked person performs bad actions and a good person good actions. We may cringe today at the generalizations suggested by such beliefs, and certainly more nuanced versions of such a creed can be extracted from the early texts of virtue theory, like the first two books of the *Nicomachean Ethics*. But my intention here is to uncover the ethotic source of the argument types involved in Socratic dialectic.

It is also the case that Gorgias's *Palamedes* is noteworthy for the several allusions it makes to Plato's *Apology* (or perhaps the allusional direction is the reverse),[19] so maybe the attitude to character is something else being copied between the texts. But a more moderated claim underlies the projects of the virtue ethicists, a group that included both Socrates and Plato. On these terms, the examples from Plato and Gorgias reflect a general way in which actions revealed character for the Greeks and their belief that if a certain character had been established—through speech or actions—then actions inconsistent with that character became unlikely if not impossible. On this reading, there is something in Socrates's character that compels him to make the proposal he does near the close of his defense because he cannot act otherwise. It is against the background of such beliefs that Aristotle's promotion of *ethos* as a persuasive force becomes plausible.

Whatever beliefs in the relation of character and action held sway in the society, an intimacy between the arguments advanced and the lives of the persons involved underlies the argumentative displays we have seen across a range of Platonic dialogues. This is more than the dramatic medium supplied by such texts (although they also serve that purpose well); it demonstrates the human roots of a logical perspective that ultimately reflects powerful ways in which reason operates to improve the lives of those who use it.

---

19. These two texts, along with Isocrates's *Antidosis*, have many structural points in common and generally exhibit patterns of imitation. Isocrates clearly drew on the earlier texts in constructing his personal defense, but the chronology of the other two remains unclear, and it is possible that they both point to an underlying "Ur" text. See Tindale (2010, 121–28).

Chapter 3

Contentious Arguments

Preconditions for Aristotle's Theory of "Fallacy" in the Dialogues of Plato

> To consider how we may speak in defense of what is false, or even what is unjust, is not without its use, if for no other reason than we may expose and refute fallacious arguments with the greater ease.
>
> —Quintilian (*Institutes of Oratory*, 12, 1, 34)

Raising the Question of Fallacy for Plato

In raising the question of fallacy in Plato, it is not my intention to explore, as others have done, the presence of fallacies in the dialogues, although we cannot avoid taking note of some of them. Nor do I argue that there is anything as comprehensive as the theory Aristotle begins to provide in the *Sophistical Refutations* (*SR*). Rather, I consider the degree to which Plato expresses a firm understanding of bad reasoning that could amount to something theoretical and serve as a precursor for what Aristotle later develops and, generally, for later fallacy theory in Informal Logic, where traditional fallacies have received rigorous attention.[1] After all, Aristotle is

---

1. In his paper "The Roots of Informal Logic in Plato," James Benjamin calls Plato's role in the origins of Informal Logic "complicated" (1997, 33). But beyond noting that Plato provides "the foundation for an examination of fallacy in informal logic" (29), no details of such a foundation are suggested. Nor is there any mention of the *Euthydemus*

explicit in his claim that he is the first to provide the kind of treatment that he does, for with respect to the inquiry into fallacies (paralogisms)[2] it is not a question of it having been previously elaborated only in part because it had not existed at all (*SR* 183b35). On the other hand, it seems unwise to expect the theory of fallacy that commentators attribute to Aristotle to have had no precedents at all. Moreover, as we began to see in the debates of the *Euthydemus* discussed in chapter 1, one of the particular concerns motivating Plato is the consideration of the question of fallacy and how it should be understood. It is also my intention, then, to explain and explore that concern. In this way, the earlier discussions of positive Socratic argument are complemented by an investigation of bad argument.

Of course, to ask about any rudimentary theory of fallacy in Plato invites a number of preliminary questions and qualifications, the answers to which can themselves be insightful. What, after all, would count as a theory of fallacy for Plato? Following again from Robinson's (1953) cautions, we should not expect Plato to hold the kinds of contemporary notions that prevail today. The suggestions of other historians of philosophy, like Ian Hacking and David Owen, are useful here: just as Descartes did not seem to share our sense of inference (Hacking 1973) or Hume to use reasoning as we do (Owen 2002), nor might a Platonic concept of fallacy have any deep connections with our current evolved understandings. Furthermore, if we are to take a theory of fallacy to be the counter-side to a positive theory of reason (as our appreciations of an oppositional thinker like Plato would invite), then a study of fallacy in Plato should shed further light on his understanding of argument per se. If we take fallacies to be in a central sense flawed arguments of some repeatable kinds (Hamblin 1970), then this reinforces the importance of Plato's view of good arguments.

What Counts as a Theory of Fallacy?

In contemporary parlance, we are likely to think of "fallacies" as arguments that fail to meet or exhibit some key criteria of correctness or as violations of rules that govern good argumentation. These ideas reflect the way appreciations of the theory and practice of argumentation have developed

---

or *Sophist* (beyond observing that the method of composition and division found there will influence Aristotle [30]).

2. The translation of this term is discussed below.

in the Aristotelian tradition. But in certain strange ways (which we will not explore here) that "tradition" is often removed from its own roots in Aristotle's milieu. Aristotle was concerned first and foremost with *sophistical* refutations, which appear to be real refutations but are not.[3] Thus, the standard against which they are judged is the refutation or *elenchus* that we explored in the last chapter. Given this familiarity, we can consider whether there is some significant difference between the earlier *elenchus* and the refutations of the *SR*.

The argumentative practice that focused on refutation is related to the method of question and answer by which Socrates conducts his examinations and which Aristotle calls "peirastic": "those [arguments] which are based on opinions held by the answerer" (*SR* 165b3–6). A thesis is refuted only when its negation is derived from the answerer's own beliefs. This reflects Socrates's repeated request of his interlocutors that they say only what they believe.

Focusing on the *elenchus* contrasts somewhat with the treatments of previous writers on this theme, like Robinson (1942) and Sprague (1962). Sprague manages to produce an entire study of fallacy in Plato's work (primarily looking at the *Euthydemus* and with the goal of saving Plato from the charge of having committed fallacies)[4] without really defining her central term. Her final chapter does suggest that fallacies are "bad arguments," but in the context of the eristic arguments she has been exploring, the specific nature of this badness remains unclear. Robinson has a more contemporary view implicit in his treatment. As evidence that Plato must have had some awareness of fallacies, he writes: "When the greatness of a great man expresses itself frequently in highly formalised and explicit chains of deduction, it stands to reason that the possibility of fallacy must occur to him in some shape" (1942, 102). But he surmises that Plato has no word or phrase that means "fallacy," offering only vague notions like antilogical, eristical, and

---

3. I am interested here with "fallacy" as it is understood in the *SR* and not in the later logical works or the *Rhetoric*. The treatment in the *SR* is Aristotle's earliest and involves the identification of a list of thirteen. In the *Prior Analytics* two of these are omitted (Begging the Question and Many Questions) because they are strictly dialectical, and he provides a formal analysis of the rest. Then, in the *Rhetoric* we find a final list of nine, which are given very short discussion. The root theory, then, is that of the *SR*, which is also the most detailed.

4. On a similar note, Lutoslawski (1897) judges it a measure of Plato's growth as a logician that logical fallacies are found often in the early dialogues but rarely in those that are judged to be late (525).

sophistical.[5] Even Aristotle, he notes, could understand the latter only by means of "unsatisfactory phrases" like "Sophistical refutation" (103). But it is exactly in the direction of such "unsatisfactory phrases" that we must look if we are to appreciate Plato's engagement with fallacy as a topic of inquiry.

Aristotle's treatment of fallacies in the *SR* focuses on dialogical exchanges. This partly accounts for some of the awkwardness of modern treatments of fallacy that have tried to retain Aristotle's labels while avoiding the specific dialectical context of their origin. In his seminal work on the subject, Charles Hamblin (1970) recognized that the nature of many fallacies is understood better "when we come to put [the concept] in the context of disputation on the Greek pattern, as Aristotle originally intended it" (33). As we have seen in the previous chapter, refutations arise as the goal of examinations, where one participant puts forward a thesis and another introduces questions for that thesis. The statements involved are examined in a conversational exchange with each move agreed upon. The goal is to arrive at a refutation of a thesis, that is, a contradiction.

This practice appears to have been central to the procedures employed in the Academy, where structured games or exercises involved attempts to defend and refute a thesis (Tindale 2007, 7), and it is also a practice that we see in the early Socratic dialogues, which involve examinations of statements that usually result in refutations of the theses put forward (and, hence, the dialogues are seen as aporetic). The kinds of refutation we saw in Socratic practice would have been viewed as acceptable by Aristotle. Insofar as it is correctly exercised, a refutation is not sophistical.

The failure to achieve this end in a reasonable fashion, to circumvent the process in some way, means the refutation is only apparent and not real. This is what Aristotle means by "sophistical." The fallaciousness in this stems from disruptions in the natural moves of the dialogue toward a contradiction. Take, for example, the very basic *ignoratio elenchi*. This translates as "ignorance of what a refutation is" and is understood as the failure to prove what should be proven. While it is first introduced as one

---

5. Sprague takes Robinson to task for concluding that Plato can have no consciousness of fallacy (or of individual fallacies) if he had no general term for fallacy. She insists that Plato's general reluctance to utilize technical language undermines this argument (1962, 5n5). Since both adopt modern meanings for the individual fallacies they identify in Plato's texts, then asking whether Plato thought in such terms seems simply anachronistic. This is particularly strange with respect to Robinson given his criticisms of exactly this kind of thinking in his *Plato's Earlier Dialectic* (1941) published around the same time.

of the thirteen sources of fallacious reasoning, in chapter 6 of the *SR* it is revised as *the* alternative way of accommodating all the other twelve, since each of them is a violation of some part of a refutation. So in broad terms a fallacy can be defined as a failed refutation. Of course, there is more to a fallacy *as* a sophistical refutation. Deception seems at stake and, depending on the degree to which eristics is brought into the mix, there is almost a willfulness in avoiding any serious outcome.

To talk about sophistical refutations as "fallacies," as the tradition invites, is to take a stand on how best to translate Aristotle's terms. Part of our difficulty involves the various words that he employs and that translators designate as "fallacy." At the outset of the *SR*, they (sophistical refutations) are described as arguments that appear to be refutations but are really paralogisms instead. This term (*paralogismos*) is rendered by Forster in the Loeb translation, for example, as "fallacies," as opposed to *paralogisontai*, which is translated as "false reasoning." But later (the start of chapter 3), when Aristotle identifies five aims of those who compete and contend in argument—refutation, fallacy, paradox, solecism, and the reduction of one's opponent to babbling—the word rendered as "fallacy" is *pseudos*. As Schreiber (2003) points out in his study of the *SR*, we have difficulty understanding Aristotle's position on fallacies and false arguments because he uses a number of terms interchangeably, or without consistency, but a case can still be made for reading paralogism as fallacy or false argument. Poste (1866) contends that Aristotle distinguishes paralogisms as fallacies from sophistical refutations. But it is difficult to see the case for this in light of what is stated at the outset of the *SR*. On this point, I am inclined to agree with Schreiber that Aristotle does not distinguish sophistic (or eristic) argument from paralogism (false argument). This is particularly clear in the concluding chapter of the *SR*, where Aristotle describes all the preceding false arguments, whether deceptions or errors, as paralogisms. For us, perhaps the most important feature of the Aristotelian account at this point is that a fallacy is the *appearance* of a correct argument (or, strictly, refutation). In light of this, and given the early dating of the *SR*, we have a fairly clear idea of what could count as a concept of fallacy for Plato. The significance of Aristotle's theory of fallacy is that its attention is directed toward a distinction between reality and appearance that underlies statements about real and apparent refutations.

One last preliminary point concerns the status of the *SR* in Aristotle's work. Generally, this book is taken as the last book of the *Topics* and so needs to be understood in relation to that larger project. Aristotle's *topoi* are distinctive in that they are opinions rather than positions of certainty (*apodeictic*) drawn from the everyday. Insofar as the *Topics* reflects the dialectical practices of the Academy, *topoi* are "places we go for arguments," or in Ryle's (1968) analysis "lines of argumentation" commonly used to defend and attack well-known theses. Hence, as an example, it seems there were standard ways to defend and attack the existence of the Forms, and members of the Academy would become practiced at using these lines of argumentation in debates. Innovations would involve adding new lines to this common fund of argumentation or further nuances to old ones. In contemporary terms, we might think of the standard lines of argumentation used in pro and con arguments around, say, the abortion debate, and the ways students are taught these standard lines and encouraged to add to them.

What is controversial about this is the clear break with what Plato would accept as *topoi*. His concern is not with argumentation drawn from opinion but with argumentation aimed at the acquisition of truth. Thus, the places one might "go" for lines of argument are far less accessible than those available to the Aristotelian student. Yet while Plato's dialectic, as we will see in later chapters, is aimed at accessing the truth of the Forms, it is not so clear that the same would have held for the investigations of the historical Socrates.

Plato's Positive Account of Argument

Remarks like those of Robinson (1942) that attribute chains of deductive reasoning to Plato may be guilty of the error that Robinson himself identifies ([1941] 1953) of reading back onto Plato's practices that are more modern in their formulation and could not have been consciously employed by an author writing prior to Aristotle. On the other hand, the dialectician of Plato's later dialogues, who grasps the unity of things through an appreciation of the Forms, sees the connectedness of ideas and is able to exact divisions through a process of logical categorizing that appears to abstract particulars from universals. This is to point ahead to the fuller account of argumentation that is present in the Platonic corpus; it requires adding understandings of rhetorical and dialectical arguments to those apparent in the practices of Socrates in the early and middle dialogues. It also requires appreciating a development in Plato's thought that will have implications for any conception of bad reasoning.

Still, we might ask now whether Robinson's attention to "inferencing" (1942, 102) is sufficient in determining a Platonic attitude toward argument. In spite of the cooperative venture that characterizes philosophizing in the dialogues, Plato's remarks on the persuasive processes of argument are really quite individualized. In the *Theaetetus*, for example, Socrates asks Theaetetus whether he defines thought in a particular way, namely as speech, which the soul has with itself (*Tht.* 190a). Here, "the soul is conversing with itself, asking itself questions and answering, affirming and denying." This "interior *elenchus*," as it appears, reflects the public practice we examined in chapter 2; it would aim to allow a person to arrive at an understanding on which to form a judgment.[6] The same attitude is borne out in the famous defense of arguments and attack on misology in the *Phaedo* (*Phd.* 89d–91a), where no greater evil could befall us than to hate arguments. Socrates develops the analogy between humans and arguments both of which may become subjects of hatred because they betray our trust and turn out to be other than as they seem. That is, implicitly, the appearance of correctness misleads because the person has not learned how to distinguish good from bad arguments and ends up hating both. A fuller statement of what Socrates says will help us here:

> It would be pitiable, Phaedo, when there is a true and reliable argument and one that can be understood, if a man who has dealt with such arguments as appear at one time as true, at another time as untrue, should not blame himself or his own lack of skill but, because of his distress, in the end gladly shift the blame away from himself to the arguments, and spend the rest of his life hating and reviling reasoned discussion, and so be deprived of truth and knowledge of reality. (*Phd.* 90c–d)[7]

Socrates blames this attitude on those who study disputation, caring not for the truth but intent only on persuading their audience. For this reason, the value of the same interior reasoning of the *Theaetetus* is avowed: "I shall not be eager to get the agreement of those present that what I say

---

6. The same point is made later in the *Philebus* (*Phil.* 38c) in the analysis, this time, of false judgment. We will return to these remarks about self-deliberation in the next chapter.

7. The translation is by G. M. A. Grube (Plato 1997a).

is true, except incidentally, but I shall be very eager that I should myself be thoroughly convinced that things are so" (*Phd.* 91a–b). Implicitly, it is the Sophists, as Plato understands them, who stand accused in this passage from the *Phaedo*, and we see no less when Socrates engages specific Sophists. Hippias, for example, is repeatedly exhorted to make his arguments about the fine clearer because they need to persuade a shadowy dissenter to whom Socrates must report. The man who Socrates must convince is finally identified as Sophroniscus's son, that is, Socrates himself, "who wouldn't easily let me say those things without testing them" (*H.Ma.* 298c). Plato's reasons for employing this strange distancing device (since Socrates could just as easily directly contest Hippias's claims) seem to again lie in the direction of stressing a preference for private argumentation, where conviction must take place internally, over the Sophist's public displays.

This gives us some larger appreciation of what Plato values in argumentation, both building on and extending the account that has been laid out in the earlier chapters: a discourse that aims to reveal knowledge of reality, that aims at truth and provides inner persuasion. However we are to make sense of the dialectical argumentation of later dialogues, judgments derived from this interior reasoning seem core to it.[8] Against this positive appreciation of arguments, we can begin to explore "fallacy" in Plato.

Eristical Argument in the *Euthydemus*

To continue the investigation into bad reasoning, we must return to the *Euthydemus* dialogue, this time to consider the Sophist brothers' alleged penchant for eristical argument. The term "eristics" is another that requires some definition. This will largely develop as we look at its expression in this dialogue, but some preliminary points are in order. Sometimes translated as "contentious arguments" (*SR* 183b35), "eristic" is described by Kerferd (1981) as seeking victory in argument and marked as not involving any concern for truth,[9] and Chance (1992) calls it the pseudoscience of argument. Debra Nails (2009) goes further, dismissing the Sophists' performance "as little more than a hilarious use of fallacies" (3). Interestingly, against a tide of negative appraisals of this practice, William Grimaldi (1996) offers

---

8. We will return to this in a discussion of that later dialectical argumentation in chapter 11.
9. See Kerferd (1981, 63.ff) for a discussion of the distinction between eristic and antilogic.

a relatively neutral definition of "eristic" ("disputatious argument wherein one person seeks to make the other give absolute answers to statements which demand qualifications," [28]) and argues that it is not something to be dismissed out of hand because "it is a kind of intellectual dueling that develops a sharpness of mind, clarifies problems, and helps to specify and define issues. Even in its bad sense it encourages the person subjected to the trickery to develop these qualities in self-defense" (29). All agree that the place to best witness it in practice is the *Euthydemus*.

As previously noted in chapter 1, the drama of the dialogue involves a series of exchanges between Socrates and members of his party (Cleinias and Ctesippus) and the Sophist brothers Euthydemus and Dionysodorus, centered and bookended by conversations between Socrates and Crito. Socrates professes admiration of the brothers' proficiency at fighting with arguments and refuting whatever may be said, whether it is false or true, to the extent that he is prepared to hand himself over to them for instruction in this skill and also invites them to persuade the young Cleinias that he ought to love wisdom and have a care for virtue. Previously, I focused on Socrates's demonstrations of hortatory argument (that is, an argument designed to exhort the nonphilosopher to take up the philosophical life); now my attention shifts to the Sophists' demonstrations of eristic argument that are interspersed with those Socratic arguments.

In the first sophistic episode, Euthydemus asks Cleinias whether it is the wise or the ignorant who learn. Cleinias hesitates before opting for the wise as the learners. But as Dionysodorus whispers to Socrates, it does not matter how he answers, he would be refuted whichever alternative is chosen. It seems a feature of eristics that the respondent is confronted by opposites with no middle ground, either of which can be refuted. Indeed, first Euthydemus refutes Cleinias's thesis by showing that it is the ignorant who are the learners because learners do not know what they learn and those who do not know are not wise, and those who are not wise are ignorant. And then, before the boy can recover, Dionysodorus steps in to show Cleinias that he should not have agreed that it is the ignorant who are learners because when boys are learning writing dictation, it is the wise and not the ignorant who learn.

When Socrates begins his first episode, he calms the boy by drawing his attention to the different meanings of "learn" that were involved in the previous argument (thus, apparently, illustrating Plato's awareness of at least what becomes the fallacy of equivocation) and then examines Cleinias's ideas on what is worthwhile, concluding that he has thus illustrated a hortatory argument (*Euthd.* 282d) and inviting the Sophists to continue in a more serious vein by developing matters along a similar line.

The contrast between what Socrates seeks and what eristics offers is maintained in the second sophistic episode, however, as Dionysodorus argues, this time with Socrates, that in wanting Cleinias to be wise Socrates wants him to be other than he is, and in wanting him to no longer be what he is now, he wants his death. Ctesippus, for whom Cleinias is a favorite, takes umbrage at this, insisting the suggestion is a lie. To which a puzzled Euthydemus asks whether Ctesippus thinks it is possible to tell lies, and the brothers proceed to show not only that it is impossible to say what is false but that contradiction itself is impossible (since all they would be doing is speaking different descriptions of the same thing, because they can only say what is the case).

When Socrates begins his second episode, this time to calm Ctesippus, he is able to turn the table on the Sophists, arguing that if there is no falsehood, then no one makes mistakes and there are no ignorant people (contrary to earlier conclusions) and no refutations (again contrary to earlier conclusions). The Sophists, however, are unfazed by this turn in the discussion and simply stop answering, in response to which Socrates proceeds with his next hortatory argument for philosophy (the one that ends aporetically with the failure to find the statesman's art).

In the third and last sophistic episode, the brothers argue that Socrates knows everything, and has always known this. The exchanges here often turn on the proper way to answer questions and the refusal (by the Sophists) to allow qualifications—another important feature of eristics. The claims become more and more outrageous, with arguments like the famous dog/father argument that Aristotle will employ in the *SR*, building to an absurd climax at *Euthd.* 303a. Along the way, Socrates draws the Sophists into further apparent contradictions and Ctesippus shows how well he has learned from the brothers by using some of their strategies against them. Yet, at the end, Socrates is still praising the brothers' skills to Crito, suggesting, as many commentators observe, that the similarities between dialectic and eristics are actually quite strong.

The dialogue itself is generally dated between BCE 390 and 380, between Plato's first Sicilian period of BCE 388/387 and the writing of the core books of the *Republic* around 380. Given Aristotle's dates (BCE 384–322), we can place the production of the *Euthydemus* well before the *Topics* and *SR*.

The Presence of Fallacies in the *Euthydemus*

Starting with the first display of the two brothers, I want now to delve further into some of these exchanges to explore what might be seen as fallacies and why they might be so considered. In the first demonstration, the brothers claim to show that neither the wise nor the ignorant are learners, with Euthydemus and Cleinias exchanging the following questions and responses.

Euthydemus: Which are those who learn, the wise or the ignorant?

Cleinias: The wise.

Euth: Are there some whom you call teachers or not?

Clein. There are.

Euth: And the teachers are teachers of those who learn?

Clein. Agreed.

Euth: And when you were learning, you did not yet know the things you were learning, did you?

Clein: No.

Euth: And were you wise when you did not know these things?

Clein: By no means.

Euth: Then if not wise, ignorant?

Clein: Very much so.

Euth: Then in the process of learning what you did not know, you learned while you were ignorant?

Clein: Yes.

> Euth: Then it is the ignorant who learn and not the wise. [Apparent refutation of Cleinias's claim.] (*Euthd.* 275d–276b[10])

Dionysodorus then follows at 276c:

> When the writing master gave you dictation, which of the boys learned the piece, the wise or the ignorant?
>
> Clein: The wise.
>
> Dion: Then it is the wise who learn and not the ignorant. [Apparent refutation of Cleinias's agreement at 276b.]

How has Cleinias become confounded by the argument? Plato accounts for the problem with points that will later be reflected in Aristotle's treatment of equivocation in the *SR*. In a response that indicates Plato's awareness of the fallaciousness at stake, beginning at *Euthd.* 277d, Socrates explains to Cleinias that *manthanein* (learn) can mean not only to get information about something but also to use information to understand what was previously known. Thus, the same word can be appropriately applied to both the one who knows and the one who does not. It is this ambiguity that the Sophists exploit. In the notes to her translation, Sprague (Plato 1965) sets down the argument to make this apparent: "Those who understand are those who know. (The learners are the wise.) When Cleinias got information about music, he was not knowing about it. Those who get information are the not knowing. (The learners are the ignorant)" (Plato 1965, 10n16).

The "success" of the Sophists's first demonstration depends on the equivocation of this central term.[11] In this example ambiguity is suggested as the dominant "modern" fallacy appreciated by Plato. If we want to develop such a treatment of fallacy in Plato along the lines of Sprague (1962), this is the route to take. It is this understanding of fallacy that is reflected in the comments of several translators of relevant works. In his introduction to the *SR*, E. S. Forster (Aristotle 1955), for example, insists that "Aristotle

---

10. This précis of the exchange and the one that follows are both based on Rosamund Kent Sprague's translation (Plato 1965).

11. As various commentators point out, the Sophists's arguments also involve the ambiguity of "wise" and "ignorant," although Plato does not draw attention to this.

is carrying on the Socratic and early-Platonic tradition by attacking the Sophists, who taught the use of logical fallacy in order to make the worse cause appear the better" (5).

These kinds of comments, however, seem to encourage the backward reading onto these texts of current understandings of fallacy. In the contexts from which the texts emerged, where the ability to refute another's thesis was so central to the curriculum of the Academy, it seems more appropriate to adopt the language that will characterize the *SR* of real versus sophistical refutations. In these terms, what the brothers do that Plato is emphasizing is simply fail to provide real refutations, and hence they begin to illustrate what is to be meant by "sophistical refutations." The applause and laughter that greets the "refutation" of the boy (*Euthd.* 276c) seems to confirm that the audience judges him to be refuted, and cleverly so. Important here also are the ways in which Plato's text presents parallels between eristics and Socratic argument. This is part, surely, of Plato's ongoing defense of his mentor, further distancing his practices from those of the Sophists. But at the same time, Plato indicates how the casual onlooker might have been confused by the two: both involve an investigation through questions and answers to a refutation of the thesis, and both solicit the agreement of the respondent at each step. To *appear* real, the sophistical refutation must imitate its legitimate counterpart, be parasitic upon it, and, of course, be seen to do this (Gonzalez 1998, 119).

The contrast between bad refutations and what we are encouraged to recognize as *real* refutations is demonstrated in the exchange between Socrates and Dionysodorus, after the latter has proposed the thesis that no one speaks falsely (*Euthd.* 286c). In this exchange, we are indeed seeing an example of the *elenchus* in the *Euthydemus*, an argument that is very different from the hortatory arguments with which Socrates engaged Cleinias. This further illustrates the different goals of the two types of argument (hortatory and elenctic) and, of course, the very different kind of interlocutor.

> [Socrates:] The argument amounts to claiming that there is no such thing as false speaking, doesn't it? And the person speaking must either speak the truth or else not speak?
>
> He [Dionysodorus] agreed.
>
> Now would you say that it was impossible to speak what is false, but possible to think it?

No, thinking it is not possible either, he said.

Then there is absolutely no such thing as false opinion, [Socrates] said.

There is not, he said.

Then is there no ignorance, nor are there any ignorant men? Or isn't this just what ignorance would be, if there should be any—to speak falsely about things?

It certainly would, he said.

And yet there is no such thing, [Socrates] said.

He said there was not.

Are you making this statement just for the sake of argument, Dionysodorus—to say something startling—or do you honestly believe that there is no such thing as an ignorant man?

Your business is to refute me, he said.

Well, but is there such a thing as refutation if one accepts your thesis that nobody speaks falsely?

No, there is not, said Euthydemus.

Then it can't be that Dionysodorus ordered me to refute him just now, can it? [Socrates] said. (*Euthd.* 286c–e)

On the terms we have been exploring, the Sophists are refuted. Having proposed the thesis (*A*) that there are ignorant people and that Cleinias was earlier refuted, they are now led to agree that there are no ignorant people and no refutation (*not-A*). At least, this is what they should be agreeing to accept if they would just commit themselves. Socrates's question "Are you just saying this for the sake of argument, or do you honestly believe it" is crucial. The integrity of the *elenchus* depends on the underlying commitment of those engaged in the discourse to the statements being explored. Hence the ethotic nature of these arguments that was identified in the last chapter. If the brothers believe what they are saying, then they are inconsistent in their beliefs and we have had demonstrated for us a real refutation. On these terms, several things are indicated: that Plato has in mind a distinction between a sophistical refutation and a real refutation; that this is similar to the distinction that Aristotle will later develop; and that this hinges on the respondent being committed to the statements he puts forward. What prevents the earlier refutation of Cleinias from being real on these terms is the structure of the opening question that demands a choice between stark alternatives (wise or ignorant) with no room for middle ground. In accepting those terms, Cleinias is not asserting what he believes but only what he is told. The point is emphasized in the third sophistic episode when the Sophists question Socrates and become repeatedly frustrated with his insistence on qualifying his answers. As Socrates recounts, using the metaphor of the Sophist as hunter that will characterize the descriptions in the *Sophist*, "I realized he was angry at me for making distinctions in his phrases, because he wanted to surround me with words and so hunt me down" (*Euthd.* 295d).

Something far more suggestive than the distinction between real and sophistical refutations is at work here. Throughout his dialogues, Plato returns to the threat represented by various Sophists to his metaphysical project, a threat that is seen in two epistemologies at odds with each other. Here, it seems quite apparent from what is said that the two Sophist brothers are not assuming the same principles and the same understanding of the nature of discourse as Socrates is assuming. Most suggestive of this is the central exchange (in the second sophistic episode), which bears on the very nature (and possibility) of fallacies themselves, if they are to be understood as involving the saying of what is false.[12] If false speaking is impossible, then what are we to say of fallacies? Here, we might appreciate how the *Euthydemus* points ahead to the problematic of the *Sophist* and what has to be accomplished there (that is, to show that there is a sense in which we can say what is not the case).

To explore this further, consider Euthydemus's argument as it develops. Ctesippus believes it is possible to tell lies (*Euthd.* 283e). Euthydemus counters

---

12. Fallacies as sophistical refutations do say something that is false. This is clear about the early account of the fallacies. Later, the concept is extended to include notions like that of irrelevance (which does not, strictly, involve falsehood). But at this point Plato does not seem to understand them in that developed sense.

by asking whether this is done when the person speaks things spoken about or when they do not speak it? To which Ctesippus responds that it is when they speak it. So, proceeds Euthydemus, if the person speaks this, he speaks no other of the things that are, except this one. And the thing he speaks is one of those that are. Hence, the person speaking the thing speaks what *is*. But someone who speaks what is, and the things that are, speaks the truth and tells no lies. Ctesippus again counters that a person who speaks these things does not speak things that are (284b). But Euthydemus insists that the things that are not do not exist. They are nowhere. When someone speaks, they do something; they make something. So, "nobody speaks things that are not, since he would then be making something, and you have admitted that no one is capable of making something that is not. So according to your own statement, nobody tells lies" (*Euthd.* 284c).

Here we have another refutation, this time of Ctesippus's original claim, although it is harder to judge whether this is a sophistical refutation. The language involved is complex, as if Plato's characters are themselves having difficulty speaking about the subject under review. Bluck (1957) suggests a fallacy "lies in the ambiguity of τὸ ὄν (or τὰ ὄντα) which can refer either (i) to an existing person or thing or (ii) to truth" (184). The ambiguity is lost when translators commit themselves to one side or the other, as Rouse (Plato 1961) does in translating *ta onta* as "the facts." But a similar ambiguity (and potential fallacy) might also be seen in the meaning of *legein x* (speaking *x*), which may mean to mention or refer to *x* or to say something about *x*.

On either front we have suggested for us an underlying epistemological difference between Plato and the Sophists, which complicates the earlier conclusions about fallacies in the *Euthydemus*. It suggests that the brothers simply do not recognize an account of the exchanges that would render their reasoning as fallacious. After all, they seem indifferent to the refutations aimed at them, which readers generally take as an indication that they are not serious. Much depends on how subtle we expect Plato to be in depicting the Sophists here. It is possible that he is providing no more than a thoroughly fictional description of their behavior and responses. But, on the other hand, the seriousness that Plato extends to sophistic thinking across his dialogues, and the threat the Sophists represent to his project, suggests that he would be strongly motivated to provide as accurate a picture as possible. If a person wants to ultimately defeat a philosophical other, the burden of proof is on that person to cast the other in a fair light, or else the victory is merely notional (and possibly fallacious!).

The ambiguity involving *legein* is resolved if we choose it to mean a use of language to refer to things that are along with a commitment to the existence of those things. In his first elenctic appearance, Socrates had pointed out that even if one learned everything the brothers teach, such a person would be no more knowledgeable about the way things actually are (*Euthd.* 278b). The value of real discussion, in contrast to its sophistical variant, lies in its ability to disclose a truth about things. But the Sophists seem not so much incapable of doing this as fundamentally uninterested in such a project. They revel in the sensual power of logos, valuing the experience for itself and not for any aperture it opens onto a world of things. If this is one of the positives to associate with eristics (Grimaldi 1996), then it would need to be countered (if it is to be countered) by bringing the words back into a context where they mean something, and this we see Socrates attempting throughout.

A deeper reading of the disagreement apparent in the *Euthydemus* brings to the surface a question regarding the existence of things over time. Several remarks made by the Sophist brothers suggest this is a concern for them. Mary Margaret McCabe (1994) addresses this, asking whether "the argument about being and dying turns on whether you admit, or refuse to admit, that there are continuants underneath change. On such an interpretation it is not a fallacy at all, but a valid argument from the extraordinary premiss that nothing persists" (83). It seems a basic principle of common sense that for any change to occur there must be something that persists over time. Dionysodorus responds to a Socratic charge of inconsistency between what was then being maintained and what had been asserted earlier by saying: "Really, Socrates . . . are you such an old Cronus [dinosaur] as to bring up what we said in the beginning? I suppose if I said something last year, you will bring that up now and still be helpless in dealing with the present argument" (*Euthd.* 287b). We noted this exchange in the last chapter (note 7), because the refusal of an interlocutor to commit to what was said deviates from the procedural path of the Socratic *elenchus*. Here, the implication is that what was previously said only applied then, while what is said now only applies now. These two distinct moments in time are unconnected. If the Sophists do not believe that there are persistent things, so that a Cleinias who is not what he is now is dead, then this further emphasizes that the focus of their interest is language and what can be done with it.

Some of McCabe's further conclusions are also of note with respect to the subject of false arguments. "If," she writes, "this sort of theory is the basis for Euthydemus and Dionysodorus' lack of interest in consistency in the *Euthydemus* then the dispute between the Sophists and Socrates is no longer a matter of what kind of argumentative tricks they are prepared to use to achieve their ends" (1994, 76). In fact, what emerges is a claim that fallacies are theory-bound, arising in relation to a series of beliefs about the standards of what is true. We recognize the existence of fallacies, and a notion of "fallacy," in the *Euthydemus* because we have been brought up in a certain epistemological tradition. Plato himself stays with the task at hand. He has recognized that to fully meet the challenge of the Sophists he must show that sophistical refutations (fallacies) are "real" by showing that when we speak falsely, we speak about something. That is a task taken up in the *Sophist*.[13]

False Argument and the *Sophist*

In spite of the *Sophist* following on the heels of the *Theaetetus* where Socrates has contested the statements of Protagoras, including the second part of the measure maxim, which speaks of things that are and that are not, Socrates is not the principal speaker in this dialogue.[14] Perhaps if the claims underlying eristics are to be put to rest here, then we should not be reminded of similarities with the elenctic method (and its practitioner).[15] In this late dialogue, a new sense of dialectic, which we have yet to explore, has emerged, one that aims beyond the limits of the *elenchus* to an achievable truth. On the morning following the meeting reported in the *Theaetetus*, Theaetetus, Theodorus, Socrates, and his younger namesake gather again, along with an Eleatic visitor introduced by Theodorus as "a sort of god of refutation" (216b),[16] or at least this is how Socrates describes him. Platonic argument has a new champion.

---

13. At this point we will continue the study of Plato on "fallacy" by following the argument into the *Sophist*. But the discussion also invites a different study, one that considers the prospect of recovering a more positive appreciation of eristics and sophistic argument in general and asks about the fairness of equating "fallacy" and "sophistical refutation." I pursue such a path in Tindale (2010).

14. I discuss the roles here of Socrates and the Eleatic visitor at the start of chapter 12.

15. If the method of the philosopher can be confused with the method of the Sophist, then it is not only the methods but the practitioners (philosopher/sophist) who need to be distinguished. As set out in the prologue (*Sph.* 216a–218c), this is the project of the *Sophist*.

16. The translation here is by White (Plato 1997d). In the following discussion, I depend on this translation and that of Benardete (1986) unless otherwise noted.

Structurally, the dialogue falls into three parts (Notomi 1999). While the beginning (*Sph.* 216a–236d) and the ending (*Sph.* 264b–268d) concentrate for the most part on the various definitions of the "Sophist," the middle part (*Sph.* 236d–264b) focuses on the problem of what is not and falsehood. It is to this part that I limit my discussion. It is not my intention here to discuss the various definitions of the "Sophist" that are put forward by the Eleatic visitor and his respondent, Theaetetus,[17] nor to consider some of the problems with the theory of Forms that this dialogue brings to light, nor the question of whether Plato involves both existential and copula senses of being. My focus at this point is solely on the import of this dialogue for the problematic brought to light by the *Euthydemus*.

The crux of the problem is clearly carried over from that earlier dialogue. The Eleatic visitor observes: "This is a very difficult investigation we're engaged in. This appearing, and this seeming, but not being, and this saying things, but not true things—all these issues are full of confusion, just as they always have been. It's extremely hard, Theaetetus, to say what form of speech we should use to say that there really is such a thing as false saying or believing, and moreover to utter this without being caught in verbal conflict" (*Sph.* 236e–237a). No explicit reference is made back to the *Euthydemus* here, but it should be clear to us what is at stake. It is only in the absence of such a backward glance that we can understand the puzzlement of commentators at the Eleatic visitor's (and Plato's) own puzzlement here.[18] As far as problems go, this is as real as they can get for Plato as he struggles to establish his ideas against the popularity of the Sophists. To hold a false opinion, it seems, is to think something that is the opposite of what is real. But this is to think things that are not, which the interlocutors agree is impossible. The Sophist has caught them in contradiction on their own terms (*Sph.* 241a–b).

To solve this puzzle, in the first instance, they must overturn the edifice of Parmenidean thought (which the Eleatic visitor does with reluctance) by identifying a set of basic or primordial Forms by virtue of which other Forms (and particulars) are possible. And to accomplish this they work with Plato's own dialectic as it has developed. Dialectic now involves understanding the nature of Forms by determining their relations to each other through collection and division. The *Sophist* gives us a succinct definition of this:

---

17. These will form part of the study of definitions in chapter 12.
18. Runciman (1962, 99) calls the problem "unreal," because Plato knew that denials could be made.

dialectic is the ability to "divide things by kinds and not to think that the same form is a different one or that a different form is the same" (*Sph.* 253d). This is a way to approach the truth that is more reliable than the Socratic *elenchus*, since it trades in the reality of the Forms, about which the *elenchus* seems agnostic. It also contrasts with the dialectic of Aristotle, which draws on popular opinions.[19]

The Eleatics, following Parmenides, would hold that there is only one Being. But the discussants of the *Sophist* determine that since change (or motion)[20] and rest are opposed to each other, and since both exist, then neither can be Being but must be separate from it, as from each other (*Sph.* 250c–d). Being, of course, blends with both these other Forms, but they cannot blend with each other. In being separate from each other, they each partake in Difference or Otherness (*to héteron*). And, finally, both of these are the same as themselves and so both partake in Sameness (Identity). These *basic* Forms are those by which all others (and particulars) can be understood.

In establishing the role of *to héteron* the discussants have made a major advance in resolving their puzzle. Change, for example, is not Sameness (or Identity) and yet it is the same as itself. So a sense of not-being emerges. As the Eleatic visitor observes, when they say that it is the same and not the same, they "aren't speaking the same way" (*Sph.* 256a). Change is in a sense Other (or Different) and also in a sense not-Other. Hence, Change really is not, and also is, since it partakes of Being. The conclusion they must draw is that in relation to Change, "not-being is," and this must extend to all the classes or kinds. That is because "as applied to all of them, the nature of the Other [or Different] makes each of them not be by making it other than that which is" (*Sph.* 256c). All of them "are not" in this same way. Not-being emerges not as the opposite of Being but as what is Other than Being: "When we say *that which is not*, we don't say

---

19. I postpone the full discussion of Plato's dialectic to focus here on the problem inherited from the *Euthydemus*. Suffice it to note that Plato's dialectic depends on different methodological principles to those of Socratic dialectic that we have already encountered. The method of composition and division is counted among these.

20. Change is the preferred translation of *kinesis* because Plato's meaning would encompass not only movement of position (locomotion) but also changes in the quality of a thing (like sunlight through a window as the afternoon progresses). Thus, "motion," a popular alternative in many translations, seems not to convey enough. Unfortunately, what seems to encourage the choice of "motion" is that the contrasting term, *stasis*, has no clear corresponding word in English, and hence the choice of "rest." Hence also, my preference for White's translation (Plato 1997d).

something contrary to *that which is*, but only something different from it" (*Sph.* 257b). Hence, they deny that the negative signifies the opposite and allow only that the particle "not" indicates something other than the words to which it is prefixed (or the things denoted by those words that follow the negative). The Other has existence as a kind of non-being, "for it does not signify something contrary to *that which is* but only something different from it" (*Sph.* 258b).

It is the case, as commentators have noted (Runciman 1962, 100), that Plato provides nothing like an account of negation that would satisfy contemporary logicians. In fact, he is extending the sense of assertion rather than explaining negation. But that larger task was not Plato's goal: he was seeking a way in which it was sensible to talk about falsity, and he seems to have found it. This is the second part of the resolution of the puzzle: having established a way in which not-being is, they must finish the question of how they can speak not-being.

The Eleatic visitor and Theaetetus have discovered a set of primary or foundational Forms that blend or mix (Being, Change, Rest, Other, Same). They have also found that not-being is a class of being that permeates all being (*Sph.* 260b).[21] This has allowed them to make the remarkable claim that the complete separation of each thing from every other thing would be "the most complete way to make all speeches (*lógon*) disappear" (*Sph.* 259e).[22] Our power of discourse is derived from the mixing of classes or ideas. Runciman, as an example, finds this claim puzzling. We can agree with his observation that what Plato means here "is extremely difficult to establish with any confidence" (Runciman 1962, 107) yet still remark on the contribution this would make to the insistence of Euthydemus and Dionysodorus that things *are* separate or discontinuous and therefore they are not committed to any consistency with regard to what they say at different points in time. Insofar as Platonic discourse requires consistency of terms as well as beliefs, then this remark of the Eleatic visitor is not so puzzling.

If not-being permeates all being, then it is not a stretch to expect it will also mingle with all speech and will create a background of otherness against which speech emerges and is possible. When Theaetetus questions this idea, the Eleatic visitor points out the consequence that we have also seen from the *Euthydemus*, that if it does not mingle "then everything has

---

21. I leave aside here the more troubling question of whether Plato is asserting a Form of Not-being. See Seligman (1974) for a discussion of this topic.

22. As rendered by Benardete (1986).

to be true," as was the case for the Sophist brothers, but if it mingles "then there will be false belief and false speech" (*Sph.* 260c), as is now the case for Plato. And with falsehood arises deceit and with deceit, the problems of appearance, that region in which Plato believes the Sophist hides.[23]

Of course, the Sophist could raise an objection here and insist that some ideas do not partake of not-being, with speech and opinion being among them. The sentences "Theaetetus sits" and "Theaetetus, with whom I am now talking" are investigated in order to both complete the resolution of the general puzzle and counter this objection.

A statement is always about something, about *this* Theaetetus, for example. And a statement has a quality of being either true or false. The one Theaetetus statement has the quality of being true, the other false. The true one states the facts or what is.[24] The false one states things that are other than the facts (*Sph.* 263b).[25] The false statement, while meaningful, speaks of what is not as if it were. Having agreed earlier that of each kind both many beings and many not-beings *are,* they now demonstrate that statements can partake of what is not. This refutes the Sophist's denial of falsehood. In sum, false discourse and false opinion[26] have been found much sooner than they expected.

Of course, a false statement like "Theaetetus flies" is not a sophistical refutation. That is, there seems a far remove from Cleinias's conclusions that the ignorant are the learners or the wise are the learners, and the false assertion about Theaetetus. But, in the first instance, Cleinias's conclusions were refutations of his claims because they were contrary to them, and the account in the *Sophist* focuses not on the contrariness of the conclusion but on its otherness from what was first asserted. Thus, it counters the charge of the *Euthydemus* that refutations, whether real or sophistical, are impossible.

---

23. Barbara Cassin (2014) sees here the full Platonic indictment of the Sophists: "The sophist is not concerned with being but seeks refuge in nonbeing and what is accidental; logically, because he is not in pursuit of truth or dialectical rigor but merely opinion, seeming coherence, persuasion, and victory in the oratorical joust" (30).

24. The same ambiguity arises here as in the *Euthydemus* of translating *tò ónta* as "the facts."

25. Not "opposite," note; it does not say that it is not the case that Theaetetus sits.

26. The argument to establish false opinion is a little lengthier: Thought is the silent inner speech that the soul has with itself; when speech arises this way it has the name of opinion; and when this condition is brought about in a person through sensation, it is called "seeming"; hence, some opinions, being akin to speech, will be false (*Sph.* 263e–264b).

Plato has countered the Sophists's claim that speech cannot say what is not the case by showing that otherness is possible. The explanation we are given, that mistakes involve the misidentification of the Form being partaken of, is idiosyncratic of Plato's project, but it allows for the first coherent understanding of what a "fallacy" might be. On Plato's understanding, a "real" refutation would not make that mistake. Speech about a class is refuted by staying within what is appropriate to say about that class, by drawing on ideas consistent with it. A false refutation asserts a conclusion that is other than about that class or outside of it. The *Sophist* is explicit in its (or Plato's) conclusion that the person who confuses or denies distinctions by "constantly trotting out contraries like that in discussion" (like, we may believe, the oppositional choices characteristic of eristics, i.e., wise/ignorant) provides "no true refutation" but only, we must imagine, a sophistical one (*Sph.* 259d). Also, this has the perhaps surprising result of allowing us to expand the concept of fallacy. Up until this point we may have been thinking about it in a very rudimentary sense as the *opposite* of truth because that was the direction in which the Sophists led us. But now it is presented as the *other* of truth, or other than the true. This would seem to open up the concept to include *irrelevance* insofar as the conclusion of an irrelevant argument is other than what should be concluded. Even Plato's earlier recognition of equivocation is consistent with this observation. We then have the philosophical groundwork laid for a broader appreciation of sophistical refutation in Aristotle's work of that name, including his all-encompassing account of the *ignoratio elenchi*, which accommodates a range of confusions about what a refutation is, all amounting to something *other than* a correct refutation.

Consequences for Our Understanding of "Fallacy"

Beyond the ideas we can now relate to Plato and his (emerging) role in the history of argumentation, we can draw some further provisional conclusions that are relevant to the interests of fallacy theory generally.

Fallacy is to be understood against not just a concept of "good" argument but a model of rationality that supports that concept. Thus, the study of fallacy in any particular tradition should reveal as much about the conditions for good argumentation as it does about bad. Assumptions that there is only one tradition (our own) grounded in the Aristotelian can obscure this insight and what we might benefit from it. Because it follows, as McCabe has hinted here, that we may have other traditions (or communities) of "rationality" that define good and bad reasoning on their own terms. We have traced the story of fallacy in Plato's dialogues on *his* terms but left aside was another story that might have been told on the part of the Sophist brothers who appear clearly to reject the assumptions along which Socrates and Plato are proceeding in the *Euthydemus*. What "that" other tradition might have looked like (and what would count as good and bad reasoning within it) is not the focus of this study (Tindale 2010). But we may be confident that it would appear in relation to the different goals (ones more public and human-centered) addressed by sophistic reason and practice. We see something similar, perhaps, in Andrea Nye's (1990, 174) observation that in her assessment of the history of logic she has likely committed a number of fallacies. She says this not as a confession or apology but, like the brothers Euthydemus and Dionysodorus, unconcerned for what it suggests. This is in part because she does not see herself writing "inside" that tradition, and what counts as fallacious for her would be something else altogether. It follows further from this that "fallacies," being tradition-bound, are not measures of objective reason but relative to the account/community in which they are recognized. Fallacies are violations of norms of rationality and will vary according to the model of rationality involved.

Secondly, a theory of fallacy must also explain why/how errors arise. This Plato's understanding does, albeit, as I have noted, idiosyncratically. But it is incumbent on those who provide accounts and treatments of various fallacies to explain both how they could be committed and (if we are to take them seriously) how people could be misled by them.[27] Some of the examples Aristotle provides in the *SR* seem to fail at least this last requirement.

Finally, and on a more positive note, we might return to the question of why we should be interested in, and even concerned by, the question of fallacy. Plato has an implicit response to this: fallacies impede our movement toward the truth and for that reason should be identified and avoided. But there is a further, fuller dimension to this. In spite of frequent appearances, Plato is not concerned with the acquisition of truth in the abstract. It fits into a comprehensive appreciation of how best to live life to the fullest. In

---

27. Hans-Georg Gadamer (1980), for example, lays the stress on the sense of dialectic involved (which we will explore in part III). We may find "all manner of violations of logic" in Plato, but he believes this points to the "reasonable hermeneutic assumption" that we are dealing with discussions, and such violations readily arise when any of us engage in the "live play" of discussion (5).

relation to this we might say that reasoning well and being able to conduct good argumentation is an essential part of *eudaimonia*, of well-being. Hence the stress placed on practicing argumentative debates in the Academy, done not just to prepare young people for interactions in public fora but for the development of their characters, for improving the self. Thus, at one of its roots, argumentation has ethical and social consequences. Bad reasoning affects our quality of life. As Plato's theory of argument indicates, it is in the internal conversation with our selves that the merits of good argumentative principles come to bear and bad ones have effect. Thus, like the Socratic arguments of the last chapter, the study of fallacy is not one of abstract logical interest but has deep associations with the most important projects of the human endeavor: to improve ourselves and the environments in which we develop.

Chapter 4

Strong Arguments

Do not examine words when you are judging virtue, but rather actions. For a battle too is decided not by word but by action. You cannot contradict your enemy: you fight, and either you win or you get enslaved—in silence.

—Antisthenes (*Ajax*, 7)[1]

Introduction: The "Socratic Dialectic"

The focus of these chapters has been Plato's engagement with argument, particularly the logical nature of his arguments. But the question naturally suggests itself, How much of this derives from Plato's own position and how much reflects the activities of the historical Socrates? After all, we have been discussing Socratic dialectic and, with the exception of the last chapter's focus on the Eleatic visitor, the principal figure of interest has been the Socrates of these various dialogues. Of course, insofar as Plato adopts these types of argument and effectively endorses them through his use, the question is moot. Our interest rests with Plato's reasons. But the figure of Socrates remains *the* arguer for most of the dialogues at issue and the method of using questions and answers to lead, encourage, or refute remains the common denominator shared by these types of argument.

---

1. Antisthenes's competing speeches *Ajax/Odysseus* are translated in Boys-Stones and Rowe (2013, 23–27).

Among other Socratics, Plato inherited Socrates's propensity for questioning organized in the form of Socratic dialogues (Kahn 1996, 1–35; Vander Waerdt 1994). We take these dialogues as descriptive of Socrates's dialectic.[2] It seems unlikely that this practice was unique to the historical Socrates. Protagoras, while primarily associated with oppositional arguments, is also alleged to be the first to introduce the Socratic type of argument (*DK* 80, A1; plus *DL* 1853, 398). And, of course, Plato has Diotima use a version of this method as she teaches a younger Socrates "the art of love" in the *Symposium* (201d).[3] But the existence of the method alone does not indicate that it was used to achieve the same goals that were noted with the three types of Socratic arguments in previous chapters.

As the discussion of maieutic argument indicated, this one type does seem to derive from Plato's own usage. In distinction to the hortatory and the *elenchus*, the maieutic is one of the ways in which knowledge is brought into (or revealed in) the world, and this is a serious concern for Plato in the middle dialogues and beyond. If the other two types of argument accurately reflect practices of the historical Socrates, they have their limits. Each brings the interlocutor to a point, albeit a serious and constructive point, but no further. Ignorance once uncovered and recognized invites, necessitates even, the next step in philosophical inquiry. The experience of having been moved to action invites the activation of that of which one has been persuaded. But maieutic inquiry involves a commitment to knowledge that cannot easily be attributed to the historical figure, even with the stress on the barrenness of the midwife. While Plato abandons the Socratic *elenchus*, or at least supplements it with further argumentative strategies, he never abandons the power of a dialectic that focuses on the ways in which thought can rise above the tendencies of language to impede rather than assist the processes of inquiry. As Deraj (2013) notes, "Despite the fact that in Plato's early aporetic dialogues, Socrates uses [*dialeyesthai*] to investigate an interlocutor's character in the same way as Xenophon's Socrates, Plato begins to transform it step by step into a dialectical art" (31). This we will see in part III.

---

2. Where dialectic, even if translated in terms of conversation (as per Sachs 2009) involves thinking through a question to explore an issue or a claim.

3. In this secondhand speech, Socrates uses *erōtika* for "love," which may recall the asking of questions (*erōtan*). We will return to the figure of Diotima below.

Speaking with the Sophists

The powerful other against the ideas and arguments of which Platonic positions are set in motion and with whose representatives Socrates feints and parries with persistent patience is sophistry. We have seen two figures of this "movement"[4] in Euthydemus and Dionysodorus, but on the basis of what is demonstrated in other Platonic dialogues it would seem unwise to take them as representative of anything more than eristics and equally unwise to equate fifth-century Greek sophistry with eristics (Enos 1993). Moreover, there is a danger that we become so distracted by the treatment of the Sophists in Plato's work and the associations of rhetoric with their practices that we overlook Plato's own adoptions of rhetorical devices in his dialogues (Rossetti 1989, 234).

Plato's mimicry of the Sophists is as astute as it is varied. Beyond portrayals of the characters of the men themselves, we have finely honed descriptions of their practices and the positions they held presented through a variety of Platonic devices. This creates a problem for some commentators, led to ask whether and why we should trust the portraits he gives. John Dillon and Tania Gergel (2003) are wary of Plato's depictions because of the depth of enmity he nurtures toward the Sophists. They recognize, though, that on occasion he may allow them "to speak more or less in their own words" (xix). Such mixed observations lead to the advice that he always be consulted with caution. In a similar vein, John Poulakos (1995, 78) notes the inevitability of personal perspective and bias in the way Plato presents the Sophists. Because of this, he suggests shifting away from the question of accuracy to asking why he provides the representations in the first place.[5] Indeed, there must be an important connection between such questions, and if we acquire a satisfactory explanation for his adoption of this strategy, we may have a better sense of how reliable he is. Håkan Tell, in the provocatively titled *Plato's Counterfeit Sophists* (2011), challenges Plato's general categorizing of the Sophists and their place in a Platonically constructed history, identifying differences between "Platonically designed sophists" and "historical individuals" (8). Thus, Plato is "not necessarily a

---

4. In spite of the title for Kerferd's (1981) study, scholars are agreed that it is difficult to assign enough commonalities to the beliefs and practices of the fifth-century Sophists to warrant referring to a movement per se.

5. In a similar vein, Patricia O'Grady (2008) asserts that we will simply not be able to judge the degree to which this "hostile witness" relied on the original works of the Sophists.

trustworthy witness of the meaning and application of σοφιστής because he has his own agenda to promote" (29). That agenda involves dissociating the Sophists from the sage tradition and associating them with groups like poets. Thus, Tell questions Plato's focus on the Sophists' monetary practices. But this all relates more to their categorization and characteristics than to their argumentation and styles of expression.

One of the strongest dismissals of the accuracy thesis comes from Eric Havelock (1957). The judgment is harsh: "No philosopher in his senses will take the trouble to report with historical fidelity views which intellectually he cannot accept" (165). Elsewhere, he applies this judgment to discussions of individual Sophists. With respect to Protagoras's "Great Speech," for example, we should not expect that it reports Protagoras's own views. Plato was not a reporter, asserts Havelock; he was in the business of replacing current views with his own, not repeating them. He conveys his dismissal with a rhetorical question: "Why in particular should such a genius take the trouble to advertise in his own writings a system already in circulation and put out by a representative of a school of thought which he distrusted?" (88). Of course, Havelock may himself suggest an answer in what he says. If you are in the business of replacing a view, it is a viable (even advisable) strategy to present that view accurately in order to then demonstrate its inferiority to the (new) position that opposes it. That Plato distrusted the views of the Sophists and disputed their worth is not itself reason for believing he would not agonize over the accuracy of his portrayals.

In future chapters we will explore Plato's stylistic mastery, casting his discourse in metaphor and simile, co-opting the voices of orators (*Phaedrus*) and tragedians (*Symposium*), evoking ideas through telling drama and biography and the suggestive narratives of several major myths (*Phaedo, Gorgias, Republic*). But his imitations of the Sophists convey both style and method and demonstrate more than literary accomplishment; they also suggest a deep desire to get it right, to show them for what they were, at least in his mind.

The meaning of "sophistry" and the membership of that cadre of itinerant teachers we term Sophists vary according to the assumptions we employ (Crome 2004, 16). There is a conundrum involved: to decide the membership we must first have a (relatively neutral) definition of "sophistry," and yet scholars routinely derive their definitions from the activities of those they identify as Sophists. George Kennedy (1999), for example, extends the membership to include Isocrates (31), which must certainly have a bearing on how "sophistry" is understood. Current notions of sophistry view it as a form of radical philosophy, with the postmodern Sophists reacting and rebelling against the orthodoxies. But the Sophists of concern to Plato could hardly have been such rebels since there was very little in the way of orthodoxy. In retrospect, we find Plato and Aristotle judged the orthodox philosophers of the day, but that is very much a post-facto judgment. At the time, ideas like "philosopher" and "Sophist" were fluid categories, still being populated, and such populations depended on whose judgment was involved. While the origin of rhetoric (*rhetorike*) has been attributed to Plato (Schiappa 1999), Barbara Cassin (2014) goes further in her attribution, including "*eristikê, antilogikê, dialectikê*, and probably *sophistikê*" (77).

I will address the problem of meaning and membership by confining myself to Plato's texts, since this is the relevant context of these explorations. There, "sophistry" is an intellectual position with clear philosophical import that stands as the opposite to Plato's positions on epistemology, metaphysics, ethics, logic, and language. Those we count as Sophists are simply those Plato identifies as such as he brings them into conflict with the figure of Socrates. This does not resolve all the issues—the matter of Isocrates's status will be considered in a later chapter, for example—but it gives us clear ground on which to work. And in this decision, we will not stray far from what amounts to the influence of the classification provided by Hermann Diels (1903), and with Walther Kranz (1952), and carried over into the English translations of Rosamund Kent Sprague (1972) and Kathleen Freeman (1948), since this classification "is a decision, a discrimination, which originates with Socrates and Plato, and with Plato's recognition of the specificity of what comes to be called 'philosophy' " (Crome 2004, 18).

It is clear, and the example of the *Euthydemus* begins to show this, that the Sophists, individually and as a group, represented a serious threat to Plato's project. While their practices involved much more than deception, this aspect is never far from Plato's concerns. For him, it is indeed true to say that their speeches lie "as low as valleys and slowly fill with fog" (Gass 1985, 257). Insofar as he thought them wrong in their claims, he sought to counter them. But insofar as he thought them pernicious in their influence, especially on the young, this concern would have been elevated to almost campaign status. The irony of one of the charges brought against Socrates would not have been lost on him and no doubt contributed to the efforts made in the writing of the *Apology* to distance Socrates from the Sophists. As Socrates states there, Gorgias, Prodicus, and Hippias can enter any city and persuade the young (*Ap*. 19e). These three alone would extend the interests of Sophists beyond the eristics of the *Euthydemus*. Gorgias served as a political emissary as well as an exemplary producer of fine speeches

(*DK* 82A); Prodicus (who receives perhaps the most respectful treatment from Plato) was renowned for his teaching on language and the use of words (*Cra.* 384b; *Lch.* 197d; *Prot.* 340a, 341a; *Chrm.* 163d; *Meno*, 75c), and Hippias is presented as a Greek man-of-all-trades who makes his own clothes, shoes, and jewelry (*H.Mi.* 368b–d).

The threat of sophistry during Plato's time in Athens manifested itself in several distinct ways. Chief among these is the apparent relativism captured in the measure maxim attributed to Protagoras in the *Theaetetus* (152a), the claim of several Sophists to be able to teach virtue (*Meno* 71c–d), and the further claim that they could take the weak argument (or case) and make it strong. This latter claim is the most relevant to our current interest in argument and it will be specifically addressed in the next section. Alexander Sesonske (1968) asserts "we may justly take the phrase 'to make the weaker argument defeat the stronger' as a summary of Plato's complaint against the Sophists" (218). One other claim related to the use of language and argument is the apparent Sophistic championing of the extended speech.

Plato's Socrates professes a preference for the exchanges of questions and answers against repeated protests from his Sophistic interlocutors. Gorgias (and Polus), for example, insist on using long speeches (*Grg.* 449b) rather than questions and answers. This is a pattern of choice repeated throughout the early and early-to-middle dialogues, where the Sophists are frequently in attendance. The discussion between Protagoras and Socrates in the *Protagoras* is almost derailed over the difference of method, with Socrates threatening to leave because he does "not have the ability to make long speeches" (*Prt.* 335d). In fact, this is a principal divide commonly noted between Sophistic and Socratic uses of speech. The contrast is perhaps best seen in the *Hippias Major*, where the Sophist Hippias both professes his love of the large fabric of the longer speech while dismissing Socrates's preference for the "flakings and clippings of speeches" (*H.Ma.* 304b). Of course, as we saw in earlier chapters, it can be a matter of suiting the speech or argument to the goal, and the Sophists' goals involved addressing larger audiences in public fora. Socrates, while still operating before a smaller public, essentially works in the private domain, as the ethotic element involved has indicated.

The environment could not get more intimate than the inner workings of the thinker himself, but, as has already been noted, that is actually Socrates's favored space, the one that matters most since it is himself that he looks to convince. We have already seen how Socratic argument serves as an invitation to self-deliberation. Whether it involves investigating a claim one espouses, following a course that provokes action, or giving rise to one's own ideas, each argument encourages introspection and evaluation. In line with this, in dialogues like the *Phaedo* and the *Theaetetus*, we see Socrates's own internal deliberation. In the *Phaedo*, we recall, after accusing Sophists of encouraging a hatred of argument, Socrates advocates the use of good arguments (*Phd.* 90d). Then he continues: "I shall not be eager to get the agreement of those present that what I say is true, except incidentally, but shall be very eager that I should myself be thoroughly convinced that things are so" (*Phd.* 91a). Public persuasion is secondary to personal conviction. Likewise, in the *Theaetetus*, where thought is seen as logos that the soul has with itself, "the soul is conversing with itself, asking itself questions and answering, affirming and denying" (*Tht.* 190a). We see a hint of this view in the opening moves of the *Republic*, as Christopher Rowe suggests,

> Socrates in fact said near the beginning of Book II that he himself was satisfied with the arguments he had already developed in Book I, in favor of justice, in response to Thrasymachus; but he says that he'll obviously have to try harder to persuade Glaucon and his brother Adeimantus, who had gone on, at the beginning of Book II, to restate the case for injustice. The whole of Books II–IV are thus designed to convince others about something Socrates says he himself is satisfied he has given sufficient grounds for believing. (Rowe 2009, 21)

While we can see obvious similarities in using questions and answers, the tasks are quite distinct, and we will later explore some of the difficulties involved in persuading others of what one has already become convinced.

In spite of the different manners of speaking preferred by the Sophists and Socrates, in the *Gorgias* and elsewhere the participants will also slip into each other's chosen mode of speaking. Socrates is not averse to the long speech after all,[6] and he actually shows a facility with it. Of course, it is Plato exercising his imitative muscles when he has Socrates master the funerary speech in the *Menexenus* or convey long narrative myths to complement his logical argumentation. But in fact Socrates has no difficulty matching the longer speeches of a Gorgias, Polus, or Thrasymachus. Maybe that training at the feet of Diotima was more telling than we thought. Armand

---

6. We will recall his entry into the courtroom and his insistence that he is outside of his comfort zone there, unaccustomed to long, elegant speech and needing to resort to the extemporaneous (*Ap.* 17a–c).

D'Angour (2019) advances reasons for thinking the unknown Diotima is actually a mask for Aspasia, the very real woman who teaches Socrates the art of the funeral speech. It is no more than a passing historical novelty, and not one that could be verified either way, but D'Angour's argument would see Socrates's abilities in both the public and private discourse tracked to the same source.

The Mystery of Crowds

Difficulties remain, though. How does one shift from reasoning with an individual to reasoning with a group? To a certain degree, the authenticity of *Alcibiades I* hinges on this question.[7] At issue is a passage (114b–d) where Socrates warns Alcibiades that when he speaks in the assembly, he will have to persuade each man individually.

> Socrates: And the only difference between the orator speaking before the people and the one who speaks in a conversation like ours is that the former persuades men in number together of the same things, and the latter persuades them one at a time?
>
> Alcibiades: It looks like it.
>
> Socrates: Come now, since we see that the same man may persuade either many or one, try your unpracticed hand on me, and endeavour to show that the just is sometimes not expedient. (*Alc.* 114c–d)[8]

Here, although Socrates distinguishes between a private speech such as they are conducting between themselves and a public one in the Assembly, he effectively reduces the latter to the former in his insistence that "you will have to persuade each man singly." Lévystone (2020) accepts the passage (and dialogue) as authentic and discusses the advantages of breaking down the crowds into the individuals (145–46). But Nicholas Smith (2004) sees

---

7. See David Johnson's (2003) introduction to his translation for a review of some of the reasons behind the doubts over inauthenticity, none of which he finds conclusive (xiv n7). This is a view shared by Patricia Fagan (2013) who appeals to the Neoplatonic tradition in starting her study of Plato with this dialogue.

8. Translation is from Lamb (Plato 1955).

in the passage itself a clear reason (one of several he delineates) to discount the authenticity of the dialogue. He is alarmed both by the suggestion of persuading many people at once and by the practice of speaking in the Assembly in general. Both counter what is said elsewhere. There is merit to the second point; indeed it is at odds with the advice Socrates gives in the *Apology* (31e–32a). But it is the first point that is of relevance to our discussion.

It matters how we translate *kai ekei toi se deēsei hena hekaston peithein*. Smith covers it rather too hastily in remarking "that Socrates says that the only difference between discussions between two people and addresses to the Assembly is the number of people being persuaded at one time" (Smith 2009, 103). But this interpretation retains an emphasis on numbers that the actual text elides. Socrates is just as plausibly stressing that persuasion always occurs on an individual basis (as each person persuades themselves having heard what is said) rather than *en masse*. On such terms, the difference disappears. This interpretation, consistent with the line in Greek, is also consistent with the emphasis on self-deliberation that we have noted elsewhere and above.

After all, how does a speaker address a crowd? This is a problem taken up by Aristotle in his *Rhetoric* (on civic discourse). But the difficulty of the answer reinforces the difference between the larger fabric of a speech and the clippings of Socratic discourse that Plato has taken pains to emphasize. Socratic argument controls the message, measuring its terms and molding it for each recipient. Sophistic argument, as captured in the extended speech, escapes some of the ethotic aspect important to Plato—the commitment of the interlocutor on which the structure of the argument can be built. Sophistic speech may well convey the power of the character of the speaker, but its necessary generality cannot address the individual on her or his own terms. Hence, each person must be persuaded singly.

Weaker and Stronger Arguments

Disagreement over public and private discourses is not the only marker that separates Platonic arguers from their Sophistic counterparts. And as noted earlier, an important ability attributed to the Sophists was making weaker arguments strong. Something of a commonplace has built up around the claim that the Sophists could make a weak argument *appear* strong. The thinking here seems to be that an argument either is or is not strong, hence it cannot be made to be other than it is, so any success in doing so must involve no more than an appearance. This further supports the belief that the Sophists were deceptive in their practices. The source of the "appearance" interpretation may lie more with Aristotle's *Rhetoric*, or translations of it, than with Plato himself. A key passage in question (in chapter 24 of Book 2) involves Protagoras and the account of the notorious weak man versus strong man assault that is attributed to Tisias in Plato's *Phaedrus* (273a–b). Trading on likelihoods (*eikota*), it is deemed unlikely that the weak man would have assaulted the strong just because he is weak, but nor is it likely that the strong man would have started the altercation simply because the blame would likely fall on him as the stronger man. Aristotle concludes that while both outcomes *seem* likely, only one *is really* likely. It will not be lost on us that the difference between strong and weak men will shadow that between strong and weak arguments. The final line of the account in George Kennedy's (Aristotle 2007) translation of the *Rhetoric* is rendered: "And this is to make the weaker seem the better cause'" (1402a23)[9]. In a corresponding note, Kennedy observes that this "is what sophists were accused of doing," (189n204) and cites Aristophanes's *Clouds* (889–1104) and Plato's *Apology* (18b). Elsewhere, Kennedy (1999) has reinforced this reading: "Because of its newness, [rhetoric] tended to overdo experiments in argument and style. Not only did it easily seem vulgar or tasteless, it could seem to treat the truth with indifference and to make the worse *seem* the better cause" (41, emphasis mine). Kennedy is not alone in suggesting it was the appearance that mattered. He follows Freese's (1926) translation of the *Rhetoric*, where the line from Book 2 is given as: "And this is what 'making the worse appear the better argument' means." Cope (Aristotle 1877, 321) and W. Rhys Roberts (Aristotle 1924 provide similar translations.[10]

All translators translate from the perspective of a particular understanding of a text and the theoretical assumptions behind it. In this case, there is an understanding of arguments (causes, or cases) that sees their strength or weakness as fixed properties they possess. Perhaps these translators are influenced by their understanding of the epistemological beliefs that united Plato and Aristotle against the Sophists. The philosophers were committed to an underlying truth to things (even if they uncovered it in

---

9. Here, Kennedy translates *logos* as cause; others (like Freese—Aristotle 1926) provide "argument."

10. This understanding is not limited to translators of the Greek texts: hence, Milton in *Paradise Lost* (II, 113–14) "and could make the worse appear/The better reason."

quite different ways), while the Sophists were seen to be more relativistic in their outlooks, as witnessed in the Protagorean measure maxim.[11] Whatever the motive, it remains the case that any reference to what appears or seems is absent from the Greek. Aristotle's text simply reads *kai to ton hēttō de logon kreittō poiein tout' estin*. No appearance is present.[12] In fact, this interpretation seems to reflect a generational divide. Jonathan Barnes (1982) and Rosamund Kent Sprague (1972), for example, along with three recent translations of the *Rhetoric* (Bartlett [Aristotle 2019]; Reeve [Aristotle 2018a]; Waterfield [Aristotle 2018b] all stick to the actual Greek text and avoid any reference to appearance. For each of them, the weaker argument is made the stronger argument.

Kennedy's cross-references to Aristophanes and Plato do not actually support his reading. In both texts (*Clouds* and the *Apology*) the weaker argument is actually made the stronger and not just to appear so. A similar discussion in the *Phaedrus* (267a–b), related again to the practices of Tisias, does include a claim that sophists make things appear (*phanesthai*). What is at stake, though, is not an argument or case. The passage attributes to Tisias and Gorgias an ability "to make small things appear great and great things small by the power of their words." Here, logos reframes the ways *things* appear. We have no example by which to judge the appropriateness of this for Tisias, but several of Gorgias's extant speeches might fit the charge. In his *Encomium to Helen*, for example, where logos is a powerful lord, Gorgias boasts in conclusion that by means of words he has altered the image of Helen. "I have by means of speech removed disgrace from a woman" (*DK* 82, B11, 21). This does little to resolve the central question of whence translators received the authority for their choice of "seeming" in their translations. In focusing on the object of a discourse rather than the discourse itself, the *Phaedrus* passage, while it might support the view once it is already held, is less clear as a source of that view to begin with. And of course, it should not distract us from the fact that the other candidate passages make no reference to what seems or appears. Perhaps Gorgias's

---

11. Where the *human being* is the measure of all things.

12. A reviewer for the press observes that the line not only omits the appearance but also omits the copula; that is, there is no "to be," either. So if we are to add the "to be" as understood, we might also add "appears." The same would hold for the instance in the *Apology*. This provides a more charitable explanation for the earlier translations and a more modified issue for the later ones. It remains the case that recent resolutions of the ambiguity have favored my reading.

Helen serves as an example of the alleged sophistic practice of making the weak argument strong. If so, there seems no obvious deception involved; its success reflects the skill of the rhetorician who produced it, and it illustrates the way minds can be changed once a case has been re-examined.

Setting aside, then, the "appearance" question, it seems more pertinent to ask how exactly a weak argument is made strong. What is at stake in doing so? On Platonic terms, the Sophist accomplishes the impossible: he makes something (the weak argument) into something it is not (the strong argument). He modifies reality in a way that can only be deceptive because something cannot be its opposite. He challenges the function of the refutation, rendering the move from *not-A* to *A* reasonable. Afterall, Socrates turns the apparently strong argument (*A*) into the weak argument (*not-A*). That was the force of the *elenchus*.

Implicated here is the larger issue of what counts as a *strong* argument for Plato. It is unlikely that there is a definitive answer to this. Plato's understanding of argument strength changes over the course of his works and depends on whether matters are viewed from a logical, rhetorical, or dialectical perspective. A strong argument may be one that successfully discloses what is true or, from a practical point of view, a different sense of strength would be assigned to the argument that successfully moves someone to the right kind of action. It is more helpful to match strength to outcome, as we have seen in the hortatory and maieutic arguments, and in the distinction between real and sophistic refutations. The latter would indicate that success alone is not sufficient; that success must be achieved in the right way.

Alexander Sesonske (1968) uncovers one sense of strong argument in his study of the *Apology*. His discussion will prove instructive on a number of fronts, including offering further explanation for the judgment of those who interpret the weak argument as only appearing to be strong. Sesonske is influenced by Havelock's (1963) thesis involving the transitions from oral to written cultures.

Havelock sees Plato's disaffection toward the poet to lie in the ways in which the oral tradition depends on memorization. Such repetition did not allow for individuality to emerge; nothing could be questioned, nor could any personality arise that was responsible for its own thought. For that to happen, what was needed was something like the Socratic dialectic, where people had to explain what they said. There was no such requirement in the poetic tradition. With Socrates (or Plato's depictions of Socrates), we can see the Greeks wake up from a kind of "hypnotic trance" (Havelock 1963, 208). Thus, the pre-Socratic thinkers serve as a prologue to Platonism, setting the stage for a writer "who would explore the rules of logic," in turn providing encouragement to a disciple who "could correct and systematise the logic of his master's discoveries" (305). The trail from orality to logicality is neatly marked, but is this a narrative to be endorsed? Elsewhere, Havelock (1986), reacting to the studies of Alexander Luria and his colleagues,[13] wondered whether all logical thinking as it was then understood was no more than a product of Greek alphabetic literacy (39). It is an important question for our deliberations. In his conclusion, and like Robinson (1953) in his promotion of an evolutionary account of logic, Havelock challenges later logicians who are taken to assume that the procedures of logic are rooted in human nature rather than rising, as Havelock suggests, as a literary discovery. Analytic philosophers (who he judges to be synonymous with these logicians) must therefore either downplay the role that the technology of the alphabet played in the organizing of logic or dismiss the power of pre-alphabetic orality as merely primitive (1986, 122–23).

Sesonske sees Havelock's linking of individuality, logical ability, and writing to provide an understanding of how weak and strong arguments are set in contest with each other in Plato's *Apology*. The text illustrates the transition from an oral frame of mind where a certain form of persuasion held sway to what will become a logical frame of mind where a different sense of strong argument prevails. As the drama of the trial unfolds, Socrates details the charges that have been leveled against him, including the charge of making the weak argument strong (*Ap.* 18b, 19b). This charge, notes Sesonske, is the only one left unanswered and given no discussion at all. He finds significance in this: "For this accusation, far from being trivial, is the important one, the one upon which the verdict of the jury hangs" (1968, 222). On these terms, the trial itself becomes a test of how Socrates delivers himself argumentatively. Plato/Socrates, in line with Havelock's thinking, had seen in their Athenian peers a failure of individual responsibility, which amounts to a failure to "say what they 'knew' in logically-connected, abstract terms" (223). This is the recipe for "strong" arguments: those that are "logically strong, with the strength of

---

13. Alexander Luria (1976) and his colleagues in 1930s Uzbekistan explored cognitive development through a series of studies that tested the ability of nonliterate subjects to "reason logically." Restricting this logic largely to the Aristotelian syllogism, they were met with repeated failures to draw the "logical" conclusion.

valid logic connecting true statements, contrasted to the spurious psychological strength of persuasion" (223). By contrast, the "weaker" argument is this spurious variety. When speaking of the Sophists who are named early in the text (*Ap.* 19e), Sesonske claims that for them "arguments are entertainments and the consequences of argument are slight" (221).

Socrates is thus propelled down dual tracks: he is alert to what counts as persuasive for his traditionally oriented hearers and must speak to that,[14] but at the same time he represents a shift to a kind of argument adoption that those same jurors would judge weak.[15] In endorsing this, Socrates does indeed make the weak argument strong. And we are better for it, thinks Sesonske. What the jurors would recognize as strong arguments—those with "the spurious psychological strength of persuasion"—Socrates believes are weak. So, his accusers speak persuasively, but he advocates for the truth. Here, Sesonske suggests, the "distinction Socrates intends is clear to *us* . . . truth follows the logical strength of abstract argument and persuasiveness characterizes any argument which does not proceed in valid logical form and yet calls forth assent" (225). Socrates's real appeal to Athens is to recognize the strength of abstract argument and accept its conclusions (230). It is *this* that must happen before the transition from oral to literate culture is complete; a new genre of philosophy must dominate the argumentative culture of the state.

This is a compelling narrative because, as Sesonske rightly notes, *we* see it. The subsequent path of argument has reinforced it. Socrates as an advocate of abstract logic is indeed a familiar figure in the history of Western logic. But this is not a picture that has been particularly borne out so far by this study. Yes, we see an interest in an underlying standard of truth that captures the ideas explored. But the persuasiveness of arguments, even in this context, returns again and again to the personal commitments of those involved. By restricting the Sophistic argument to those served up for light entertainment (221), Sesonske looks no further than eristics and does the Sophists an injustice. Thus, from the start, his conception of weak argument is impaired.

---

14. "Assuming that Socrates' accusers were men still close to the oral tradition, we can say what such argument would be for them. Familiar terms would be the concrete, image-making, descriptive terms of the oral record: appropriate patterns of speech, those of the rhythmic, formulaic, narrative style spoken by the wise men who conveyed to them all the knowledge which the culture treasures and preserves" (Sesonske 1968, 224).

15. "The weaker argument, the abstract, logical Socratic talk which compels assent but carries no conviction" (Sesonske 1968, 230).

We may have a larger dispute over the other party in the contrast—the truth. In the context of a text relating a trial speech in which the principal speaker claims to be unwise, the existence of an abstract logic may be hard to discern. We may rightly question Sesonske's claim that "truth follows the logical strength of abstract argument." The truth that Socrates provides is a redescription of his philosophical practice and the life that both informed that practice and is informed by it. Perhaps the contrast is to be seen between words and deeds. Socrates does, after all, offer the jurors what they prefer over words, namely actions (*Ap.* 32a). But he does this to make more vivid the truth of his claims about just and unjust actions. *This*, like his duty and other virtue-related matters, he does *know*. But the private nature of virtue can only be demonstrated in the public displays that stream from them. Hence, the actions show Socrates disobeying both the tyranny and the democracy because in each case they required him to do something that he judged (that he *knew*) to be unjust. This is a truth that cannot be conveyed better in words, and certainly not in abstract logic. Or perhaps abstract logic conveys truth in the elenctic exchanges between Socrates and Meletus? We have seen, though, that such displays, wrestling the contradictions of a life into the open, are far from abstract but once again expose what is private to public scrutiny. These exchanges may *suggest* a reading of the *elenchus* that the tradition has subsequently provided and that encourages abstraction in the pursuit of "What is F?" questions. But that, as we have seen in chapter 2, was never the core of the *elenchus*.

We can agree that "Socrates' speech is not devoid of persuasive devices," while still questioning whether "all of them are used to weigh the psychological balance against himself" (Sesonske 1968, 230). Any exception would prove the counter case, like the use of a *praeteritio* at *Ap.* 34d, refusing to adopt the custom of bringing his family before the court in support of an acquittal. Because, of course, in this refusal he does exactly that, but more emphatically and persuasively than if he had brought them forward in person. In calling attention to the custom, he effectively invites the jurors to conjure up those family members for themselves, bringing them alongside him. This seems more a strategy to further his interests than weight the balance against him. Likewise, the appeal to his sign, likely to infuriate rather than quell his audience, is made to support his presence at the trial (and presumably the manner in which he has conducted himself). Puzzlingly, it did not oppose him. But that was because the experience is not harmful: "I have strong evidence of this, since there's no way my usual sign would have failed to oppose me, if I weren't about to achieve something good" (*Ap.* 40b). Strong evidence, indeed.

Like Havelock, Sesonske harbors a belief in Plato's commitment to abstract logic. As we come to explore the inferential nature of Plato's dialectic in later chapters, we will see the grounds for this position. But that it is evident in early texts like the *Apology* and reflected in the illustrations of Socratic argument there and elsewhere is far from clear. Logic requires rules, and Aristotle will provide such rules. So far, we have seen procedures, and these have been crucial for the correct conduct of arguments. But the focus on procedures indicates something dialectical rather than logical in nature. In fact, it is the dual sense of "dialectical" that has characterized the nature of Socratic arguments: first, the thinking through that "dia" indicates, and second, the other party with whom the thinking through is conducted, indicated by the sense of "dialogue." On one level, Socrates does invite the jury to think through the case with him, but the *Apology* indicates little else of the pure dialectical method (beyond those exchanges with Meletus)—for that we must look elsewhere. The *Apology* is, after all, a trial speech and not an easy fit into the genre of Platonic dialogue.

Dialogues and Dialectic

When, in the context of a dialogue, Socrates appeals to a very different jury, "members of the jury[16]—for this is really what you are" (*Symp.* 219c), he addresses men who have shared in the Bacchic frenzy of philosophy (*Symp.* 218b), sitting in judgment over the character of Socrates and frankly ensorcelled by him. No abstract logic impedes this appeal or issues from it. It is to their experience that he speaks and on which the strength of his argument depends. It is through their personal experience that they have encountered philosophy.

Although the charge is stated there, perhaps the *Apology* was not the best text for Sesonske to explore Socrates's relationship to weak and strong

---

16. Is there ever a time when Socrates is not being judged by a jury of some description? However we answer that, it remains the case that Plato takes pains to specify different juries with particular compositions, from that of the *Apology* to this jury in the *Symposium* and a similar "receptive" jury in the *Phaedo*: "I want to make my argument before you, my judges, as to why I think a man who has truly spent his life in philosophy is probably right to be of good cheer in the face of death" (*Phd.* 63e).

arguments. Outside of the trial speech where the dialogue form does prevail, in the ambivalent medium of the written word, argument has a specific, concrete application. As Tushar Irani (2017) insists in a discussion of the art of argument in Plato, "a genuine lover of argument, must be a lover of others" (25). It is the personalized nature of argument that gives it its force, that makes it strong. In each of its varieties, as we track it from the early into the middle dialogues, the goal of an argument is to bring about some kind of awareness in an individual: to lead them to action, assist them to see the measure of their own ideas, or refute claims that cannot withstand examination. These kinds of analyses invite the vehicle of a literary form that can capture the drama in individual lives as ideas are themselves brought alive in conversation. And for this reason, our discussion suggests, Plato wrote dialogues. In time, those dialogues would evolve along with Plato's own thought. The drama would diminish, and the urgency of ideas would come to the fore with attention to a very different dialectic. And then the nature of argument and what Plato considers a strong argument would also change, while never completely losing sight of its roots. These transitions await us in later chapters.

Writing detaches ideas from the voice that expresses and defends them. It renders statements accountable for their own meaning. The dialogue form retains the oral tradition in its insistence on commitments to the statements expressed, statements that are associated not just with contexts but with the lives of those who utter them. Even here, in the transitional medium of the dialogue, writing is to be heard as much as read: writing "rises up immediately in its readers to the level of the ear, and becomes a vital presence in their consciousness" (Gass 1985, 263). The extemporaneous speeches championed by the Sophist, the kairotic moments glimpsed and immediately grasped, all fall prey to the intransigence of the written word. The tension between interior and exterior arguments with their different measures of strength finds resolution in a form about which Plato remains ambivalent. With the advent of writing, language tumbles onto the page in neat sequences and formulae, inaugurating a linear consciousness (Flusser 2002, 22) that lays the foundations for an abstract logic. But for the early Plato, any possibility of this kind is in the future, and the logical remains a feature of the human in all its individuality. In this respect, the rhetorical features inherent in Plato's reasoning start to take on significance. It is to considerations of these features that we turn in part II.

Part II
The Rhetorician

Introduction to Part II
Plato's Style

> And Athens it is that has honored eloquence [*logos*], which all men crave and envy in its possessors; for she realized that this is the one endowment of our nature which singles us out from all living creatures, and that by using this advantage we have risen above them in all other respects as well.
>
> —Isocrates (*Panegyricus* 47–48)

To speak of Plato's style is to confront his true ambivalence toward rhetoric, to see the anti-rhetorical in force. If style involves the presence of the author (writer; speaker) on the page, then Plato's style conjures an acute problem. He appears invisible, voiceless; his absence distracts us. He is a master of silences, using them to manipulate the mind, draw it into crevasses that might otherwise be passed over, divert it down passages not entered, cause it to dwell on the unspoken as it resonates in the ear. Hiding within the shells of his characters, he imitates *their* styles, a true Borgesian divinity: everything and nothing.

Persuasive Power

The power of persuasion in the tradition may have an able competitor in the power of tradition itself. Thus, once a view is fixed in history it acquires a presumption in its favor that is difficult to dislodge. Friedrich Solmsen (1975) conveys something of this inertia in his response to the puzzle created by Gorgias's last thesis in his treatise *On Not-Being*. Thus, while nothing exists, and even if it did exist it could not be grasped, still even if it could be grasped it could not be communicated. Gorgias fills out the reasoning by saying that we reveal things through logos, but we only perceive (see, hear) things that are external substances, and logos is not an external substance (*DK* 82, B3, 83). There is something of the eristical display at work here. But Solmsen takes it at face value in asking why Gorgias would lend such importance to the power of speech if nothing could be communicated (Solmsen 1975, 47), even though the target of Gorgias's reasoning is the reality of external things and how to talk about *them*. We might recall a similar position that is attributed to Protagoras: that we can only entertain a certain agnosticism regarding the existence of the gods owing in part to the obscurity of the subject matter (*DK* 80, B4). If the domain about which we can know (about which we are the measure) and of which we can communicate is that of human experience, then of what lies beyond that sphere we must remain silent.

In Gorgias's *Helen*, Solmsen finds the roots of the traditional association between persuasion and emotion, associations reinforced in early texts from thinkers like Antiphon and Euripides. Logos works insofar as it arouses (or allays) the appropriate emotional responses in an audience. Thus, Solmsen understands that for the Greeks "to persuade a person" is to produce "in him the necessary emotional condition." He proceeds to anticipate Plato by remarking that "to see a distinction and concepts not yet known at the time—although the basis for them is laid in it—some speeches are addressed to the rational element of man's soul, others to the emotional" (Solmsen 1947, 49). Indeed, the consequences of such a divide will be seen in Socrates's disingenuous "offer" to poetry (or her champions) to present an argument for her entry to the state, having previously explained that poetry by nature addresses emotions not reason (*Rep.* X, 607c–d). So, any argument that might be forthcoming would need somehow to close a divide that Plato leaves gaping in his *Republic*. It is not until Aristotle's association of emotion with judgment that the divide begins to close. Still, what Solmsen reiterates is a traditional story of Plato's disdain for persuasion.

Plato's Anti-rhetoric

To speak of Plato having a rhetorical style necessarily invites discussion of his relationship to rhetoric—both that of the handbooks and that of his own work. Indeed, here is another thread of the traditional story, strongly encouraged in contemporary textbooks that highlights Plato's anti-rhetorical stance. Yet Plato is critical of other things that he still in some way adopts:

he expresses disdain for the epic poets yet borrows their lines and tropes to the degree that scholars will speak of Plato's own poetic nature; he dismisses the value of writing yet is himself praised for his ability to produce some of the most compelling texts of our tradition. Why would we then take his criticism of rhetoric to be the end of the discussion?

With rare exceptions, the judgment of the literature is that Plato's reaction to rhetoric is generally negative and that the dialogues in which rhetoric is at issue are the *Gorgias* and *Phaedrus*, with the latter allowing a more positive conception.[1] Tom Conley (1990), for example, in his well-received study of rhetoric in the European tradition, promotes the definitive judgment that "Plato had nothing good to say about rhetoric or its practitioners," a sentiment that strongly echoes that of Brian Vickers's (1988) indictment of Plato. This is a conclusion that simply cannot be sustained if we pursue Plato's discussions of rhetoric beyond the *Phaedrus* and through to later dialogues like the *Statesman* and the *Philebus*.

James Herrick (2001), commenting on the *Phaedrus* in his history of rhetoric, finds the issue to be rhetoric's relationship with truth. "Scholars have often noted that in *Phaedrus* Plato hints at a true art of rhetoric. Clearly, this would not have been the same art as that practiced by the Sophists and criticized in *Gorgias*. In fact, this Platonic art of rhetoric may not have been practiced by anyone in Athens, except Plato himself." (63). George Kennedy (1963) allows that in the *Phaedrus* "the art of rhetoric is conceivable for use in advancing truth, which must, however, be known by the orator first" (78).

Indeed, in the *Phaedrus* Plato proposes a true art of rhetoric in which the rhetorician is transformed into a philosopher. But, as we will see, this is the *atopic* philosopher, because he is out of place when taken beyond the activities of the *polis* and has no audience other than himself. Returning to the city after his time in the sun, the philosopher-rhetorician of the *Phaedrus* must then find the language and strategies with which to address others. The task is not leading them to philosophy per se (that

---

1. There are a few exceptions. One is Wardy (2009), who reads the *Phaedrus* account as consistent with that of the *Gorgias*. The sense of "rhetoric" confirmed in the *Phaedrus* is so far from what is "recognizably practiced" as to represent something that only "perfect philosophers" could acquire (55). Another exception is the view of Golden et al. (2000) that is mentioned below. Then there is Ernesto Grassi's (1980) generous reading of the *Phaedrus* that judges true philosophy to be rhetoric and true rhetoric to be philosophy (32). And finally, I would add Halliwell (1994), who allows that many other dialogues supplement or qualify what we find in the *Gorgias* and *Phaedrus* (225).

is, not hortatory argument), since so many of the lessons learned "in the sun" are not applicable to the wider populace. In this respect Susan Jarratt (1991), contra Kennedy above, is correct in pointing out that rhetoric's role is not the discovery of truth; that is always the role of dialectic. She sees rhetoric's role to lie in advocacy. But then how, if at all, does this fit into Plato's later philosophy, where, as Rosenstock (1997) observes, "Plato seems to have shifted from a view of philosophy as practice to a view of philosophy as theory" (84)? And so from Plato onward, the ruling judgment finds rhetoric and philosophy pursuing separate paths (Bonazzi 2020, 61) and encountering very different fates.

Vickers's Treatment

In titling one of the chapters of his seminal work *In Defense of Rhetoric* "Plato's Attack on Rhetoric," Brian Vickers makes no attempt to hide his own judgment. Halliwell (1994, 242n5) finds this a "harsh account" of Plato's views of rhetoric, and as the chapters of this part of the book will demonstrate, there is little reason to disagree with that assessment. Yet given the influence that Vickers's work has had on rhetorical studies, it is important to weigh the details of his treatment of Plato and judge the fairness of his remarks.

The treatment begins with the *Gorgias*, a dialogue that, claims Vickers, treats rhetoric "as subservient to politics, being indeed the main tool of politics in Athenian democracy" (1988, 84). Indeed, it is the main tool, and would not be otherwise. And as we will see, Plato does not stray from this judgment in later dialogues. But as a tool of politics, it is not necessarily subservient to it. We might equally observe that without rhetoric, politics could not succeed. But Vickers accuses Plato of stacking the deck against rhetoric by, for example, enlisting incompetent people to defend it, a strategy that he puts down to Plato's strong desire to discredit rhetoric (93). He finds the *Phaedrus* to be "Plato's longest exposition of a reformed, philosophical rhetoric" (133), without fully acknowledging what has been accomplished there.

And there Plato's engagement with rhetoric effectively ends. Vickers enlists the judgment of E. L. Hunt to suggest that Plato's "'later utopia' allowed 'no freedom of utterance,' so denying rhetoric any chance to develop" (138). Yet he fails to consider the chronology of the dialogues in order to explore the possibility of any development. His treatments of dialogues after the *Phaedrus* are cursory and confused. He thinks the Socrates of the *Statesman* is Socrates when he was younger, which is an odd suggestion given that both Young Socrates and Socrates are present. And he observes of that dialogue that while oratory is distinct from statesmanship; it "is openly given the task of state propaganda" (142). I will correct that judgment below.

On the last page of the chapter (147) Vickers mentions the *Philebus*, but it is a vague reference that accomplishes little. He recognizes the return of Gorgias and the citing of rhetoric's greatness, but without exploring the context in which these things occur. After all the details of the treatments of earlier dialogues, it is disappointing to see such a minimal discussion of the later Plato, and with no appreciation of the development of Platonic dialectic to which the later prospects of rhetoric are inextricably linked. In fact, one of his confusions concerns the nature of the Platonic dialectic, which, like other commentators before him, he reduces to the *Socratic* method of dialectic. He talks of Plato's privileging of the Socratic *elenchus* (125), never allowing that Plato's own method is distinctively different. This puts into question much of his interpretation of how rhetoric stands to philosophy in Plato's work, since the latter cannot be understood without a full appreciation of Plato's own dialectical method.

It is in discussing the role of rhetoric in *Laws* that Vickers is most insightful and comes close to crediting the role that it must play. If he was not predisposed to conclude otherwise, he might recognize the value of what he observes. With reference to a passage at 719e–720a he says, "The appointed lawmaker must not just 'tell us curtly what we are to do or not to do, add the threat of a penalty, and then turn to the next enactment, without one word of exhortation or advice to the recipients'; rather, he must add a 'prefatory statement in front of his code,'" and then: "So, ironically enough, he now needs rhetoric again!" (143). In fact, he never stopped needing it and consciously so; a more objective analysis would have recognized this.

Revising the Narrative

While the forgoing captures the tone of what might be judged a "traditional" reading, there is a growing awareness that Plato's engagement with rhetoric is far more nuanced than this narrative allows. In the seventh edition of their history of rhetoric in the West, James L. Golden and his authors (2000) report: "We have found that the general subject of rhetoric is featured with varying degrees of emphasis in every dialogue Plato wrote. In these writings, he touched on all aspects of human discourse." They then detail some of these "aspects" as they appear in dialogues from the *Apology* through to the *Theaetetus* and the *Statesman* (22). This is welcome recognition and accords with the story that will unfold in the chapters of part II.

James Kastely (2015; 1997) comes closest to giving the subject of rhetoric in Plato the kind of treatment it deserves. While not exploring the later dialogues as will be done here, he does raise questions about the relationship between refutation and persuasion (1997, 51–52). As we have seen, refutation is at the heart of Socratic dialectic, involving the examination of an interlocutor's statements in a way that results in the contradiction of his initial thesis. But the dialogues also raise questions about what persuasion involves and how it should function in the everyday life of the polis. The contrast suggested by Kastely is important. It is one that appears to be overlooked by those who claim that Socrates is actually the true politician because the one-on-one discussion of his dialectic (the refutation) is the only authentically political sort of talk (Wardy 1996, 82–83). This ignores the failure of Socratic dialectic to meet the general needs of the polis, where a positive discourse is required (rather than Socrates's negative nay-saying). It is this need to address the polis, to lead people to a just life, that I would suggest is on Plato's mind in the later years of his career. This is long after he has abandoned the method of Socratic dialectic with its failure to move beyond *aporia* and replaced it with his more distinctive brand of dialectic. At this later stage, rhetoric is rehabilitated and called upon to play an important role. The philosopher discovers truth through dialectic, but dialectic cannot itself suffice for communicating ideas informed by that truth. It for this reason that expressions of truth will always be conveyed through a mix of genres, and "the philosophy within Plato's dialogues is always rhetoric" (McCoy 2008, 19).

In the chapters of part II, I first explore the details of the traditional narrative that dwells on the *Gorgias* and *Phaedrus* while exhibiting a reluctance to move beyond considerations of those dialogues. I then follow Kastely and others in looking at the nature of persuasion in the *Republic*. This leads naturally to considering the place of rhetoric in Plato's political philosophy generally, and in his later political dialogues specifically. The more convoluted entanglements of rhetoric with Platonic dialectic are reserved for part III.

Chapter 5

Plato's Attack on Rhetoric

Fractures in the Standard Narrative

> Again, it is a fault to disparage an art or science or any occupation because of the faults of those engaged in it, as in the case of those who blame rhetoric because of the blameworthy life of some orator.
>
> —Cicero (*Rhetorica Ad Herennium*, II, 27, 44)

> [From the *Gorgias*] I conceived the highest admiration of Plato, as he seemed to me to prove himself an eminent orator, even in ridiculing orators.
>
> —Cicero (*De Oratore*, 1.47)

Rhetoric through a Moral Lens: On the *Gorgias*

All about Athens

As parodies go, the *Menexenus* leaves a few things to be desired.[1] Its provenance, while attested to by Aristotle, continues to be controversial, not least

---

1. In describing it thus, I break with Schofield (2006, 94n64), who insists it is a pastiche and not a parody because there is no humor in the speech. What we might lack, he suggests, is the right appreciation of "pastiche." Of course, we might also lack an appreciation of parody, as captured in a more neutral definition: "Any cultural practice which provides a relatively polemical allusive imitation of another cultural production or practice" (Dentith 2000, 9).

because Socrates delivers the speech several years after his own death.[2] But as a parody, suggests Scott Consigny (2001), its imitations indicate an appreciation of Gorgias's funeral oration (*epitaphios*) as representative of the genre. And as a piece of rhetorical discourse, we cannot ignore the identity of the rhetor who delivers it. Insistent on the power of language couched in short answers to questions, yet equally comfortable with the expansive terrain of the longer speech, Socrates is portrayed not just as a lover of speeches (*Phdr.* 228c) but as an accomplished speaker in his own right. In fact, George Kennedy judges the *Menexenus* to be a model of a good speech and sees the intent behind that of showing that a philosopher can be a successful performer of a powerful rhetorical speech (Kennedy 1963, 160–61). The subject matter of the speech in question is Athens and her history and the values that attach to both. This focus is relevant to the way I approach the *Gorgias*.

It is Eric Dodds who draws attention to the *Menexenus* as a companion dialogue to the *Gorgias*, a judgment reinforced by Schofield (2006, 72).[3] Both texts deal with rhetoric and its use by Athenian politicians (Plato 1959 [trans. and rev. Dodds], 23;) and both convey criticisms of Athenian democracy. One text provides the theory, the other the practice. This marks an important link between the interests of the *Gorgias* and those of later political dialogues, unlike the *Phaedrus*, where Socrates is specifically placed outside of the city and its political concerns.

If Dodds is correct in judging the *Menexenus* as a follow-up text to the *Gorgias*, then this places the composition of the latter about 387–85 (Plato 1959 [Dodds], 24). Stylometric analyses of the dialogues have placed it between the *Euthydemus* and the *Cratylus* and after the *Protagoras* and *Meno* (Lutoslawski 1897, 215). On this view, the *Gorgias* is a dialogue showing the transition from the concerns and method of Socrates to those of Plato.

The Socrates of the *Menexenus* gives full responsibility to his instructor who "is by no means weak in the art of rhetoric" (*Menex.* 235e)[4] and

---

2. Eduard Zeller (1839) sees such to indicate the spurious nature of the dialogue. But in this he is going against the stronger testimony of Aristotle's *Rhetoric* (1367b and 1415b).

3. Zuckert (2009), by contrast, sees a closer association with the *Phaedo* "on the basis of the indications of the dramatic date" (817). Menexenus is present at Socrates's death (*Phd.* 59b), and Zuckert sees in the conversation between Socrates and Menexenus an attempt on the part of the former to restrain the latter's political ambitions. This association, it should be noted, plays down the role of rhetoric, although Zuckert insists that a similar critical attitude to that in the *Gorgias* is present (2009, 818).

4. I draw here and for subsequent quotes from the *Menexenus* of R. G. Bury's (1929) translation.

suggests that, as a consequence of such training, it should be no surprise that he "should be clever at speaking" (*Menex.* 236a), a remark that grinds against the excuses of the *Apology*. And it is speaking that is the key issue here. Like in the *Phaedrus* (to which we will turn in the next chapter), the speech of importance will be delivered by someone who was not the author, so the skill in question is delivery not invention. And also like in the *Phaedrus*, the central issue is memory. Here, the transition from the oral to the written inaugurates new challenges for the memory. In the *Phaedrus*, a prepared text (hidden from public view) has been memorized for delivery; in the *Menexenus*, the memorization is of an aural experience:

Menex: Could you repeat from memory that speech of Aspasia?

Soc: Yes, if I am not mistaken; for I learnt it, to be sure, from her as she went along, and I nearly got a flogging whenever I forgot. (*Menex.* 236b–c)

Such coercive memorization may not be the ideal, but the point here is to reinforce the idea of Socrates as a figure of the spoken word, a lover of speeches who can repeat what he hears.

The speech itself, befitting the funeral genre, is thoroughly epideictic in character, while still serving as an example of historical discourse (in spite of omissions and inaccuracies [Zuckert 2009, 824]). The primary goal is to promote values like courage and moderation and reinforce them in the hearers "to give kindly exhortation to the living, appealing to their children and their brethren to copy the virtues of these heroes" (*Menex.* 236e) since it would be shameful to be judged only for the glory of one's ancestors and not for oneself (*Menex.* 247b). The mixture of praise and potential blame dominates the descriptions of historical facts, culminating in the ideal person who is best prepared for life: that person is temperate, courageous, and wise (*Menex.* 248a). It is "of such a character" that friends are exhorted to be "even as we now display ourselves as such" (*Menex.* 248b). It is important to recognize the emotive power of these passages, because if this is a text that illustrates what the *Gorgias* argues, then also on display is the nature of the threat that Plato judges rhetoric to represent.

In the *Gorgias*, Socrates asks not just for a definition of rhetoric but to have its specific power explained to him (*Grg.* 456a). At stake are two modes of refutation (*Grg.* 458a, 472c, 500c) and the kinds of lives that support these modes. At 500c, for example, Socrates sets the contrast most strikingly. Addressing Callicles, he asks him which course of life is best: "Whether it should be that to which you invite me, with all those manly pursuits of speaking in the Assembly and practicing rhetoric and going in for politics after the fashion of you modern politicians, or this life of philosophy; and what makes the difference between these two." One of the tensions that recur in Plato's early and middle dialogues is between these two lives, always presented as mutually exclusive: different ends require different means.

The *Gorgias*

In spite of some attempts to cast the narrative of the *Gorgias* in a light more amenable to the prospects of rhetoric (Wardy 2009), it remains the dialogue (and the only dialogue) in which the practice is severely critiqued.[5] Against the escalating defenses of Gorgias, Polus, and Callicles, Socrates marshals Plato's most serious objections in a rigorous investigation of the claims and alleged accomplishments of the rhetorical "art." In fact, of course, it is not judged an art, or at least the practitioners cannot supply a strong argument for believing it to be such.

If one of the primary concerns driving the dialogue is to name the power that rhetoric has and how to control that power, then Gorgias is a fitting Sophist to involve. It is he, as we know, who judges logos a powerful force (or lord), alert to the ways in which it moves audiences (*DK* 82, B11, 8). And the Gorgias of the *Gorgias* is presented in ways that suggest an effort to accurately portray the historical figure.[6] When Socrates first encounters him at Callicles's house he is invited to put to Gorgias any question he has on any subject (*Grg.* 447c), an apparent reference to Gorgias's ability to speak extemporaneously on any topic (*DK* 82, A1, 3).

Why would Plato be interested in controlling the power of rhetoric? Why not just dismiss it as he will do with some types of poetry in the *Republic*? One reason is that it presents itself as a candidate for advancing one of the argumentative projects in which he (and perhaps the historical Socrates) is engaged. Of the types of argument we explored in part I, the

---

5. Granted, the *Phaedrus* critiques the handbook tradition and the practices associated with it, but I would judge the attitude toward rhetoric generally to be less severe. This is taken up in the next chapter.

6. Brad Levett (2005) shows how the accuracy of the portrayal extends to a parody of Gorgias's own use of a particular rhetorical figure (the *polyptoton*, or repetition of a word in different cases) that is used against him (218). See also Luzzatto (2020, 190).

elenchus and the maieutic do not require any obvious persuasive force. But the hortatory is a different matter altogether. Here, an interlocutor is turned to the practice of philosophy and needs to be persuaded of the value of doing so. Any strategies that might facilitate this program in a reasonable way are to be recommended for adoption. In this regard, I think certain commentators are correct in suggesting that the Socrates of the *Gorgias* is interested in enlisting the Sophist's assistance in promoting the value of philosophy (Plato 1998a [trans. Nichols], 131, 148–49). And the concern with the hortatory will also find expression in the *Phaedrus*.

The Definition

The first reference to *rhētorikē* is made at 448d, and if we accept Edward Schiappa's view (1999, 14),[7] it is the first instance of the term available to us, suggesting that its coinage lies with Plato himself. Yet as it is introduced, in reference to the practice of Polus, the implication ("Polus has had more practice in what is called rhetoric," *Grg.* 448d) is that the term is common, and a prior usage is being drawn upon. And along similar lines, it becomes evident that Socrates has reflected on the nature of rhetoric before and has some clear ideas about it. Of course, assigning its origin elsewhere would imply there is a prior meaning that can be drawn upon. This seems to be what Socrates pursues in the famous definition that promotes a general dismissal of rhetoric as a useful art.

Having disagreed over the subject matter of rhetoric, with one party addressing the *logoi* themselves (*Grg.* 449d) and the other addressing what the *logoi* are about (*Grg.* 451d) (no slight difference), Gorgias offers—again consistent with the expressions of the historical Sophist—that rhetoric is "being able to persuade people by *logoi*" (*Grg.* 452d).[8] Rhetoric has the

---

7. "The word *rhētorikē* simply cannot be found in any text that has been dated prior to Plato's *Gorgias*, usually dated to 380s B.C.E." Laurent Pernot is more cautious on this, given the large number of texts that are simply no longer available to us. But he does allow that the word was probably rare prior to Plato's adoption (2005, 22–23). Stephen Halliwell (1994) is more insistent that the term predates Plato because of the way Socrates first references it in the *Gorgias* ("so-called *rhētorikē*" [*Grg.* 448d]). Schiappa (2017) agrees that the term could have been in oral use before Plato or used in texts that are now lost (38). Schiappa (2022) stands firm in his position, countering the view of Luzzatto (2020) that the term can be assigned to the historical Sophist.

8. Unless otherwise noted, quotes from the *Gorgias* are from Nichols's translation (Plato 1998a).

power to produce persuasion in the soul; it is the art of persuasion as seen in the law courts and among other crowds (*Grg.* 454b). Here, is the first of several contrasts of note: Socratic discourse addresses the one; Gorgias addresses the many.

Another contrast immediately follows, between a type of persuasion that provides belief without a foundation in knowledge and a type of persuasion that provides knowledge itself (*Grg.* 454e). Given that the vast majority of the polis will be fine with the former as long as they are led by philosophers who have acquired the latter, then this anticipates the ways rhetoric will operate in the *Republic*. It is the first of these—believing without knowing—that then receives attention, with Socrates drawing a contradiction from Gorgias's agreement that this is a plausible sense of the subject. After all, if the rhetorician were to become more persuasive than the physician, he would be more persuasive than the one who knows. The same holds for carpentry and music. And most important of all, it holds for justice, since Gorgias has allowed that the rhetorician must be just and will never wish to do injustice. But earlier, Gorgias had said that "the rhetor might use rhetoric unjustly as well" (*Grg.* 461a). Gorgias has been refuted, although Polus will immediately interject that Socrates has been leading Gorgias on (*Grg.* 461b–c).

The discussion now shifts: Polus takes up the questions and Socrates the answers, and there is a hint of *aporia* with respect to the inquiry to this point when Polus suggests that, in Socrates's view, Gorgias "is at a loss concerning rhetoric" (*Grg.* 462b), a judgment reiterated at 463a. We are clearly beyond the limitations of the early dialogues as Socrates is now offering his own opinion of the nature of rhetoric. It is not an art but a type of experience "of the production of a certain grace and pleasure" (*Grg.* 462c). Polus takes from this that Socrates believes it a fine thing, but Socrates responds that the same can be said of cookery. Pressed by Polus, Socrates is reluctant to finish the definition for fear of offending Gorgias. But given that he still does not really know what Gorgias thinks it is, he proceeds, responding directly to Gorgias:

> It is a certain pursuit that is not artful but belongs to a soul that is skilled at guessing, courageous, and terribly clever by nature at associating with human beings; and I call its chief point flattery. Of this pursuit there are, in my opinion, many various parts, and one of them is cookery; it seems to be an art, but—as my argument goes—is not an art but experience and

routine. I also call rhetoric a part of this pursuit, and cosmetic too and sophistry, these four parts directed to four kinds of business. (*Grg.* 463a–b)

What might we say of this definition? First, as Dodds points out in his commentary, it is not specifically a definition of rhetoric but of a whole of which rhetoric forms a part (1959, 224). Indeed, given how central definitions are to Plato's later dialectic, there is at least an anticipation here of the method of collection and division, if not a full example. The stress on guessing is also of note since it corresponds with points made in other dialogues that would contrast the precision of mathematical techne with a less reliable opinion.

The whole to which the definition is directed is "flattery" (*kolakeían*). This is a term that resonates far differently for us than it may have in Plato's time when it conveyed a negative moral tone. Later in the dialogue it will acquire the sense of pandering to the multitude.[9] This advances the moral concern. Aristotle will see in such panderers an insincerity that warrants blame (*NE* 1127a7). This is reinforced by Socrates's further statement after being pressed by Polus to clarify in what part of flattery rhetoric consists and responding that it is "a counterfeit (*eídōlon*) of a branch of politics" (*Grg.* 463d).[10]

Rhetoric, as Socrates presents it here, has two failures: it is unscientific (lacks exactness) and it is morally suspect (cares little about justice). Both deficiencies are open to remedy, however. The subject is unscientific because it cannot give an account, as all arts must do, about what it makes use of or on what it is used (*Grg.* 465a). Arguably, this concern will be addressed in the *Phaedrus*. It is the moral question that receives the bulk of attention in the remainder of the *Gorgias* and that will track on through the *Republic* and the *Statesman*.

A Question of Method

In many ways the dispute with the rhetoricians of the *Gorgias* is a dispute over how to use language. And both with Gorgias and in the exchanges with Polus, the debate hangs on the matter of method. Of all the issues

---

9. Which would justify Sachs's (2009) decision to render *kolakeían* as "pandering."
10. I suggest "counterfeit" rather than "phantom" to maintain the contrast that is at issue (*Grg.* 465c).

at stake in this dialogue, the right way to use language to achieve an end judged valuable is continuously brought back into the frame. At 449b, for example, we find:

> Socrates: Would you be willing, then, Gorgias, to continue just as we are talking now, asking and answering, and to put off until afterwards this lengthiness of speech that Polus started? Don't play false with what you promise, but be willing to answer what is asked briefly.
>
> Gorgias: Some answers, Socrates, must necessarily be made in speeches of great length; but I shall nevertheless try, at least, to speak as briefly as possible.

And, indeed, he does try, as does Polus, who is repeatedly challenged in similar terms. As a consequence, both Gorgias and Polus operate in unfamiliar territory and express a certain discomfort at doing so. Speech may be a powerful lord, but he who has mastered its use in a particular form controls that power and is able to lead interlocutors down paths they might not otherwise choose to follow.

Socrates shows himself adept at both the long speech and the short dialectical exchange. The same cannot be said for a figure like Polus, who when drawn outside his preferred mode of discourse becomes easily confused. But at issue is not just the ways they approach language but also what they draw on to support their respective positions. In this regard, a tension over the nature of refutation is instructive.

Polus and Socrates disagree over a key moral claim—whether the person who commits injustice can be happy. Socrates's position on this means that he would rather suffer injustice than do it (*Grg.* 469c). Polus makes clear that he holds the opposite position and draws on examples to make his case (*Grg.* 471a–c). Socrates resists not just the assertion but, as importantly, the way it is supported. He regards Polus to be well versed in rhetoric but to have neglected disputation (*dialégesthai*) because he believes he has refuted Socrates (*Grg.* 471d–e). Socrates then accuses Polus of trying to refute him rhetorically, the way they do in the law courts. Noteworthy here is that the reference is not to a sophistical refutation, as we saw this in chapter 3. While rhetoric and sophistry are both among the four parts of pandering, they are clearly considered distinct from each other even with respect to the ways they use language. Polus's "rhetorical" refutation is made by means of bringing witnesses against Socrates's position (from across the political range: Pericles, Aristocrates, and Nicias [*Grg.* 472a–b]). The contrast is with the familiar *elenchus* that involves examining the statements themselves and seeing where they lead. This method of refutation was illustrated earlier when Socrates invited Gorgias to examine the argument whether the rhetorician was in the same condition with respect to justice as to health (*Grg.* 459c–d). On these terms, Polus should be examining the claim that the unjust person cannot be happy. Instead, he is "providing many false witnesses against" Socrates and attempting to expel him from his "reality, the truth" (*Grg.* 472c). Polus's argument has presented Socrates the opportunity to identify two types of refutation and set them side by side for comparison. On the one hand, refutation is aimed at the many; on the other, refutation is aimed at the individual. As Socrates explains his procedure: "For I know how to provide one witness for what I say, the man himself to whom my speech is directed, while I bid the many farewell; and I know how to put the vote to one man, while I don't converse to the many either. See then if you'll be willing in your turn to give occasion for refutation by answering the things asked" (*Grg.* 474a–b). Once Polus concedes to this, he is on the well-worn path of Socratic refutation, arriving at the contradictory position to the one he first asserted. They agree—Polus with reluctance—that the unjust person is not happy. This is also judged a refutation of rhetoric because *it* led to a position that they are now agreed is wrong. "Polus, what is the great use of rhetoric?" (*Grg.* 480a).

The Moral Import

The discussion with Gorgias results in the failure to understand what rhetoric is. The discussion with Polus results in the failure to see what value it has. Now Callicles steps forward. In this figure, we are presented with one of Plato's more enigmatic characters. We know nothing about him beyond what is provided here—a young Athenian of the deme of Acharnia (*Grg.* 495d) in the early stages of a political career—leading some to suggest he is fictional (Hamilton in Plato 1960, 11). If he was a real person, it would seem that his political life was short and unsuccessful, or we would have heard of it. And this failure might be a reason for Plato's choice. Yet again, if he is a fiction, one may wonder why Plato was unable to attribute the position he holds to any actual politician. If rhetoric is so threatening, that threat would be best demonstrated through the example of a real figure. And yet, on one level, the position Callicles holds is not itself unknown.

That it is natural that the strong should dominate the weak and the weak should submit to the strong is the position Athens took in its dealings with Melos.[11] If there are echoes of the unjust argument still resounding after the exchanges with Polus, then the contemporary reader would hear them here, in Callicles's voice. He is real insofar as Athens is real; he personifies the city, or at least a dark moment in its political history. The indictment of Callicles that Plato has Socrates deliver is an indictment of Athenian political power and the use of rhetoric by the Athenian envoys in exercising that power. If this supposition is correct, then the Melian arguments can be judged one of the most problematic uses of rhetorical discourse in Athenian history. Thus, nowhere is their consideration more appropriate than in the *Gorgias*, where the merits and demerits of rhetoric are being weighed with careful deliberation.[12]

Callicles believes conventional laws are those set down by the weak, while the strong appeal to what is natural. In Socrates's exchanges with Polus, when the latter spoke of things of nature, Socrates asked about convention, and when Polus spoke of what accorded with convention, Socrates "pursued the argument according to nature" (*Grg.* 483a). Thus, Callicles is suspicious of the Socratic way of arguing; he believes it leads the interlocutors where they would not choose to go, and he will later complain to Gorgias that Socrates focuses on things of little worth and refutes them (*Grg.* 497b). Criticism of the Socratic method of short questions and answers has come from all three interlocutors of the *Gorgias*, but with Callicles the concern reflects a

---

11. As related by Thucydides in his *History of the Peloponnesian War* (bk. 5, chaps. 84–116), the Athenian envoys argue for the submission of the city of Melos on the grounds that it is natural for the weak to submit to the strong. No matter how the Melians argue their case, appealing among other things to what they deem just, the Athenians persist in their position. The arguments of the Melians failed, and the Athenians subsequently massacred the men and sold the women and children into slavery, a response that sent shock waves throughout the Greek states and received condemnation from friend and foe alike. Isocrates would later identify Melos as a black mark on Athenian history (*Panathenaicus* 62–64). So, it is no surprise that Plato will also find the occasion to add his reaction. In fact, the failure of him to do so would be a greater surprise. When Callicles begins by criticizing Socrates for switching between references to nature and to convention in his questioning of Polus (*Grg.* 483a), the allusion to Melos starts. And when he argues for the supremacy of the stronger over the weak (*Grg.* 488c), it is complete.

12. Simon Blackburn (2006) ties the siege of Melos and the Melian debate to the position of Thrasymachus in the *Republic*. For reasons argued here, I see the details of the debate to have greater relevance for the critique of political rhetoric in the *Gorgias*. I will address Blackburn's position on Thrasymachus in a chapter 8.

general mistrust that will reoccur in the *Republic*. The counter-side is that Socrates is putting himself on a trajectory to self-harm by pursuing a subject that does not teach him how to defend himself with a speech appropriate for the law courts (486a–b). By bringing philosophy under scrutiny in this way, not only does Callicles set rhetoric on the higher ground, but Plato is also given an opportunity to defend philosophy against rhetoric rather than just pursuing an attack on the latter.

A Rhetoric without Practitioners

The question accordingly turns to the life that is best pursued: the kind of person one should be and what course one ought to pursue (*Grg.* 487e–488a). But, given the contrast that has been introduced between philosophy and rhetoric, it is clear that rhetoric is still at issue; it somehow characterizes one of the lives of concern. In advance of this, Socrates clarifies Callicles's position as to what is just according to nature—that the stronger carry off the things of the weaker by violence; "how big cities advance against small ones in accordance with the just by nature, because they are stronger and mightier, on the grounds that the stronger and mightier and superior are the same thing" (*Grg.* 488b–c). What is just, on these terms, is equals sharing equally (*Grg.* 488e). Callicles confirms that this is his position. And this is the position that recalls Thucydides's description of the Athenian envoys at Melos. Speaking to the Melians, they remark, "You know as well as we do that right, as the world goes, is only in question between equals in power, while the strong do what they can and the weak suffer what they must" (*Thuc.* 5.89.1). Later in the exchanges, the Athenians claim that it is "by a necessary law of their nature" that the strong rule. They found this law existing before them, and it will continue to exist after them (*Thuc.* 5.105.2). It is difficult not to see the commonality of positions between these Athenian representatives and Plato's Athenian representative, just as it is difficult to avoid seeing how this compounds the concerns of the dialogue between Socrates and Polus over the suffering of injustice.

Socrates observes that many customarily believe that doing injustice is more shameful than suffering injustice, and that this is so not just by convention but also by nature, so that Callicles was wrong to criticize him for opposing nature and convention. But Callicles is dismissive of Socrates's "driveling" (*Grg.* 489b), twisting his own words to suggest the strong are other than the superior. At the same time, Socrates remains unclear on exactly what Callicles means by the superior, since he is clearly not thinking of numerical supremacy. They consider intelligence, and whether the superior man would get more in the way of food and clothing and shoes. While Callicles sees this as further driveling, the reader understands Socrates's concern for the finer details of definitions and the ability to distinguish similar things from each other. Again, we see a mixture of the method of refutation applied to the one who supposedly knows and the growing quest for precise definitions that drives the later Platonic dialectic.

Callicles, however, insists that he is restricting the sense of stronger to those who rule the affairs of cities, that he is interested in political strength and the intelligence and courage associated with it (*Grg.* 491c–d). Still, Socrates shifts the discussion from the ruling of many to self-rule, bringing the concern back to the kind of life an individual leads and that individual's self-knowledge. On this matter they differ the most. And, importantly, in continuing to promote his position, Callicles is "now saying distinctly what the others think but are unwilling to say" (*Grg.* 492d), with the contrast between the two lives coming into view. One life is the "insatiable and intemperate life," of speaking among larger groups of people, practicing rhetoric and politics; the other, "the orderly life, sufficient and satisfied with the things that are ever at hand" (*Grg.* 493c–d), speaking to one other person at a time and practicing philosophy. Cookery and medicine are illustrative of the two distinct lives: the first is an experience (not a techne) and proceeds irrationally without examining the nature of what is involved; the second "examines the nature of he who it cares for and the cause of the things it does, and it has an account (logos) to give of each of these things" (*Grg.* 501a). Callicles hesitates to accept Socrates's conclusions here but allows them for the sake of the argument. Activities that address the many are grouped together because of the pleasures they give, from flute-playing to poetry. Stripped of tune and rhyme, they are no more than *logoi*, but *logoi* that are popular in nature, addressing the crowd. In this, suggests Socrates, they have identified a certain kind of rhetoric but one they agree is not admirable because it is a pandering one (*Grg.* 502d). But Callicles still hesitates to extend the same judgment to the political rhetoric that is addressed to Athenians and those of other free cities, because while some fit the description Socrates provides, others care about the citizens when they speak.

Socrates pounces on this; it is an observation he had been waiting for Callicles to make. And from it emerges the prospect of a valuable political rhetoric, albeit one that is yet to be seen. One part of rhetoric, as they have described it, deals with pandering and popular speaking; the other part, as Callicles now has identified it, would be fine or noble (*kalon*), "making preparations for the citizens' souls to be as good as possible and fighting to say the best things" (*Grg.* 503a). Callicles offers some candidates from the past who may fit the bill here: Themistocles, Cimon, Miltiades, and Pericles. They calmly examine each of these leaders in light of the teleological outcome at which such an artful rhetor should aim (ordering the soul in a lawlike manner similar to health within the body), only for the earlier politicians to fail to make the grade once the role of justice is brought into the discussion.[13]

The true rhetoric must lead people to justice and remove injustice from the soul, a step that allows punishment to be good for a soul. This echo of the earlier discussion causes Callicles to balk at where they are going, and he refuses to continue. Socrates is left to complete the discourse himself, even though he does not say what he says with knowledge (*Grg.* 506a).

Socrates again becomes the self-deliberator, demonstrating a model of argument in which the others cannot engage, investigating the idea of a strong rhetoric. The moderate soul is the ordered, good soul since it is just, courageous, and pious. And the better city will be held together in just this way. What follows are the things for which Callicles had accused Socrates of being unserious: that "one must accuse oneself, one's son, and one's comrade, if he is doing injustice, and one must use rhetoric for this" (*Grg.* 508b). Unmentioned but implicit here we should hear a similar indictment of "one's city." Because it also follows that it is not shameful to be treated unjustly but treating another unjustly is "more shameful and worse" (*Grg.* 508e). The Melian venture haunts these remarks. Plato may not have agreed that the Melians were just men, but he would have agreed with them that they were fighting against the unjust (*Thuc.* 5.104.1). The greatest of evils is the injustice of the doer of injustice, and even greater still (if that is possible) is for the doer of injustice to avoid the just penalty (*Grg.* 509b).

It is a long route from Callicles's identification of the key politicians of the past as candidates for the strong rhetoric that he and Socrates have discovered (*Grg.* 503c) to the rejection of those very same politicians because they who were incapable of making anyone just (*Grg.* 515d–517a). The Athenians did not become better for the efforts of any of these. Each of

---

13. See, though, Aristides's powerful defense of the four in his third oration (Aristides 2021).

them—Pericles, Cimon, Themistocles, and Miltiades—suffered at the hands of those they had ruled. It follows that neither contemporary politicians nor those Callicles picked out were rhetoricians who used the true art of rhetoric (*Grg.* 517a). Rhetoric, on these terms, is no different than sophistry and the rhetors are simply Sophists, because in both cases they have "conferred no benefits on those whom they say they benefit" (*Grg.* 520b). By contrast, and against the persistent warnings given by Callicles, Socrates promotes himself as a lone practitioner of politics insofar as he does nothing unjust (*Grg.* 521d).

Character and Consequence

To sum up his argument, Socrates offers a rational account that Callicles will judge a myth. The differences between these two types of discourse we shall consider elsewhere; for now it suffices to consider what makes this story of the judgments meted out on humans by the sons of Zeus a *rational* account. In this eschatological tale, souls are stripped of their identities, so no one can hide behind power. And they therefore become defenseless in the face of justice and receive the punishments their actions warrant. And those most likely to receive the severest treatments are "those who engage in the affairs of cities" (*Grg.* 525d)—the politicians.

Socrates is persuaded by such discourses to the degree that it directs his current actions. And he exhorts Callicles to be persuaded (*peithomenos*) and follow him. But it is not the myth alone that recommends this; it is the myth set against the other arguments that have been reviewed—of Gorgias, Polus, and Callicles himself: "Among so many speeches, the others are refuted and this speech alone remains fixed" (*Grg.* 527b). Interestingly, Plato sets this account on equal footing with those of the three rhetoricians, more than just equal in fact, since it "wins out." What remains fixed is that "one must beware of doing injustice more than suffering injustice, and more than everything, a man must take care not to seem to be good but to be so, both in private and in public" (*Grg.* 527b), and those who are unjust must pay the penalty by being punished. These, of course, are the principles of the Socratic position as it has been maintained throughout the dialogue.

This rational account also holds a final lesson for the value of rhetoric, since fleeing from all pandering, whether it concerns few men or many, is the goal to which all should aspire. And the tool to help accomplish this is rhetoric itself, rhetoric against rhetoric, against pandering: "One must use rhetoric thus, always aiming at what is just, and so for every other action" (*Grg.* 527c). This is not, then, a dismissal of rhetoric; it is a championing of a kind of rhetoric, a true political rhetoric, which so far has no adherents or practitioners. It is a rhetoric that, if successfully established, will lead people to justice.

Eric Voegelin (1966) detects a revolution in the closing myth of the *Gorgias*. Moral authority is removed from Athens, a city state that has lost its soul, and transferred to Socrates/Plato. Callicles has warned Socrates many times of the fate that awaits him at the hands of the Athenians, but it is the fate that awaits Athens that the myth brings to light (Voegelin 1966, 39).

ATHENS

With Athens and Athenian politicians receiving such severe criticism in the *Gorgias*, we might wonder at the praise that was bestowed on the city in the *Menexenus*. Of course, that example of epideictic rhetoric was careful not to stray from the conventions of the funeral speech. It is also a text, Kennedy reminds us, that emphasizes the happiness of those who have done their duty for their country (1963, 162). Political speeches, minimally, should assign happiness to the just and unhappiness to the unjust, a point emphasized by Socrates in the *Gorgias* and reiterated in the *Republic* (392b). Dodds judges the *Gorgias* to be the result of Plato's reflection on the causes that brought about Periclean Athens, a city in material and spiritual ruin (Plato 1959 [trans. Dodds], 32–33). The blame for the collapse of Athens lies not with the generation of Alcibiades, "the ultimate responsibility rested in [Plato's] view on Pericles himself . . . what he attacks in the *Gorgias* is the whole way of life of a society which measures its 'power' by the number of ships in its harbours and of dollars in its treasury, its 'well-being' by the standard of living of its citizens. Such a society, he holds was Periclean Athens" (33). This is obviously a shift in expressed attitude from the *Protagoras* and *Meno*, where Pericles is spoken of as a great and wise man.[14]

If Periclean Athens extends to the end of the Peloponnesian war and not just the death of Pericles—as seems likely because the ethos, the city's self-conception, its political and social institutions would all continue beyond his departure—then this is the leadership that looms over the Melian siege. Under this leadership, military power is prized and praised. This is an added,

---

14. Which would be another reason for judging the composition of the *Gorgias* to be later than both the *Protagoras* and the *Meno*.

deeper dimension to the criticism of political leaders, the bulk of which is leveled against Pericles himself. Of the four Athenian political figures singled out by Callicles as good men, Socrates directs developed comment against only one of them. Drawing on hearsay and what he knows, Socrates charges Pericles with making Athenians "lazy, cowardly, babbling, and money lovers" (*Grg.* 515e) and notes how the city turned against him, "clearly on the grounds that he was base" (*Grg.* 516a). People should have "become more just instead of more unjust through him" (*Grg.* 516c), to which Callicles must agree, although with reluctance. As the closing myth makes clear, the unjust men face "fearful suffering," but justly so (*Grg.* 525c).

This criticism gives us further reason to believe the target of the dialogue here is the political rhetoric of the Athenian empire, essentially Pericles's Athens, rather than the more contemporary Athens that has committed the equally egregious act of condemning Socrates to death. The premonitions about Socrates's fate that haunt the dialogue simply indicate the ongoing struggle between justice and injustice in the lives of the citizenry. The dialogue begins with Socrates addressing two non-Athenians, but its arguments culminate against an Athenian.

CALLICLES

It is worth repeating that we know nothing at all about Callicles beyond what Plato tells us in the *Gorgias* (Dodds in Plato 1959, 12) and that what he tells us describes him in terms that makes him a natural heir to the ideas of Periclean Athens, if not the ambitions. And for this reason, I forbear against adopting Dodds's judgment that because of the pains Plato takes to give depth to his character, identifying his deme and three of his associates (*Grg.* 487c) (who are all known personages) so Callicles must have been a real historical figure.[15] After all, it is perfectly consistent with Plato's realism to find any character detailed in this way. Such a portrait is also consistent with viewing the character of Callicles as a plausible representative for a type of Athenian that has both historical and contemporary relevance.[16] The

---

15. John Beversluis likewise accepts his "implied" historicity (2000, 339n1), and Robin Waterfield in his translation of the dialogue (Plato 1994) insists that he is "surely a historical person, rather than a Platonic fiction" (168) because Plato gives details about his deme. In her study of Plato's characters, Debra Nails follows Dodds and adds further details, while acknowledging the difficulties involved (Nails 2002, 75–76).

16. Beyond the puzzle of his existence, the question of Callicles's political affiliation (democrat or demagogue) has attracted considerable scholarly attention. Kerferd (1974)

presence of two renowned rhetoricians like Gorgias and Polus in the opening sections of the dialogue may distract us from Callicles's nature. But in a dialogue in which Athenian politics is so heavily implicated, the presence of a politically astute Athenian is a significant addition.

The significance involved lies in the distinctively Athenian position that he espouses. Whether or not Callicles was a real figure (whose political career may have ended too early for any record of it to have been made—Dodds in Plato 1959, 13) is now beyond us to determine. But his argument retains historical presence. An advocate of nature and critic of what is decided by convention, Callicles asserts the supremacy of those who are strong by nature: "But nature herself, I think, reveals that this very thing is just, for the better to have more than the worse and the more powerful than the less powerful" (*Grg.* 483d). As Socrates reframes it: "That the stronger carry off by violence the weaker men's things, that the superior rule the worse men, and that the better have more than the lowlier" (*Grg.* 488b). Richard Enos observes of Callicles that, unlike Gorgias and Polus, he "has little to contribute to the understanding of the nature of rhetoric" (Enos 1993, 96), which is ostensibly *the* subject of the dialogue. Instead, he serves as an example of the misuse of rhetoric. Whatever rhetoric Pericles and others used—and we are told it was not the true art of rhetoric (*Grg.* 517a)—minds like Callicles's are the result.[17]

Gorgias

To the forgoing it may be objected that the dialogue is not called the *Callicles*, so the real attention should be on Gorgias, whose visit to the home of Callicles is the occasion for the dialogue and whose role as teacher connects him with the other speakers.

Undoubtedly, Gorgias moves back and forth into view in the dialogue, and even when he remains "behind the scenes" of a discussion the criticisms advanced by Socrates may still be relevant to him. Something similar will hold for Thrasymachus through the middle and later books of the *Republic*. Afterall, if Callicles's associations are with the ideas of the Athens that Pericles brought into being, Gorgias had associations with Pericles himself. Philostratus in his *Lives of the Sophists* (1921) reports on the admiration

---

reviews the matter, noting Callicles's links with Pericles and concluding that Plato considered him a democrat (52).

17. On this reading, it cannot be Callicles with whom Plato's sympathies lie (Cooper 1998).

Gorgias received when he spoke in Athens, although already an old man, drawing the attention of equally admired men like Pericles, who was also already old. Gorgias's *Olympic Speech* dealt with political matters, as did the *Funeral Oration* that he delivered at Athens. In the first of these speeches, Philostratus tells us, he praised victories over the Medes "because he was addressing the Athenians, who were eager for empire, which could not be obtained unless they adopted extremism" (Philostratus 1 9, 1). Perhaps erroneously, Pericles is also counted among Gorgias's students, further cementing the association (Consigny 2001, 7; Enos 1993, 75).[18] It may suffice for us to observe a likely connection between his rhetorical performance in support of a political cause and his popularity. Insofar as this display was concordant with the political ambitions of the city, the historical allusions that Plato inserts into the *Gorgias* supply the links between Callicles, Periclean Athens, and Gorgias.

The key for us, though, is not so much the men involved but the art that they do or do not possess. The failure of those who "know" to give a definition of rhetoric gives way to a need to divide political rhetoric so as to distinguish the pandering kind from the true art. Gorgias, for all his power (and probably because of it), can never be viewed as a proponent of the latter. Enos goes further in marking the concern that never leaves Plato's treatment throughout the dialogue: "Plato had no choice but to denounce Gorgias, for to acknowledge his philosophical position and his view of rhetoric would mean that Plato would have had to renounce the fundamental tenets of his own philosophy" (Enos 1993, 83). What the *Gorgias* does bring to the fore, though, is the impossibility of divorcing the political and the rhetorical. This realization drives the discussions of the *Republic* and retains its importance through to the *Statesman* where rhetoric will again be called upon to lead people to justice (*Stm.* 304a). It is within the city that the impact of rhetoric is most forcefully seen. Perhaps that is why Plato has to take his philosopher outside of the city in the *Phaedrus* in order to further his investigation of rhetoric in and of itself.

---

18. As is often the case with such matters, what constitutes being a student may be questioned here. Given that Gorgias's first visit to Athens, as an emissary from Leontini, seems to have occurred only a few years before Pericles's death, then any formal relationship of teacher and student seems unlikely. But the admiration of Pericles for Gorgias that a number of sources report may well be translated into the kind of influence that emerges from such relationships.

Gorgias himself will also return. Direct and indirect references to Gorgias occur in a number of dialogues,[19] but his most telling appearance is in the *Philebus* (58a). Here, a kindlier treatment of Gorgias is suggested, albeit at a time in Plato's career where rhetoric has been assigned its natural position, one appropriately subordinate to the rule of dialectic.

Lessons of the *Gorgias*

The *Gorgias* contributes many ideas to our study of Plato's use of argument and his roles as logician, dialectician, and rhetorician. Most pronounced are his proposals in relation to the latter, with the rejection of a political rhetoric that had proved popular in the city in which Plato was raised and his advocacy of a rhetoric that will promote justice over injustice. It is a dialogue in which the Socratic *elenchus* is still powerful, but also one in which a method of definition is on display that will receive more attention through the middle and late dialogues.

---

19. By indirect references I have in mind the Gorgianic style of Agathon's speech (*Symp.* 198c) and what I take to be an earlier mention of his method of learning that was passed on to Meno (*Meno* 71c–d).

Chapter 6

The *Atopic* Philosopher

[For the philosopher] it is in reality only his body that lives and sleeps in the city. His mind . . . pursues its wingéd way, as Pindar says, throughout the universe.

—Plato (*Theaetetus* 173e)

Entering the *Phaedrus*

The *Gorgias* opened with Callicles and Socrates exchanging pleasantries around the "feasting" that had been enjoyed on the many fine things that Gorgias's speeches had provided (*Grg.* 447a). The *Phaedrus* opens with Phaedrus and Socrates observing that Lysias would have been "feasting [Phaedrus] with all his fine speeches" (*Phdr.* 227b) in the house of Epicrates. If this allusion were not enough to suggest kinship between the two dialogues, then it is reinforced by Socrates's explanation for why he is outside the city wall: having been persuaded by the physician Acumenus to take walks along country roads (*Grg.* 459a).

Lysias was a speech writer of fifth-century Greece, one of the ten Attic orators of the Alexandrian canon, of whose work only thirty-four speeches are still available. Tradition suggests that he was friendly toward Socrates.[1] The interests that Gorgias and Lysias had in logos would have been quite

---

1. It is in the house of his brother, Polemarchus, that the action of the *Republic* takes place. We know very little of the historical Lysias. See Viidebaum (2021) for a recent review of the evidence and for an examination of the "Lysianic" rhetorical tradition.

different in nature. While both wrote speeches, one of them was more renowned for his extemporaneous inventions, offering to speak on any topic that his audience requested (*Grg.* 447c); the other crafted texts that others could learn and declaim. But allowing Gorgias to haunt the opening of a dialogue in which Lysias's work comes under scrutiny serves to emphasize a primary interest of the dialogue: already in this opening, then, we have a focus on speeches, their construction, and their delivery; on texts and their memorization. In fact, memory will be an enduring theme of the whole work.

Yet for many the *Phaedrus* stands out from among other Platonic dialogues for the uncertainty of its unity and because of its nonpolitical setting, as commentators disagree over exactly which theme ties the work together, if any does (Hackforth in Plato 1952b). Charles Griswold Jr. (1986), for example, looks to the theme of self-knowledge, while others see the problem of writing as the central concern. In a similar fashion, translators emphasize different interpretations in the choices they make. Christopher Rowe (2006; Plato 1986 [trans. Rowe]) opts for the nature of *eros*; James Nichols Jr. (Plato 1998b), for the power of rhetoric.

Further confounding these problems of interpretation is the Socrates that this dialogue offers us. Drawn out from the comforts of the city, he speaks and acts in ways not usually associated with Socrates. In contrast to the central figure of the *Apology* who professes unfamiliarity with long speeches, the Socrates of the *Phaedrus* claims to be a lover of speeches and is eager to hear the long Lysianic speech that Phaedrus has concealed beneath his cloak. After Socrates has given a colorful, evocative description of the place where they have arrived, Phaedrus describes him in terms variously rendered as "extraordinary" (Plato 1986 [trans. Rowe], 27), "amazing" (Plato 1998b [trans. Nichols], 30) and the "oddest of men" (Plato 1952b [trans. Hackforth], 25). The term being translated here is *atopos* (*Phdr.* 230c), and we would be better to stay closer to its literal meaning. While the descriptions of "extraordinary" and "oddest of men" recall Alcibiades's similar way of separating Socrates from other human beings in the *Symposium*, the literal "out of place"[2] or "out of one's element" separates Socrates from his environment and emphasizes how unexpected it is to find him outside of the city with its human relations and ensconced in nature. This removes the action and the central figure from the political concerns of the city. And, accordingly, the rhetoric that will be reviewed and modified is not the specific political rhetoric of the *Gorgias* but the more general "art" that was first pursued in

---

2. Thus, Nehamas and Woodruff (Plato 1975c) come closest in their translation: "And you, my remarkable friend, appear to be totally out of place" (*Phdr.* 230c).

the exchanges between Gorgias and Socrates. Being "out of place" the *atopic* Socrates of the *Phaedrus* is free to do and say surprising things. And he will grasp the opportunity to embrace this freedom to the fullest.

The Speeches

The *Phaedrus* addresses a moment in the development of Greek thought when the power of the oral is confronting the emergence of the written text (Ong 1982, 45).[3] This confrontation is prefigured in the literal cloaking of Lysias's text by Phaedrus. He claims to have memorized the speech, as would have been the custom. But Socrates detects it beneath Phaedrus's cloak and draws it out for attention (*Phdr.* 228d). In the hidden text, "Lysias is also here."[4] It is the written discourse that will be the subject of the opening inquiry, just as its nature will occupy the closing concerns.

Phaedrus/Lysias

Socrates did not expect to learn much from country places and trees—from nature, essentially. His real lessons are drawn from the people of the city. But to counter this apparent disappointment, and incite Socrates's interest, Phaedrus has found a drug (*pharmakon*) in the logos he offers (*Phdr.* 230d–e).

This first speech of the *Phaedrus* is Lysias's speech in praise of the non-lover. A list of reasons is given for gratifying the non-lover over the lover: in fact, a series of contrasts is provided. For example, lovers when desire has ceased rue the neglect of their own interests and the damage done because of their love, but non-lovers do not have such troubles to face and so can perform whatever actions they think will please the other person (*Phdr.* 231a–b). The growing list of benefits that follow from favoring the non-lover (whose friendship, unlike that of the lover, will outlast desire, for example) begins to sound like the friendship based on utility that Aristotle will criticize in his *Nicomachean Ethics* (bk. 8, chap. 3); it is an argument

---

3. Walter Ong observes: "The agonistic dynamics of oral thought processes and expressions have been central to the development of western culture, where they were institutionalized by the 'art' of rhetoric, and by the related dialectic of Socrates and Plato, which furnished agonistic oral verbalization with a scientific base worked out with the help of writing" (1982, 45). Alternatively, the "oral state of mind" has been judged Plato's main enemy (Havelock 1963, 41).

4. Unless otherwise noted, quotes are drawn from the Rowe translation (Plato 1986).

built on benefits with little attention to the affection that binds lovers. Lysias's speech has a mercenary quality to it, albeit with advantages to both parties.

Phaedrus asks how the speech has appeared to Socrates, clearly inviting a positive response. And Socrates provides it, overcome by what he has heard, or rather by what he has seen, because it is the way the delivery has energized Phaedrus that is remarked upon, leading Phaedrus to question the seriousness of the reaction (*Phdr.* 234d). In fact, Socrates will separate the content of the speech from the rhetorical effect; it is the latter that has caught his attention. This suggests that even the most paltry of content (as this first speech is so regarded) can *appear* as something it is not if the rhetoric is powerful. Socrates admits he "was only paying attention to the rhetorical aspect of it" and doubts that "even Lysias himself thought the speech good enough." In fact, he seemed just to repeat himself several times over (*Phdr.* 235a).

Phaedrus demurs: no one could say anything better on the subject. But Socrates in turn is unpersuaded and appeals to the lyric poets like Sappho. This elicits a challenge to Socrates to counter with a speech that supports his judgment.

Socrates's First Speech

In spite of professing himself a layman at such things, Socrates will deliver two speeches in the dialogue. Not short, focused pieces of dialectical exchange—the "clippings of speech" of which Hippias accuses him elsewhere (*H.Ma.* 304b)—but extended pieces of discourse in response to the Lysianic speech delivered by Phaedrus. While judged as little more than a bridge between the dialogue's first speech and the speech that will matter—the palinode—Socrates's initial speech is noteworthy for at least two things. In the first case, it advances the underlying interest in rhetoric. Socrates missed many of the details of Lysias's speech because he was only paying attention to the rhetoric involved. Thus we, in turn, are invited to pay attention to the rhetorical aspect of Socrates's first speech, as it avoids the disorganization of its predecessor and insists on a "starting point" (*arche*) for all inquiries in the form of a definition or standard from which details of the speech can follow or to which they can be compared. The methodology thus used both anticipates the organization of speeches that will be advocated later in the dialogue and reflects the practice of other dialogues in seeking first to understand the terms that are at issue.

Secondly, the first Socratic speech is noteworthy for the compulsion that instigates it and the way Socrates seeks to escape responsibility for it because of this compulsion. In this way the manner of the speech's delivery reflects the tension within the speech between the compulsion of desire and the deliberations of judgment. Socrates attributes the details of the speech to things he has heard, perhaps in the poetry of Sappho or Anacreon (*Phdr.* 235c). This is in keeping with his usual protests of ignorance and his tendency to attribute ideas to others, as he does, say, to Diotima in the *Symposium*. But unlike the latter case, here he speaks unwillingly and only, in the end, because Phaedrus threatens never again to share further speeches with him. This is too much for an avowed lover of speeches and he is forced involuntarily to comply. With his head covered to hide his shame, he delivers an "improvised" speech in contrast to the written speech previously delivered by Phaedrus. And this first Socratic speech centers on a bipartite psychology: "In each of us there are two kinds of thing which rule and lead us . . . the one an inborn desire for pleasures, another an acquired judgement which aims at the best" (*Phdr.* 237d). Like the concealed lover of this speech, Socrates, beneath his cloak, has been drawn by desire and struggles to bring himself under the control of judgment. The lesson suggested here has to do with the persuasive power of speech and the effort that must be exerted to control it. The fear of this power drove Plato's concerns in the *Gorgias*, and they are no less relevant in the first Socratic speech. What will need to be learned is how to submit desire to the control of judgment.

Extemporizing, Socrates has no text to read, but of course, beneath his cloak he is effectively unsighted and could not read. He will need to recover his sight and aims to do so, following the lead of Stesichorus[5] by composing a palinode to appease the gods for the offense he has committed by speaking of Love as he has. He had thought to depart the place, but his inner voice checked him and drew his attention to the need for expiation.

Before this, however, Phaedrus greets the end of Socrates's first speech by expressing surprise, not at what has been said but at the fact that no more is to be said; the "other half" of the speech has not been given. As he says, he "thought it was just in the middle, and would go on to say an equal amount about the non-lover, to the effect that one should rather grant him favours, mentioning all the good things he has on his side; why then are you stopping now?" (*Phdr.* 241d). Commentators tend to pass over this remark, focusing on why Socrates might be reluctant to say more (Hackforth

---

5. A sixth-century lyric poet who was deprived of his sight for libeling Helen and thus composed verses to recant what he had said (*Phdr.* 243a). Thus, he inaugurates discourses that retract an earlier position.

in Plato 1952b, 53; Griswold 1986, 70). But given the dialogue's interest in the nature of rhetoric, we should first be asking from where does Phaedrus derive this expectation? Because this tells us how he (the internal audience) is hearing the speech, what his assumptions are about such speeches, and thus his expectations for this one. Socrates doesn't challenge him on this, so he too understands speeches to require such a balance.

It would seem, then, that they both recognize certain matters of form governing the construction of speeches. That is, they are both aware of a rhetorical tradition that expects speeches to review both sides of an issue. What might this tradition involve? Diogenes Laertius writes of the sophist Protagoras that he was the first to claim that "on every issue there are two *logoi* opposed to each other" (*DK* 80, A1). This in turn invokes thought of the *dissoi logoi* and the extant text of that name, a text that was reviewed in the introduction to part 1. The text strikes the same tone that Plato will evoke later in the *Phaedrus* (261d). It states: "The same thing is good for some but bad for others, or at one time good and at another time bad for the same person" (Robinson 1984, sect. 1, para. 1). As we have seen, technically, it is the single author of the *Dissoi Logoi* who marshals opposing arguments. The author does not *assert* both sides but relates what "some" say against what "others" say.[6] Still, this may be enough to explain an expectation that speeches will need to look at both sides in order to be "complete." What this in turn indicates is that Plato is well versed in the nature of rhetorical speeches and the form they should take. Such an understanding is clear in Aristotle's *Rhetoric* (bk. I, chap. 1) where the encouragement is given to "argue persuasively on either side of a proposition." This is done there in order to discover the real case of affairs (since Aristotle assumes both sides cannot be correct). That Plato would have agreed with Aristotle's motives reinforces Phaedrus's expectation here that the other side will be given.

Socrates's Second Speech

Socrates's speech of retraction, the palinode, is itself a contrast of a different kind. The first part with its exploration of the nature of the soul takes the reader beyond the human world up to that of the gods and the Forms. The second part, with its concentration on the nature of eros, brings us back down into the human context to apply what has been seen elsewhere. In many ways this speech will anticipate what is to be discussed and learned

---

6. For a more detailed analysis of the *Dissoi Logoi* text and its relation to the tradition of opposing arguments see Tindale (2009).

about persuasive rhetoric and the leading of souls. But in the first instance it raises the question of the appropriate audiences for speeches. On this front, the palinode is ambiguous; it offers several audiences. Let me just provide three suggested audiences, to which we can return later.

The obvious audience of concern is the god of love, who, having supposedly taken offense at the earlier speech, has required the recantation. But there is also internal to the speech the "boy" who was the ostensive audience of Socrates's first speech: "Where then is that boy I was talking to? I want him to hear this too" (*Phdr.* 243e). Thus, the speech that discusses both divine and human matters will have both divine and human imagined audiences. The third audience is the real one present in the person of Phaedrus, who is expected to learn the lessons of *eros* and particularly those relating to how the beloved can be led to philosophy by the lover. In appeasing the god, Socrates asks him to make Lysias cease the composition of speeches like the one first presented and turn him instead to philosophy, like his brother Polemarchus. The intent is that Lysias's favorite, Phaedrus, may then in turn make the right choice between philosophical and nonphilosophical speeches (*Phdr.* 257b). There is, then, an element of the hortatory argument and the goal involved that we explored in chapter 1, but it is recast here in a rhetorical light.

Characteristically, Socrates assigns the origin of the speech he is about to give to someone else: his "former speech was that of Phaedrus . . . the one I am going to speak is of Stesichorus" (*Phdr.* 244a). The first part of the palinode addresses a mistake over the nature of madness. For this is the source of the greatest of good things, as various examples illustrate. The "mantic art" seems to capture the way divine things can be revealed. It excites a "Bacchic frenzy" in the souls of the young, turning them toward different types of composition.[7] This, in turn, requires a "rational account of the soul" (*Phdr.* 245e) that invokes Plato's metaphysics at least indirectly, explaining the immortality the soul must possess. From the rational account we turn to an image: that of the team of winged horses and the charioteer, the vehicle that allows the mind of the philosopher to pursue "its wingéd way, as Pindar says, throughout the universe" (*Tht.* 173e). The course of the chariot above the heavens brings it into sight of the Forms, setting up the dialogue's later concern over opinion and the importance of memory.

---

7. Both references provide links to the *Symposium*, where Socrates again delivers the speech of another person (the mantic woman, Diotima), and the presenters of speeches in that dialogue are unified by their common experience of the Bacchic frenzy of philosophy (*Symp.* 218b).

The first of these matters, concern over opinion, arises because few can emulate this "gods' life" and the knowledge it possesses (*Phdr.* 248a). Thrown into confusion by their horses and the difficulties involved in beholding the Forms, many become maimed and have broken wings: "And despite their having much toil, all go away unfulfilled in respect to the sight of being, and having gone away, they make use of opinion (*doxa*) for nourishment" (*Phdr.* 248b). Having failed to achieve insight, they necessarily lack the memories that they can draw on later to be reminded of what is true.

"Truth" here is understood in strict Platonic terms and again implicates the method of the later dialectic: "A human being must understand that which is said in reference to a Form, that which, going from many perceptions, is gathered together into one by reasoning. And this is the recollection of those things that our soul saw once upon a time" (*Phdr.* 249b–c). This collection into one through reasoning (*ek pollōn ion aisthēseōn eis hen logismōi suniaroumenon*) is the primary accomplishment of the philosopher; it will make possible the processes of division central to the later searches for definition. But of equal importance in this dialogue, it sets a prerequisite for any true rhetoric; it must be informed by this knowledge.

By this route, Socrates has arrived at the definition of the lover, the one who participates in the most important kind of madness that has been identified and loves beautiful things. This is the person who can recollect what has been seen, and so this is the one that can lead others to philosophy. Socrates has retracted his earlier speech and shown why it is the lover and not the non-lover that should be the target of affections. The friendship of utility has been replaced by the most important type of any friendship—that which harbors the prospects of being led to philosophy. There is no greater good than this way of life (*Phdr.* 256b). The contrast between the earlier options has now been made as stark as possible: "Such great gifts as these, boy, and divine ones, will friendship from a lover thus present you. But intimacy from the nonlover, watered down with mortal moderation . . . producing in the friend's soul illiberality that is praised by the multitude as virtue, will make it roll mindlessly around" (*Phdr.* 256e–257a).

Eikotic Rhetoric

The first half of the *Phaedrus*, through to the completion of Socrates's palinode, has tracked the examination of the lover and non-lover to the question of the turn to philosophy and the choice involved. It is also a choice that requires the appropriate speeches for the task. The examination has further occasioned negative remarks about opinion and the attitudes of the multitude. And so, almost naturally, the theme of the dialogue switches to the nature of rhetoric in relation to the discourse by which one may best be led to philosophy.[8] Because they have identified two types of speeches and their related modes of composition—one beautiful, the other not—Socrates, echoing his own method, proposes to examine the question they have now set themselves and study "in what way it is beautiful to speak and to write a speech, and in what way not" (*Phdr.* 259e). At the same time, he immediately takes charge and poses what amounts to a rhetorical question, since it already assumes the account that was conveyed through the image of the horses and charioteer: "For things that are going to be well and beautifully said, must not the speaker's thought already exist, with knowledge of the truth about the things that he is going to say?" (*Phdr.* 259e).

In reality, it is not so much a switch as it is a recentering, because the theme of rhetoric and appropriate discourse has been there from the start, beneath the surface, present in the various practice speeches brought out to illuminate the lover and non-lover. Some aspects of these early speeches have been more successful than others, and we might expect them to be recalled in the analysis that follows.

There is also a new audience for the change of discussion in the form of the cicadas singing in the noontime heat. The myth of their origin that is now related ties them to the Muses. Important in this respect are Calliope and Ourania, one concerned with the divine, the heavens, and philosophy; the other concerned with the human and speeches. The cicadas will be addressed on both levels; they will listen and report. The palinode told of souls witnessing the heavens and returning to report what they had seen. The cicadas listen to the speeches of the human world and return to the divine to report what they have heard. The report of the *theoroi*, those who return from elsewhere to report what they have witnessed, is a unifying motif of the *Republic*, seen especially in the narratives that Er reports of his near-death experience and that of the philosopher who returns to the cave, burdened with a hardly expressible narrative of what has been seen outside (Nightingale 2004). The reports of such witnesses are an important kind of

---

8. There is a definite conceit on my part in stating things in this way since the unity of the dialogue (or its apparent disunity) is a repeated concern in the literature. But I hope to reinforce in what follows my opening claim that rhetoric has been the unifying theme from the outset.

discourse for Plato with their implications for questions of credibility and trust. These reports also further the theme of speaking from memory, that most reliable type of discourse, as the dialogue will later reveal.[9]

The subject matter becomes explicitly what it has always been implicitly—rhetoric, and not the negative political rhetoric that we saw in the *Gorgias* that could not even achieve the status of a techne. Here it is a techne involving truth and one of a division of *logoi*, along with two other terms of Platonic invention, dialectic and antilogic (Schiappa 1999; Cole 1991). Of course, what is new with Plato is how these things are christened. There was a tradition of antilogic prior to the interest Plato takes in it, just as there were handbooks in what we would now deem rhetorical practice. But Plato brings a conceptual clarity to these things by labeling them as he does. With the method of collection and division, which is also announced in the second half of the *Phaedrus*, discourses are brought together in one category and then differentiated by style and aim.

Rhetoric itself, insofar as it has a past, has dealt only with preliminaries (*Phdr.* 269b). This includes all the innovations in speech contributed by great names like Tisias, Gorgias, and Protagoras, along with a number of others. These are adherents of what might be called an eikotic rhetoric. They value *eikos*[10] over truth, manipulating the power of words to make what is weaker seem stronger. In fact, it is to such a view that Phaedrus has appealed in response to Socrates's rhetorical question at 259e.

While Socrates may believe a speaker must already have knowledge of the truth about the things involved, Phaedrus appeals to what he has heard in suggesting otherwise: "There is not a necessity for one who is going to be a rhetor to learn things that are in reality just but the things that seem so to the multitude who will give judgment, nor the things that are really good or beautiful but that will seem so. For persuading comes from these, but not from the truth" (*Phdr.* 260a). Before the examination can continue, this false step must be addressed, and it is aided by rhetoric (or, at least, the "art of speeches" [*lógon téchnen*]) speaking up on her own behalf: "I do not compel anyone who ignores the truth to learn to speak; but . . . when he has acquired that, thus let him take me up. Now then,

---

9. I will consider the myth of the cicadas further in the next chapter.

10. There is a general tendency to render this term "probability." But the confusion this encourages, especially when *eikos* is set in contrast to truth with its contemporary senses that suggest a rigorous inductive procedure, argues more for the weaker "likelihood."

what I am saying is this big thing:[11] that without me, he who knows the things that really are will not at all be able to persuade by art" (*Phdr.* 260d). This is a big advance in the discussion. The implication is that the knowledge of the philosopher is not sufficient to lead people to justice or philosophy. Rhetoric is also required.

However, as Socrates quickly insists, recalling the *Gorgias*, mention here of rhetoric assumes that she is an art, and that has by no means been established by an appropriate method. To match rhetoric's big thing, a genuine art of rhetoric must be identified, and its parts elaborated, blending philosophizing with speaking well.

RHETORIC'S "BIG THING"

A general definition of rhetoric emerges: that of *psychagogia* (leading the soul) by speech (*Phdr.* 261a) in public and private,[12] and so passing on conviction and excellence by means of words (*Phdr.* 270b). Thus, the expert in rhetoric must know the soul in all its varieties, along with the types of speeches that can match those varieties, and the *kairotic* moment in which it is best to speak or be silent (*Phdr.* 272a). This places rhetoric in a particular environment removed from the more human concerns that involve the *eikotic*. The rhetoricians of that brand, captured under the parental figure of Tisias, infect the law courts with a concern for what is likely rather than what is true (*Phdr.* 272d), taking the likely to be what most people think is the case (*Phdr.* 273b).

There remains here, though, a hint of unfairness. Plato's target and the manner in which he categorizes it serves to mark the sharp contrasts involved. If we turned for an understanding of this law court rhetoric to, say, Antiphon, we would find the practice cast in a more positive and even necessary light. In his *Tetralogies*,[13] for example, Antiphon provides contrasting arguments for and against positions, all of which rely primarily

---

11. I follow James Nichols's (Plato 1998b) translation here, preferring it to those that include "boast," because it *is* a big thing that is being said.

12. The inclusion of the private here clearly marks the generality of the account and identifies its wider applicability beyond the interests in political rhetoric that occupied the *Gorgias*. See Asmis 1986, who argues that this concept gives the dialogue its underlying unity.

13. Antiphon, another Attic orator, was a contemporary of Socrates. His *Tetralogies* are generally recognized to be models of argumentation devised for the instruction of students.

on *eikos* evidence.[14] A man has been accused of murdering another in the night. But since he is a known rival, it is not likely he would have committed the crime given that suspicion was very likely to fall on him.[15] But then the other side of the argument insists that, given this, it is likely he *would* have committed the crime, assuming he could not be suspected of something so obvious. Each tetralogy proceeds with a series of likelihoods and counter-likelihoods aimed at establishing what is most likely to have happened in situations where there is no direct access to the truth of events. This is the "speaking well" that the eikotic rhetoricians teach. Juries hearing such arguments must rely on the reasonableness of their common experiences in weighing likelihoods. The rhetoric is egalitarian and invitational. It does not assume an underlying (or overlying, heavenly) truth to things but insists on working out that truth in discourse. Thus, we see examples of the human measure that is reflected in something like the Protagorean maxim ("The human is the measure of all things. Of things that are that they are and of things that are not, that they are not"). The claim that the majority opinion determines the likely seems unfair here because it suggests an arbitrary, purely relative measure. But *eikotic* rhetoric reveals the only measure available in specific cases and insists that, rather than an arbitrary standard, the view of the many must be corroborated by the experience they share, as we see in the judgment of Antiphon's juries. Thus, *eikotic* rhetoric can address large audiences without worrying about determinations within them. The point here is not so much to challenge the division of rhetorics in the text as to rehabilitate what is being relegated as valueless. It is clear that, from Plato's perspective and with his goals in mind, the promise of rhetoric on *eikotic* terms is scant. But from another perspective, like that of Antiphon, the promise remains.

Still, this illuminates the contrast with Plato's "true" rhetoric, where the expert must know the souls and the speeches that will match them. To what end? The closing of the palinode stressed the importance of leading the loved one to philosophy. And the conception of Platonic philosophy

---

14. Another example of the dependency on *eikotic* argumentation is Gorgias's speech *Defense of Palamedes*, a text that, as we will see in the next chapter, was used by Plato as a model for his defense of Socrates.

15. It will be observed that this is the same strategy of reasoning (it is unlikely x would have committed the action because x is the most likely to be suspected and knows this) that Plato attributes to Tisias at *Phdr.* 273b (and exactly the same argument is attributed by Aristotle to Corax [*Rhet* 1402a20–24]).

as *psychagogia* reinforces this. When we explore the *Republic*, we will need to consider whether this rhetoric can engage large audiences as the *eikotic* aspires to do (and as was the case for the Gorgian and will be the case for the Aristotelian), whether it can talk to the multitude with its necessary mix of souls. Like Platonic philosophy itself, it is dialectical in the limited sense of encouraging a dialogue with one other. It leads toward philosophy the other person who is naturally suited to the task. Here, most clearly is that link between the discourse of the hortatory argument so well illustrated in the *Euthydemus* and the discourse of the true rhetoric now under discussion. This discourse develops in an atmosphere of intimacy. By contrast, *eikotic* rhetoric may still retain that political force of the *Gorgias*. It can be taught to anyone who pays the money, regardless of talent. It is equally at home in the law court and political arena with their lack of intimacy.

Now we see why we are outside the city, beyond the political environment in an *atopic* space, because the discourse that is the subject of the dialogue is *not* a civic discourse. It is not, after all, the rhetoric of the philosopher ruler who must lead the polis. It is the discourse of the philosopher who must lead another toward what is true, upward on the heavenly round toward the Forms. A fitting primary audience, then, is Phaedrus, alone, whose love of discourse may make him susceptible to the speech that Socrates decides will match his soul and lead him to philosophy.

This can also give partial explanation to a remark made by Socrates that cannot be ignored but demands comment. The approach to the right art, claims Socrates, is not the direction taken by Lysias and Thrasymachus. To which Phaedrus naturally asks what direction should be taken. In answer, Socrates praises Pericles, who may have become "the most perfect of all in rhetoric" (*Phdr.* 269e). James Nichols observes in a footnote: "The contrast with Socrates's critique of Pericles at *Gorgias* 515d–516d is striking" (Plato 1998b, 79n168).[16] It is more than striking; on the face of things, it is contradictory. A figure roundly condemned in one dialogue is praised in another. The answer lies in Pericles's status as an orator rather than as an exponent of political rhetoric. This passage in the *Phaedrus* better reflects the praise of the *Menexenus*. There, Pericles is "the one outstanding orator among the Greeks" (*Menex.* 235e). No irony attends this remark, and a subsequent reference to his funeral speech (*Menex.* 236b) further identifies

---

16. Beversluis (2000) finds curious the similar praise of Pericles as a good politician in the *Meno* (93a) in light of what has been said in the *Gorgias*. But he also offers no further comment (364n36).

the context. In the *Gorgias*, rhetoric within the polis that addresses political matters is condemned and particular exponents of that rhetoric condemned with it. In the *atopic* environment of the *Phaedrus*, with its discussion of pure concepts unsullied by the political rhetoric of the polis, rhetoric *in itself* is explored, with the lessons derived to be taken back into the city. If Socrates is to name exponents of *this* kind of rhetoric to aid Phaedrus's understanding (and that of the dialogue's readers), then Pericles's reputation may indeed suit him for the kind of praise this rhetoric receives.

Kairos

Among the qualities of the true rhetor is one that is often overlooked or played down, that is the ability to grasp the *kairotic* or opportune moment. This introduces a temporal element into the examination of rhetoric and further emphasizes the extemporaneous nature of certain rhetorical discourses. Ostensibly, this was a contrast seen in Lysias's written text hidden beneath Phaedrus's cloak and the speeches of Socrates prompted by the occasion. But as a concept, *kairos* lacks the clarity afforded others in the rhetorical tradition. It is, suggests Barbara Cassin, "one of the most untranslatable of Greek words" (2017, 148).

James L. Kinneavy (2002; 1994; Thompson and Kinneavy 2000) has provided detailed studies of the concept, identifying its importance to several Greek thinkers, such as Aristotle, Plato, and Isocrates. The concept he uncovers is rich with diverse strands of meaning, but it is certainly not one restricted to temporal measures. Beyond the temporal sense, there is alleged to be a sense common to both Plato and Aristotle that focuses on what is "proportionate." This is the sense that forms the basis of the theory of the mean (the right thing at the right time in the right respect) that is developed in Aristotle's ethics and has its origins in Plato's *Republic* (443d–e). This pushes the meanings into the ethical realm, where the sense of "rightness" associated with *kairos* refers to appropriate behavior. Of course, there is more than just the ethical involved here. The full sense speaks to "appropriate, as in the right balance" (Sipora 2002). While promoting the importance of the ethical implications of *kairos*, Kinneavy adopts a definition that embraces these two distinct strands: "the right time and due measure" (Thompson and Kinneavy 2000, 75). And it is Kinneavy who traces the importance of the term back to the constructive account of rhetoric in the *Phaedrus*.

Socrates identifies *kairotic* insight as the final piece in the rhetor's toolbox: "When he now has all of this,[17] and has also grasped the occasions [*kairos*] for speaking and for holding back, and for speaking concisely and piteously and in an exaggerated fashion, and for all the forms of speeches he may learn, recognizing the right and the wrong time for these [*eukairos* and *akairos*], then his grasp of the science [techne] will be well and truly finished, but not before that" (*Phdr.* 272a–b). Along with the right time to speak comes the wrong time, and we can match these with the experience of the speaker who recognizes when an audience is receptive to a point and so presses it accordingly, and when not. There is nothing abstract about this culminating feature to the art of rhetoric: it speaks explicitly to the contexts of address, to the intimacies arising there between speaker and audience.

Eric Charles White (1987) traces the concept of *kairos* to the ancient practice of archery, where an archer's arrow must follow a particular, narrow path to its target. Here, with the importance of accuracy comes the power required for penetration, and it is this second aspect that can inform our reading of Plato's dialogue. Drawing on these two related senses, White concludes: "One might understand *kairos* to refer to a passing instant when an opening appears which must be driven through with force if success is to be achieved" (White 1987, 13). The *kairotic* moment is that passing moment of opportunity in which a point can be pressed, along with the material that supports it. Such skill must be learned from experience, and while it can be described and illustrated, it is difficult to see how it could be taught.[18] It encourages us to reflect back on the many times Socrates grasps an opportunity to press home a point with an interlocutor, having observed that the individual is ready to receive it.

Some commentators judge that the view of rhetoric in the *Phaedrus* is no more positive than in the *Gorgias*. Indeed, both dialogues dismiss the *eikotic* rhetoric that addresses the multitude and panders to its views.

---

17. That is, knowledge of the nature of speeches and the types of receptive audiences for each.

18. The idea unfolding here does not fit easily into a fixed formula of theory; there is extemporaneity involved that escapes prediction or rote application. One early promoter of such an idea was Isocrates, whose pedagogical advice is replete with evocations that fit this model (Sipora 2002, 7–14). In his *Antidosis*, for example, rhetorical success depends on an "understanding of *kairos* as a *dynamic* principle rather than a static, codified rhetorical technique" (Sipora 2002, 10).

But while Plato's rhetor has been equipped with philosophical tools and understanding, the account of rhetoric itself stands apart from this. Rhetoric emerges from the *Phaedrus* as an artistic skill necessary for leading human beings toward Platonic goals, essentially, toward philosophy and justice. Having established the techne involved, thus complementing the positive ideas of the *Gorgias*, the refrain of 260d resounds more forcefully: "Without me [rhetoric], he who knows the things that really are will not at all be able to persuade by art." The philosopher must communicate, must be artful about speeches. But the knowledge that informs the art is separate from the different things that might be conveyed through the art (*Phdr.* 277b). It matters, then, that speeches can be matched to audiences because both are multiform in nature. This is a point that will characterize Plato's own rhetorical practice, as he adjusts his message to different audiences. Which is to say that knowing the principles of justice and how it appears in the state is a quite separate knowledge from knowing how to construct discourses that lead people to actions that conform to those principles or to an understanding of the principles themselves.

Return to the *Atopic*

The Socrates of the *Phaedrus* is extraordinary, but, paradoxically, that itself is not surprising. That he is *atopos* may be. Since the focus placed on *topos* by Aristotle, there has been a lot of attention given to that concept. But less has been paid to *atopoi* (Reeves 2013, 312). *Atopos* announces a radical change of experience, a reorientation, which invites a shift in understanding. Glaucon uses it in the *Republic* to describe the prisoners in the cave: "It's an *atopon* image, and they are strange [*atopos*] prisoners" (*Rep.* 515a). A double dislocation is suggested here: the prisoners are out of place, and so is Glaucon in relation to the experience that he is supposed to grasp. That is, he has no experiential resources by which to appreciate the allegory. Removed from his natural environment in the state, Socrates is out of place in the countryside setting of the *Phaedrus*. In that place, the philosopher is at liberty to gather ideas that can be taken back into the state to inform the practice of others who also return, like *theoroi* reporting a similar message of what they have seen beyond the limits of *eikotic* experience. The supernatural atmosphere of the place in which Socrates and Phaedrus conduct their conversation befits the ideas encountered there.

Thus, we might describe the rhetoric advocated in the *Phaedrus* as an *atopic* rhetoric. It is not limited in application to political concerns, and it calls for a new understanding of the use of language, beyond the *eikotic* rhetoric of the law courts. The one type will draw, as we have seen, on human experience and use the elements of a pseudo-techne involved to describe and modify that experience. The other type will draw on the divine and the techne involved will be of divine matters, more obscure just as it is more intimate.

Socrates himself emerges as a bridge between the two, as both the lover of speeches and the expert in rhetoric—not only *eikotic* rhetoric, the traditions of which he fully understands, along with its contemporary power, but *atopic* rhetoric, which is the necessary speech required to translate the message of the palinode into terms understandable by the uninitiated.

For Phaedrus himself, the lessons of the dialogue are promising. He is the audience whose responses readers will most closely observe. At the close of the *Phaedrus*, he is issued with the charge to become a *theoros*, to return to the city and to Lysias and report on the *logoi* that he has heard at the shrine of the Muses (*Phdr.* 278c). To do this well—and nothing suggests such a task is beyond him—he will have to rely on his memory. But this is a memory no longer fixed on written discourse, as it was with the speech of Lysias hidden within his cloak. The myth of Thamus and Theuth (a myth to which we will return in the next chapter) has conveyed Plato's misgivings over the written text, that external repository for ideas that serves simply to remind. Instead, Phaedrus will need to recall what he has heard—messages for the speechwriter (Lysias), the poet (Homer), and the politician (Solon). These messages report that if the three individuals have insight into the truths of things about which they write, so that when challenged by "refutative examination" each is able to help his composition, then they will warrant a title beyond that of speechwriter, poet, and politician/lawmaker—something like that of philosopher.

The two rhetorics of the *Phaedrus* are not mutually exclusive. As the closing discussion makes clear, the one who has mastered the artful can better see the connections between things and thus speak well in all situations. But then we must believe that this excellent rhetor is no longer dealing with *eikos* since he or she draws directly on the truth. Thus, the *eikotic* is to be subsumed within the *atopic*, a new whole no longer recognizable to the tradition. This is always Plato's intent, to place the relativism of human reason, of likelihood, under the authority of the fixed truths of the divine realm. But in the course of this he indicates that he knows well that of which he disapproves. Or at least, he knows it to fail the tests he would put to any discourse. But that it has merits on its own terms, we have also seen.

While Phaedrus is commissioned to go back to the state and report to Lysias, Socrates has a different audience to address. He is directed by Phaedrus to report to "the beautiful Isocrates" (*Phdr.* 278e), with Phaedrus inquiring what Isocrates should be called.[19] Socrates replies that Isocrates is still young but offers a prophecy that, given his understanding of the natures of the things he talks about and his noble character, as he grows his speeches will excel, because "a certain philosophy is present in the man's thought" (*Phdr.* 299b).

Perhaps here we see the hope of a future philosophical rhetorician who may practice the kind of rhetoric that Plato champions in the dialogue. As R. C. Jebb explains, irrespective of its date of composition, the dramatic date of the *Phaedrus* is around 410 BCE. Isocrates was then about twenty-six years of age (and Lysias more than two decades older). What the passage indicates is the possibility of a friendship between Socrates and Isocrates[20] and the further possibility that this prompted Plato to see promise in Isocrates. What we do know is that Plato and Isocrates came to lead major schools in Athens and contested the nature and meaning of "philosophy." Of course, the term did not have then the associations it holds for us today, hence the attribution of "philosopher" to Lysias, Homer, and Solon in the earlier passage. In the ordinary usage of the day, such men were "wise" or "lovers of wisdom" and no more. It is worth emphasizing, then, that, as with "rhetoric," a certain amount of fluidity surrounds the meaning of the term "philosophy." It was clearly to remain a contested term for Plato and Isocrates as their careers developed. Each used the word to describe what they were doing, just as each denied the label to the other. In general, Isocrates eschewed the abstract metaphysical thinking that characterized Plato's work.

In his middle and later periods Plato will often suggest the label "dialectician" for his "philosopher." As for the label "rhetorician," it is equally clear that this was not a name Plato reserved for himself. But there is a difference that matters between adopting a role as rhetorician and developing a model

---

19. For a discussion of the respective styles of Lysias and Isocrates, see Jebb (2016, 42–46).

20. A friendship that may have encouraged Isocrates to model himself after Socrates in his *Antidosis* (Yun Lee Too [1995] suggests that this text "constitutes Isocrates's attempt at being Socrates," 108). We will explore the relationship of this text to the *Apology* in chapter 7.

of rhetoric adequate (even necessary) for one's projects. And this, at the end of the *Phaedrus*, is where we should see Plato: rhetorically proficient and equipped with a model of rhetoric that can be taken back into the state to remedy the deficiencies of the political rhetoric of the *Gorgias*. As a means to an important end—that is, leading others to justice—rhetoric takes on serious value once it has been given the qualities of a techne.

Chapter 7

Platonic Devices

> It seems to me irrational for Plato not to be ashamed of criticizing rhetoric, even though he himself may have been something of a rhetorician.
>
> —Aristides (*Orations*, 1.2.15)

Introduction: Style and Stylometrics

The importance of knowing the development of Plato's ideas has led naturally to attempts to identify the order in which the dialogues were produced. While there is general agreement on three periods of Plato's life to which various dialogues can be assigned—early, middle, and late—there is still disagreement over the exact place of many of the dialogues in relation to others of the same period. There are a few internal references that help, such as the action of the *Timaeus* occurring after the close of the *Republic*, or the *Sophist* and *Statesman* following the *Theaetetus*, and we also have the advice of various knowledgeable contemporaries on the order of other dialogues, like Aristotle's indication that the *Laws* was written after the *Republic* (*Pol.* II, 6, 1264b24–27). Beyond this, the literature is filled with disagreements about the ordering, fueled by different readings of how the ideas of various dialogues anticipate or rely on each other.

A more promising method arose with the attention to stylometry by Lewis Campbell, who studied the word choices of different dialogues, collecting lists of distinct words (often rare words), some of which seem to originate with the author (that is, with Plato). Campbell's student, Wincenty Lutoslawski (1897) subsequently analyzed Campbell's work along with that of other scholars who focused on stylometry, like Engelhardt, Kayssler, Dittenberger,[1] Droste, Ritter, and many others. The interest did not die in the nineteenth century. Recent attention to stylometrics in Plato include the work of Leonard Brandwood (1992; 1990) and Gerard Ledger's (1989) computer analyses. What counts as style, relative to the goal of deciding chronology, beyond the identification of words at specific stages in a corpus, includes the varying use of reply formulae (a feature that necessarily disadvantages dialogues like the *Menexenus* and *Apology*, which involve limited use of dialogue itself [Brandwood 1992, 115]) and the rhythm of Plato's prose. Taken together, such features led to the three chronological groups that are generally now accepted by most scholars. The ordering of dialogues within groups, especially that of the early dialogues, has so far eluded the best stylistic studies.[2]

As noted above, the primary goal of stylometric analyses has been to determine a "correct" chronology of Plato's dialogues in order to then appreciate the development of his thought. Lutoslawski himself is interested in the growth of Plato's logic. But he also allows that aspects of style may figure in more than just word choice. It is by no means an easy subject to investigate, as he notes: "Most readers think that style is indefinable" (1897, 65). Among the other essential marks of style (beyond the word choices of a person's vocabulary), he lists the following: "The length, construction, and interdependence of phrases; the rhythm produced intentionally or resulting naturally from the order of words selected; the recurrence or exclusion of certain phonetic effects, as, for instance, avoidance of the hiatus or the repetition of syllables with the same vowels or consonants; a preference for certain sounds; the use made of quotations and proverbs; the frequency of rhetorical figures and tropes; and many other points" (Lutoslawski 1897, 71–72). It is an exhausting if not exhaustive list. But it indicates the complexity involved with questions of style. My interest is not to examine style in order to determine any development of ideas in Plato but simply to identify some of the chosen stylistic strategies that characterize his work, because in these strategies we gain a glimpse of the rhetorician within the philosopher. An individual's style, whatever else it may prove to be, is captured in the choices they make in approaching the construction of a text. Style is reflected

---

1. Brandwood (1992, 91–94) singles out Dittenberger's work, along with that of Lewis, as particularly valuable.

2. Alternatives to stylometric analyses include classifications based on the "character" of the dialogues, an approach championed by Thrasyllus (Tarrant 1993) and preferred by Marion (2021).

in the devices used. It may matter whether that text is written to be read or heard, as with a speech that is to be delivered. But in both cases, the author, if in control of the art, is conscious of how what is said will be *received* by the audience. And so, of course, on the same terms, they must be conscious of their audience. In fact, in the case of Plato the question of audience comes to the fore in the decision to write, and to write dialogues, because Plato gives us what we might call a "dialogical style." The dialogue form lends itself to certain kinds of devices that cannot be used in other types of discourse. We will see this illustrated later in the chapter in Plato's use of silence as a rhetorical device. Such devices support the judgment that Plato excelled as a rhetorician, perhaps against his own impulses.[3]

Christopher Rowe (2009) identifies an awareness of audience in Plato when he writes "Plato's turning to the bigger scale (in the case of the *Republic*, the monumental) might suggest a shift in his attitude to his *audience*—and/or in his view of the kind of audience he needs to address: perhaps a larger, less specialized one, to the extent that the larger works tend to be more accessible, and intelligible, at least at some level, than the shorter ones" (18). Indeed, there are two aspects to this concern with audience. Rowe here imagines how Plato himself imagines the consumers of his texts, how his dialogues will be read and by whom. And so we might imagine (to join the exercise) how different choices—myth over argument, for example—might reflect this awareness. Secondly, because of the dialogic nature of the texts, where participants are being addressed, we can locate certain audiences *within* the texts. Here, we have the possibility of seeing how strategies can be adopted to address different types of audience. I have in mind here rhetorical figures or the use of images and analogies. In this chapter, I want to pursue Plato's rhetorical choices with both of these audience considerations in view.

The Early Rhetorician

In his *Helen,* Gorgias boasts that words have a powerful agency. Speech can "stop fear and banish grief and create joy and nurture pity" (*DK* 82, 11, 8). And as speech writers know, with the right composition and delivery, it can move juries. On these terms at least, Socrates's ability to speak failed him when he most needed it. At his trial, the warnings of Callicles

---

3. "Plato was one of the greatest rhetoricians of all time, though he . . . would have bridled at the label" (Booth 2004, 503).

come to pass (although that was a bit of retrospective prophesy on Plato's part).

The details of the actual trial of Socrates aside, the depiction of it in the *Apology* by Socrates's "scribe" (McLuhan 1962, 25) has been judged a "rhetorical masterpiece" (Sansone 2012, 220), indicating that one does not need a thought-through account of rhetoric to write rhetorically. Whatever views Plato harbors when he comes to treat rhetoric as a subject of investigation in the *Gorgias*, his own writings across his corpus are replete with rhetorical devices and strategies that give some insight into his style.[4] We can approach this subject by exploring more closely David Sansone's claim.[5]

Socrates famously enters the courtroom with an excuse that few in attendance were likely to have judged as serious: that he is not, as his accusers insist, a clever speaker (*Ap.* 17a). He must therefore speak in an unaccustomed manner: "Extemporaneously, in whatever words come to mind" (*Ap.* 17c). And, indeed, if the measure of a speech is the result, then this one is spectacularly unsuccessful. Notwithstanding this disclaimer, as Sansone observes, "Plato's Socrates employs very many of the standard rhetorical commonplaces in his speech for the defense" (2012, 188). At the same time, Plato's skill in composing the *Apology* would lie in what Aristotle will call *entechnic* ("whatever can be prepared by method and by us") rather than *atechnic* features (*Rhet.* 1355b36). That is, Plato is constrained by the facts of the historical event—who was present, what charges were brought and countered, and what outcome ensued. These were non-negotiable. What mattered was what Plato chose to *do* with these features, how he approached *invention*.

Chapter 4 included a discussion of Alexander Sesonske's (1968) treatment of the *Apology*, during which several nontraditional modes of argumentation were identified in Socrates's speech. The attention in this chapter is less on the reasoning of the historical Socrates and more on the way the early Plato adopts or accommodates rhetorical expectations. To

---

4. And this may even be the case in the *Gorgias* itself. According to Brad Levett (2005), Plato has Socrates employ rhetorical language "that persuades without being true" (215) in order to defeat the rhetorician.

5. While generally accepted as a text belonging to the earliest period of Plato's career, at least one stylometric study places the *Apology* around 386 BCE (Ledger 1989). This puts it close to the dates of texts like the *Menexenus* and the *Gorgias*, a placing that acquires significance in light of my discussion of these texts in chapter 5.

this end we might compare it to three other similar versions of the "trial," by Xenophon, Gorgias, and Isocrates.[6] But before turning to those texts, I want to review some of the features that Sansone collects in support of his "masterpiece" claim.[7]

As a trial speech that conforms to the expectations of the genre, the action of the *Apology* involves the three principal participants: accused, accuser, and jury. Thus, the accused speaking in his defense will address his accuser and the jury, and sometimes both. The need to address the charges and the accuser invited the use of several commonplaces. We see, for example, Socrates adopting the strategy, approved by Aristotle (*Rhet.* 1419b4–5), of ridiculing his accuser, Meletus, playing on the idea that he cannot really be serious in what he says: "You're presenting us with a riddle and playing around" (*Ap.* 27d). In an earlier chapter, we saw Plato here introducing an illustration of the Socratic method of refutation (into a text that does not otherwise involve dialogical exchanges). But in leading Meletus into the contradiction involved in holding Socrates both to believe in new deities and also to be an atheist, Plato achieves the rhetorical effect of holding Socrates's accuser up to ridicule.

Another common strategy of trial speeches involving the accuser is the turning of the charges back onto them and so indicting them in similar terms. Gorgias, as we will see, gives a vivid case of this in his *Palamedes*. In the *Apology*, Socrates is quick to turn the tables on Meletus: he "says, then, that I commit injustice by corrupting the young. But I, men of Athens, reply that it's Meletus who is guilty of playing around with serious matters, of lightly bringing people to trial, and of professing to be seriously concerned about things he has never cared about at all" (*Ap.* 24c). Of course, answering charges with a counter-charge could be judged a fallacious move, directing attention elsewhere. But the point here is to identify ways Plato observes rhetorical conventions, not to judge their quality.

Plato also has Socrates adopt common strategies for addressing the jury. For example, he makes use of the strategy of anticipating an argument that

---

6. Michael Gagarin (Antiphon 1997, 249; Gagarin 2002) sees parallels also between Plato's *Apology* and Antiphon's trial speech. But it is difficult to conclude too much given the fragmentary nature of the evidence. Antiphon's defense at his trial occurred a decade before that of Socrates, and like the latter he took the opportunity to defend his whole career and not just the charges brought against him.

7. In the following discussion I draw from Sansone 2012, chapter 9.

the prosecution may use. This is important to the defense case given that Socrates believes so much of the enmity against him derives from rumor and is difficult to locate in any particular person's position. Thus, Socrates believes himself authorized to formulate the accusations against him made over time by people who are largely anonymous: "One cannot bring any of them to court or cross-examine them. One must literally fight with shadows to defend oneself and cross-examine with no one to respond" (*Ap.* 18d). This he proceeds to do, stating the alleged charges in his own terms (*Ap.* 19b). The strategy of anticipation is one he will resort to on several occasions: "But perhaps someone may say, 'Aren't you ashamed, Socrates?'" (*Ap.* 28b), even giving expression to what he believes the jurors are thinking: "Now, perhaps when I say this, you may think I'm speaking in a quite wilful manner. . . . That's not so, men of Athens" (*Ap.* 37a). In speaking so, the accused maintains control over what is said and what is thought.

A further strategy involving the audience (here, the jury) is the use of the figure of apostrophe, where a speaker addresses one audience directly in order to address a second audience indirectly. This is a common strategy of forensic rhetoric, popular among Attic orators (Usher 2010, 352). It can arise simply, as with Socrates's question to Meletus: "Are you that contemptuous of the jury?" (*Ap.* 26d), or the more developed cross-examination of one's accuser. Socrates begins addressing the jury then switches to interrogate Meletus, thereby illustrating to the jury that his accuser is unreliable and certainly unpersuasive. Having led Meletus to his contradiction regarding Socrates's belief in gods, Socrates shifts between audiences: "Please examine with me, gentlemen, why it seems to me that this is what he's saying. And you, Meletus, answer us" (*Ap.* 27a).

Apostrophe, suggests Usher, can arouse indignation or anger (2010, 352), thus being employed to stimulate an emotional response. Perhaps the most interesting strategy of an emotional nature used in trial speeches, and one that Plato adopts, is the *praeteritio* (or passing over). The accused, in the course of completing their defense, would routinely introduce an emotional plea by bringing forward their dependents. Less frequently, they might insist they will not do so (passing over them) while simultaneously drawing attention to the fact. Thus, Socrates ends his defense but adds a further anticipation that one member of the jury might resent the fact that he has not invoked his family: "Perhaps when he was contesting even a lesser charge than this charge, he positively entreated the jurors with copious tears, bringing forward his children and many other relatives and friends as well, in order to arouse as much pity as possible" (*Ap.* 34b–c). That is what is expected in such trials. But, Socrates proceeds: "I'll do none of these things, even when I'm facing what might be considered the ultimate danger . . . I do have relatives, sons too, men of Athens, three of them, one already a young man while two are still children. Nonetheless, I won't bring any of them forward here and then entreat you to vote for my acquittal" (*Ap.* 34c–d). The conventions of the figure involved have a speaker claiming that he will pass over doing something that, in the course of so saying, he actually does do. Here, Socrates generously supplies the details of his three sons, effectively bringing them before the minds of his audience. They "see" what Socrates says he will not produce. And, arguably, in seeing this for themselves, the spectacle is all the more effective.

Compare these details to the way Xenophon approaches the same event of Socrates's trial. Structurally, his account is quite different; shorter and based not on firsthand observation but the secondhand narrative of Socrates's friend Hermogenes. Xenophon admits that he "had not made it a point to report the whole trial" (Xenophon, *Apology*, 22) and describes as much as he shows. He also enters the text reflectively to pass his own judgment on those involved. The exchange with Meletus is not elenctic in nature, involves no ridicule, and has no counter-charge of wrongdoing on Meletus's part. The few passages where Socrates addresses the jury are direct and without rhetorical device. This text is stark in comparison to the Platonic version of the same events, and it certainly would not be described as a rhetorical masterpiece.

The same could not be said of Gorgias's *Defense of Palamedes*. The principal difference between this text and Plato's *Apology* lies in the fictive nature of the events relayed by Gorgias. The subject matter of the speech involves events from the Trojan War after Odysseus accused Palamedes of treachery. Gorgias tells the story of Palamedes's trial and imagines his defense before the jury and his accuser, Odysseus. In spite of its fictional subject, the text parallels Plato's *Apology* in interesting ways. Here, I will address just the points I identified above in Plato's text.[8]

For most of the speech, Palamedes addresses the jury (members of the army), but in sections 22 to 27 (*DK* 82, B1, 11a) he turns to his accuser, Odysseus. Unlike the *Apology*, there is no exchange between the two—Palamedes is the only speaker—but like the *Apology* the accuser is ridiculed and

---

8. Elsewhere, in a discussion of allusion, I have explored ten parallels between the two texts (Tindale 2010, 122–25). McCoy (2008) examines the two texts in detail and identifies ways in which they both exceed the *topoi* of the genre.

himself accused. The ridicule is clear: "It is worth examining the kind of man you are who says the kind of things you do, like the worthless attacking the worthless" (22). What incites the ridicule is the perceived contradictory nature of Odysseus's charge: "You accused me through spoken words of two directly opposed things, wisdom and madness, which the same man cannot have . . . how can one trust a man of the sort who in a single speech says to the same man the most inconsistent things about the same subjects?" (26).

The counter-accusation is perhaps less clear. How did Odysseus come to learn about the events of which he accuses Palamedes? "If it is with knowledge, you know either from seeing or participating or learning from someone <who was participating>. If then you saw, tell these judges <the manner>, the place, the time, when, where, how you saw. If you participated, you are liable to the same accusations" (22). The implication is strong that Odysseus would have had to be present in some way and thus party to the alleged crime. Some blame is to be shared. In this manner, Palamedes adopts the strategy of turning onto his accuser what is believed of him.

The speech contains several anticipated objections to which Palamedes responds proleptically. A few examples will suffice, and the strongest instances of this are a series of questions posed and answered in support of his claim that he was incapable of performing the alleged action: "How could there be discussions unless there had been some meeting? And how could there be a meeting unless the opponent sent to me or <someone> went from me to him? . . . How do we listen and talk with each other? By ourselves? But we do not know each other's language. With an interpreter then? A third person is an added witness to things which need to be hidden" (6–7). Then later, "Someone might say that I ventured on this out of a desire for wealth and money. But I have a moderate amount of money, and I have no need for much" (15). Generally, Palamedes adopts the strategy of showing how unlikely it is that he could be guilty because the treachery would have been so difficult to perform. Thus, he is asking the jury to reflect on their own experience of likelihoods and judge accordingly.[9]

The strategy of apostrophe is adopted in the general way that turning to question the accuser is a means to make further points to the jury. And that the intent is to address one audience through another is made clear through statements like the one noted earlier: "How can one trust a man of the sort who in a single speech says to the same man the most inconsistent

---

9. It is, of course, such *eikotic* rhetoric that Plato seeks to replace in the *Phaedrus*.

things about the same subjects?" (26). It is only for the jury that Odysseus's trustworthiness is an issue.

It is in the same section in which Palamedes addresses his accuser that we find a *praeteritio* to match the one used by Plato. Here, it does not involve an emotional appeal to the jury but it is used to cast aspersions on the character of his accuser. As the section closes and before turning to address his judges, Palamedes says to Odysseus: "I do not want to introduce in reply the many enormities, both old and new, which you have committed, though I could" (27). Of course, by explicitly declining to mention them, he brings them to the jury's attention, encouraging the more effective result of having the judges actively conjure up the spectacle in their own minds.

Given Plato's challenge to the power of Gorgianic rhetoric in the *Gorgias*, the common rhetorical patterns shared by the *Apology* and the *Defense of Palamedes* present a puzzle. Who is the imitator here? We know Plato prides himself in his ability to imitate the style of others: he does it for Gorgias in the *Gorgias*, *Meno*, and *Symposium*. So, it is quite plausible that a younger Plato, keen to adopt the best vehicle for the defense of his mentor, would feel no hesitation at turning Gorgias's speech to his own ends. Commentators generally judge the *Palamedes* to be the earlier speech (Sansone 2012; McCoy 2008; Coulter 1979; Calogero 1957), so the question is not the who but the why. Guido Calogero suggests that it was the historical Socrates who was enamored of Gorgias's work and who made the allusions and that Plato was simply repeating what he heard. Marina McCoy (2008) takes a different tack in stressing the nonfictive nature of the *Apology* that sets it apart from the *Palamedes*; she sees Plato composing "an encomium disguised as a piece of forensics" (53). For Sansone, the appropriation is also deliberate on Plato's part, but he sees it as part of a superior accomplishment: "He produced a dazzling rhetorical display that rivaled and, indeed, eclipsed his Gorgianic model, at the same time elevating Socrates to heroic status by associating him, both implicitly and explicitly (41b), with the mythical Palamedes" (2012, 220). The explicit association is worth noting, with Socrates mentioning Palamedes at 41b as someone he might engage with in the afterlife who had met his end because of an unjust verdict.

If Sansone is right on Plato's motive, then he might find for support Isocrates's choice of model in his defense speech. With the *Antidosis* the question of primacy does not arise. We know it was written and delivered after the *Apology*. But it takes its place in a series of imitative texts adopting the same rhetorical strategies.

Isocrates composed the speech to defend himself and his life after losing a case brought by another Athenian who argued that Isocrates, rather than he, should bear the cost of financing a trireme because he could better afford to do so. I will not delineate here all the parallels with the *Apology* since they are readily accessed elsewhere.[10] What the adoption does is reinforce the indications of friendship between Socrates and Isocrates that were noted in chapter 6. It is not an incidental reference to Isocrates that Plato is making at the close of the *Phaedrus*. Isocrates was quite interested in modeling himself on the Socratic character, resulting in another association between Athenians who had been victims of injustice. And it further serves to emphasize how natural it is for the name of Isocrates to join that of Gorgias in any discussion of Plato's rhetorical interests and abilities.

In the *Apology* we have Plato's growing awareness that rhetoric can be used in the service of justice. But it cannot be simply a matter of rhetorical efficiency. It needs to be informed by ideas that collectively constitute the measure of an art for which associated skill can be identified. Thus, the *Apology* gives us a vivid example of rhetorical practice, not rhetorical theory. It would also indicate that Plato's interest in the power of words and rhetorical devices was not restricted to his criticisms of Gorgianic rhetoric in the *Gorgias*. It began earlier, flowing from his own experience. And, as we will see, it extends beyond not just the *Gorgias* but also the *Phaedrus*.

Mythical Discourse

Good communicators show an awareness of their audience, matching their message and their mode of messaging accordingly. Both the *Gorgias* and the *Phaedrus* involve the use of myths, and this points to another form of discourse that Plato readily adopted in addressing different audiences, and thus another aspect of his dialogical style. Of course, the use of myth to communicate ideas does not require the dialogue form. But under Plato's direction, it is facilitated by it.

Plato adopts, adapts, and devises myths as the need arises. It would seem that if the appropriate narrative was already available, he would simply draw on it, modifying it to his ends (Halliwell 2007, 447). That would have the added benefit of being a discourse that was already familiar to

---

10. See Tindale 2010, 126–28.

his audience. But there was no concern for fidelity, and a number of his adoptions of mythical elements or poetic lines were wrong (see, for example, *Rep.* 457b). Most interesting are the myths that seem to originate with Plato. This gives him greater range as an author and speaks further to his powers of invention. But on these occasions he cannot rely on the audience being familiar with what he relates. So these cannot involve an appropriation of meaning from one circumstance to another. Since my interest here is not so much in what Platonic myths *mean* but in why he uses them and how they work rhetorically, I will restrict this discussion to myths of Platonic origin, and in particular to three myths we have seen in the *Gorgias* and the *Phaedrus*.

I return again to the myth at the close of the *Gorgias*, having already given some thought to it in chapter 5. It belongs to a series of eschatological myths that come at the end of major works, akin to what we see at the close of the *Phaedo* or in the last book of the *Republic*. In each of these cases, Plato reframes ideas he has discussed in a different format, dressing them with a moral message. After the abstractions of the investigation, the myth reduces the idea "to terms of image and fable" (Burke 1950, 200). In the myth of the *Gorgias*, we recall, the powerful politicians were stripped of their clothing when they came before their judges after death, thus becoming defenseless in the face of justice and receiving the punishments they deserved (*Grg.* 525d). It is a lesson that summarizes what Socrates has insisted about injustice and punishment.

It is important to note that Plato communicates no sense that he considers *muthos* inferior to logos.[11] Even though he will often insist on a rational account in the sense of a *logos*, in some contexts logos and *muthos* do the same work (Lloyd 2018, 91). Evidence of this was seen in Socrates's claim that what he was offering as a rational account, Callicles considered a myth (*Grg.* 523a). What rendered this the "rational" account was its power to refute so many speeches delivered by Gorgias, Polus, and Callicles. In the terms deliberated there, this power must derive in part from the truth of the account, but it is also conveyed through the persuasive packaging of that truth. Given that Socrates explicitly notes that Callicles will not take the narrative

---

11. For Geoffrey Lloyd (1990), *muthos* simply means a narrative account. Some commentators retain the assumption that there was a natural evolution from myth to reason (logos). But see Most (1999) for a persuasive challenge to that assumption. Stephen Halliwell (2007, 453) argues against reading a simple *muthos/logos* dichotomy into Plato's work.

as intended (judging it a *mere* myth), then we may surmise that, although he was being directly addressed, Callicles was not the principal or only audience. Plato has in mind another audience for whom mythical discourse is attractive.

The *Phaedrus* is replete with mythical elements befitting its staging outside of the city and involves several full, if short, myths. The myth of the cicadas is interesting for the way in which it anticipates the end of the dialogue (since we so often view a myth as a supplement to a previous position). Formerly men, the cicadas listening in the trees sing until they expire. Then they become *theoroi*, reporting back to the Muses about divine and human speeches. Among the Muses to whom they will report is Urania, who will be told of "those who spend their time in philosophy" (*Phdr.* 259d). Various meanings are assigned to the myth, from identification of a difficult task ahead and the need for divine support (Hackforth in Plato 1952b, 118), to G. R. F. Ferrari's interesting and apt observation that "the aims of philosophy are ill-suited to the restrictions of a single format, and can be most strikingly captured by the peculiar multiplicity of formats exhibited in the dialogue as a whole" (1987, 30), which is surmised from the cast of Muses involved. Indeed, the *Phaedrus* is renowned for its apparent disparate parts, contributing to debates over the actual theme of the dialogue. But as a myth, what the cicadas episode surely does is anticipate the closing discussion when Phaedrus and Socrates will themselves be tasked with reporting back to other philosophically inclined logographers, thus emphasizing the importance of "those who spend their time in philosophy" (*Phdr.* 259d). Here, Plato uses myth as a device to connect sections of the dialogue, reminding the reader of what has been "heard."

More central to the general concerns of the dialogue and our interest in discourses is the myth of king Thamus and the Egyptian god Theuth. Its details are widely known and appreciated: an apparent gift for remembering—writing—is revealed as a recipe for forgetting, hence the ambivalent attitude of Socrates and Plato toward the written word.

We should remember that it was misgivings about the written word that began the inquiry into rhetoric. Plato's repetition of the term *pharmakon* that was used to describe the written text when Phaedrus was first enticed to disclose the text he has hidden beneath his cloak encourages that remembrance in the reader. And so the first speech delivered in the dialogue has been written to be read. The speeches that follow, extemporaneous in nature, exhibit weaknesses and strengths of spoken discourse. The myth of Thamus and Theuth collects the concerns with writing and expresses them in a different form, allowing access for a different audience while reinforcing the points made for the "philosophical" audience. At its heart, the myth provides further comment on the problem of memory, a theme that recurs whenever a speech is being delivered and that has implications for any reports that are taken back to their respective audiences. In the context of the time in which Plato writes, where the transition from oral to written would affect different audiences in different ways, memory is a powerful force in contest with the force of speech itself. It too needs to be preserved and protected, and the myth invites a marriage of discourse and memory that may do this. The spoken word emerges as the thing of value, even if the sentiment is conveyed through the medium that threatens it.

What is going on in these myths? Who is Plato addressing? The move from the oral to the written was not a smooth one, as the misgivings over writing in the myth of Thamus and Theuth indicate. Plato was sensitive to the tensions involved and would be aware that any readership of his "popular" works would be diverse in background, some more able to grasp the arguments of the dialogues, others more inclined to appreciate the power of the narratives. As the myth of the *Gorgias* makes clear, reason is still operative in myth. But it operates at a different level and speaks to a different audience. If Plato hopes his philosophers will learn the skills needed for leading people to justice, then he must equip them with a full range of strategies and discourse types to do so. A lesson of the *Phaedrus*—to match the speech with the soul—reverberates here. Jean-François Mattéi (1988 captures this understanding in the choice of "theater" in the title to his essay on myth in Plato. *Muthos*, suggests Mattéi, "engenders the natural movement of the soul that enables it to see the theater of Ideas" (68). Thus, he invokes the spectacles that myths present, among which must be counted the winged team of horses and charioteer from the *Phaedrus*. In the next chapter, we will consider the needs of those who "see" images better than they "reason" from propositions. For now it suffices to suggest how Plato's dialogical rhetoric with its variety of devices on display anticipates Aristotle's definition of "rhetoric," with the available means of persuasion that the mind sees (*theorein—Rhet.* 1355b26–7).[12] The etymology at work here, encompassing as it does the spectacle of theater, accommodates the variety of minds that see in different ways and the demand on the rhetorician to meet these accommodations.[13]

---

12. Thus, in Book 3 of the *Rhetoric* figures "bring things before the eyes," making them conceptually (rather than visually) alive (*Rhet.* 1401b31).

13. In closing this discussion, it is appropriate to observe that the use of myth is no less potent with the emergence of Platonic dialectic in later dialogues. In the *Statesman*, for example, a myth is introduced to correct an argument and show how the dialectic has gone wrong.

Platonic Silence

Diskin Clay (2000) called Plato the Silent Philosopher, ostensibly due to his noted absence from the dialogues. But on a more practical level, Plato's descent into language from the heights of the abstract requires the adoption of diverse strategies of communication, and one of the more interesting is his choice of silence to convey ideas. I draw attention to this device because this one may most illustrate the dialogical nature of Plato's rhetoric.

There are some general ways in which we can note versions of this strategy. Socrates's silence in later dialogues, like the *Statesman*, has attracted attention as an apparent deliberate rhetorical strategy, inviting the reader to wonder what Socrates is thinking (Eades 1996). On similar terms, I would suggest, we can find significance in the fact that Thrasymachus does not leave the company of the *Republic* after the first book. But except for a brief interjection (and one further mention), he remains silent and unacknowledged throughout the lengthy discussions that ensue, even during the critical attacks on Sophists and their influence on the masses.[14] This seems on par with the "technical silence" that Taplin (1972, 80) sees throughout Greek drama. Are we here invited to wonder how Socrates's arguments register with this silent observer? Or what, from his perspective, the challenges involve? Again, we might consider the crucial moment at the close of the *Symposium* where the heavily fatigued and unreliable witness, Aristodemus, fails to catch the argument that Socrates presents to Agathon and Aristophanes, that the same poet can write both tragedy and comedy. Is the reader invited to reflect back over the speeches and drama that has preceded to reconstruct such an argument?

Beyond these cases, there is the moment at the end of the *Euthydemus* that was observed back in chapter 2, when we see Crito (to whom Socrates has related his encounter with the Sophists Euthydemus and Dionysodorus) in a closing quandary over what to do with his sons. One is still quite small, but Critobulus is at an age where he needs someone who can improve him. But when Crito looks around at the men who set up to educate the young, all of them strike him as unsuitable. He laments in conclusion "that I cannot see how I am to persuade the boy to take up philosophy" (*Euthd.* 307a). We judged this an amazing confession given what has taken place in the dialogue. There is little doubt that the Sophist brothers, who claim to educate,

---

14. Similarly, Theaetetus is present for the conversation of the *Statesman* but remains silent throughout.

are vivid examples of the unsuitable kind. They failed, after all, to provide a hortatory argument designed to lead someone to take up philosophy. But in the exchanges between Socrates and young Cleinias, Socrates has both provided such an argument and seen it bear fruit in the boy's responses and insights. Yet Socrates listens to Crito's concerns without comment.

Plato's indirectness is never in question. Had he wanted to present clear and unambiguous messages in his exoteric works, he would have chosen a different medium than the dialogue. As it stands, the wealth of literature agrees on the merits of this form and recognizes that things can be achieved that could not be so readily achieved by other means. Moreover, it amply reflects the communal nature of scholarly investigation prior to the rude interruption of the book.[15] But my target here is a different use of silence that becomes apparent in the dialogues, one that Plato seems to deliberately adopt as a rhetorical strategy. I am interested in places where Plato uses this device of silence to suggest an answer that the text does not explicitly provide, and to that end I explore two cases in detail.

THE *LYSIS*

The first case is drawn from the early dialogue *Lysis* and the crucial moment when Lysis resists speaking out and correcting his friend Menexenus, who is about to fall into a Socratic trap that had earlier ensnared Lysis himself. The dialogue ensues after Socrates has been enticed into a wrestling school to show Hippothales the proper way to speak with the object of his affections (namely Lysis). Thus, the dramatic context sets up a contrast between the pair Hippothales/Lysis and the young friends Lysis/Menexenus. Three principal discussions develop. The first one (*Lys.* 207d–210d) is between Socrates and Lysis after Menexenus has been called away. Socrates humbles Lysis, showing him that he should not have a high opinion of himself. The lesson is intended for Hippothales, lurking in the background (apostrophe again), who might register that one should humble a favorite rather than puffing him up. Then Menexenus returns and Lysis quietly asks Socrates to tell Menexenus what he has been saying to Lysis. Socrates declines (since Lysis is capable of doing it himself) but agrees to take a different tack. This second discussion (*Lys.* 211d–213c), between Socrates and Menexenus,

---

15. Think, for example, of the apparent alarm that Aristotle's acquisition of a library seems to have caused his colleagues, since it allowed him to conduct solitary investigations without conversations with others (Natali 2013, 20, 96).

involves the nature of the "friend." The conclusion is reached that neither the loving person nor the loved one is a friend, at which point Menexenus cannot see the way forward. The last conversation (*Lys.* 213d–222d) involves both the boys but arrives at a previously discounted position that friends belong to one another, being alike. They have reached the ridiculous position of considering themselves friends but being unable to say what a friend is.

The dialogue has divided commentators, some dwelling on the failed (and sometimes sophistic) arguments (Grote [1867] 2010; Guthrie 1962), and others seeing its positive elements as precursors for the arguments of the *Symposium* or *Phaedrus* (Versenyi 1975). Some of the more constructive treatments, such as Gadamer's (1980), have focused on the play between what is said and what is done (*logos* and *ergon*). If attention is given only to what is said, then crucial elements of the dialogue may be overlooked. Gadamer focuses on a passage where Lysis falls silent. It is the crucial moment in the dialogue. Both boys are both responding to Socrates, and at 221e they agree that the objects of love and friendship are among one's belongings and so they both, as friends, belong to one another. Socrates continues:

> And in a case where one person desires another, my boys, or loves him, he would never be desiring or loving or befriending him, unless he somehow belonged to his beloved either in soul, or in some disposition, demeanour or cast of soul.
>
> Yes, to be sure said Menexenus;
>
> But Lysis was silent. (*Lys.* 222a)[16]

Gadamer's judgment on this is that while he has the premonition of friendship, he does not apprehend it (1980, 20). I would take the position further and suggest that the moment of silence *is* the apprehension, and that Plato is deliberately encouraging the reader to consider what is implied there.

If we focus on the actions of the dialogue, along with the discussions, then one thing of importance that should be stressed is the *absence* of Menexenus during the first conversation between Socrates and Lysis. A. E. Taylor (1960, 67) calls the going and coming of Menexenus "by-play," a device to separate the issues of the dialogue. But this does not give due

---

16. From Lamb's (Plato 1925) Loeb translation.

consideration to what occurs in Menexenus's absence: in being called away he misses both the details of the conversation and the humbling of Lysis. The contrast between Hippothales/Lysis and Lysis/Menexenus is brought into focus here. Hippothales's words and actions are not in harmony: he builds up the one he ostensibly loves, but in order that glory should reflect back on himself. Now, on Menexenus's return, Lysis asks Socrates to repeat with Menexenus what he had done to him. In the context of the wrestling school, where competition abounds, Lysis puts forward his friend for a challenge. As one candidate relationship for friendship is discounted, another is brought into view for consideration.

Lysis sits back and allows Menexenus to become engaged in a conversation that Lysis can see, given the avid attention he pays to each move, goes off track. Lysis does not interject until Menexenus hesitates and Socrates suggests they have gone wrong. Then he blushes at his outburst, since it betrays a recognition of the problem that had developed but about which he had remained quiet. This could be perceived as excitement prompted by his friend's failure. But since they are friends, and this failure would reflect also on Lysis, we might look for a different meaning. Lysis had been keen for Menexenus to experience what he, Lysis, had encountered firsthand. He saw the impasse into which his friend was heading but allowed him to proceed.

More pronounced is that later behavior after Lysis and Menexenus are drawn into a further discussion with Socrates. The boys respond, agreeing or doubting, mostly in unison. But when Socrates suggests that someone desiring another would never desire him or befriend him if he did not belong to him in some way (*Lys.* 222a), while Menexenus responds with firm agreement, "Lysis was silent." No insightful outburst this time. The silence here (*sigē*) has the added sense of "keeping secret," and this suggests a deeper reaction on Lysis's part. He has something to say but does not speak it. It seems to me that he sees where the discussion is leading and what is to come. Rather than speaking up and preventing Menexenus's error, he allows him to continue. And Plato explicitly marks his silence, drawing our attention to it.

On one conception of friendship, the friend might speak up if he sees the other is heading for a painful experience. But on the conception unveiled here, the friend's silence, as painful as it might be, is one that allows the other person to discover something for himself. While Gadamer suggests that the logos "has not yet revealed something in deed (*ergoi*) to this boy," the opposite seems to be what has happened: the silence of Lysis is an action on his part; it is the act of not intervening in what is happening

172 | Plato's Reasons

to Menexenus. Lysis falls silent and allows Menexenus to proceed on his own into Socrates's conclusion.

Plato's use of Lysis's silence is instructive. He wants to demonstrate something through the action (or inaction) of the dialogue. How do friends treat those with whom they are friends? What do they allow them to experience and what do they prevent? Lysis's silence shows a maturity of insight on his part—he has learned something in the process of participating in Socratic dialectic. But it also gives an example of friendship in a dialogue where the concept is proving elusive. In contrast to Hippothales's candidacy as friend, Lysis qualifies on all fronts. He does not love for the sake of himself, and he shows concern for the other in appreciation of the value of the experience of failure in this Socratic exercise.

The *Parmenides*

The second case that illustrates Plato's use of silence as a strategy is less explicit in terms of what is stated in the text and concerns the *Parmenides*, a later if not late dialogue, and the opening exchange between Parmenides and the young Socrates. This dialogue raises problems for the commentators because of the rigorous and apparently unanswerable critique to which the theory of Forms is subjected (Gill 1996, 1). That Plato continues to hold to that theory in notably late dialogues (albeit with the revisions of the *Sophist*) would suggest that he did not consider the critique definitive but saw ways around the arguments that he has Parmenides deliver. How might we understand this?

The relevant section of the dialogue discussion begins with a display by Parmenides's companion, Zeno, and the interjections of the young Socrates (that is, supposedly the historical Socrates during his younger days[17]). Zeno has argued that if things are many, as the pluralists insist, then they will be both like and unlike, but unlike things cannot be like, nor like things unlike, and so the position is absurd. Socrates, however, counters that the position is credible if the theory of Forms is recognized and we allow that there are Forms and particular things that participate in them. It is at this point that the elder Parmenides, who had been listening to the exchange,

---

17. Perhaps such an encounter could have taken place; the dates of the respective participants would allow this. But that this actual conversation could have ensued is implausible given that the young Socrates is asked to defend the mature theory of Forms.

steps in and asks, with a hint of incredulity, whether Socrates believes that the same thing can be at the same time in one thing and in many.

The following exchange ensues:

> Parmenides: "But tell me this: is it your view that, as you say, there are certain forms from which these other things, by getting a share of them, derive their names—as, for instance, they come to be like by getting a share of likeness, large by getting a share of largeness, and just and beautiful, by getting a share of justice and beauty?"
>
> "It certainly is," Socrates replied.
>
> "So does each thing that gets a share get as its share the form as a whole or part of it? Or could there be some other means of getting a share apart from these two?"
>
> "How could there be?" he said.
>
> "Do you think, then, that the whole form as a whole—one thing—is in each of the many?
>
> Or what do you think?"
>
> "What's to prevent it being one, Parmenides?" said Socrates.
>
> "So being one and the same, it will be at the same time, as a whole, in things that are many and separate, and thus will be separate from itself."
>
> "No it wouldn't," Socrates said. "Not if it's like one and the same day (*hēmera*). That is in many places at the same time and is none the less not separate from itself. If it's like that, each of the forms might be, at the same time, one and the same in all."
>
> "Socrates," he said, "how neatly you make one and the same thing be in many places at the same time. It's as if you were to cover many people with a sail, and then say that one thing as a whole is over many. Or isn't that the sort of thing you mean to say?"

"Perhaps," he replied.

"In that case would the sail be, as a whole, over each person, or would a part of it be over one person and another part over another?"

"A part."

"So the forms themselves are divisible, Socrates, he said, and things that partake of them would partake of a part; no longer would a whole form, but only a part of it, be in each thing."

"It does appear that way." (*Prm.* 130e–131c)[18]

The key moment of this exchange comes when Socrates responds to the crucial challenge ("So being one and the same, it will be at the same time, as a whole, in things that are many and separate, and thus will be separate from itself") with the analogy of the day. This is something, he suggests, that is in many places at once.

Parmenides's response to Socrates's example of the day involves the shift to a very different category of physical analogue in order to explain the relationship of Forms to things that participate in them. "It's as if you were to cover many people with a sail, and then say that one thing as a whole is over many. Or isn't that the sort of thing you mean to say?"

Socrates's response to this is hesitant, "perhaps," or "I think so." We are expected to observe the dynamics involved in a conversation between a philosopher of eminence and a novice disarmed by the other's authority. A day and a sail are qualitatively quite different. Parmenides's shift from one to the other reinforces his very physical conception of the relationship between the One and the Many. It is difficult to dispute that should a sail be laid over several people, each of them would indeed be under part of the sail. But what Parmenides fails to do in making this shift is address the actual analogy that Socrates advances, which is far more promising. On a certain level, it seems absurd to speak of part of a day being over one person and a different part being over another, because a day is a more abstract concept. Moreover, it takes its place among a collection of similar Platonic referents that have to do with illumination, whether it is the sun itself or the light drawn from a fire (for revealing figures in the cave or testing ideas in the *Theaetetus*). It is *this*

---

18. The translation is drawn from that of Mary Louise Gill and Paul Ryan (Plato 1997f).

analogy that needs to be investigated, and it is on this that the text remains silent. Socrates does not have the status to insist that his analogy be addressed, and so the discussion goes off on another track altogether.[19]

In fact, it is Socrates's passive reaction to the shift in analogy and what goes unsaid as a result that sets the subsequent discussion on a path that is detrimental to the theory of Forms, whereas Socrates's silence suggests a different path with a different consequence for the theory. The path taken retains the "physical" conception of the Form/particular relationship. The next criticism in the dialogue regarding Largeness confirms this. But the path not taken is suggestive in its absence. Surely Plato expects the attentive reader to observe the shift from day to sail and wonder why Socrates allows it? Surely, also, there is an invitation to the reader to pursue that untaken path for themselves?

Guthrie (1978) points out that while "the young and inexperienced Socrates" has no response to Parmenides's sail example, "in fact a material object like a sail is very different from a period of time, which provides no bad analogy for a relationship which, as Plato saw and Aristotle deplored, can only be described analogically or metaphorically" (41). This is promising. But in an accompanying footnote, Guthrie states he has no doubt *heméra* meant period of time in ordinary usage, and that references to light or the sun are irrelevant (41n1). The reason for Guthrie's certainty is unclear, nor is it clear why we should look for any "ordinary usage" of a term when the discussion is technical and philosophical.[20] But this aside, it remains the case that the text pursues one direction and ignores the other. And it is this strategy (on the writer's part) that is of interest. Is Plato drawing attention to the participants' failure to address the first example? Is this silence a further invitation to go where the discussion does not go? Crombie suggests that Plato is indicating here that Forms should not be thought of in pseudo-concrete terms (1963, 333), and this indeed appears the most plausible interpretation, given Plato's proficiency as a writer (where nothing seems unintended) and his interest in retaining the theory that is under review.

---

19. Cornford (1957), in his otherwise excellent commentary, makes no comment on either analogy.

20. Moreover, in a related footnote (41n2), Guthrie refers us "for further on this" to Crombie (1963, 330ff). Surprisingly (given Guthrie's skepticism), Crombie does take the day analogy seriously: "For the principle of individuation of a day is different from that of a physical object . . . Socrates ought never to have accepted Parmenides's illustration in place of his own (his hesitant agreement shows that he himself had doubts), and it must surely be significant that he is rail-roaded into accepting it" (331).

Texts create a certain set of expectations. They follow according to patterns of necessity or probability. This is the point Aristotle makes about plots (*Poet.* 1451b), but it should be extended to other texts. Thus, the failure of a text to follow the direction expected of it stands out as a particular type of misdirection, calling attention to itself and inviting our scrutiny.

If I am correct, and we have a clear strategy being employed here, then we should consider what value such a strategy possesses. As a rhetorical strategy "silence" has the advantage of denying the reader a passive response. As one audience (Parmenides) falls away, another audience (the reader) steps forward. This audience engages the text, interrogates it, to discern the meanings available. Plato's dialogues have often been considered "invitational" (see Griswold 1988). Along with the *aporetic* nature of the early dialogues, the general tendency to withhold points and make specific demands of the reader indicate ways in which they invite us in.

This strategy should also tell us something about Plato's understanding of his audience, how he conceived their capacities and what he expected of them. In the *Statesman*, the Eleatic visitor explains that a definition in words is a better description than any model. And he then elaborates: "A better description, I mean, for those capable of following such a definition: for those who cannot do so the model or visible illustration is appropriate enough" (*Stm.* 277c). Clearly, presentations can be adjusted according to what is appropriate for an audience, which recalls the important remarks on knowing psychology and of *psychogogia* that were made in the *Phaedrus* (*Phdr.* 271a–e).

Again, at various points in the dialogues the difficulty of the methods employed is stressed, from the *Meno* through to the *Philebus*. These may be exoteric works, but a number of their strategies still anticipate a sophisticated audience, able to match the demands of the text with their own intelligence. Plato's deeper philosophy is not egalitarian; it is not open to all (notwithstanding the wider accessibility that opens up when he resorts to myth). And rhetorical strategies like this tend to stress this point. Thus, Plato draws in one audience, inviting them to follow a conversation along its unspoken pathways to firsthand discoveries, while presumably accepting that other audiences may miss the invitation altogether.

Dialogical Rhetoric

Whatever Plato's reasons for adopting the dialogue form (and several are implicit in these chapters), the choice makes possible (encourages, even) strategies like the use of silence that would not work as effectively (if at all) in a different form. In their introduction to a collection of studies of the dialogue form as drama (and in contrast with what they claim to have been a dominance of "analytical" readings of the dialogues), Fossheim, Songe-Møller, and Ågotnes (2019) propose that "argumentation in the strict sense does not exhaust the philosophical meaning of a dialogue" (1). Setting aside the meaning of "strict sense," what is welcome here is a recognition that argumentation can accommodate a wider range of features than might traditionally be thought.

None of the preceding is meant to suggest that the strategies adopted in dialogues dictated the use of the dialogue form itself, but it shows how ready Plato was to exploit the rhetorical possibilities of the dialogue format. As we turn in the next chapter to the *Republic*, we will see further evidence of this, as Adeimantus's challenge for Socrates to find a persuasive argument for being just (rather than merely appearing just) involves the introduction of devices that push him beyond his professed comfort zone, all in the interests of justice. There, the warnings of the *Gorgias* and the insights of the *Phaedrus* are brought together with telling effect.

Chapter 8

Back in Plato's Labyrinth

The Rhetorical Challenges of the *Republic*

> A simile is also a metaphor, with little to tell them apart. . . . Examples of similes are: . . . In Plato's *Republic* despoilers of corpses are compared to dogs that snap at stones but ignore the man throwing them; and he likens the citizens of a democracy to a ship's captain who is strong but hard of hearing; and he likens poems to boys who have youthful bloom but no real beauty, on the ground that, once they have lost their bloom and the poems have lost their metres, the impression they give is quite different.
>
> —Aristotle (*Rhetoric* 1406b20–38)

Discourse for Minotaurs

The early dialogues of Plato involve elaborate labyrinths of speech in which interlocutors become lost, finding their statements moving around beyond their control. These are labyrinths from which they despair of escaping. The *Euthyphro* makes clear that the escape, à la the lessons of Daedalus, is upward, toward the sun. But the philosophers of the middle dialogues return to the labyrinth to fulfill their political role, part of which is to engage the polis with ideas of justice (Yunis 2017, 129). Back in the labyrinth, the first task is to tame the savage beast that rules there, presented in the *Republic* in the person of Thrasymachus. Bound by arguments that tame him, Thrasymachus must play the role of the bystander for the rest of the work, usually without making a comment.

Beyond the taming of Thrasymachus, the domain of the labyrinth (in which language has no fixed bases and commitments are under threat) is still the lair of a great beast, this time reflected in the population of the city. People are no longer enamored of the discourse that operated so effectively in the early dialogues (if they ever were). Now Plato must find a different way of speaking and different devices for conveying ideas—a discourse for savage minds, for Minotaurs.[1] This is not so much a labyrinth from which to escape, but one to colonize with ideas from outside, brought back by the philosophical *theoroi* but conveyed through the language devices most fitting for the polis.

Dialogue as Labyrinth

The *Euthyphro*'s investigation into the standard for measuring pious actions led Socrates and Euthyphro through several attempts at definitions, arriving at the characteristic puzzlement that befalls all interlocutors subjected to the trials of the *elenchus*. Euthyphro discovers that he has no way of telling what is in his mind "because whatever I put forward for us always wanders off and doesn't want to stay where we put it" (*Euthphr.* 11b). These ambulatory statements, in turn, puzzle Socrates, who compares them to the animated statues of his "ancestor" Daedalus. The statues were so lifelike that they refused to stay put (*Euthphr.* 11c–d). There is humorous by-play as they disagree about which of the two of them is the Daedalus. But the predicament in which they discover themselves is far from a joking matter. Looking for a fixed definition, they find themselves caught in a labyrinth of words, where each attempt to escape with a definition leads them back to the center of the maze.

The *Euthyphro* remains an aporetic dialogue, its ending clothed in the ambiguity of Euthyphro's destination: rushing off either to withdraw the charges against his father or to continue to press them. The failure of either participant in the dialogue to state what piety is makes it also unclear

---

1. Pausanias (3.18.11): "I cannot say why Bathycles has represented the so-called Bull of Minos bound, and being led along alive by Theseus." Scholars are attracted to the fact that Socrates's execution was delayed by a festival that had its roots in the myth of Theseus and the Minotaur (see Futter 2014; Crooks 2000; Burger 1984; Dorter 1982). Thus, associations between Socrates and Theseus, along with the labyrinth, are seen to echo particularly in the mythical subtext of the *Phaedo*. Flutter even argues for Socrates as both hero and Minotaur (2014, 89), as he accepts the cup of poison looking up "like a bull" (*Phd.* 117b5).

whether Euthyphro has any real insight into his own ignorance on the matter and its consequences for his actions. But the references to Daedalus had suggested a way forward, because beyond the construction of his statues, the legendary Daedalus is also renowned for escaping the labyrinth by moving upward in the direction of the sun. In this allusion we have a harbinger of the movements of the *Republic* and the images that await us there.

The turn to *Republic* involves a return to the labyrinth, the environment of words and arguments. This is the environment where Plato struggles to bring the fixed truths of the forms into the flux of language. This is the environment in which a persuasive argument must be developed that *shows* the effect that each of justice and injustice has and thereby the merits of the just life (*Rep.* 367e).[2] But before this argument is constructed, Socrates is to encounter and perhaps defeat one of the major rhetors of his day, because this is also a labyrinth with a new monster, the great beast that is Thrasymachus.

Thrasymachus and the Beast of the *Republic*

Thrasymachus is a figure of the polis, an animal who must be tamed, entering the discussion "like a wild beast about to spring" (*Rep.* 336b).[3] In this he shares the passionate character of the city itself, identified in similar terms later in the dialogue (*Rep.* 496d). He is the rough beast who slouches in the background of the action, a watching check on what transpires.

Commentators assign multiple themes of importance to the *Republic*, variously seen in the emergence of the dialectical method and the resistance to the charms of poetry. But as James Kastely observes, Thrasymachus is neither politician nor poet; he is a rhetor (2015, 9). In choosing him as the central interlocutor of the first book and retaining his presence throughout the remaining books, Plato announces that rhetoric will be at least as important as these other themes.

---

2. There is a further persuasive argument developed in the later parts of the *Republic*—the argument that would persuade people to subject themselves to the rule of philosophers. See Scott (2020, pt. 1) for a discussion of this argument and its persuasiveness.

3. Occasionally, people wonder *which* wild beast is at issue. Perhaps Socrates answers this when he remarks at 341c that he is not crazy enough "to try to shave a lion and quibble with Thrasymachus." Lions do represent ferociousness for the Greek, but as G. E. R. Llyod reminds us, they have also represented courage since the time of Homer (1966, 184). Citations from the *Republic* are from the Reeve translation (Plato 2004) unless otherwise noted.

Thrasymachus represented the kind of rhetorical handbook and *eikotic* rhetoric that was challenged and eventually supplemented in the *Phaedrus* (261c, 266c, 267c–d, 269d, 271a). And here in Book I he will offer an argument that echoes much of what Callicles promotes in the *Gorgias* (Beversluis 2000, 340). In such ways at least clear links are made between these important "rhetoric-focused" dialogues and the start of the *Republic*.

Very little is known of Thrasymachus's life and writing. But he was judged to be an accomplished orator with an ability to condense thought through an appropriate diction (*DK* 85, A3). And his reputation for pugilism in argument had Aristotle quoting the punster Herodicus's retort to Thrasymachus: "You are always *thrasymakhos* [bold in fight]" (*Rhet.* 1400b21).[4] Plato had clearly given careful thought to "the Chalcedonian Man's" speeches, with their clever ways of angering the many, and of beguiling and slandering (*Phdr.* 267c–d).[5] And Philostratus, in his *Lives of the Sophists*, insists that the reference to shaving a lion rather than bearing witness against Thrasymachus (*Rep.* 341c) is a taunt at Thrasymachus for spending so much of his time in the law courts trumping up cases for the prosecution (Philostratus 1921, I, 14).

The first book of the *Republic* is aporetic in nature and some commentators judge it an early dialogue reframed to fit the larger project of the main work. That the discussion begins afresh at the start of Book II but with more acquiescent interlocutors encourages this thinking. At the same time, Nightingale (2004) notes how the story of the *theoros* that had drawn Socrates and his companion Glaucon down to the Piraeus and the festival in honor of Bendis anticipates the similar episodes of *theoroi* in the allegory of the cave and the myth of Er, thus tying the work together. As Polemarchus notes in setting the scene: "There will be an all-night celebration that is worth seeing. We will get up after dinner and go to see the festivities. We will meet lots of young men and have a discussion" (*Rep.* 328a).

---

4. Here I follow Kennedy's (Aristotle 2007) translation of the *Rhetoric*.

5. Stephen White (1995) suggests that the Thrasymachus of the *Republic* is a caricature of the diplomat from Chalcedon who had defended his city's position after a failed rebellion against Athens in 407. He argues that this is the side of Thrasymachus to be analyzed, not Thrasymachus the orator. White believes Thrasymachus did not visit Athens before 418 and his unexplained presence in the *Republic* may be due to the negotiations between Chalcedon and Athens in 407 (324–25). While this may provide another connection to the Melian debate, it is not a popular interpretation (see Frank 2018, 61). The developing interests in rhetoric in the *Republic* and the attention to the threat of sophistry would tell against White's claim of caricature.

Of course, anything in the first book could be a later revision. Suffice it to note that, while Thrasymachus may be "tamed," the inquiry of the first book is itself a failure. Thus, it is appropriate for Thrasymachus to hold his place as an observer for the rest of the work; he has an interest in the outcome.

When Thrasymachus enters the fray as a wild beast intent on its prey (*Rep.* 336b), roaring into the midst, he gives vent to a pent-up frustration from failed attempts to break into the discussion earlier, having been clearly exercised by the course the inquiry was taking. In particular, he is alarmed by the elenctic method that has been employed to refute Polemarchus (*Rep.* 334b) and so challenges Socrates: "If you really want to know what justice is, don't just ask questions and then indulge your love of honor by refuting answers. You know very well it is easier to ask questions than to answer them. Give an answer yourself and tell us what you say the just is" (*Rep.* 336c). This is the first (but not the last) challenge the elenctic method will receive in the *Republic*. Thrasymachus's demand that Socrates provide his own definition is a demand that he give up the method of refuting the ideas drawn from others and proceed on a different course. He will demur for now; he cannot give an answer if he does not know or claim to know (*Rep.* 337e). In this way, Socrates resists the shifting of the burden of proof onto himself. It stays with Thrasymachus, who, encouraged by the company, gives his own definition: "Justice is nothing other than what is advantageous for the stronger" (*Rep.* 338b). The stronger hold power in the state and pass laws that are to their advantage. Justice requires obeying those laws. Thus, justice advantages the rulers.[6] But this needs adjustment; sometimes rulers make laws that are not to their own advantage. Thrasymachus clarifies: "A ruler, to the extent that he is a ruler, never makes an error and unerringly decrees what is best for himself" (*Rep.* 340e). Simply put, at the time of making a mistake, the practitioner of any craft is not *at that moment* actually a craftsperson since the knowledge is absent. So, justice remains obedience to the law.

After Socrates has led a reluctant Thrasymachus to a refutation of his first thesis (the ruler in fact does what is advantageous to his subjects), the Sophist rebounds with a further clarification of justice and injustice that illustrates how the so-called just man is disadvantaged in the state, paying his taxes, neglecting private affairs, and so forth, whereas "the opposite is

---

6. Reeve (1988) gives a gloss on the details, drawing out the parts of the argument in ways that fit a contemporary reading of the logic of the case (see my chapter 1).

true of the unjust man in every respect. I mean, of course, the person I described before: the man of great power who does better" (*Rep.* 343e). Assuming this is the strong person who rules, it follows that this is the happiest person:

> When someone appropriates the possessions of the citizens, on the other hand, and then kidnaps and enslaves the possessors as well, instead of these shameful names he is called happy and blessed: not only by the citizens themselves, but even by all who learn he has committed the whole of injustice. For it is not the fear of doing injustice, but of suffering it, that elicits the reproaches of those who revile injustice.
>
> So you see, Socrates, injustice, if it is on a large enough scale, is stronger, freer, and more masterful than justice. And, as I said from the beginning, justice is what is advantageous for the stronger, while injustice is profitable and advantageous for oneself. (*Rep.* 344b–c)

There are overlaps here with some of Callicles's position from the *Gorgias*: for it is both better to do injustice than to suffer it and happiness is acquired accordingly. In our investigation of the Calliclean position, we saw Plato offering an indictment of the Athenian action toward Melos, where the argument of the strong imposed an unjust judgment on the weak. Does this indictment reoccur here?

Simon Blackburn (2006) suggests it does. "In Plato's drama, Thrasymachus is in effect the spokesman for the Athenian envoys [at Melos]" (34). He assumes more than he shows here, tracing the writing of the *Republic* (*en masse*) to the probable date of 375 BCE, forty years after the Melian siege occurred.[7] It seems clear to Blackburn that a state built on the principles that Plato will unfold in the *Republic* would not have treated Melos so harshly, nor would they have sent envoys to argue as they did. Plato did not share the views on justice and injustice that were espoused by Periclean Athens. But, as we have seen, this case was made fully in the *Gorgias*. Thrasymachus does not suffer the same fate as Callicles; while "tamed" by a Socratic method that he continues to criticize, he does not see his arguments met in Book I and must await (silently, observantly) for the later discussions to unfold.

---

7. In fairness to Blackburn, his book is not a close-reading scholarly study of the *Republic* but a popular "biography."

Stephen White (1995) sees in Thrasymachus not the immorality of Callicles but a refreshing idealism, since "his claims express the outrage of a man disillusioned and embittered by the brutal realities of fifth-century power politics" (322). Pursuing his thesis that Thrasymachus's greatest concern is Athenian imperialism (particularly with respect to Chalcedon), he draws heavily from the opening to one of his speeches preserved by Dionysius of Halicarnassus (*DK* 85, B1). The context is actually unknown, but White makes a case for it belonging to the Chalcedon/Athens disagreement.[8] Thrasymachus begins by noting that in ancient times the city was managed properly. But he lives in a time in which "we submit to <the government of> our city <by others> but <bear> its misfortunes ourselves" (*DK* 85, B1). Blame lies with some within the government and not with the majority of citizens. As White submits, there is nothing to preclude this being a plea made on the part of a city that has fallen foul of Athens (White 1995, 313). Thrasymachus proceeds to present a contrast between his city's past and the virtues expressed by the citizens and the current state of affairs, which is not representative of them. White concludes that Thrasymachus's "political sympathies, in B1 and his other efforts alike, bear directly on issues of justice, and they make him an apt spokesman for the ideas Plato has him espouse in the *Republic*" (321). Thrasymachus draws attention to the inconsistencies involved when people claim to value justice but prefer the results of injustice (*Rep.* 343d–e) and notes that the extreme case of tyranny sees injustice receiving the greatest reputation and success (*Rep.* 344a–c). But what recommends this reading most to White is the passage late in the discussion when Socrates shifts to speaking of actions between cities:

> Socrates: would you say that a city may be unjust and try to enslave other cities unjustly, and succeed in enslaving them, and hold them in subjection which it enslaved in the past?
>
> Thrasymachus: Of course. And that is what the best city will especially do, the one that is most completely unjust.
>
> Socrates: I understand that that is your argument, but the point I want to examine is this: will the city that becomes stronger

---

8. The speech directly addresses Athenians. Since only a citizen could address the assembly, the suggestion is that it was never delivered. In fact, most analyses focus on the stylistic features rather than the content. Of course, if the occasion was diplomatic and Thrasymachus an envoy to Athens, he could have been invited to address the assembly (White 1995, 311).

than another achieve this power without justice, or will it need the help of justice?

Thrasymachus: If what you said a moment ago stands, and justice is wisdom, it will need the help of justice; but if things are as I stated, it will need the help of injustice. (*Rep.* 351b–c)

Thrasymachus draws attention to the contrast between what Socrates has just said and what Thrasymachus has been saying. In the latter, one city achieves it power over another with the help of injustice. White further insists: "At no point, however, does [Thrasymachus] express clear approval for self-serving by the strong" (1995, 322).

In the Platonic text, Socrates has "defeated" the positions that Thrasymachus put forward. But neither of them has discovered the nature of justice, having been diverted by discussions of whether it is a virtue and whether it promotes happiness. What disturbed Plato in the *Gorgias* was the power that rhetoric wielded, detached from any moral anchor. It was the Melian *debate* that came into focus; the use of arguments by the envoys to overpower the arguments of the weak. To a certain degree, Thrasymachus rehearses the arguments of the strong, well aware of the power that words have to reinforce matters. This is, after all, his craft. So, the impasse that Book I represents, where neither Thrasymachus nor Socrates is satisfied by the outcome, points to the need for a nontheoretical argument that can correct the distorted political views on justice and injustice that prevail.

Another Silence

After his central role in Book I, Thrasymachus remains as a background presence throughout the discussions of the other nine books, and, of course, there is the matter of what he says in Book VI. Few commentators remark on his continued attendance (Kastely 2015, 124; Roochnik 2003, 49; Strauss 1964, 123). But the larger question is why he is there and what Plato intends by the periodic references to his presence. After all, there are also others present from the start, most with no subsequent role. Polemarchus provides a whispered prompt at the start of Book V (*Rep.* 449a–b), but no more is heard from the rest of the company; Socrates proceeds with Adeimantus and Glaucon as his interlocutors. But the complex figure of Thrasymachus—rhetor/rhetorician, Sophist, and diplomat—poses a continual question regarding the nature of justice in the city (and perhaps between cities), and his identification as a wild beast, albeit now tamed, cannot be forgotten.

The metaphor of the beast returns with force in Book VI. As a metaphor, the beast points to a threat that Plato takes seriously and to which he responds accordingly. This seriousness is not perhaps as fully appreciated as it could be. As part of her study of comedy in the *Republic*, Arlene Saxonhouse (1978) finds the animal images laughable. Indeed, as elsewhere, we do find comic images. But also as elsewhere, there is a serious, even tragic, edge to what is suggested. And Saxonhouse presses the merits of seeing how comic elements "appear at certain points in the dialogue and illuminate the philosophic content" (890). In like terms, John Harris (2018) studies animal imagery in Plato and other Greek authors, noting how it can be used "to elevate or denigrate" those to whom it refers (491). Sometimes we see both, as when the education of the guardians is designed to produce tame dogs rather than savage wolves (*Rep.* 416a–b). The savagery into which the state can collapse is always a concern for Plato.

Behind these threats, there is the ongoing question of the power of political discourse within the state, how to provide the practical persuasive argument asked for at the start of Book II. So, in his discussion with Adeimantus in Book VI, Socrates's reference to how an anonymous individual addresses people within the city strikes a note of importance. He says there:

> It is just as if someone were learning the passions and appetites of a huge, strong beast that he is rearing—how to approach and handle it, when it is most difficult to deal with or most docile and what makes it so, what sounds it utters in either condition, and what tones of voice to soothe or anger it. Having learned all this through associating and spending time with the beast, he calls this wisdom, gathers his information together as if it were a craft, and starts to teach it. Knowing nothing in reality about which of these convictions or appetites is fine or shameful, good or bad, just or unjust, he uses all these terms in conformity with the great beast's beliefs—calling the things it enjoys good and the things that anger it bad. (*Rep.* 493a–c)

The *Apology* had also compared Athenians to a beast; there it was a horse, roused from its slumber by a gadfly; here it is huge and strong. The passage from the *Republic* echoes the concerns raised in the *Phaedrus* over the *eikotic* interests in opinion. Plato there dismissed the idea that what matters "conforms to the opinions of the multitude" (*Phdr.* 273b), contrasting it with knowledge of the truth. Now in the *Republic*, the point is reiterated, this time in the presence of Thrasymachus.

And it is Thrasymachus who is key here; he represents the kind of "populism" depicted, raising the *rhetorical* question of the origins of political thinking, and he would seem to be a good candidate for the "someone" to whom Socrates is referring. For him, political thinking is egalitarian and not the exclusive task of a cadre of philosopher-rulers. He opposes the elitism involved: "He calls this wisdom, gathers his information together as if it were a craft, and starts to teach it," conforming to the beliefs of the great beast, the polis. I noted in chapter 1 that the populism that we associate with the various Sophists appears as a humanism, a judgment now to be reinforced by the position of Thrasymachus.

It is easy to forget that Thrasymachus is still there, listening to the discussion. His silence in Book VI invites us to watch and listen through his eyes and ears. We can do this in light of the ideas he put forward in Book I, or in light of the wider appreciation of him as a rhetorical, sophisticated Sophist (or both). The view Socrates recounts is consistent with Thrasymachus's recourse to commonly held views in Book I. Here Plato resorts again to the device of silence, this time to encourage a different perspective on the action. Perhaps the wild beast of *Republic* I has indeed been made gentle (*Rep.* 354a) and so rendered mute. Or perhaps it is simply that there is nothing for him to dispute here: it is an accurate description of the gulf between two positions, the Sophistic and the Platonic. We might recall Friedländer's description of Thrasymachus as "the prototype of the Sophist, the exact counterpart of the genuine philosopher" (1958, 143). The association between Thrasymachus and this polis is confirmed by the description they share: one beast drawn from a collective beast. The unruly power of the polis is difficult to approach and requires caution. But working from within, the Sophist draws on what is known of human nature and experience. The human being here is the measure of all things, the standard by which things are to be judged. So, it is this collective that needs to be understood, along with how to address it. This is the "wisdom" of the Sophist, humanistic in root and nature. He "gathers his information together *as if* it were a craft." But Plato is skeptical of this because it lacks the grasp of reality that dialectic is to bring. The *Phaedrus* made clear why this is unacceptable. But it is equally clear to see how recognizable and reasonable it would seem to Thrasymachus. He would accept this as an accurate description of two approaches, one of which he endorses. There is no need for him to speak, and watching through his eyes (as the text invites) we can see why. And in so seeing, we appreciate the crux of the issue that confronts Plato. He must accommodate a rhetoric that addresses people on their own terms yet is informed by insights they will not grasp. Socrates and Adeimantus agree that this majority cannot possibly be philosophic (*Rep.* 494a), and so those who practice philosophy are likely to be disparaged by them.

The Platonic position that was detailed in the *Phaedrus* is that any rhetorical argument worthy of adoption will be informed by the "reality of things." That is, it will be subservient to dialectic. This anticipates the more rigorous dialectic that is yet to be introduced. The absence of that dialectical influence leaves a discourse drawn from human experience and couched in the strategies of *eikotic* rhetoric.

Plato's Revision to the Socratic Image

Adeimantus had demanded not a theoretical argument that justice is stronger than injustice but a practical one (*Rep.* 367e). In his middle and later work, as he recognizes the need for a rhetoric controlled by the insights of dialectic, Plato looks for different strategies of argumentation. As we saw back in part I, the method of Socratic refutation had reached its limits. Thrasymachus also indicated this at the start of the work. Its usefulness lay in uncovering ignorance and thereby encouraging people to turn to philosophy to discover in fact what they previously believed they knew. But beyond this, it is clearly inadequate for leading people to justice. Shifts occur in various dialogues that cross the threshold to Plato's middle period. And in the *Republic* one such shift arises when Adeimantus highlights the negative public reaction to Socrates's practice.

> No one, Socrates, would be able to contradict these claims of yours. But all the same, here is pretty much the experience people have on any occasion on which they hear the sorts of things you are now saying: they think that because they are inexperienced in asking and answering questions, they are led astray a little bit by the argument at every question, and that when these little bits are added together at the end of the discussion, a great false step appears that is the opposite of what they said at the outset. (*Rep.* 487b)

190 | Plato's Reasons

The perception of a false step lies with others, but Socrates does not challenge the reaction.

> Socrates: Do you think that what these people say is false?
>
> Adeimantus: I do not know. But I would be glad to hear what you think.
>
> Socrates: You would hear that they seem to me to be telling the truth.
>
> Adeimantus: How, then, can it be right to say that there will be no end to evils in our cities until philosophers—people we agree to be useless to cities—rule in them?
>
> Socrates: The question you ask needs to be answered by means of an image.
>
> Adeimantus: And you, of course, are not used to speaking in images! (*Rep.* 487d–e)

We observed the importance of this passage in chapter 1, and this is the place to explore it more fully. Plato here marks the newness of what is to come, a shift of method that will take the discussion beyond the limits of the Socratic method. Added to the repertoire of Platonic devices is the "image," or *eikōn* (and Socrates's own discomfort with this is immediately stressed[9]). The shift is being made to a wider range of devices necessary for the rhetorical task that Plato faces. Of course, it will matter how we understand "image" here, since on the face of things it is nothing new for Socrates (or Plato): the image of the ship's captain and sailors that is about to be considered was already in use in Book I (*Rep.* 342d). And what else is the beast of the polis than an image? The dialogues are replete with images of various types. What changes here is that they become part of a shift in

---

9. Unlike Gonzalez (1998, 131), I do not read Adeimantus's remark as ironic. Yes, Socrates has used images before and this may have been a known method of the historical Socrates (Xenophon, *Memorabilia* I, 2, 32–37), but henceforth it will take on an important methodological role in the education of young philosophers and it marks a notable shift away from the use of the *elenchus*.

methodology.[10] Plato is speaking here again of likelihood, of comparisons. Images (icons) here are similitudes of the truths, as the discussion of the "divided line" will stress. Through Socrates, we understand, Plato would prefer to reach for the level of the truths themselves. But here he must be brought down to the lowest level of representation in order to address an audience that operates with comfort at this level. It is by first understanding the image that one might be led to look beyond it. This has been the cautious approach of the *Republic*'s discussions after the exchanges with Thrasymachus where the whole project becomes predicated on a comparison between the justice of an individual and the justice of an entire city (*Rep.* 368e). This is the method of search to be employed when one's vision is not very keen (*Rep.* 368d).

No scholar has done more to advance our understanding of images and comparisons in Plato's work than G. E. R. Lloyd (1966). In exploring such different modes of argument in Greek texts, he looked to shed light "on some of the broader issues of the place of informal logic in early Greek thought[11] before the invention and discovery of formal logic" (3). Lloyd is interested in two types of argumentation. The first involves oppositional thinking, and this I have explored in earlier chapters. The second involves comparative thinking, and that is what I will explore further here, because the images in question are used as comparators to bring ideas into relief and help the participants (and readers) explore features that might otherwise be missed.

There are places where the use of an image is clearly the less preferred means of making a case. In the *Phaedo*, for example, where Simmias's use of the image of the lyre to suggest that like the harmony of a musical instrument so the soul may be the harmony of the body, that image is judged problematic. As Simmias admits to Socrates: "I adopted the [image] without proof [*apodeixeis*], because of a certain probability and plausibility, which is why it appeals to most men. I know that *logoi* of which the proof is based on probability are pretentious and, if one does not guard against them, they certainly deceive one" (*Phd.* 92c–d). This is not a dismissal of all images but a warning that they can deceive if they are used incautiously. The distinction between image and proof, though, is not one we see elsewhere.

---

10. I do not intend to explore every image that is used in the dialogue. Such a task is beyond the scope of this study and has been ably accomplished by McCoy (2020), whose detailed study reinforces the importance of images in Plato's rhetorical argumentation.

11. And later in comparison with Chinese thought, see Lloyd (2018; 2015).

As Lloyd observes, in the middle and late dialogues there are passages "in which the use of analogies is *recommended* in certain contexts" (1966, 395; italics in the original), usually to instruct someone or reveal a truth. We have shifted here from talk of images to analogies; what ties them together is the role of comparison. A further device to be added to these is the example or paradigm. As we shall see in the next chapter and in part III, an account of the method of analogy and of examples is developed in the late dialogues in relation to the mature theory of dialectic. So, I will reserve the fuller discussion of these until then. Here, we stay with the image, while recognizing the way images are usually employed to show comparisons.

Of course, it is one thing to identify the importance of images in Plato's dialogues and to explain *how* he uses them. It is another matter to suggest *why* he turns to them, and particularly why they begin to serve as a replacement for what would appear to be a more rigorous method of analysis like that traditionally associated with Socrates. The shift to a Platonic dialectic is usually seen to involve the adoption of a Hypothetical method (Robinson [1941] 1953; Vlastos 1991). We see it announced, for example, in the *Meno* as a response to Meno's paradox. No longer does Socrates insist that any interlocutor is committed to the ideas that are examined; instead, they will proceed to examine a hypothesis (*Meno* 87a–b). But Robinson points out in his study of Plato's earlier work that as much as the hypothetical method is discussed in the middle dialogues, it is images and analogies that are used: "What the middle dialogues really rely upon, in order to persuade us and apparently also in order to intuit the truth, is analogy and imagery" ([1941] 1953, 204–5). More perplexing still, these features receive very little discussion. Robinson calls the *Republic* (along with the *Gorgias*) one of the most "analogical dialogues of all" (205). It is also, we might suggest, one of the dialogues that is most reliant on images.

In his examination of the images that describe the cosmos in the *Timaeus* (biological images, for example), Lloyd (1966, 267) shows how they are often an extension of earlier beliefs and myths, which suggests they may be designed to fit patterns of thought with which audiences were already comfortable. In addition to this, they serve to elucidate what may be obscure (360). This fits with the kinds of didactic and heuristic functions images have in the *Republic* (397), and in the later dialogues a further function of discovery will emerge (399).[12]

---

12. The method of the Example (paradigm), for example, is developed in the *Statesman* to assist in the discovery of the kingly art.

Plato's use of images covers those that we might describe as literal as well as others that are clearly figurative. Thrasymachus, after all, was not a lion; he was alleged to possess qualities of a lion, and the image drew attention to those qualities. But the diagram that Plato has Socrates draw in the *Meno* (82b) *is* more directly like the geometrical shape that the boy is being encouraged to recover in his mind. Seeing the image on the floor helps him correct what he sees in his mind's eye. And what he sees in his mind is closer to the thing itself, just as the drawing on the floor is further away. It is the connection between these "images" that matters to Plato. In the *Republic*, we witness the use of both kinds of image.

The Platonic Socrates of the *Republic* starts to employ different rhetorical devices, at first with reluctance, then with growing strength. When Adeimantus draws attention to Socrates's ambivalence toward images, Socrates fears he is being mocked, but he then seems to agree when he responds: "Listen to my image, and you will appreciate all the more how I have to strain to make up images" (*Rep.* 488a). He finds it necessary to use many sources to construct images and defend the best philosophers, just as painters combine the features of many things to paint goat-stags. This association with painting seems to anticipate the reservations that will be expressed about the craft later while also stressing the fictive nature of the whole enterprise. The portrayal of the goat-stag, after all, is an exercise in imagination. But once produced, the viewer sees the artist's intentions.

In this instance, Socrates returns[13] to the image of the shipowner and the sailors to illustrate how citizens treat the true philosopher, and he uses it to apparent success, since Adeimantus is quick to see what he means (*Rep.* 489a). The image is of a tall and strong shipowner whose knowledge of seafaring is impaired by poor hearing and sight. The sailors discuss the role of captain, each wishing to assume it, even though none of them has been taught the craft. In fact, they claim it cannot be taught at all and try to persuade the shipowner to turn over the ship to them. And having succeeded in persuading the shipowner to give up the ship, they rule to disastrous effect and yet still honor whoever was successful in persuasion and assign him the title of "expert." In such a context, anyone who was a "true captain" would be dismissed by the sailors (*Rep.* 488a–489a).[14]

---

13. *Republic* 342d–e, where the owner is captain and ruler.

14. The image of the shipowner/captain, once established in the *Republic*, does some heavy lifting in his later political writing (even as the method of dialectic is developed). The Eleatic visitor adopts it to illustrate the practices of the rulers of the best state (*Stm.*

After Adeimantus's ready grasping of the image, Socrates's next remark is instructive: "*I do not think you need to examine* the image to see the resemblance to cities and how they are disposed toward true philosophers" (*Rep.* 489a; emphasis mine). How often in earlier dialogues has Socrates pursued a discussion with some variant of the question "Shall we examine this idea/statement?" That was the Socratic method in action; this is not.

Here, "images" are conceptual tools. There is a visual aspect to them, but they are essentially images in the mind. The "shipowner" and its related structures of authority and responsibility provide comparative support for the ideas of how the state should function. And while Socrates may be easing into such usage, Plato himself has shown no such reluctance (hence, the "beast").

Devices of Persuasive Argument

The turn to images is a turn to a kind of mimesis[15] where, Kastely argues, what is imitated is not justice but rhetoric (Kastely 2015, 44). On these terms, for Kastely, the *Republic* "demonstrates how to speak persuasively when one returns to the cave. It argues for a philosophical rhetoric that employs images to allow its audience to begin the process of transcending those images" (145). As I have approached the dialogue, the driving concern remains the need for a persuasive argument to show that it is better to be just than to be unjust. On these terms, and contrary to some views (Morrow 1953; Warman 1983),[16] Plato possesses a positive conception of persuasion (McCoy 2020, 85). But we cannot overlook the concomitant interest in leading young people to philosophy, in promoting an attractive role for philosophers in the state. Hence, the importance of how Adeimantus

---

297a), before he identifies the third art of statecraft (Rhetoric) as that which "persuades men to justice and thereby helps to steer the ship of the state" (*Stm.* 304a). All of which underlines the importance of the persuasive argument first requested by Adeimantus and the role of rhetoric in providing it.

15. This allows that there are kinds of mimesis, at least one of which Plato embraces. Tate (1928) identifies two basic kinds, one dismissed as based on ignorance, the other adopted insofar as it is enlightened (21).

16. Warman (1983) finds the theme of a new rhetoric "conspicuously absent from the *Republic*" (49), while Morrow (1953), compounding the criticisms of Popper and associating persuasion with enchantment, asks: "Who could fail to share Mr. Popper's apprehension at this device that Plato calls persuasion?" (142).

and Glaucon are addressed and taught. The persuasive argument at issue is a type of hortatory or protreptic argument,[17] and we are now in a position to see this as a truly rhetorical argument (compared to the *elenchus* and the maieutic argument).

As we saw in chapter 1 with the example of Cleinias in the *Euthydemus*, persuasive arguments lead people to philosophy and to justice. And, thus, arguments of these kinds must use the devices rhetorically suited for the audiences involved. Different audiences emerge here, among whom we must count the accomplished rhetor Thrasymachus. Warning Adeimantus in Book VI not to start a new quarrel between him and Thrasymachus, Socrates says: "You see, we won't relax our efforts until we persuade [*peíthō*] him and the others" (*Rep.* 498d). But more specifically there is the audience of prospective philosophers like Adeimantus and Glaucon. Charles Kahn (2003) proposes an interesting division of the dialogues between those that were exoteric and for a wider audience and those later dialogues that were esoteric and intended for philosophers. Among the first group he includes dialogues like the *Phaedrus* and *Republic*, which involve a "protreptic stance"; that is, they use hortatory arguments to persuade and to draw people to philosophy (Kahn 2003, 159–60). We saw this earlier, with the exploration of hortatory arguments in part I and the example of the young man Cleinias. Now, this can be illustrated further through the treatments of the two most promising interlocutors in the *Republic*: Glaucon and Adeimantus. They are the ones who have asked for the protreptic argument, and on the face of what ensues, they do need it.

The Educations of Adeimantus and Glaucon

Socrates begins his instruction of Adeimantus with the direction to teach the image of the shipowner and sailors to the person who is surprised that philosophers are not honored in the city, and he extends the lesson of the image by having Adeimantus agree that just as it is not natural for the

---

17. The two might be used interchangeably; they are both persuasive arguments (as opposed to refutation arguments, for example), but their focus is slightly different. Hortatory arguments exhort, encourage, and advise. I found this to be the best description of the arguments used by Socrates in the *Euthydemus* (chapter 1). Protreptic arguments are more didactic in nature, with a stronger emphasis on teaching. I find this more appropriate for the pedagogic treatment of Adeimantus and Glaucon in the *Republic*. See Halliwell (2007) for the role of protreptic in the *Republic*.

captain to approach the sailors and ask to rule, so it is not natural for the philosopher to ask to rule the state (*Rep.* 489a–b). To further explain the negative attitude extended to philosophers in the state, Socrates develops an opposition between those led by truth and the surprising majority who are corrupted. Encouraged to gather a more precise understanding and grasp the correct principle, Adeimantus follows along (*Rep.* 491c). For all things, nature must receive the right nurture, and this is no less the case for philosophers. This way, the failure of philosophers in the state is down to education. As Adeimantus sees this he comes to exemplify the very point being made. Having a philosophical nature, he has access to the right kind of education. All this stems from the lesson of one image soon to be supplemented by the image of the great beast (*Rep.* 493a–b) and then an image of a blacksmith (*Rep.* 495e). Adeimantus is growing in insight. He sees what a "sweet and blessed possession philosophy is" and the contrasting "insanity of the masses" (*Rep.* 496c). And he recognizes the direction the discussion needs to take in order for the examination to be complete (*Rep.* 497d).

Socrates's argument is an argument for the muse of philosophy to gain command of the city (*Rep.* 499d). This is the muse, concerned with "the heavens and with both divine and human speeches" (*Phdr.* 259d) recognized by Adeimantus but still veiled from the masses. The vision of the philosopher that has emerged, who imitates things of the rational order and who, once compelled, aims to stamp this order on the souls of the polis (*Rep.* 500c–d), takes on another image—that of the painter of constitutions: the painter/philosopher, working on a slate wiped clean, uses the divine order for a model and writes laws that calm the characters of the people. Once angry, the people become, as Adeimantus says, "much calmer"; once angry, they "become altogether gentle and persuaded" (*Rep.* 501c–502a). The great beast of the polis is tamed by a change of character imitative of the divine nature; like it, but not actually it. The difference between the true belief that this represents and the corresponding knowledge that the few possess is not quite clear to Adeimantus, as his closing disagreement with Socrates suggests. Here Adeimantus presses Socrates to say what he believes even if he does not know the matter (*Rep.* 506c). Still, Adeimantus has been led a long way, image by image, from the shipowner to the painter/philosopher. He sees the reason for the negative view of the philosopher in the city and what needs to be done to replace that image, to replace that philosopher, with one modeled on the divine. Adeimantus has grown in insight and understanding as he has reflected on the method of images arrayed before him.

As Glaucon takes his turn in the discussion, the images start coming in fast succession, from the simile of the sun to the divided line and the allegory of the cave. The reader would do well to consider Plato's intention in switching interlocutors as these images approach. In a text that we now see to be following the advice of the *Phaedrus* and which matches argumentative device to audience, the shift is not likely to be accidental. Plato is suggesting something about the strengths and competencies of the minds involved. So, we watch how Plato casts Glaucon's responses. Glaucon will struggle with what he hears, particularly when the description of the line moves into the intelligible realm and dialectic is introduced (*Rep.* 510b).

In fact, Glaucon is exhorted to pay close attention and not let any unintentional deception escape him (*Rep.* 507a). Following this, he manages well with the sun/Good analogy, appreciative of the parallels being developed. When the shift comes to the intelligible realm, there is the first note of hesitancy in the request to be told more (*Rep.* 508c). This is obviously new to him. And the workings of the Good, in line with those of the sun—the giving of power to sight and the growth of ideas—elicits the first strong reaction: "And Glaucon very ludicrously said, 'Apollo save us, hyperbole can go no further'" (*Rep.* 509c, Shorey translation, adapted).[18] Why is this a ludicrous (*geloiōs*) response? Perhaps because such exaggerations are not new to the text; the wild beast of the polis alone would fit the description. So either Glaucon has not been paying attention or has not bought into some of the earlier discussion. Socrates proceeds into his explanation of the divided line, pausing after the first division to check that Glaucon understands (*Rep.* 510a).

Glaucon has no difficulty grasping what is involved in the sections of the visible realm, but again the shift to the intelligible confounds him: "I don't fully understand what you mean by this" (*Rep.* 510b). But Socrates's detailed elaboration of what is involved seems to hit the mark. Although Glaucon again expresses a lack of conviction, the explanation he repeats receives praise from Socrates; it is judged a sufficient understanding (*Rep.* 511d).

The next stage of the explanation, the one that brings education into the equation, occasions the recounting of the allegory of the cave. Education

---

18. Paul Shorey insists that there is no good English equivalent for *huperbolēs*, hence his choice of the limit metaphor. He also believes this is mere banter to relieve the strain of the interrogation (Plato 1935, vol. 2, 107n).

provides the "turning around" from image to reality that the *Republic*'s protreptic rhetoric is encouraging. Here, Glaucon proceeds with ease, providing the appropriate responses. Socrates then ties together the images they have reviewed: "This image then, dear Glaucon, we must apply as a whole to all that has been said, likening the region that has been revealed through sight to the habituation of the prison, and the light of the fire in it to the power of the sun. And if you assume that the ascent and the contemplation of things is the soul's ascension to the intelligible realm, you will not miss my surmise" (*Rep*. 517a–b, Shorey translation).[19] Image upon image reinforces the philosophical lesson, facilitating Glaucon's understanding.[20] This is, after all, the first time Plato has stressed a dialectic that reaches the Forms. In fact, the more accessible allegory of the cave is intended to help Glaucon grasp the journey of dialectic couched in imagistic terms (*Rep*. 532b–c).

The next step is to leave the images behind and rise to the things themselves. But Glaucon has reached his limit. Although he requests a description of how the power of dialectical discussion works, Socrates declines to provide it: "You will not be able to follow me further . . . if I could, I would show you no longer an image and symbol of my meaning, but the very truth . . . nothing less than the power of dialectic could reveal this, and that only to one experienced in the studies we have described" (*Rep*. 533a). Perhaps the message here is that Glaucon needs further help to make the final discovery, and rhetorical devices, while facilitating the process, can only take him so far. The discussion of dialectic in chapter 12 will suggest as much. Or perhaps at this point he lacks the requisite experience for which this foray into the preliminaries of dialectic has now prepared him. How we judge this will answer how we judge Glaucon: a young man of promise, or one constrained by a deficient nature.

Stephen Halliwell (2007) suggests that neither Adeimantus nor Glaucon are philosophers; they serve as philosophically inclined examples to readers who can be prepared for such an education through the protreptic devices of the text (4, 23–24). This is to view the primary audience of Plato's concern to be the readership of the *Republic*. But we have already extended the audiences of importance to include Thrasymachus, and the educational

---

19. See Robinson ([1941] 1953, 185–89) for a discussion of whether Plato held the Line and Cave to be parallel explanations. He suggests that they are not.

20. Roochnik (2003) worries that it is difficult to correlate the terms of the three images (31–32). But the point seems not so much replication (and thus correlation) but supplementation. Plato is building an imagistic argument composed of quite separate components.

progress of Adeimantus and Glaucon is for his edification as much as anyone else. And insofar as insight is registered in the responses of both of Socrates's primary interlocutors, they exemplify what the rhetorical force of Plato's writing can accomplish. Here, we recognize what Plato has achieved through his "mimetic art" (Badiou 2012, 83). In his "hyper-translation" of the *Republic*, Alain Badiou gives a clear preference for "proofs, and more broadly speaking, rational argumentation" (301) as the philosopher's tools, rather than rhetorical devices.[21] But the recognition of rhetorical power is unavoidable, even irresistible, even in such a critic of these devices as Badiou shows himself to be. Metaphor is ubiquitous, for example, and *muthos* is a natural point on a path from mathematics to metaphor (366n4). Missing from Badiou's treatment is an appreciation of how such a path would accommodate the interests and capacities of a range of audiences.

Philosophers have no one method to communicate. Later detailed discussion of the method of example and the illustrations of the method of division and collection makes this clear. What matters is the audience. In the *Statesman*, the preference is to use the description of dialectic when explaining things, but those who cannot follow such descriptions are quite adequately served by "the model or visible illustration" (*Stm.* 277c). And the audiences at stake may not be clearly demarcated by the designations "philosophical" and "nonphilosophical."

Glaucon is philosophically astute but he struggles with the description of dialectic, and Adeimantus, also philosophically able, is seen to require a model or illustration to grasp the point of Socrates's argument in the same book. Each in his own way is experiencing persuasive argument in some of its diverse styles because each is being presented with an argument that aims to train a person to turn to the insights of philosophy and to justice (rather than just the appearance of justice). These insights may be incomplete (McCoy 2020, 124), but they are just what the occasion, and audience, requires.

As they move in and out of the discussion of the *Republic*, each interlocutor requires different strategies of argument to be persuaded. Socrates

---

21. This is in keeping with Badiou's general anti-rhetorical attitude that encourages a number of "adjustments" in his hyper-translation (an expansion and updating of the text that uses Badiou's own philosophical lexicon—2012, xxiv). Among the many innovations he adopts is the altering of the gender of Adeimantus to allow for gender-specific discussion to enter the text. In general, though, his translation is more a vehicle for Badiou's own philosophical perspective on metaphysical Truth and political Marxism than any attempt to accurately portray Plato's thought. Still, his version remains relevant to this project because of the treatment provided of Plato's rhetoric.

measures the soul of the one he is persuading and employs an appropriate argument to match it. They in turn acquire argumentative tools to support their role in the state.

Plato uses different methods across the dialogues and adapts those methods according to the audience. The message of the *Phaedrus*—know the souls and speak accordingly—is illustrated within the dialectic of the dialogues. The same would hold at a meta level for Plato himself, who adopts different strategies of argument and presentation according to the purposes he has. Halliwell judges that one of the more compelling things about the *Republic* is not the argument itself but the means through which it is cast, designed to attract and persuade as many readers as possible: "By utilizing an unprecedented array of stylistic, rhetorical, imagistic, narrative, and other artistic devices . . . the *Republic* represents an expansion of Plato's literary art" (2007, 17). On a similar track, but emphasizing the argument of the *Republic* itself, Harvey Yunis judges that "the argument on justice (*dikê*) that constitutes the core of the work is conveyed to the interlocutors, and thus to readers, by means of the most concentrated use of rhetorical art in Plato's corpus" (2017, 129). The devices of this art combine to express the diversity of rhetorical argumentation in which Plato is versed. And in his political work, Plato's rhetorical argument has a primary purpose: turning people to action by a variety of persuasive means.

Rhetoric is most effective when it modifies the cognitive environment of an audience, bringing them into the presence of ideas toward which they may be previously disposed and that enhance their well-being. This requires the rhetor's knowledge of that environment, and in Plato's case it would include an understanding of the literature to which his audiences have been exposed through oral storytelling or written text. Thus, we see him drawing on a common pool of poems to illustrate points. And we see him taking aspects of the poetic tradition and presenting them in new ways. The example of Odysseus at the end of Book X illustrates this. As Er relates his experience in the afterlife, Odysseus is seen searching for a new life to take on and choosing the quiet life of an individual "who did his own work" (*Rep.* 620c). At the end of the *Republic* Plato's rhetorical skill brings the just person back into focus, now accessible to a wider audience.

Chapter 9

Rhetoric in the Middle Plato and Beyond

> In his dialogue *Politicus* . . . Plato agrees directly with what Hesiod was manifestly telling us earlier, since he is saying that rhetoric cooperates with kingship in the cause of right
>
> —Aristides (*Orations* 1, 2, 438)

Beyond the *Republic*

The attention to audiences and rhetorical devices in the *Republic* indicates ways in which, as James Kastely expresses it, Plato "embodies rhetorical practice both within his dialogues and as an essential feature structuring his different dialogues" (1997, 51). The question now is the range of dialogues to which this judgment should be applied. Any deep study of a dialogue is likely to disclose rhetorical features that reflect the understanding of its power at the time of writing.[1] The attention to speeches in the *Symposium*, for example, identifies a flourish of stylistic imitations but also marks the appearance of a philosophical rhetoric insofar as the speeches attributed to Diotima and Alcibiades are read as "corrected versions" of earlier rhetorical speeches (Pernot 2005, 50).

My interest in this chapter is the middle-to-late work of Plato and particularly those dialogues widely considered to have been composed in the

---

[1]. It is impossible to be exhaustive here, but consider Rosenstock on the "true rhetoric" of the *Phaedo* (Rosenstock 1997) or Wayne Thompson's study of rhetorical ideas in the *Symposium* (Thompson 1972).

last period of Plato's life. These include the *Sophist, Statesman, Philebus*, and *Laws*. These are also dialogues where the practice and expression of Platonic dialectic has reached its height, and although that is a subject for the later chapters of this book, any detailed inquiry into the nature of rhetoric in those dialogues will inevitably see it arise in relation to dialectic.

This is material largely passed over by investigations of rhetoric in Plato (Tindale 2021a). Much of the literature sees Plato's interest in rhetoric begin with the *Gorgias* and die with the *Phaedrus*, understanding the issue to be settled by the latter's revision of the ideas in the former. As we have seen in recent chapters, this is an overly simplistic view of the matter. And as we will see in this chapter, rhetoric continues as a concern for Plato during the later dialogues. Edward Black (1958) is among the few to acknowledge this continuing interest in the social utility of rhetoric, particularly in the *Statesman* and *Laws* (373), although he makes his observation in the context of an examination that focuses largely on the *Gorgias* and *Phaedrus*.

Both the *Sophist* and *Statesman* are dated around 360 BCE, and both depend for their success on the central role of dialectic as a method. But the *Statesman* fits the interest in political rhetoric that began in the *Gorgias* and continued through the *Republic*. In fact, the *Statesman* is one of the final statements Plato will make on the value of rhetoric to statecraft. Persuasion is not only present in but also crucial to the success of the state. So, it is the *Statesman* that will receive most attention in this chapter. We will explore its relationship to the *Sophist* in part III.

Images in the *Statesman*

There are a number of themes that link the *Statesman*, through the *Republic*, back to the *Euthydemus*, a dialogue that was explored in chapter 1, from Cleinias's expansive comments on generalship and hunting (a metaphor throughout the *Statesman*) to the quest for "a kind of knowledge which combines making and knowing how to use the thing it makes" (*Euthd.* 289b) and also to whether this knowledge is the art of the statesman (292a).

As we enter this late dialogue,[2] Socrates has taken to the sidelines along with the dialectic for which he was famous. Some vestiges of the arguments associated with that dialectic are still present, but Platonic dialectic in the form of the method of Collection and Division is now prominent,

---

2. Numbered among the last dialogues, succeeded by the *Philebus* and *Timaeus*, and dated between 366 and 362 (Skemp in Plato 1952a, 17).

along with the methods of example and analogy that will receive more of our attention here. Certainly, in the eventual successful definition of the statesman there is the reminder of the early *elenctic* search for definitions, and the Young Socrates could be seen to be responding to the maieutic arguments of the Eleatic visitor,[3] but the principal method employed is a purer dialectic, as this has been promised since its intimation in the *Phaedrus* and introduction in the *Republic*.

The method of Collection and Division proceeds by the philosophers involved (still working together as in earlier dialogues, posing questions and answering them) making cuts or cleavages to concepts that have been collected under a unified term. It is this methodological procedure that they value above all else, and it consists "in the ability to divide according to real Forms" (286d).[4] Like all methods employed in the dialogues, it is not straightforward, and missteps are always possible. The first part of the dialogue indicates just this danger as the various "natural" divisions in search of statecraft, with the splitting of knowledge into more precise categories, lead them astray, requiring a myth to see the error of their ways and put them back on track.

Unlike the myths discussed in earlier chapters, this one serves as a corrective to the dialectical line of inquiry. It is interesting to see *muthos* playing such a vital and innovative role so late in Plato's work. The Eleatic visitor and Young Socrates had reached (prematurely, we recognize) their conclusion and discovered the nature of statesmanship, summarized at 267a–c. It is said there to be a kind of tending to the herd. But they immediately worry that their definition is inadequate because there are other herders who nurture the herd and yet practice different arts, like merchants, farmers, and so forth (*Stm.* 267e). So, the statesman cannot, on these terms, be the lone shepherd of the human flock, as they had concluded. "Then we must begin all over again," says the Eleatic visitor, "from another starting point and travel by another road. . . . We have to bring in some childish stories to relieve the strain. There is a large part of a big myth [*megalou muthou*] which we must now use for our purposes; after which we must go on as before" (*Stm.* 268d; adapted from Skemp).

Briefly, the myth explains that the rotation of the universe was set by a god but then later released and so proceeded according to its own nature to rotate in reverse. Thus, there is an underlying principle of rotation during

---

3. Of the three types of Socratic argument explored in part I—the *elenctic*, the hortatory, and the maieutic—it is the last of these that seems transformed under Plato's later dialectic.

4. Unless otherwise noted, translations are those of Skemp (Plato 1952a).

different eras, and humans will undergo changes according to the era in which they live. In fact, each living creature will grow forward or grow backward accordingly. With such a reversal, humans are born directly from the earth, and a god is placed as shepherd over each group of living creatures. "And now the pilot of the ship of the universe let go the handle of its rudder and retired" (*Stm.* 272e), with the minor gods also relinquishing their duties. The subsequent deterioration encourages the god who started it all to retake the helm.

Those are the details of the myth, but the Eleatic visitor wants to clarify its relevance to their quest for the statesman. Under the changed regime all creatures took responsibility for their own procreation and nurturing. Humans "had to manage their lives and fend for themselves in the same way as the whole Universe was forced to do" (*Stm.* 274d). And there ends the myth.

The lesson to be drawn from the myth is then explained by the Eleatic visitor. It discloses two mistakes they had made in their reasoning, one big and one small:

> We were asked to define the king and statesman of this present era, and of humanity as we know it, but in fact we took from the contrary cosmic era the Shepherd of the human flock as it then was and described him as the statesman. He is a god, not a mortal. We went as far astray as that. Furthermore, we showed him as a ruler of all the life of the state but did not specify the manner of his rule. Here too, what we said was true, but it cannot be regarded as the whole truth or as a clear and sufficient description. We have gone wrong in this also, though not as badly wrong as on the other issue. (*Stm.* 274e–275a)

There are detailed and provocative interpretations of the myth, most tying it to the background thinking of the Greeks at that time and the ways they would have viewed the parallels between leaders and shepherds (see Bernadette in Plato 1984, 94ff; Skemp in Plato 1952a, 52–66; Kahn 2009). In such readings, all agree that the political argument of the *Statesman* anticipates the *Laws*.[5] My interest is in the use of myth as a counter to other methods. If the myth is directed toward an audience, it is to those who trace their understanding of the way humans should be ruled to the patterns observed in mythology. There, the divorce between divine and mortal dominates

---

5. On this point, see also Kahn (2013, 234).

the relationship. But it was wrong to assume the statesman of the inquiry would be a dominator of the ruled on such parallel terms. The myth draws attention to an old way of thinking that was obscured in the first part of the inquiry. Once revealed, its tendencies can be avoided in what is to come.

Plato might have made the same point by having the Eleatic visitor simply note the error and correct it. But such directness has never been a feature of the dialogues, no matter who is leading the inquiry. The Socrates of the earlier dialogues routinely led his interlocutors on circuitous paths to understanding, leaving no point unnoticed. But in the later works of Plato, we have new methodological tools being refined and developed. When the importance of rhetoric to the processes involved in grasping what should be done is revealed late in the dialogue, it in turn invites reflection back on the rhetorical devices that have been employed to get to that insight.

Although I have not gone into the details of the commentators' readings, something of Skemp's conclusion deserves acknowledgment because it is related to method. He agrees that the myth serves as an ultimate rejection of the shepherd/herd conception of the ruler and ruled. What the *Statesman* will present to readers is a royal weaver, not a royal shepherd, someone who binds together rather than dominates. So, the use of myth combines with the use of analogy to keep the dialectical inquiry on the right course once that course has been found. As Skemp observes in a note: "The nominal connection with 'concern for herds' really counts for nothing, however, once the weaving analogy comes to dominate the dialogue" (Plato 1952a, 57n3).

Appropriately, then, it is at this point (after Plato has demonstrated that the dialectical method can go wrong) that the methodological focus of the dialogue shifts. First, it provides a complementary method of example that itself has rhetorical resonance. As the Eleatic visitor explains, a definition in words is a better description than any model, a point he then qualifies: "A better description, I mean, for those capable of following such a definition: for those who cannot do so the model or visible illustration is appropriate enough" (*Stm.* 277c). Clearly, presentations can be adjusted according to what is appropriate for an audience, which recalls once more the important remarks on knowing psychology that were made in the *Phaedrus* (271a–e), and the various devices employed in *Republic* and elsewhere. In fact, we learn that it is difficult to demonstrate anything of real importance without the use of examples, perhaps recognizing the less philosophical bearing of most audiences.

Like other Platonic methods, that of example, once elaborated, reflects a refinement of something that has earlier instances in the dialogues.[6] Plato has always shown an interest in analogical thinking (Lloyd 2015; 1996), as it was present in the comparative images of the last chapter. But in the *Statesman* the emphasis is explicit:

> Have we not gathered enough information now to show how the method of Example proceeds? It operates, does it not, when a factor identical with a factor in a less-known object is rightly believed to exist in some other better-known object in quite another sphere of life? This common factor in each object, when it has been made the basis of a parallel examination of them both, makes it possible for us to achieve a single true judgment about each of them as forming one of a pair. (*Stm.* 278c)

The parallel thinking here draws together objects from quite different spheres of life in order to arrive at a single judgment about them. The Example is the common factor possessed by these disparate things but clearer in the better-known object. This way of reasoning highlights imagination and creativity in an explicit way. We have associated Plato himself with an array of creative devices, from metaphors and similes to imitating styles of discourse and argument. But here we see this creativity presented in a method for others to employ. Success at this method would seem to require expansive experience of spheres of life (in the visible world) and the ability to identify similarities in disparate things. It is a type of reasoning for which the Greeks certainly had interest and facility (Lloyd 1966, 176). Here, it supplements the efforts of dialectic, and, on many occasions, will be the preferred necessary method used to communicate ideas to those who are not "capable of following . . . definition" (*Stm.* 277c). These would be the unphilosophical.

We should recall here Socrates's reluctance in *Republic* VI when Adeimantus's challenge regarding the way society dismisses philosophers required "an answer expressed in a comparison or parable" (*Rep.* 487e), for which he

---

6. The term used is *paradeigma*. As Rosen (1995, 83) points out in his discussion, Liddell and Scott give both "example" and "model" as separate meanings for this term. So, this does not help us in understanding the sense involved in this passage. As my discussion indicates, I lay stress on the importance of the comparison that is sought here and elsewhere and thus gives importance to analogy. Lloyd (1966) simply employs "paradigm," and weaves it into his examination of analogy in Plato. The actual term "analogy" (*analogian*) arises only once in the dialogue, in reference to mathematical proportion (*Stm.* 257b).

supplied the image of the shipmaster to compare to the philosopher.[7] No such concerns haunt the method by the time we reach the *Statesman*. Plato is resigned to the necessity of such rhetorical means of communication to nonphilosophical audiences.

Having been thus introduced, the method of Example is then applied. They need an example that is sufficiently small (and hence manageable) but which has the same kind of activity as statesmanship (*Stm.* 279a). And they take at random the art of weaving, specifically the art of weaving wool. Importantly, though, they proceed to apply the method of division to weaving. As always in the later Plato, other methods are subordinate to the method of Collection and Division when the examination is conducted by philosophers.

The "commonality" that they are interested in discovering, scientifically by means of the method of Example, is the nature of "tendance" or superintending as this applies to the whole community (*Stm.* 278e). Weaving works as the other analogue in the Example because "when the section of the art of combination which is also a section of the art of wool-working produces a fabric by the due intertwining of warp and woof, we call the finished fabric a woolen garment and the art superintending its production the art of Weaving" (*Stm.* 283a).

The judgment drawn from the two analogues (weaving and statecraft) emerges later after they describe the way the statesman must oversee the education of the young and combine the core characters in the state into a common fabric: "This is exactly like weaving. The art of weaving hands over the materials it intends to use for the fabric to the carders and others concerned with preparatory processes, and yet it watches their work at every stage, retaining the direction and oversight itself and indicating to each auxiliary art such duties as it deems that each can usefully perform to make ready the threads for its own task of fashioning the web" (*Stm.* 308d). The statesman takes characters that are predominantly courageous and others that are predominantly moderate and weaves together the two groups. The one thing that most occupies this political weaver as the web of state is constructed is to ensure that gentle characters are not separated from brave ones. To this end, the fabric is woven closely together "with perfect agreement" in the hearts of each type of citizen (*Stm.* 310e). How is this done? This must be a role for rhetoric, the art that aims at such agreements.[8]

---

7. The Eleatic visitor uses the same example of the shipmaster later in the *Statesman* (297a).

8. Ostensibly, we have here an answer to the question of the *Euthydemus* regarding the double art that knows both what is involved and how to use it. Crito had suggested this

How good is this analogy between weaving and statecraft? The difficulty involved in answering this question is the difficulty involved in knowing what criteria of "goodness" to apply. As we have seen in earlier chapters, it is rarely appropriate or helpful to impose contemporary standards of logic and argumentation back onto Plato's dialogues. There is more of a sui generis status to his modes of reasoning, as they arise according to his needs or the needs of his audiences. David Hume, for example, judged that the further apart two analogues were in nature, the weaker the analogy: "Wherever you depart, in the least, from the similarity of cases, you diminish proportionally the evidence; and may at last bring it to a very weak *analogy*, which is confessedly liable to error and uncertainty" (Hume [1779] 1980, 16). This is the measure that has proven popular in subsequent accounts of analogical reasoning. But Plato seems to explicitly eschew such rigor. His illustrative (or explanatory) analogies, while argumentative, do not aspire to establish the kinds of conclusions at which Hume is directing his critique.

Robinson ([1941] 1953) worries that there is an incoherence between the Hypothetical method that replaces the Socratic method and Plato's reliance on images and analogy. On his reading, the middle dialogues should rely on the Hypothetical method, whereas "what [they] really rely on, in order to persuade us and apparently also in order to intuit the truth, is analogy and imagery" (204–5). We will return to the importance of the Hypothetical method in a later chapter. Here it is worth noting the assumption Robinson makes about audience. Does Plato write to "persuade us," or does he write to persuade a series of audiences all of which are closer to his own context than to ours? The question is deliberately rhetorical because we have already seen enough to be confident in asserting the latter. Robinson further observes how important analogy is to central dialogues like the *Gorgias* and the *Republic*. Much of the *Republic*, for example, is an extended comparison between the human individual and the collective of the polis, intended to illustrate the individual against a larger canvas, and within this there is the less obviously similar comparison between the guardian class and dogs. Indeed, the parallels between the health of the body and the health of the soul are given forceful expression there and elsewhere. It is clearly a methodological strategy that has always been present, indicating simply

---

was the art of statecraft (*Euthd.* 292a), but the answer was then unclear. The weaving of the strands (of the gentle and the brave) of the web of state is, I suggest, the use of the knowledge of the art of statecraft. And this use requires persuasive argument to achieve the required agreement.

how fundamental analogical reasoning is to any discussion that is remotely philosophical in nature. What happens in the middle dialogues, as we have seen, is that there is deliberate reference to the use of images and analogies. That this occurs in dialogues in which political concerns are in the forefront is no coincidence since it is here that Plato is most conscious of the task that any philosophers face in speaking generally, in finding the persuasive argument to move people to action. The analogy between the rhetor and the doctor has its force in delineating the areas of influence of each (*Grg.* 479a–b), but for contemporary commentators the more instructive analogy might be with the teacher-surgeon who leads students around the wards, going case by case, speaking to them over the patient as if the patient was not present and did not have something crucial to contribute to what is being said. The parallel to this would be the rhetorician instructing students in the invention of speeches without any attention to the audience who is to be addressed, as if that audience has nothing to contribute to how the rhetoric is to be formulated and the strategies that might best work.

In his study of analogy as a method, Robinson ([1941] 1953) notes the case-by-case nature of the examples rather than any concern for the universal. In this way, I think he captures the essence of Plato's use of analogy perfectly:

> Analogy seems to be essentially an argument from a single case to a single case. However many cases are available, the argument, if it is an analogy, chooses only one of them, or at any rate treats all that it takes as being for the purpose of the argument a single case. It is essentially not perfect epagoge; for that ascends to the universal. It is essentially not probable epagoge from a plurality of cases either; for it professes to be intuitive in character, to see into one thing by an insight obtained on another. (Robinson [1941] 1953, 207)

Indeed, Plato's analogical reasoning would fail to meet contemporary standards on a number of fronts, with analogues too far apart and little in the way of general knowledge being drawn about one on the basis of what we know of the other. The analogy opens up a case by revealing aspects of its nature through the comparison. In the *Statesman*, we have been introduced, after all, with a method of "example" (*paradigma*), or "model or visible illustration" (*Stm.* 277c) that we then choose to interpret as analogy. Or, as Robinson phrases the matter, the intuition associated with analogy "slides imperceptibly" into the form of an example or image as it explains or illuminates ([1941] 1953, 208). The analogy between the weaver and the politician, with all the importance of unifying and braiding, illustrates the value of this approach. It shifts attention away from the concern with ruling and onto more fertile ground. All Plato requires is a common factor in each analogue "which is made the basis of a parallel examination," and this allows us to judge them as a pair for the purposes at hand (*Stm.* 278c).

The Place of Rhetoric and the Absent Rhetor

Returning to the *Statesman*, after the long excursion into the divisions of weaving, the discussion reapproaches the central subject of the statesman (*Stm.* 287a), separating out the other arts according to natural divisions. Like the shipmaster, the rulers of the best state use their art as a stronger power for good than any written laws. This helps to determine the "second-best" when the ideal is not available. The other constitutions will preserve themselves by adhering to a code of laws. Because simply following written laws, rather following than generalship or the other arts, does not result in the best states. And it would be even worse if each art was forced to function according to a legal code and placed under a judge, because such an individual could ignore law and become a tyrant.

Dividing each of the available constitutions (the rule of one, the rule of a few, the rule of many) they arrive at six, according to whether or not they are well ruled. But the true constitution, the rule of philosophical statecraft, is a seventh (*Stm.* 302d). This brings us to the heart of their discussion (and close to the definition sought), as the Eleatic visitor asks what arts are left after all the previous separations. The answer is that there are three (beside statecraft), and the relationships between those three are what should interest us as we continue to unfold Plato's late attitude to rhetoric: "These include the art of generalship, the art of administering justice and that department of the art of public speaking which is closely allied to the kingly art. This last persuades men to do what is right and therefore takes its share in controlling what goes on in a true community" (*Stm.* 303e–304a). So, there is the art of generalship, the art of justice, and a third—the art that persuades.

The quotation here is from the Skemp translation (Plato 1952a), which stresses the art involved rather than the person who holds it. Thus, he talks of generalship and administering justice rather than the general and the judge. While I have found the Skemp translation most serviceable in the course of this study, on this point the Fowler translation in the Loeb edition (Plato 1925b) is closer to the Greek in stressing the general and judge, since "arts of the general" (rather than of "generalship"), for example, is the better translation. Moreover, in place of Skemp's description of the third art—"This last persuades men to do what is right and therefore takes its share in controlling what goes on in a true community"—Fowler offers "persuades men to justice and thereby helps to steer the ship of the state." Both "justice" and "steer"[9] better capture the sense of the words used, and we might prefer to retain the ship analogy because it has such a strong Platonic pedigree, finding its source back in the discussion of the *Republic* and elsewhere.

These three arts closest to statecraft after all others are cleaved away and dismissed through dialectical discussion, and the positions that hold them, all have important roots in earlier dialogues. We recall previous searches for the general, implicated in the *Laches* and pronounced in the *Euthydemus*. And the importance of the judge tracks much of the political discussion of the *Republic*. Of course, we have not *found* either here. Such discoveries would require separate dialectical investigations employing Collection and Division. But we are expected to recognize the importance of these arts in support of, but subordinate to, statecraft.

It is the third art, however, that should be of greater interest to us. Several things are of note in its regard. The first of these is the curious case of the absent rhetor: this art is not assigned a figure that exercises it like the other two; there is no rhetor standing beside the general and the judge in support of the statesman. Furthermore, finding this art here in such an overt political context might occasion surprise in the reader, given its apparent dismissal in the *Gorgias*. The exchange between the Eleatic visitor and Young Socrates over this art is revealing:

> E. V. The art which decides whether we learn a skill or not ought to have control of the art which actually teaches us that skill. . . . Then in the same way the art which decides whether persuasion should or should not be used ought to control the operation of the art of persuasion itself. . . . Which is the art to which we must assign the task of persuading the general mass

---

9. Seth Benardete (Plato 1984) supplies "piloting the actions in the cities."

212 | Plato's Reasons

> of the population by telling them suitable [or edifying] stories rather than by giving them formal instruction?
>
> Y. S. I should say that it is obvious that this is the province to be assigned to Rhetoric. (*Stm.* 304c–d)

The protreptic arguments illustrated in the *Euthydemus* have not disappeared from Plato's repertoire as he shifts from using Socratic dialectic to employing methods like that of Collection and Division that reflect his own dialectic. The argumentation that persuades people to turn to specific actions retains a central role in the best state. A necessary role, in fact.

It is also really not such a surprise to find rhetoric so prominent this late in Plato's career. The *Republic* had emphasized its necessity. The *Phaedrus* had found, outside the city, a "philosophical" rhetoric that could be brought back in and matched against the rhetoric of the Sophists.[10]

So there is precedent (or corroboration, depending on the chronology of dialogues here) for the importance of rhetoric in the *Statesman*, where the discussion raises the new question of *who* uses this persuasive argument. The exchange between the Eleatic visitor and Young Socrates continues:

> E. V. But to which art must we assign the function of deciding whether in any particular situation we must proceed by persuasion, or by coercive measures against a group of men, or whether it is right to take no action at all?
>
> Y. S. The art which can teach us how to decide, that will be the art which controls rhetoric and the art of public speaking.
>
> E. V. This activity can be none other than the work of the Statesman, I suggest. (*Stm.* 304d)

This quickly separates Rhetoric itself from Statecraft, just as the other two arts had been separated earlier. Consistent with the message of the *Phaedrus*, rhetoric is to be a subordinate art. But we are no wiser as to whose art it is. The general and the judge have their arts. The philosopher, it seems,

---

10. And the *Philebus* (from the same late period as the *Statesman*) will allow rhetoric, and even Gorgias himself, a place in the state, as long as it is subject to the rule of dialectic.

works in dialectic, to which rhetoric is subordinate. And the Statesman's particular art is spelled out in the closing discussions of the *Statesman*, when the analogy with weaving is brought back into play. The temptation is to read rhetoric as a general art that can be employed by different people. This runs the risk of violating Plato's principle that each person has but one art or skill that they know well. But on the other hand, we have precedents scattered throughout the earlier dialogues.

The *Statesman*'s detailed discussion of the method of example and the illustrations of the method of Collection and Division make clear what I stressed in the last chapter: there is no single method preferred for philosophers to explore ideas and communicate the results. Once again, what matters is the *audience* being addressed. And those audiences may not be clearly demarcated by the designations "philosophical" and "nonphilosophical." As we have seen, Glaucon is philosophically astute but struggles with the description of dialectic at the end of *Republic* VI. And Adeimantus requires a model or illustration to facilitate his understanding in the same book. The diverse styles of protreptic argument are matched to the variety of minds for whom they are best suited.

This point (that the philosopher can employ different arguments for different audiences) is reinforced in the lessons of the *Euthydemus*. Cleinias has philosophical potential, but he cannot be presented with any philosophical argument until he has first been led, protreptically, to see the advantages of the philosophical life. Then, we might believe, he is prepared for the kind of training experienced by the Young Socrates of the *Statesman*.[11]

The general and the judge, those other "survivors" of the dialectical cleaving, also need a set of strategies to persuade their particular audiences. Courage and justice are virtuous qualities of the soul. Those with the appropriate natures need to be encouraged in these dispositions. But a discourse with associated strategies is required for such encouragement. The text does not set any rhetor beside the general and judge, preferring to stress the art itself, because both of these become the rhetor as they play their parts in helping to steer the ship of the state. Statecraft is an art in itself, but it cannot operate without the aid of subordinate arts, all woven together by the practices of rhetoric.

In this late dialogue, then, we see both the natural place of rhetoric within the state and the tools needed to weave together and govern the

---

11. Or by Protarchus and the young men with him in the *Philebus*.

disparate parts, as well as first the discussion and then the illustration of rhetorical strategies themselves.

The Return of Gorgias

The *Statesman* firmly demonstrates Plato's late engagement with rhetoric. But among the dialogues of the late period it is not alone in doing so. Turning to the *Philebus*, we find a similar discussion and illustration of dialectic before some poignant remarks about rhetoric are introduced. Recognized as another late work in Plato's corpus, the *Philebus* is connected through a number of themes to the *Timaeus* (Hackforth in Plato 1972, 3) and reflects the same illustration of method that we find in both the *Sophist* and *Statesman*.[12] The focus is on the nature of the better life: whether it is that of pleasure (Philebus's position) or intelligence. In examining both the nature of pleasure and of intelligence, Socrates and the younger man Protarchus perform the role of dialecticians and apply the method of Collection and Division to each. This will be important to the discussions of Plato's late dialectic in future chapters. But that is not the focus here.

The *Philebus* applies the method of Collection and Division to the notion of knowledge itself and arrives at something that is the pure kind. The discussion there is between Socrates and Protarchus (rather than Philebus), and when the latter hears mention of a pure kind of knowledge he responds that he thinks this is the art of rhetoric of which Gorgias spoke: "On many occasions when I used to listen to Gorgias, he regularly said, Socrates, that the art of persuasion was greatly superior to all others, for it subjugated all things not by violence but by willing submission, and was far and away the best of all arts" (*Phil* 58a–b).[13] Socrates's response suggests that there is, indeed, a usefulness to rhetoric, but he clarifies his meaning: "What I wanted to discover . . . was not which art or which form of knowledge is

---

12. Not all commentators agree to the late dating of the *Philebus*. Zuckert (2009, 385), for example, treats it immediately after the *Republic* because she sees it expanding the argument of that dialogue for the life of the mind. But for reasons I will address, this is hard to accept. Justin Gosling prefaces his translation (Plato 1975a, xx–xxi) with a refusal to commit to a date because the considerations, including stylometric ones, are complex. Lutoslawski (1897, 470) places it close stylistically to the *Statesman*.

13. I take this and other lines from the *Philebus* from the Hackforth translation (Plato 1972).

superior to all others in respect of being the greatest or the best or the most serviceable, but which devotes its attention to precision, exactness, and the fullest truth" (*Phil.* 58b–c). In this, Socrates concedes that Gorgias's art may indeed be "the greatest or the best or the most serviceable." And Socrates would seem to confirm this when he goes on to explain: "You won't give offense to Gorgias, if you allow his art the property of doing paramount service to mankind, while assigning to the procedure to which I have just referred just that property of possessing paramount truth" (*Phil.* 58c).

Seth Benardete (Plato 1991) does not see Plato endorsing rhetoric here. He views Protarchus as advocating for a rhetoric of self-knowledge, the art that allowed him to do whatever he wanted. But this rhetoric, suggests Benardete, "seems to be comedy, which Socrates had argued was always grounded in self-ignorance" (Plato 1991, 224). This agrees with Scott Consigny's decision to place the passage among those in which Plato criticizes or satirizes Gorgias (Consigny 2001, 217n5), although he declines to elaborate on his grounds for categorizing it thus.

In his commentary, Justin Gosling (Plato 1975a, 129) is influenced by the "persistent hostility" that Plato shows to rhetoric in the dialogues and follows Gilbert Ryle (1966) in seeing the reference to Gorgias as an allusion to the ongoing dispute between Plato's academy and the Isocratean school. Gosling does observe the positive reading of Hackforth (Plato 1972), who recognizes a change of attitude toward rhetoric (at least, a change from the attitude of the *Gorgias*). But this too Gosling disputes: he judges the dialogue to be arguing that it is dialectic that promises the greatest practical value, and secondly "the passage puts rhetoric in its proper place" beneath the power of philosophical (that is, dialectical) knowledge (Plato 1975a, 129). This seems too hasty a dismissal of a reference that deserves more attention. Even if the passage is intended to place Isocrates's efforts beneath those of Plato, it is still marking a definite change of tone from the *Gorgias*. That rhetoric is subordinate to dialectic does not detract from it now being accorded an appropriate domain. To suggest that dialectic is of comparable *practical* value to rhetoric grinds against the picture of dialectic that is emerging in the late Plato. I will explore this further in the chapters devoted to dialectic.

Of course, one could insist that all Socrates is doing in the passage is inviting *Protarchus* to allow that Gorgias's art is of paramount service to humanity (which, indeed, he had just done). But this would then fail to appreciate the statement in the context of the division of knowledge that has been performed. Nor does it explain why Plato should phrase things as he does and not grasp the opportunity to reinforce the earlier negative view of the *Gorgias*.

In fact, the text recognizes what the late Plato has been drawn to see, that grasping the fullest truth with precision and exactness, while having great personal value, has no social currency unless the dialectician can then communicate the insights gained in a way that informs society at large and thereby improves the nature of that society. The subsequent advocacy in the *Philebus* of the mixed life would seem to acknowledge as much (*Phil.* 61b). Hackforth's gloss on this is instructive: "We now proceed to select the ingredients of the mixture. First as to knowledge, we must of course have the 'truest part' of this, namely the knowledge of true, immutable Being; but it is agreed that an inferior kind must be included as well; in fact we shall allow any and every sort of intellectual ability . . . a place. This decision is taken out of regard for the needs of the practical life" (Plato 1972, 127). For example, as he explains things, knowledge of pure arithmetic is not sufficient to build houses. Indeed, we can make a parallel case for the discourses required to govern. The pure is not sufficient; mixed discourses matched to different audience types is what we would now expect. The only strict provision in taking all the other sorts of knowledge is that the first sort must be in place before the others (*Phil.* 62d). This powerful reading proceeds on the understanding that rhetoric does have a place in the taxonomy of knowledge types, but in doing so it answers the less considered remarks of the commentators noted above who seem, I would suggest, to have allowed the usual story of Plato's negative view of rhetoric to require them to find a more convoluted explanation for the positive position granted it here.

Given the disagreements over the dating of the *Philebus*, we cannot even be sure that the remark about not wanting to offend Gorgias is even a reference to a living thinker.[14] What should strike us now is not the inconsistency between the attitude here and that conveyed in the *Gorgias* but the consistency of attitude toward rhetoric in this dialogue and the *Statesman*. In both, rhetoric finds its place in relation to the theoretical knowledge acquired through the method(s) of dialectic. In both, it informs the practical life and is necessary for it to flourish.

---

14. Zuckert's comment on the passage, for example, directs her readers to "a later conversation with Gorgias and his students" (2009, 411n219).

The Methods of Articulation

The importance of rhetoric to Plato's political concerns in his late dialogues naturally requires some consideration of his *Laws*. This is the unfinished investigation by Clinias, Megillus, and the Athenian into the best legislation for the state. The discussion in Book XII makes clear that the guardians (the nocturnal council), comprising older and younger members, must practice dialectic as we have seen it mentioned elsewhere and as it will be explored in future chapters. In any field, the skilled individual should not just see many particular instances of a thing but also should "win through to a knowledge of the single central concept, and when he's understood that, put the various details in their proper place in the overall picture" (*Laws* XII, 965b).[15] This use of Collection and Division holds for things like virtue, goodness, and beauty, with respect to which the guardians should not only know that these terms are a plurality but also understand the sense in which they are unities (*Laws* 966a).

Then the Athenian asks: "What if they understood the point, but couldn't find the words to demonstrate it?" To which Clinias replies that this is absurd. So, the Athenian proceeds: "Well then, isn't our doctrine going to be the same about all serious questions? If our guardians are going to be *genuine* guardians of the laws they must have *genuine* knowledge of their real nature; they must be articulate enough to explain the real difference between good actions and bad, and capable of sticking to the distinction in practice" (*Laws* 966b). Here, we see the familiar concern between grasping knowledge and then being about to communicate what is seen. The question really is the audience to whom such things need to be communicated. In the context of this dialogue, that principal audience would again be members of the polis.

How the guardians come to master the methods of articulation is not explained, though. Earlier in Book VII their education had been discussed, and rhetoric was not included. But earlier still in the discussion of Book IV, as dawn has become noon (*Laws* 722c),[16] the Athenian recognizes that legislators cannot just impose laws by means of a "dictatorial prescription."

---

15. Quotes from the *Laws* are from Trevor J. Saunders's translation in the Hackett edition (Plato 1997c).

16. A reminder, perhaps, of the heat of the noonday sun that prompted the important action of the *Phaedrus*.

There must be a preamble such as "the spoken word, and in general all compositions that involve using the voice" employ. This is the persuasive element "analogous to that of a preamble in a speech" (*Laws* 722d–723a). As noted in the introduction to this part of the book, Brian Vickers finds this recourse to the tradition of rhetoric ironic (1988, 143) and seems surprised by it. But on my reading, it is a natural acknowledgment of the utility of what has never been abandoned; it just needed to be adapted to the right ends.

At the very end of the *Laws*, at the close of Book XII, the discussion returns to the question of education, and it is decided that no legislation can determine in advance the full nature of the education until the council's activities have been established. "Its curriculum must be decided by those who have already mastered the necessary branches of knowledge" (*Laws* 968c), and "it will be a waste of time to produce written regulations about the order in which the various subjects should be tackled" (*Laws* 968e). This discussion, then, certainly points toward the need for the guardians to be able to use language to articulate what they see. And in the context of other late dialogues, the need points toward the value of a rhetoric similar to that which we have seen advocated in those dialogues. That not just any discourse in the social arena will do had been made clear earlier in Book XI, where the Athenian observes:

> There is a certain kind of immoral practice, grandly masquerading as a "skill," which proceeds on the assumption that a technique exists—itself, in fact—of conducting one's own suits and pleading those of others, which can win the day regardless of the rights and wrongs of the individual case; and that this skill itself and the speeches composed with its help are available free—free, that is, to anyone offering a consideration in return. Now it is absolutely vital that this skill, if it is a skill and not a knack born of casual trial and error—should not be allowed to grow up in our state if we can prevent it. (*Laws* 937e–938a)

The criticism here is reinforced by the use of the same phrase that carried the barb in the *Gorgias* (463b), a knack or experience not born in knowledge. But here, as there, the context is a political rhetoric that cannot lead people to justice. Its critical tone is consistent with what we have seen throughout Plato's discussions of rhetoric and helps to further mark the contrast with the positive account with which we are now acquainted. The difference between a skilled and unskilled rhetoric is one with which dialogues subsequent to the *Gorgias* have readily acquainted us.

What is then at issue here is clearly the discourse of the Sophist—Plato's perennial foe still posing a threat in his twilight years—with his desire to use any means to win the argument, regardless of the truth of the matter. It is thus the unjust "art" of sophistry that must never arise in the state, allowing that its counterpart (rhetoric) can promote what is just. Of course, on this reading, what was most disdained in the *Gorgias* was sophistry. But this is consistent with the attempts in other dialogues, like the *Republic* and *Sophist*, to distinguish the practices of the Sophists from other practices. Plato has never lost his disdain for sophistry. But what is said here contrasts clearly with the positive rhetoric that is informed by knowledge of the truth as it speaks justice. In general terms, a judgment we have found elsewhere holds here for the guardians, that insofar as they acquire the knowledge of dialecticians, then to communicate they must become rhetors.

Rethinking Rhetoric's History

Plato's engagement with rhetoric continues past the middle dialogues. He requires it to forge the social environment in which justice can flourish. The late dialogues reflect this positive attitude in the attention given to rhetorical questions and rhetoric itself, duly understood within the contexts developed there. As we see in the *Statesman*, rhetoric has a primary role, one of three gathered close to statecraft and necessary for it to function well. It implants true opinion about matters like honor and justice and their opposites in those who have the appropriate preparation. This explains the usefulness of rhetoric acknowledged in the *Philebus* and illustrated in the *Laws*, where details of the tradition of rhetoric (discussed in contrast to "Platonic" rhetoric in the *Phaedrus*) are brought back as aids to the last project that Plato attempted in his life.

The traditional rhetoric discussed in the *Phaedrus* has not been supplanted by the new; it has been supplemented by that to which it is naturally inferior. Platonic dialectic involves individual discovery, not mass communication. But the philosopher does not just speak to other philosophers or those being led to philosophy. There is the speech of persuasion, which checks the desire to compel and speaks of justice. This is how rhetoric is employed in the late Plato.

Not only was Plato engaged with questions of rhetoric in the *Gorgias* and *Phaedrus*, but they occupied him throughout his career, from the early to the late dialogues. And as attention to the political discussions of the later dialogues indicates, it was necessary for him to do so. The challenge of the *Republic* to find a persuasive argument to lead people to justice was a challenge that he needed to address in his own more serious political writing like the *Statesman* (assuming that the *Republic* can on some level be assigned to the category of "dream" (*Rep.* 443b). This demands a reassessment of Plato's role in the history of rhetoric. If philosophical rhetoric begins in earnest with Aristotle's *Rhetoric*, a handbook for civic discourse, then to what degree is Aristotle building on what he has seen in the work of, or heard in discussions with, his own mentor? Aristotle's conception of rhetoric as well as that of the rhetor is positive. As the capacity (potentiality) to see the possibilities for persuasion in any situation (*Rhet.* 1355b26), rhetoric is essentially neutral for Aristotle; it can be employed for good or ill. But the rhetor is a character of goodwill (along with practical wisdom and virtue: *Rhet.* 1378a8). And in the psychology of Book II of his *Rhetoric*, Aristotle can be seen to "implement Plato's scheme" of matching speech to souls in the *Phaedrus* (Solmsen 1975, 243). On such terms as these, Aristotle adjusts the focus of Platonic lenses. But in harnessing the power of rhetoric in civic contexts, Aristotle continues a project that has already received firm direction in Plato's dialogues.

Part III
The Dialectician

Introduction to Part III
A New Dialectic

[Plato] was the first to introduce argument by means of question and answer, says Favorinus in the eighth book of his *Miscellaneous History*; he was the first to explain to Leodamas of Thasos the method of solving problems by analysis; and the first who in philosophical discussion employed the terms antipodes, element, dialectic, quality, oblong number, and, among boundaries, the plane superficies; also divine providence.

—Diogenes (III, 24).

Whatever the provenance of *Definitions*, its existence and the debate around its authorship is instructive. It has been variously attributed to Speusippus and other members of the Academy, but even those attributions are useful in associating the book and the activity it represents with Plato's school. And while it is a text to be approached with caution—it does, after all, contain repetitions—it may still give insight to the practices and emphases of the school. As Douglas Hutchinson observes in the introduction to his translation of the work (1997, 1677), the method of collection and division was a systematic approach to definition, and one we see practiced in the late dialogues.

This is another thread of connectivity between the practices of Socrates and those of Plato. Just as there is a continued interest in dialectic in spite of the shift between the Socratic and the Platonic understandings of method, so in Plato's concern for definitions there is a vestige of the Socratic practice. This is that one thing that Aristotle tells us can be fairly said about Socrates: the interest in defining ethical terms (*Metaph.* 987b1–4).[1] Indeed, this is a feature of Socratic practice that Xenophon insisted on emphasizing. In his

---

1. See also *Metaphysics* 1078b17–19.

Memorabilia he writes that Socrates was always reasoning with his associates about the nature of things, and that "to go through all the terms he defined, and to show how he defined them, would be a long task" (bk. 4, chap. 6, 1).[2] To be able to say what something is, is to control an account (logos) of that thing and so to know it. It is with respect to this ability to say what they believe they know that many of Socrates's early interlocutors fail. And it is with respect to this that the members of the Academy are encouraged to excel. We will see the practice advocated in chapter 11 and illustrated in chapter 12.

In his study of the Academy, G. C. Field (1930) provides the following extract from the comic poet Epicrates, an Athenian contemporary of Plato:

> A.: Tell me about Plato and Speusippus and Menedemus. What are they working at now? What deep idea and what great argument is being examined by them? For the land's sake tell me truly, if you know anything about it.
>
> B.: I know all about it and will tell you plainly. At the Panathenaea I saw a group of boys in the gymnasia of the Academy. And there I heard strange and indescribable things. They were defining and dividing the world of nature, and were distinguishing the habits of animals and the natures of trees and the species of vegetables.

The passage continues with a comic description of the attempt to define a pumpkin, to the chagrin of an abusive bystander. But the passage ends: "B.: It didn't worry the boys. But Plato, who was there, told them very kindly, without being in the least disturbed, to try again from the beginning to define its species. And they went on with their definitions" (Epicrates cited in Field 1930, 38–39).[3] Obviously, the pumpkin example (which gets so

---

2. Nevertheless, Xenophon proceeds to illustrate a sufficient number of definitions (beginning with "piety") to make his point.

3. It is interesting to note in passing that these "boys" are judged to be "roughly, the ages fifteen to eighteen" (Field 1930, 38n2). Field also refers to them as "junior students" of the Academy. We may tend to think of older figures associated with the school, but the dialectical games described in Aristotle's *Topics* are clearly meant for students who are at an earlier stage in their education. The age is relevant when considering attempts—like those of Greek archaeologist Phoibos Stavropoullos—to locate the sites of buildings of the Academy complex. One of the finds that he judges to locate the site of the school is

much attention whenever the passage is discussed) is provided for comic effect. But the underlying activity that draws our attention is the "defining and dividing" because it so readily reflects the practice of the Eleatic visitor and the young Socrates in the *Statesman* or that of Socrates and Protarchus in the *Philebus*. Working together, the experienced dialectician and the novice exhibit a dialectical procedure that emends and extends the attention to definition in the early dialogues. There, there was a failure to arrive at the accounts expected; in the later dialogues, while there are missteps as we saw in the *Statesman*, the dialectical inquiries are ultimately successful.

In the *Cratylus*, Plato challenges conventional approaches to naming because (he has Socrates state this) names belong naturally to their objects. Again, this seems to reflect the attitude behind the dialectic in which Plato engaged and for which definitions were so important. For the Socrates of this dialogue, a definition is a tool for instructing ourselves as we divide things according to their natures (*Cra.* 388a–c).

So, the text of *Definitions* is more than a novel oddity. It holds promise in its suggestiveness. It would indicate an extensive series of successful dialectical inquiries. The entries do not demonstrate the process of defining (or dividing); they illustrate the products. But in several instances, it is a product the search for which we can see elsewhere. Consider two of the definitions, for example: "πολιτικός (*politikós*), statesman: one who knows how to organize a city" and "σοφιστής (*sophistes*), sophist: paid hunter of rich and distinguished young men" (*Def.* 415b). Both of these are close enough to the definitions arrived at after the method of division has been applied in the respective dialogues devoted to these inquiries. Moreover, there are definitions that arouse interest for other reasons. Philosophy is here as "desire for the knowledge of what always exists; the state which contemplates the truth, what makes it true; cultivation of the soul based on correct reason" (*Def.* 414b), a definition that aligns the philosopher with the dialectician, lest we be tempted (as we will) to distinguish them. And the definition of knowledge reflects the rigor of the later methods: "Conception of the soul which cannot be dislodged by reasoning; ability to conceive one or more things which cannot be dislodged by reasoning; true argument which can-

---

a set of schists he identifies as school-boy slates. This interpretation has been challenged as indicating, at best, material that "might be from a school at the elementary level, but nothing more" (Murray 2020, 226). Such a young age would not align with our understanding of Academy students. See also Glucker (2020) for a study of the extant material relating to Plato and his students and what he may have taught them.

not be dislodged" (*Def.* 414b–c). As we have seen, early interlocutors like Euthyphro lament the way words move around and will not stay still for them. Later interlocutors like Meno welcome the suggestion that knowledge has a fixed nature to it. But how rigorously the members of Plato's academy might have judged that fixedness is suggested here by the insistence that it cannot "be dislodged by reasoning." Dialectical inquiry has reached its end.[4]

If that is the case, then where, we might wonder, is the starting point to which this end is conceptually related. While we will review in chapter 10 the argument that sees dialectic *(dialektikê)*, like rhetoric *(rhêtorikê)*, to be a term invented by Plato (Kahn 2013, 132; Schiappa 1999, 14), the practice of reasoning together through conversation to arrive at insight has a clear pre-Platonic history. Diogenes Laertius ascribes to Protagoras the practice of Socratic argument (*DL* IX, 53), where the term used—*logos*—could well refer to the manner of discussion as well as the type of arguing. And we know that the types of conversation captured in the Socratic dialogues of Plato were also emulated by other Socratics like Aeschines, Antisthenes, Aristippus, and, of course, Xenophon. While Diogenes believes Plato brought the form to perfection (*DL* 3.48), he accords Simon the cobbler the honor of being the first to record Socrates's conversations in dialogue (*DL* 2.123).

In a similar vein, the study of definitional reasoning has its own history, tracing back at least to the Greek Sophist Prodicus, who was renowned for being driven by a desire for precise definitions (*DK* 84, 70). And Diogenes Laertius reports that Antisthenes—a contemporary of Plato and associate of Socrates—was the first person to define discourse, describing it as that which shows what anything is or was (*DL* VI, 3), suggesting that by "discourse" he had in mind the act of defining.

What these sources reflect is the widespread influence or practice of *Socratic* dialectic as a conversational activity aimed as defining essential terms, often of an ethical nature. Over the course of the dialogues, elements of the Socratic practice recede to be replaced by a dialectic that is more recognizably Platonic. We have already seen some of the shift, but the next few chapters will record it in greater detail. It remains largely a practice of reasoning together (although we will also consider places where self-deliberation is discussed), but the goal expands beyond a search for ethical terms to include (as Epicrates noted) terms related to "the world of

---

4. Still, we can only derive so much from *Definitions*, and much remains speculative. After all, while there is a definition for "definition" (*Def.* 414d) there is none for "dialectic."

nature" and much more. These will be the fixed truths about things that cannot be dislodged by further reasoning.

So, we are entering upon a discussion of a new dialectic, one that has distinctive features that separate it from both the Socratic dialectic[5] (features that may have been present in the practices of the historical figure) and the later dialectic of Aristotle.[6] But after the exploration of earlier dialogues, where references to dialectic or different methods have arisen, we are already aware that this is a complex matter. Just as we would now be loath to simply identify Socratic dialectic with the single practice of refutation and not include the use of hortatory and maieutic argumentation, so we need to think about the various parts that comprise Platonic "dialectic," now to be understood as an umbrella term under which are gathered several related methodological processes. In the *Meno*, for example, there is an announced shift from the Socratic method to the Hypothetical method, and that method is illustrated in dialogues like the *Phaedo*. But the Hypothetical method, while clearly an important part of Plato's dialectical repertoire, itself recedes from importance and practice in the later dialogues, to be replaced by attention to the method of Collection and Division that was introduced in the *Phaedrus* (and hinted at elsewhere), as well as the method of Example with its association with analogical reasoning, hence my reference above to "dialectic" as an umbrella term under which the methods of the later dialogues can be collected. It will be one of the tasks of the next few chapters to distinguish these parts of Platonic dialectic while also exploring the relationships between them.

---

5. This claim is consistent with the readings I have developed so far and with what I will go on to develop in the chapters of this part of the study. But it is fair to note that other accounts recognize a coalescence between the different approaches. Castelnérac and Marion (2009) and Marion (2021), for example, develop an elaborate set of rules for dialectic that accommodates the three perspectives of Socrates, Plato, and Aristotle in a single account of dialectical games, as these were deemed to have been practiced in the Academy. This includes a "Socratic Rule" that prohibits the use of any premise not granted by the Answerer (Marion 2021, 76).

6. Aristotle's concept of "dialectic" is ultimately as different from the Platonic as the Platonic is from the Socratic. We will explore those differences in chapter 10.

Chapter 10

Tracing Dialectic

> His introduction of the Forms was the result of his investigation of arguments; for none of his predecessors engaged in dialectic.
>
> —Aristotle (*Metaphysics* 987b30–34)[1]

What We Mean by "Dialectic"

Among Plato's many innovative inventions is a vocabulary that captures and expresses the ideas in which he is interested. At a time when different genres are emerging and discourses are taking on distinctive features that will set them apart, Plato's introductions of terms like *dialektikē* and *rhētorikē*, and the particular dimensions he will apply to *philosophia* to distinguish it from the usages of, say, Isocrates, are fundamental to the epistemological project that he is developing. As noted in the introduction to this part, *dialektikē* and *rhētorikē* were terms invented by Plato (Kahn 2013, 132; Schiappa 1999, 14). And as was observed in chapter 5, Edward Schiappa has argued: "The term *rhētorikē* simply cannot be found in any text that has been dated prior to Plato's *Gorgias*, usually dated to the 380s B.C.E." (1999, 14). Of course, while the terms may originate with Plato, this does not mean that the practice of what any of them identifies does. But while rhetoric itself had a lively pre-Platonic life, captured by various terms (usually *logos*), the same cannot be said for *dialektikē*. Ancient writers attributed its origin to Plato, notes Kahn, a judgment strongly supported by the way "we can see the term taking shape before our eyes in *Republic* VII" (Kahn 1996,

---

1. Irwin and Fine translation (Aristotle 1997a).

325–26). While it has a range of associated meanings that can track back to types of communal inquiry or the art of philosophical conversation, Plato gives it specific meanings both as a description of Socratic practice and as a program for adoption by future philosophers (Timmerman and Schiappa 2010, 34). While a technical sense is certainly extended to the method of refutation employed by Socrates as part of dialectic in the course of the *Republic*, the sense of dialectic that was still to emerge in that dialogue is even more technical in nature, and this will be the sense fully adopted by Plato himself and developed in the late dialogues.[2] As David Timmerman and Edward Schiappa (2010) observe, "for Plato, dialectic was, above all, the activity that *enacts* philosophy" (40). They consider how Plato effectively "disciplines" *dialegesthai* as a term of art, identifying a specific skill associated with dialogue and giving it a technical force.

In his work *Plato's Earlier Dialectic*, Robinson ([1941] 1953) describes "dialectic" as an honorific title that Plato confers throughout his career on "whatever seemed to him at the moment the most hopeful procedure" (70), and he attributes the notion we find in the dialogues to Plato himself (88). In spite of this, the aim remains constant: to discover "what each thing is" (*Rep.* 533b). This also consistent, of course, with the general attention given to definitions, since it is in the account of a thing that the requisite discovery is made.[3] Because he takes dialectic to be the technical aspect of "philosophy," Robinson widens the range of references to it. But, as Hugh Benson notes, the actual occurrences of the term "dialectic" in Plato are far fewer than might be expected.

> The Greek substantive *hē dialektikē* and its cognates occur only 22 times in the Platonic corpus and only once in dialogues that Robinson considers early (*Euthd.* 290c5). Moreover, more than a third of those occurrences are concentrated within six Stephanus pages[4] in the *Republic* (531d9, 532b4, 533c7, 534b3, 534e3,

---

2. See also Havelock (1963, 280–81), who argues that "philosophy" gains a new sense in the *Republic*.

3. Robinson's own study is restricted to those elements that are common to all descriptions of "dialectic" and to the method of Hypothesis; space did not allow him to make a comparable study of division.

4. Here, reference is being made to the standard way of quoting Plato, which refers to the Renaissance edition of his works published in Geneva in 1578 by Henri Estienne (1528–1598), more usually known by the Latinized version of his name: Stephanus. This source was explained in the introduction to part I.

536d6, 537c6, 537c7). The substantive infinitive *to dialegesthai* occurs more frequently and can sometimes carry a technical sense as opposed to its more ordinary meaning of "to converse" or "to discuss." (Benson 2009, 86)

Indeed, it is the larger number of references to *dialegesthai* that presents the challenge because this surely indicates something less "technical" than what Robinson identifies. So translators have had to decide when Plato is referring to "mere" conversation and when a more rigorous method is at stake. In the *Cratylus*, for example, the more basic sense is conveyed when Socrates inquires of Hermogenes, "And what would you call someone who knows how to ask and answer questions? Wouldn't you call him a dialectician?" (*Cra.* 390c). Later in the same dialogue, in the discussion of heroes, *dialektikoi* are included (along with sophists and rhetors, it should be noted). But the sense remains as those who are good at conversation.

The *Gorgias* is a further case in point. This is, after all, a dialogue where we might expect *dialektikē* and *rhētorikē* to be brought into contrast. The first mention of "rhetoric" finds Socrates accusing Polus of having more practice at what is called rhetoric than at discussion (*Grg.* 448d). Here, the term translated as "discussion" or "conversation" does indeed mean to pick out from another in the sense of drawing things out from conversation (our term "discussion" does not quite capture this). What is at stake are two separate uses of language that might be contrasted in different ways. One involves addressing others, perhaps in larger public venues; the second involves engaging others on a more personal level, perhaps more privately. When we enter into conversation there is an intimacy that focuses attention on the other and their ideas. And this mode of conversation is being compared with Socratic questioning when Socrates immediately invites Gorgias to forgo the long speech and continue conversing as they are with "one asking questions and the other answering" (*Grg.* 449b). The same term is used for "conversing," so the drawing out from the other is explicitly understood in terms of questioning and answering—which we may take from previous investigations to be the rudimentary form of Socratic dialectic. But that term itself is not mentioned. The ultimate contrast of speeches is between the political pandering associated with rhetoric and speeches that aim to improve the population by bringing justice into their souls (*Grg.* 504d–e). This second kind of speech is aligned with the activities of philosophy and reflects its aim as it is understood in that dialogue (*Grg.* 500c).

It is in the *Phaedrus* that the rhetoricians and philosophers are joined by those occupying another role—dialecticians (*dialektikoi*). And they enter the discussion with the first clear appearance of the method of Collection and Division. Over the course of *Phaedrus* 265d–e, Socrates describes the practice or insight that should underly speeches of value. First, there is Collection: "For him whose sight comprehends things dispersed in many places to lead them into one idea, so that by defining each thing, he makes clear what on each occasion, he wishes to teach about" (*Phdr.* 265d).[5] Then, there is Division: "To be able, contrariwise, to cut apart by forms, according to where the joints have naturally grown, and not to endeavour to shatter any part, in the manner of a bad butcher" (*Phdr.* 265e). Socrates then aligns himself with this method. This is where the *atopic* philosopher of the *Phaedrus* transforms into the dialectician:

> And I myself, for one, Phaedrus, am a lover of these dividings apart and bringings together, so that I may be capable of speaking and thinking. And if I consider someone else to have the power to see the things that have naturally grown into one and toward many, I pursue this man "behind after his footsteps, as if a god's." Furthermore, those who are able to do this, whether I address them correctly or not, god knows, but however that may be, so far, I call them dialecticians (*dialektikoi*). (*Phdr.* 266d–c)

There is an ambivalence here apparent on the one hand in Socrates's love of the method and those who use it, and yet on the other hand in an uncertainty about whether he has labelled them correctly. Suffice it to note that, once introduced, the *dialektikoi* will grow in stature and take their place at the pinnacle of Plato's hierarchy of those who access the truth. Dialectic is referenced at *Phaedrus* 269b when Socrates imagines a rebuke from Adrastus and Pericles insisting that he and Phaedrus should show sympathy to those who, "being ignorant of dialectic (*dialegesthai*), proved unable to define (*horísasthai*) whatever rhetoric can be."[6] And all of this is reinforced by a summary that captures the import of dialectic for the prospects of a positive conception of rhetoric:

---

5. These quotes from the *Phaedrus* are from Nichols's translation (Plato 1998b).

6. James Nichols Jr. (Plato 1998b) renders *dialegesthai* as "discuss," but the context and the use then of *horísasthai* demands a clearer reference to the version of the method that has now been introduced.

> Until a man knows the truth about each of the things about which he speaks or writes, and becomes capable of defining the whole by itself, and having defined it, knows how to cut it up again according to its forms until it can no longer be cut; and until he has reached an understanding of the nature of the soul along the same lines, discovering the form which fits each nature, and so arranges and orders his speech, offering a complex soul complex speeches containing all the modes, and simple speeches to a simple soul, not before then will he be capable of pursuing the making of speeches as a whole in a scientific way, to a degree that its nature allows, whether for the purposes of teaching or persuading. (*Phdr.* 277b–c)

Essentially, then, until someone has become proficient at using the method of Collection and Division, they will not be able to use speech to teach and persuade. Rhetorical competence presupposes dialectical competence of a more rigorous kind than we have seen in previous dialogues.

In this way, the *Phaedrus* adds the dialecticians to the roster of those who are philosophically adept, placing them in the superior position. In fact, we may now wonder whether any distinction is being suggested between philosophers and dialecticians. At the close of the dialogue, as we saw in chapter 5, Phaedrus and Socrates are assigned the task of returning to the city and to their friends and telling them what they have learned. If those who hear the reports compose speeches in the correct way, then they should be named accordingly. But the text stops short of calling them dialecticians. Socrates says: "To call him wise, Phaedrus, to me seems to be a big thing and to be fitting for god only. But either philosopher or some such thing would fit him better and would be more harmonious" (*Phdr.* 278d). More ambivalence is suggested here in the call for a "philosopher or some such thing." What else would be comparable to a philosopher at this point of the dialogue than the dialectician? But if so, why not use the name? This may be another place where Plato thinks the point obvious and leaves it to the reader who has followed the inquiry to insert the name. But it further stretches the point to incredulity to suggest that figures like Lysias, Homer, or Solon could wear the title of dialectician, although they may qualify for the now lesser role of "philosopher." Perhaps, then, what we have is indeed the suggestion of a distinction between philosopher and dialectician, with the nature of the latter to be filled in further elsewhere.

Socratic and Platonic Dialectic

The dialecticians of the *Phaedrus* are not Socratic dialecticians. Something has happened to bring about this change. In part II, we saw a tendency among some scholars of the history of rhetoric to read Plato's contributions to an understanding of that topic in quite a restrictive way, invariably failing to take their analyses beyond the *Gorgias* and *Phaedrus*. Contributing to this view about rhetoric, I believe, are limitations in the appreciation of the nature of *Plato's* dialectic, combining it with the earlier Socratic version (Conley 1990; Vickers 1988).[7] For example, Conley writes: "Dialectic has a game-like quality to it. Two people are needed to engage in dialectic" (1990, 10). If there is any "game-like" nature to this practice it will not be true for the mature Platonic dialectic, which is treated with quite seriously even if it can involve a range of participants. What Conley describes is more characteristic of the conversations Socrates has with interlocutors who profess expert knowledge in the early dialogues, as he seeks to establish whether they know what they claim to know. As we saw in chapter 2, this activity is one of refutation, where the statement put forward by the interlocutor is examined dialectically (through the asking of questions) to the point where the examination arrives at the opposite of the statement and it is refuted.

Clearly, there are threads of connectivity between the Socratic and Platonic versions. The Socratic inquiries were definitional: What is piety? What is courage? But the results were aporetic, failing to achieve a satisfactory definition in each case. The Platonic dialectic that emerges in the *Republic* and that is illustrated in later dialogues like the *Sophist*, *Statesman*, and *Philebus* refines the interest in definitions by looking to place things under the right classes. As we will explore in chapter 11, this inquiry into classification is best understood in terms of what was described in the *Phaedrus*—the method of Collection and Division. Here, participants in Plato's later dialogues take concepts and divide them in order to find where something—the Sophist, the statesman—naturally belongs and thus discover the truth about it. Reginald Hackforth in his commentary on the *Philebus* observes that it tends to be more a method of division than of collection

---

7. I would not want to suggest that this view of dialectic is shared only by historians of rhetoric. Ample examples could be found among philosophical commentators. A case in point is Gilbert Ryle (1968), who in discussing dialectic in the Academy, and referring to the Socratic Method, writes: "Surely Plato would have transmitted to the students in his own Academy what Socrates had transmitted to him. What else, indeed, had Plato to teach?" (71). What else, indeed.

(Hackforth in Plato 1972, 26). But insofar as the participants engage in finding the correct classes, they are composing those classes (or uncovering what is collected in them). Hence, we have a clear method of Division *and* Collection. The Eleatic visitor observes in the *Statesman* that those listening to him should not make the mistake of thinking he believes that the class and part are separate from one another. Rather "when there is a class of anything, it must necessarily be a part of the thing of which it is said to be a class; but there is no necessity that a part be also a class. Please always give this, rather than the other, as my doctrine" (*Stm.* 263b).[8] Such a remark indicates an understanding of both classes and divisions within them and implies a process that has provided this understanding.

The Socrates of the *Apology* is a moral philosopher and that alone.[9] He disavows any knowledge except that associated with moral virtues. He knows his duty; he knows what actions of his are just; he knows that a good person cannot be harmed; but he knows nothing beyond these kinds of things. The Socrates of the middle and later dialogues (or those principal participants, like the Athenian stranger who occupies the "Socratic" position in a dialogue) knows about epistemology, metaphysics, aesthetics, mathematics, politics, and much more. It is at least in these knowledge claims and associated methodologies that we see a contrast between the versions of the Socratic figure that Plato portrays in his work.

In chapter 8's discussion of rhetoric in the *Republic*, we identified one place where there is a shift away from the Socratic, after the method of refutation is seen to have resulted in a widespread skepticism among those that have witnessed its practice. Because they are inexperienced at dialectic in the Socratic sense, they believe they are being led astray and eventually fall victim to one "great false step" (*Rep.* 487b). Socrates agrees, and thereafter attention is given to other methods.

Similar announcements of a Socratic/Platonic divide can be found elsewhere. There is, of course, the testimony provided by Aristotle, who twice in the *Metaphysics* notes the specific limits of Socratic inquiry.[10] As he is famously recalled saying there: "For two things may be fairly ascribed to Socrates—inductive arguments and universal definition, both of which are

---

8. From Harold N. Fowler's Loeb translation of the *Statesman* (Plato 1925b).

9. This is a widely held but not unanimous view. For dissenting voices see Talisse (2002) and Kahn (1992).

10. Perhaps reflecting problems related to the origin of the *Metaphysics* itself, an earlier mention of some of the same points is found in Book I, chapter 6. I restrict my attention to the more detailed descriptions of Book XIII.

concerned with the starting point of science. But Socrates did not make the universals or the definitions exist apart; [the Platonists], however, gave them separate existence, and this was the kind of thing they called Forms" (*Metaph.* 1078b27–31). While some commentators take the Aristotelian judgment at face value (Vlastos 1991, chap. 3; Graham 1992[11]), for others there is always an element of suspicion associated with these passages (Kahn 1996; 1992). As with the Stoics and Skeptics, for example, there was a tendency among post-Socratic thinkers to enlist Socrates as a precursor, or an ancestor even, to their own endeavors. Plato was no different in this respect. Earlier in the same passage, Aristotle provides more grounds for his judgment:

> Socrates occupied himself with the excellences of character, and in connection with them became the first to raise the problem of universal definitions . . . it was natural that Socrates should seek the essence. For he was seeking to syllogize, and "what a thing is" [the essence] is the starting-point of syllogisms. For there was as yet none of the dialectical power which enables people even without knowledge of the essence to speculate about contraries and inquire whether the same science deals with contraries. (*Metaph.* 1078b17–27)

At least two points of interest arise here. In the first instance, the technical knowledge Socrates is alleged to have sought sounds remarkably like that which we associate with Aristotelian science. In fact, were we to substitute "Aristotle" for the second mention of "Socrates," we would find nothing awry in the description provided. Secondly, the observation about dialectical power seems less controversial. Although, as we will also see, what Aristotle understands by that may differ somewhat from how Plato would read it.

Of course, as I noted in the introduction to these chapters, the principal value that may be attached to such Aristotelian testimony lies in its confirmation of Socrates's interest in definitions. But as Kahn observes in a treatment that generally questions Aristotle's status as an historian of philosophy, Aristotle seems dependent for this judgment on the early Socratic dialogues themselves (1996, 84–85). So there is something circular at

---

11. In fact, Graham hangs his understanding of the relationship between Socrates and Plato on Aristotle's testimony, seeking out indirect evidence for what Aristotle reports (1992, 161).

work in the appeal, if Aristotle's testimony is to be taken in evidence of a historical separation of Socratic and Platonic thought.

Thus, while the lack of a specific kind of dialectical reason in Socrates's thought recognized here has plausibility, the attribution to Socrates of the desire to syllogize is more difficult to credit. Of course, a more charitable explanation recognizes that once a thinker comes to see the world in a certain way, it may be natural to assign similar insights to his predecessors. And also, Aristotle's judgment may simply be pragmatic in nature. Why would Socrates want to acquire knowledge of universals if not to then draw particular knowledge from it? Still, we should be on firmer ground if we stay with the Platonic corpus for evidence of the shift in methods.[12]

Gregory Vlastos (1991) directs us to the *Meno* for just such evidence, in support of his bold thesis that the ideas of the historical Socrates can be recovered and distinguished from those of Plato.[13] Vlastos is probably the strongest recent proponent of what we might call the "two Socrates" position, providing ten theses in support of it. For him, the early definitional dialogues reflect ideas that can be associated with the historical figure and to which Plato subscribed during the period in which he wrote those dialogues. He refers to this Socrates as $Socrates_E$ (or S_E). Starting with the middle dialogues, the historically linked Socrates is replaced by one that now serves as the mouthpiece for Plato's own developing thought. Vlastos refers to this Socrates as $Socrates_M$ (or S_M). These two Socrateses mark the shift between two different, though related, notions of dialectic. As Kahn remarks of Vlastos, he is a radical when it comes to the relationships between dialogues because he views "so much *discontinuity* between early and middle dialogues that something like a philosophic conversion is required to bring Plato from his initial Socratic stance to his own position in the middle dialogues" (1992, 242). Kahn's disbelieve in the thesis includes his incredulity at the thought

---

12. Still, Kahn (1992) also acknowledges that after his arrival in Athens thirty years after Socrates's death, Aristotle would have access to a mass of Socratic literature, including works of Antisthenes, Aeschines, Phaedo, and Euclides, as well as Xenophon. So, that he "preferred the account in Plato's earlier dialogues" (236) is to some degree based on judgments about what scant texts remain of these other authors. Kahn does go on to question why any Socratic dialogues, no matter the author, should be trusted as reliable accounts of Socratic thought (238). It remains, then, a question that will continue to invite debate.

13. In fact, Vlastos supports the stronger claim that the philosophical positions endorsed by first the early Socrates and then the middle-period Socrates are "irreconcilable" (1991, 53).

that a creative thinker like Plato could have stayed fixed within a system of thought that was not his own for the length of time (twelve years or more) in which he wrote those early dialogues (240).[14]

On this—Vlastosian—reading, the *Meno* is a notably transitional dialogue. In it, we have as many as three methods on display, the first of which is attributed to Gorgias. Meno had been a paying student of Gorgias, from whom he had supposedly learned details of the subject matter in question—virtue—such that he could serve as an expert and elucidate the subject for Socrates. This qualifies him to participate in an elenctic investigation into the nature of virtue, with Meno providing the lead. During some of the apparent by-play after Meno's early failed definitions, Socrates explicitly imitates Gorgias and his method: "Would you like me to give an answer Gorgias-fashion, the way it would be easiest for you to follow?" (*Meno* 76c).[15] Of course, the topic of inquiry has shifted here to the nature of color and examples of shape, which are hardly subjects of investigation that we would associate with the historical Socrates of earlier dialogues. This is the first indication that there is something strange going on. But it is merely a precursor of much stranger "un-Socratic" behavior that is to follow in the dialogue. What Plato demonstrates here is both a further example of Gorgias's failing (assuming the teacher can be blamed for the failures of a student) and the differences between two types of pedagogy: the Gorgianic, in which students are simply told secondhand what to believe (and then like Meno have difficulty remembering), and the Socratic, where "students"[16] are encouraged to engage in a firsthand inquiry to discover matters for themselves. When Meno responds to Socrates's definition of "colour" with the exclamation that it was an excellent answer, Socrates wryly answers: "Probably because it is put in a way you are accustomed to" (*Meno* 76d). We have little doubt that any grasp Meno has of the point will be short-

---

14. Ryle (1966) offers a less radical explanation for this transition in Plato, suggesting that the Socratic method was abandoned because there were no more memories to dramatize (204). Beversluis (2000) sees in the shift different conceptions of philosophy (the Socratic and Platonic) requiring different kinds of dialectical interlocutors (378–79).

15. Translations here from the *Meno* are by C. D. C. Reeve (Plato 2012a).

16. The qualification here is in recognition of Plato's insistence in the *Apology* that Socrates was a teacher to no one. So, whatever pedagogical practices we judge him to perform, they must fall outside of a traditional model of teacher-student relations. The distinction between firsthand and secondhand inquiries may well characterize the difference that Plato has in mind.

lived. The first methodological contrast demonstrated in the dialogue, then, is between the Gorgianic and the Socratic.[17]

It is the Socratic that proceeds to dominate, with Meno's contributions to the inquiry following the pattern of early dialogues, with three attempts that all fail and a subsequent confession that he does not know what he thought he knew. This, as we saw in our examination of the *elenchus* in chapter 2, is characteristic of the early "definitional" dialogues: the interlocutors make multiple attempts at saying what courage, or piety, or virtue is before slipping into a state of perplexity and confessing that they cannot say what they had in mind. For Meno, this point comes after his last attempt to define virtue fails and he admits that, while he thought he had spoken well about virtue on many occasions in front of many people, "now I cannot say what sort of thing it is" (*Meno* 80b).[18] And here, with some appropriate closing discussion, the dialogue should end.

But it continues, moving into territory and enlisting ideas that have not been seen before. We will come to the shift in method shortly; for now, we are interested in the changes in the Socratic character himself. He had agreed with Meno (as he had with earlier interlocutors) that he was equally confounded by the failure of their investigation. But no confusion lingers as he confidently takes control of the conversation and begins to act in ways and express understandings that he has not shown in any of the dialogues that precede this one.[19]

---

17. Tarrant (1993) takes this exchange on color and shape between Meno and Socrates at face value, keen to excise the "unnecessary" second definition of shape from the text because he deems it a later addition, even though "the second definition is more mathematical in nature and thus seems to fit well into a work where Plato's great interest in mathematics is already evident" (186–87).

18. A similar point is attributed to the household boy who becomes the subject of Socrates's next investigation. Socrates describes the boy's performance: "[He] thought he knew, answered confidently as if he knew, and didn't think he was puzzled. At this point, however, he now does believe he is puzzled, and as he does not in fact know, he does not think he does either" (*Meno* 84a).

19. The *Meno* is customarily placed at the end of the early dialogues and before middle dialogues like the *Phaedo* and *Republic*. Kahn (1996) places it at the end of the first group of dialogues, before the *Phaedo* and *Symposium*, which he includes in the same group (47); Lutoslawski (1897) places it as a continuation of the *Protagoras* (207) and before a middle group consisting of *Republic* II–X, *Phaedrus*, *Theaetetus*, and *Parmenides* (189); Zuckert (2009), who does not accept the developmental thesis, places the dramatic date much earlier and before dialogues like the *Gorgias, Lysis, and Euthydemus* but after the *Phaedo* (9).

Let us first consider the appearance of a mathematically competent Socrates. Part of Vlastos's fifth thesis is that "Socrates$_M$ has mastered the mathematical sciences of his time" (1991, 48). In the *Republic*, we know the sections of the intelligible realm where dialecticians will operate is characterized in part by mathematical knowledge, specifically by "features of a mathematics that we associate particularly with geometry" (Mueller 1992, 184). But that is in the future, assuming the *Meno* does precede the *Republic*. Still, the Socrates who will so confidently lead Glaucon through those sections is already present in the second half of the *Meno* when he uses the practice of geometers to indicate how he and Meno should progress (*Meno* 86e). He then proceeds to enlist the boy from Meno's household in order to demonstrate that he (the boy) can recall a geometrical problem and thus has true beliefs in him. Over the course of this discussion, Socrates draws the geometrical form on the ground in a way that anticipates the line between the visible and the intelligible in the *Republic*, where the image serves as an aid for the mind to "see" the ideas at issue. Socrates exhibits confident geometrical knowledge as he steers the boy through his confusion to the solution. He even remarks that the line that stretches from one corner to the other is what experts call the diagonal (*Meno* 85b). For those that support Vlastos's thesis, this is a new and even unexpected feature of Socrates's character and knowledge, if we are using only the earlier dialogues as a source.

On the other hand, there is no surprise to find Plato indicating both a facility with and need for mathematical knowledge, here "preening himself on his own expertise in geometry" (Vlastos 1991, 123). The degree of his accomplishments as a mathematician remains unclear (White 2009), but the importance of mathematics to the activities of the Academy and Plato's own philosophical project is beyond dispute. On the evidence of the Line image in the *Republic* alone, it is clear that for Plato "mathematics is propaedeutic to philosophy (dialectic)" (White 2009, 230), and this is reinforced by the dedication of a full decade to mathematical training in the education of the candidates for rulers of the state (prior to five years of dialectic). The Academy boasted a number of prominent mathematicians among its members, chief of whom would be Theaetetus and Eudoxus (Field 1930, 40–41; White 2009, 229), and it was renowned as a center of innovative advances in the field. In fact, given the prominence that mathematics achieved in Plato's affairs we might wonder at the absence of mathematics from the earlier dialogues if Kahn is right and Vlastos wrong about the continuity of ideas between the early and middle periods.

A similar oddity accompanies the new religious thinking of Socrates in the second half of the *Meno* (and, as we will see in the next chapter, the companion dialogue *Phaedo*). Thesis nine of Vlastos's set includes the claim that "Socrates$_M$'s personal religion centers in communion with divine, but impersonal, Forms" (Vlastos 1991, 49). On the testimony of the *Apology*, Socrates was agnostic about an afterlife, although not the gods. While his recognition of gods is part of his defense in the *Apology* and recorded by other Socratics like Xenophon in his *Memorabilia* (1.4), in his closing comments at his trial Socrates allows that death is one of two things: "Either the dead are nothing, as it were, and have no awareness whatsoever of anything at all; or else, as we are told, it's some sort of change, a migration of the soul from here to another place" (*Ap.* 40c). Now, in the *Meno* and *Phaedo* (as well as the *Phaedrus*) the doubt has been resolved in favor of the second disjunct. Oblivion is no longer an option; migration of the soul is favored, and the theory of recollection depends on it. This theory is presented with aplomb as the solution to Meno's paradox. A person can indeed inquire into what he knows but needs to be able to recall it to mind. So, Socrates can pronounce:

> Since the soul is immortal, then, and has been born many times, and has seen both things here and the ones in Hades—in fact, all things—there is nothing it has not learned. So it is in no way surprising that it can recollect about virtue and other things, since it knew them before. For, since all nature is akin, and the soul has learned all things, nothing prevents someone who is recollecting one thing—which men call learning—from discovering all the rest for himself, provided he is courageous and does not get tired of inquiry. For the whole of inquiry of learning is recollection." (*Meno* 81c–d)

Meno is surprised. He has not heard this before and asks to be shown it, a request that leads to the illustration with the boy from his household. Recollection is not so much a theological doctrine but an epistemological one that presupposes a theological position. Mark McPherran (2009; 1996) describes Plato's philosophical theology as one that was influenced by Socrates's conception of piety as caring for the soul and the methods of the mathematicians of the day "that he took to overcome the limitations of Socrates's elenctic method" (2009, 246).[20] Add to this an infusion of

---

20. Frederick Bussell's (1896) overtly Christianized reading of Socratic and Platonic thought judges the realization of divine purpose to be the central thought in Plato's work (102) but ultimately decides his error lies in not being religious enough (117).

post-Hesiodic religious forms, and the result offered the "un-Socratic hope of an afterlife of intimate Form-contemplation in the realm of divinity" (247). Of course, as is demonstrated in the *Phaedo*, pre-existence does not necessitate an afterlife per se, but it does contribute to a theological shift in the thinking of the Socratic figure from early to middle dialogues.

Related to both the expression of mathematical knowledge and philosophical theology, and with most significance for this discussion, is the shift in methodology. The so-called Hypothetical method that we will explore in the next chapter violates at least one crucial feature of the Socratic method as represented by the *elenchus*. As we have explored in part I, what the *elenchus* investigates is statements connected to lives, and thereby the lives themselves. Hence, in each case, Socrates seeks the commitment of the interlocutors to what they say and holds them to that commitment whenever they try to stray from it. In the latter part of the *Meno*, that personal stake in what is said is ignored in favor of a "hypothetical" inquiry into statements that Socrates is now free to introduce. No longer is he restricted to what the interlocutor believes; now he can test any statement that seems plausible in the continued search for definitions. That, of course, remains the dialectical thread connecting the methods involved.

The Socratic *elenchus* was a powerful tool for uncovering ignorance and showing so-called experts that they did not know what they thought they knew. It opened a space for inquiry, inviting the interlocutor to ask questions that he had thought did not need asking. But what comes next? After the confusion and puzzlement of the early dialogues, we now have progression to correct belief and the prospect of knowledge beyond that. In the terms used by Vlastos, to adopt the method of hypothesis "is *to scuttle the elenchus*" (Vlastos 1991, 123; italics in the original).

The method is introduced after Socrates and Meno have reflected on the lessons with the boy. They return to their inquiry, which we recall involves virtue, not a geometrical problem. But the connection is there in the method championed by geometers, who investigate from a hypothesis: "When someone asks them, for example, whether a certain area is capable of being inscribed as a triangular space in a given circle: they reply—'I cannot yet tell whether it has that capability; but I think, if I may put it so, that I have a certain helpful hypothesis for the problem, and it is as follows:'" (*Meno* 86e–87a). Socrates then proceeds to suggest what might follow if the hypothesis is correct. He then applies the idea to the task at hand: "It is the same for us, too, where virtue is concerned. Since we do not know what it is or what sort of thing it is, let's consider by adopting a hypothesis whether it is something acquired by teaching, or not something acquired by teaching" (*Meno* 87b). So, hypothetically, what sort of thing would virtue have to be in the class of mental properties in order to be teachable or not? This question that they then pursue belongs to neither of them; no one is committed to its truth either way and thus the outcome of the inquiry has no direct impact on the life of either inquirer. It is in this respect that the strongest divide appears between what we investigated at the end of part I and what now develops. In part I, we saw how Socratic dialectic engaged the whole person; it investigated the logic of the lives involved and its outcomes had serious consequences for those lives. Here, we have moved quite literally to a detached form of inquiry, pursuing matters in the abstract. Those matters will be brought back to the particular later, for that is an aim of all Platonic dialectical methods, but they have first to proceed somewhere else.

So, alongside a Gorgianic method that has been shown inadequate and dismissed and a Socratic method that has served them well but is not structurally built for the next stage of inquiry, we have the Platonic Hypothetical method that represents that further stage. What this method reveals is a mediating state between ignorance and knowledge (parallels of which we see in the account of mediation in the *Symposium* [202a]). The ability to judge correctly without also being able to give a reasoned account is a significant step beyond the insights of ignorance at which the Socratic *elenchus* arrived. Correct belief or judgment is as good as knowledge as a guide to action (and virtue), but it falls short of knowledge itself (*Meno* 97c). Plato encourages us to think of what had caused the perplexity in the early dialogues when he invokes again the figure of Daedalus and the moving statues that need to be tied down (*Meno* 97d). The method of Hypothesis is a way out of the labyrinth and thus an important component of the new dialectic that is emerging in the middle dialogues. We will pursue this further in the next chapter.

The Future of Dialectic: The Academy and Aristotle

Paul Friedländer (1958) draws his picture of study in the Academy in part from the dialogues, such as the *Symposium* and *Republic*, and relies perhaps too heavily on the authenticity of the seventh letter.[21] But his account is

---

21. As the reader may appreciate, the fortunes of this letter undergo periodic revision.

useful in reinforcing the importance of mathematics in the curriculum and marking divisions between the thought there and what emerges in Aristotle's writings. Friedländer does not favor, for example, the view that the attention to definitions (which I noted earlier in this chapter) stressed systems of classification that were preparation for Aristotelian empiricism (94). This would accord with Aristotle's remarks on the lack of any Platonic desire to develop a scientific attitude that could be compared with his own.

On the face of things, Aristotle's use of the term "dialectic" seems somewhat removed from what we are coming to appreciate in Plato, even if it may have threads of connectivity similar to those that link the Socratic and Platonic (Marion 2021).[22] It becomes a question of whether the stress should be laid on the ways in which the accounts differ or the ways in which they exhibit commonalities. In Aristotle's *Rhetoric*, dialectic is presented as an *antistrophos* to rhetoric (1354a), reflecting the position of the *Topics*, which stands as a treatise on dialectic. There, "dialectic" is concerned with "opinions which are generally accepted" by everyone, or most people, or the wise, but not a method that grasps the truth of being (*Top.* 1.14). On such terms, it would hardly be counted as synonymous with *the* philosophical method for Aristotle, as it is for Plato. In fact, it appears in direct violation of Socrates's insistence to Glaucon that dialectic aims at grasping what each thing itself is, whereas all other arts have for their object human opinions (*Rep.* 533b). Like Plato, Aristotle utilizes a number of methods in support of a project that is obviously different in nature. Our interest here is solely with his use of "dialectic" as we wonder how the meaning shifts again under his gaze, while still retaining connections to the ideas that influenced him.

In his *Nicomachean Ethics*, Aristotle describes an adequate dialectical "proof" as follows: "As in other cases we must set out the appearances (*phainómena*), and first of all go through the puzzles. In this way we must prove the common beliefs (*endoxa*) about these ways of being affected—ideally, all the common beliefs, but if not all, then most of them, and the

---

Friedländer wrote at a time when it was widely accepted. But more recent examinations (Burnyeat and Frede 2015, the results of a seminar conducted in 2001) favor a negative judgment. Caution thus recommends that we not place too much reliance on what is found there and so it is largely absent from my arguments.

22. Following his work with Castelnérac (Castelnérac and Marion 2009), Marion (2021) lays stress on the process of dialectic: that is the debates and the rules involved, rather than the product, and the definitions that will form the core of the account to be given in chapter 12.

most important. For if the objections are solved, and the common beliefs are left, it will be a sufficient proof" (*NE* 1145b2–7). Where dialectical reasoning differs from other kinds of reasoning is in the nature of the premises. Here, and consistent with the above quote from the *Topics*, dialectical reasoning proceeds from *endoxa*. A method for testing appearances measures the associated *endoxa*, and if all objections are met, a sufficient proof is rendered. There is something recognizably modern about this procedure. Setting aside any aspirations for discovering the truth about things (Aristotle develops other procedures for that), this method operates in the domain of uncertainty, arriving at conclusions that have pragmatic value while also being open to revision in light of further relevant evidence. It is also apparent that important parts of the method involve investigating the puzzles and recognizing the objections.[23]

Of all the extant Aristotelian works, it is the *Topics* that gives the clearest account of how he understands and works with dialectical argument. Consider the distinctions laid out in the opening to Book I, where the goal is to find a method to reason from generally accepted opinions while avoiding contradiction. The specter of the refutation argument is immediately evoked there. Aristotle writes:

> A deduction (*sullogismos*), then, is an argument in which, certain things being supposed, something different from the suppositions results of necessity through them. It is a demonstration (*apodexis*) if the deduction is from things which either are themselves true and primary or have attained the starting-point of knowledge about themselves through some primary and true premises. A dialectical deduction, on the other hand, is one which deduces from what is acceptable. . . . A contentious (*eristikos*) deduction is one from what appears to be acceptable but is not, or an

---

23. These *endoxa* indicate what those engaged in dialectical exchanges might accept. For the premises themselves, however, we need to turn to another innovation of Aristotle's account, captured in the title of the work—the *topoi*. Unfortunately, *topos* is another obscure term, the meaning of which is assumed by the author, and we rely on later commentators to suggest how it should be understood. Cicero, for example, provides the following helpful explanation: "If we wish to track down some argument we ought to know the places or topics: for that is the name given by Aristotle to the 'regions,' as it were, from which arguments are drawn. Accordingly, we may define a topic as the region of an argument, and an argument as a course of reasoning which firmly establishes a matter about which there is some doubt" (Cicero, *Topics*, II.7).

> apparent deduction from what is actually or only apparently acceptable. (*Top.* 100a25–100b26)[24]

Three types of argument are involved here, expressed through technical terms that reflect Aristotle's specific vocabulary. The principal term that may attract attention is "deduction" since it has come to have the precise meaning in contemporary logic that was discussed back in part I. This is consistent with Aristotle's general belief that all arguments, whether demonstrative, rhetorical, or dialectical, are either deductions or inductions. When "deduction" is defined here as "certain things being supposed, something different from the suppositions results of necessity though them," it is a definition that is echoed in virtually the same terms in Book I, chapter 1 of the *Prior Analytics* (24b19–22) and in Book I, chapter 2 of the *Rhetoric* (135b15–18).[25]

The word translated as "deduction" is *sullogismos*, but this also has modern connections with the rigor of the categorical syllogism, even though its usage here points to rendering it simply as a general type of reasoning. In his commentary on the *Topics*, Robin Smith warns against conveying a more contemporary sense with the term "syllogism" because "as a translation it is seriously misleading, since the English term usually suggests this narrower meaning" (Aristotle 1997b, 42). But it is not clear that we fare much better with the choice of "deduction." Still, Aristotle's interest is in valid arguments, and he is understanding two senses of validity here. The reference to a demonstration (*apodexis*) clarifies matters somewhat. If a valid argument has true premises, then its conclusion can be demonstrated as true. By contrast, dialectical deductions proceed, as we have seen, from acceptable opinions that retain some element of uncertainty about them. The third type of argument—the contentious—captures the sense of invalidity. Demonstrative arguments will receive full attention in the *Posterior Analytics*, while contentious arguments occupy the analyses of the *Sophistical Refutations* (or last book of the *Topics*). This leaves the bulk of the *Topics* for the exploration of dialectical arguments.

We are then presented with a recognizable method of questioning and answering, with the answerer keen to avoid being drawn into contradiction

---

24. For references to the *Topics*, I draw upon Robin Smith's translation (Aristotle 1997b).

25. Of course, the complexity of the logical theory involved differs across these sources, perhaps indicating a development of Aristotle's ideas from an earlier instantiation in the *Topics* and *Rhetoric* to the more robust descriptions of forms of argument in the *Prior Analytics*. This assumes that the *Topics* is an earlier text (Smith in Aristotle 1997b; Elders 1968, 136).

(*Top.* 159a21–25). At the same time, the arguments involved take their premises as clearly hypothetical, with an interest in seeing what follows from them. Moreover, the arguments involved are interested in definitions (*Top.* 101b37–102a10).[26]

This attention to definitions brings us to consider Aristotle's apparent attitude toward the method of Collection and Division, a method that is acutely associated with the search for definitions in Plato's dialectic. In the *Prior Analytics*, Aristotle is largely dismissive of what we might take to be the Platonic enterprise:

> It is easy to see that the division by genera is but a certain small part of the method we have described: for division is, so to speak, a weak deduction; for what it ought to prove, it begs, and it always deduces something more general than the attribute in question. First, this very point had escaped all those who used the method of division; and they attempted to persuade men that it was possible to make a demonstration of substance and essence. Consequently, they did not understand that it was possible to deduce by division, nor did they understand that it was possible to deduce in the manner we have described. In demonstrations, when there is a need to deduce that something belongs, the middle term through which the deduction is formed must always be inferior to and not comprehend the first of the extremes. But division has a contrary intention; for it takes the universal as middle. (*Apr.* 1.31, 46a31–46b2)[27]

The criticism of "those who used" the method of division is explicit. But, as always in the debates between Plato and Aristotle, the criticism needs to be tempered with an appreciation of what is at stake for each thinker. Aristotle's epistemology deviates in serious ways from his mentor's, and this

---

26. And with respect to this, we cannot ignore Aristotle's predilection for classifications in his biological works and beyond. Leroi (2014), in his detailed discussion of Aristotle's practiced studies of forms of life, associates the classification of animals with the "Academic obsession" with definitions. In several of his works, believes Leroi, Aristotle is tweaking Platonic division (106). This view needs to be set against the concerns Aristotle raises about division, in *Parts of Animals* (Aristotle 1984) for example: "Some writers propose to reach the ultimate forms of animal life by dividing the genus into two differences. But this method is often difficult and often impracticable" (*PA* 642b5–7).

27. Ross's translation (Aristotle 1984, edited by Barnes).

is reflected in the methods employed. At the same time, as I have already noted and we will see throughout the chapters of part III, the dialectical method is a complex matter for Plato, harboring several related components. The same may be said for Aristotle. There is much in the account of the *Topics* through which a vestigial Platonism still shines. And in several places, he may be seen to placate the Platonists. In *Topics* Book VIII at 157a7 and 164b4–7, he implies a relationship between dialectical skill and Platonic division. In the latter, we read that "putting forward propositions is making many things into one . . . while objecting is making one thing many." Here, he is referring to the respective dialectical proficiency of the questioner and the answerer. The intent may be as revisionist as the passage in the *Prior Analytics*. Or, as Robin Smith suggests, "he may also be trying to show that his method really meets Plato's expectations for dialectic" (Aristotle 1997b, 163). We would not expect Aristotle to fully embrace Plato's dialectic, but nor is his own account likely to be free from its echoes.

In her study of the ancient commentators on Plato and Aristotle, Miira Tuominen (2009) observes, "Behind the various argument techniques, Socrates, Plato and Aristotle found a general idea acceptable to them. Arguments succeed in persuading the interlocutor (perhaps to change his mind) when statements that he accepts in the course of the discussion are shown to contradict the claim that he made at the beginning" (74). While this may overstate the case in terms of the extent of agreement over the meaning of dialectic, there is clearly an underlying correctness to the remark. Tuominen is referring to the social contexts of argumentation that were reflected in the practices of the Academy and developed by Aristotle's later logical works. The link between Socratic practice (as seen in the activities of Socrates$_E$) and Aristotle's dialectic is clear. And insofar as this is captured in the curricula of the Academy, the Platonic connection is preserved. But as we have also seen, the attention to definitions may be the better common feature of each thinker's interest in dialectic. It is this aspect of Plato's thought that will receive attention in the remaining chapters.

In part of Hugh Benson's description of the account of dialectic in the *Republic*, this distinctive Platonic focus is captured along with a vestige of the Socratic (and Academic) interest in refutation: "Socrates explains that dialectic can give an account (*ho logos*) of what it knows (531d6–e6, 534b, and 534c), and can survive against all refutations (*elenchōn*). . . . He explains that the dialectician 'tries through argument (*tou logou*) and apart from all sense perceptions to find the being itself of each thing' (532a6–7)" (Benson 2009, 91). It is to this height that Aristotle declines to ascend, and while he is as interested as Plato in the "truth of things," it is not through dialectic that such knowledge is to be acquired.

So, over the course of three generations, dialectic travels from the immediacy experienced in the logic of lives to the heights of the forms and then back "down" to the opinions of general acceptance. Whether all three figures are equally interested in deductive inference remains to be seen. In the case of Socrates, it depends in part on how persuasive we take Aristotle's testimony on this point. In the case of Plato, we need to turn to the method of Hypothesis, a method that, as it appears in the *Meno*, Charles Kahn judges to be "the earliest known theoretical account of deductive inference" (Kahn 1996, 309).

Chapter 11

The Song that Dialectic Sings

Methods in the Middle Dialogues

> Isn't this at the last the song itself that dialectic performs? It is in the realm of the intelligible, but it is imitated by the power of sight.
>
> —Plato (*Rep.* 532a)[1]

Dialectic's Methods

The last chapter ended with Kahn's observation that the method of hypothesis provides us with the earliest account of deductive inference (Kahn 1996, 309). But he quickly moderates that claim, questioning whether this is deduction as we understand it (315). The examples provided from the *Meno* express the condition of a conditional sentence (*protasis*) but not the entire construct.[2] As Kahn explains in terms that echo the warning we drew from Robinson in part I, "The difficulty here is created, I suggest, by imposing our own notion of deduction on Plato's text. When I claimed above that Plato's method of hypothesis initiates the theory of deductive inference, the notion of deduction was taken somewhat loosely. Plato's conception of inference does not have the formal precision of Aristotle's syllogistic" (315–16). So, in line with this, and our earlier qualification about the nature of logic

---

1. From Allan Bloom's translation (Plato 1968).

2. Robinson (1941, 122) had initially judged the conditional form used to denote a single proposition but revised his judgment in a second edition (1953, 118).

developing in Plato's works, we need to assess the method of hypothesis on its own terms, determining how its nature fits the role that Plato assigns it.

A similar caution will attend the investigation of the method of Collection and Division later in this chapter. Both Benson (2009, 86) and Kahn (1996, 298) see the methods interrelated. Robinson suggests otherwise. But insofar as Plato is clearly advancing these methods under the common heading of "dialectic," is behooves us to consider whether indeed they have a common thread connecting them, whether they replace each other in some way, or whether that are each designed to accomplish something that remains distinct to that particular method. Likewise, the method of example that we explored in chapter 9 should be part of this comparative investigation. We begin with the method of Hypothesis that we last saw emerge in the *Meno* as an advance beyond the Socratic inquiry into definitions.

The *Ethos* of Argument

Like many "Where were you when?" events, the opening of the *Phaedo* has Echecrates pose just such a question to Phaedo about the death of Socrates. Phaedo was present, and ostensibly Plato (who we are told was absent) reports the firsthand testimony that Phaedo provides Echecrates. This is the dialogue renowned for its central concern with immortality—a natural topic of urgency under the circumstances—and provides major tenets of Plato's maturing thought in the discussions of asceticism, dualism, recollection, and the Forms as a theory of causation. But it also conveys important ideas about the nature of argumentation and the methods involved, sometimes self-reflectively.

At a pivotal moment in the dialogue, after Socrates's interlocutors Simmias and Cebes had respectively advanced their imagistic arguments involving the lyre and coat only to see those arguments fail, the "immediate" discussants—Echecrates and Phaedo—are brought back into the frame to reflect on the nature of arguments. "What argument shall we trust?" asks Echecrates (*Phd.* 88d).[3] In response, Phaedo praises Socrates's way of managing dialectical argument and his sensitive awareness of the way arguments impacted the audience and then reports on Socrates's praise of arguments themselves.

---

3. Except where noted, quotations from the *Phaedo* are based on the Reeve's translation (Plato 2012a).

The passage has similarities with that involving unruly arguments in the *Euthyphro*, where the participants were caught in a labyrinth of statements and Euthyphro and Socrates disputed which of the two of them was the mythical Daedalus figure who might find a route for their escape. Here, the mythical figures enlisted are Heracles and Iolaus (*Phd.* 89c). Phaedo recalls how Socrates had turned affectionately to him, stressing the importance of defeating the twin arguments of Simmias and Cebes. Phaedo replies:

Ph.: They say not even Heracles could fight two people.

Soc.: Then call on me as your Iolaus, as long as the daylight lasts.

Ph.: I shall call on you, but in this case as Iolaus calling on Heracles.

Soc.: It makes no difference, but first there is a certain experience we must avoid. (*Phd.* 89c)

Which of them is Heracles and which Iolaus remains unclear; what matters is the nature of the labors that they share, and these labors involve argumentation. The experience of which they both must be wary is misology—the hatred of arguments, and here Socrates draws another important analogy.

Misologists are like misanthropes, observes Socrates, and "there is no greater evil one can suffer than to hate discourse (*logos misésas*)" (*Phd.* 89d). Given the context here, where the logos of interest is between interlocutors discoursing together, the concern is a hatred not just of arguments but of dialectical arguments, involving other people. This reinforces the parallels that Plato wants to impress here between misology and misanthropy.

In the closing chapter of part I, I noted the importance of ethos (character) to the Greek way of mind and its relationship to good argumentation. The value of trust is never far from the Greek mind, and this is no less true for Plato. Misanthropy, as Socrates explains, involves a loss of trust, the failure of ethos to retain its importance in human relations. "Misanthropy arises when a person without knowledge or skill has placed great trust in someone and believes that person to be altogether truthful, sound, and trustworthy, then . . . [the trusted person] is found to be wicked and unreliable" (*Phd.* 89d). When this happens several times, especially with erstwhile friends, a hatred toward all humans arises. That this happens to someone "without knowledge of skill" suggests there is an art involved, it is an extension of the importance of human psychology that we have seen elsewhere. In fact, this is subsequently confirmed: if people have such skill or art, they will see that the extremes in human nature are quite rare, with the characters of most people lying in between. The need to develop an ability of measuring character relative to a standard seems to echo the earlier dependence on a standard to measure other relatives like equality, and the role that Recollection played in identifying that standard.

The rarity of the extremes, however, is suggested not to apply to arguments. There, the stronger similarity is that "when one who lacks skill in arguments puts their trust in an argument as being true, then shortly afterwards believes it to be false—as sometimes it is and sometimes it is not—and so with another argument and then another" (*Phd.* 90b). Such a person, like those who study *antilogoi* (disputations), will come to think there is no trust or reliability to be placed in arguments but that they will fluctuate like a river and "not remain in the same place for any time at all" (*Phd.* 90c). Thus, a loss of trust in the ethos of arguments parallels a loss of trust in the ethos of humanity, all deriving from a failure to develop the art in question.

The consequences are serious: if a person spends their life hating and reviling dialectical argument, then they will "be *deprived of truth and knowledge of reality*" (*Phd.* 90d). I emphasize this line because it indicates the association in Plato's mind between dialectical argument and the ability to acquire knowledge and truth. In light of this, the "no greater evil" than misology claim takes on its real force.

An Inner Dialogue

Socrates then makes a statement that should cause us to pause and consider the challenges that it suggests to dialectical discussion. The course of the inquiry has reflected the regular patterns of Socratic dialogue, with several minds thinking together to achieve an outcome that benefits them all. This has always been a benefit of Socratic inquiry, where the outcomes of discussions have ramifications for the lives of those involved. And, on one level, the same holds here; nothing could be more relevant to Socrates's circumstances than determining the prospects for immortality. And Socrates allows as much when he points to the benefits of their discussion because of his "impending death," and the others' "future lives" (*Phd.* 91a). But he follows this with a more problematic admission: "I shall not be very eager to make what I say seem true to my hearers, except as a secondary matter, but shall be very eager to make myself believe it. For see, my friend, how selfish my attitude is" (*Phd.* 91a–b).

Several times in earlier chapters the question of self-deliberation has entered the discussion.[4] Here, we return to give the topic further consideration because of its significance for the themes of this dialogue. After all, how might this selfish deliberation bring him to believe what he says? Such advocacy of introspection seems quite at odds with the general Socratic practice of "reasoning together" to ascertain what is true. That is, it seems at odds with general practice until we consider that there is still a dialogue involved, but this time an internal one. This is made clear in a passage from the *Theaetetus*. There, Socrates defines thinking and judgment in terms of a speech that the soul has with itself:

> Soc.: Very good. Now by "thinking" do you mean the same as I do?
>
> Theaet: What do you mean by it?
>
> Soc: A talk which the soul has with itself about the objects under its consideration. Of course, I'm only telling you my idea in all ignorance; but this is the kind of picture I have of it. It seems to me that the soul when it thinks is simply carrying on a discussion in which it asks itself questions and answers them itself, affirms and denies. And when it arrives at something definite, either by a gradual process or a sudden leap, when it confirms one thing consistently and without divided counsel, we call this its judgment. So, in my view, to judge is to make a statement, and a judgment is a statement which is not addressed to another person or spoken aloud, but silently addressed to oneself. And what do you think?
>
> Theaet: I agree with that. (*Tht.* 189e–190a)[5]

What is advocated here is an internal, silent dialogue modeled on one's social experience. It suggests that we become more accomplished reasoners

---

4. The importance of self-deliberation arose when exploring Plato's account of argument in chapter 3 and in chapter 4's discussion of methodology.

5. From the Hackett translation of M. J. Levett, revised by Myles Burnyeat (Plato 1997b).

by taking the lessons we learn from reasoning together and adopting them strictly for ourselves. The reference to the practice of asking questions and answering them confirms what we have seen in the social group. The reference to arriving at a conclusion "without divided counsel" indicates an internal agreement that strengthens the belief.

This sense of the self as an audience for its own deliberations is especially emphasized in an extended discussion between Socrates and the Sophist Hippias in the *Hippias Major*. Hippias is an advocate of the large, expansive speech and contrasts this with the Socratic propensity for the "flakings and clippings of speeches" (*H.Ma.* 304a). The Socratic approach is criticized for taking the mass of a thing and dividing it up with words, freezing things in isolation for examination, and tearing them from the natural flow of discourse. Hippias is concerned that this separates things from their specific context.[6] What Hippias values is to be able to present a speech well and to successfully persuade others of the position at issue. In the course of this exchange between Hippias and Socrates over the relative merits of types of speech, Socrates employs a strategy that does not directly attack the points raised by Hippias but instead invokes a shadowy dissenter (someone who Socrates accuses of questioning him quite insultingly, *H.Ma.* 286c–d). Socrates then takes on the persona of that other man so that Hippias is to answer Socrates as if this other is the actual questioner (*H.Ma.* 287c). Socrates stresses how important it is that he, Socrates, be able to convince this other man, who he eventually identifies as Sophronicus's son, that is, as Socrates himself (*H.Ma.* 298c).

This indirect strategy is puzzling in itself.[7] It is only when read in conjunction with the passages from the *Phaedo* and *Theaetetus* that a rationale emerges. It is possible that the intent of the strategy is to allow Socrates to insult someone like Hippias who is so antithetical in nature to everything that Plato represents. Given Hippias's boasting of his proficiency in diverse areas, he is thought to be the Sophist who Plato sees most fit for ridicule. But Socrates states often that he agrees with the insults of this other man, so he is hardly a buffer between the insults and the person insulted. Rather, we should see in this device Plato reaffirming what we are recognizing here as having particular importance: a preference for silent, internal argumentation. Where Hippias promotes argumentation in the public domain, Plato, on

---

6. The same point is made in the *Hippias Minor* (369b–c).

7. See Woodruff (1982, 43, n47; 108) for a discussion of the controversy surrounding Plato's use of this device. Some see it as non-Platonic, but Woodruff makes a strong case for its authenticity.

this occasion, promotes the internal dialogue of self-deliberation. Socrates's venture into the public domain, on these terms, is to harvest arguments with which he can then withdraw into the private sphere and deliberate upon in order to convince himself.

The *Phaedo's* misology passage thus introduces us to another dimension of dialectical argument, one that is consistent with the earlier benefits that we saw accruing to the dialogues' interlocutors. Through the practice of reasoning together, examining commitments and—now—hypotheses, the participants become better reasoners per se. They can develop as cognitive beings more confident in their beliefs insofar as they are able to judge the strength of those beliefs. As the hypotheses develop in the dialogue, we remind ourselves of who it is who most needs to be convinced.

Hypothetically

When the investigation resumes, the arguments of Simmias and Cebes are tested again. And Simmias promptly cedes his harmony proposal to the more compelling explanation provided by the theory of Recollection, because his harmony argument "came to me without demonstration (*apódeixis*); it seemed merely likely and attractive, which is the reason why many hold it. I am aware that those arguments which base their demonstration on mere probability are deceptive, and if we are not on our guard against them they deceive us greatly, in geometry and in all other things. But the theory of recollection and knowledge is based on a hypothesis worthy of acceptance" (*Phd.* 92c–d). This hypothesis—the theory of Recollection—was introduced earlier (*Phd.* 72e–73a). In that passage, they had decided that the living come from the dead and the souls of the dead still exist. Cebes observes that further support for this is to be seen "if that theory is true that you are accustomed to mention frequently, that learning is no other than recollection" (*Phd.* 72e). *If* the theory is true, *then* they must have existed at some previous time. Cebes poses the matter in a hypothetical way even here. At Simmias's request, Cebes then recalls the arguments supporting the theory, with an implicit reference back to the *Meno* (81e–ff). Given the support provided, the theory serves as a principle on which other ideas can be built. One of those subsequent ideas is the theory of Forms, which will be introduced later but which (as Kahn notes) is *the* fundamental hypothesis of the *Phaedo* and had "served as the basis for Socrates's position throughout the dialogue" (1996, 314).

It is later, though, at 100a that Socrates explicitly addresses the method he is using when he offers a bit of feigned autobiography. To explore the truth of things, he turned away from his senses and investigated with his mind, "taking as [his] hypothesis in each case the theory that seemed to [him] most compelling, [he] would consider as true, about cause and everything else, whatever agreed with this, and as untrue whatever did not agree" (*Phd.* 100a). Fearing he is unclear, he identifies the theory in question as that of the Forms, here given as a causal theory.[8] What makes something beautiful, for example, is its unexplained relationship to the Beautiful. This is the safe answer that satisfies him and in line with which he will never fall into error. This is the self-deliberator from earlier in the dialogue exposing the results of his inner dialogue to his friends.

Accepting this, he explains to Cebes how he should proceed, warning that he must not confuse what follows from the hypothesis with the hypothesis itself, as those who engage in antilogoi do. Socrates states that the inexperienced Cebes would not accept additions and divisions, but would

> cling to the safety of your own hypothesis and give that answer. If someone then attacked your hypothesis itself, you would ignore him and would not answer until you had examined whether the consequences follow and seen whether they agreed with one another or not. And when you must give an account of the hypothesis itself you will proceed in the same way: you will assume another hypothesis, the one that seems best to you of the higher ones until you come to something acceptable, but you will not mix up the two as the antilogoi do by discussing the hypothesis and its consequences at the same time, if you wish to discover any truth. (101d–e)

To hypothesize is to put forward a proposition as a candidate for investigation and to then see where that proposition leads. The hypothesis becomes a basic premise that is not itself investigated[9] and on which is built a series of statements.

In both passages noted above (*Phd.* 100a and 101d), Plato uses a term that has occasioned disagreement among commentators and challenged

---

8. As opposed to the Forms as a theory of mimesis or a theory of illumination, which we find elsewhere.

9. In the *Definitions*, "hypothesis" is defined as "indemonstrable first principle" (*Def.* 415b).

contemporary sensibilities. When Socrates writes, for example, that he will consider as true "whatever agreed with" or is in harmony with (*sumphonein*) the hypothesis, and as untrue "whatever did not agree" with it, the meaning of the term and the relationship involved is unclear. Might it mean, for example "follow from" or "entailed by" (Robinson [1941] 1953, 129ff)? Strict logical entailment of the kind that is reflected in contemporary logical systems produces some implausible results. Could Plato seriously believe that *anything* that does not follow from a hypothesis is thereby false? On one level of course, a hypothesis as fundamental to Plato's system as the theory of Forms would have overarching explanatory force. Something not consistent with that explanation would not be accepted but the same could not be held for some of the less all-encompassing hypotheses such as that concerning the teachability of virtue in the *Meno*. Robinson sees only two plausible interpretations, neither of which is completely palatable. Either Socrates is advocating whatever is consistent with a hypothesis or what follows logically from it. In the first case, we would be justified in "adopting every proposition that is not contradicted by our hypothesis"; in the second case, any proposition not implied by a hypothesis is judged false (130). Robinson adopts the consistency reading, and I think this is correct. This itself is consistent with our (and Robinson's) earlier reluctance to impose modern-day requirements on Plato's texts, which a choice of, say, an "entailment" reading would seem to involve. This preferred interpretation also accords with the general advocacy of "harmonizing" ideas found elsewhere (*Phdr.* 270c; *Prt.* 333a; *Grg.* 457e). In support of this reading is David Gallop's recourse to the context in which Socrates's remarks are to be applied (Plato 1975b, 181). Gallop takes the ensuing passage (*Phd.* 100b–101c) not only to illustrate what is judged to be the strongest hypothesis but also to establish as true whatever is in harmony with it. Judging beautiful things beautiful because they accord with the Beautiful is thus an illustration of how harmony or "agreeing with" (*sumphonein*) should be read here. And this in turn should be understood in light of Socrates's "autobiographical" needs. He wants arguments that will convince himself in his current situation. As Gallop suggests, we need to attend to the method's "role in the quest for 'reasons' " (181). The hypothesis involved includes both the existence of the Forms and their primary function in causing the nature of particulars: the Beautiful exists and causes beauty in beautiful things. Propositions that are in harmony with *this* are acceptable to Socrates; those that are relevant to the Form-particular hypothesis but are not in harmony with it are not acceptable. On this reading, *sumphonein* is not equivalent to logical consistency and does not commit Socrates to any judgment about other, irrelevant propositions. Gallop again: "The great mass of propositions, having no relevance to the issue about which any given hypothesis is put forward, will be neither 'in accord' nor 'not in accord' with it" (181).

Both Robinson and Gallop in their own ways provide a less rigorous reading of the manner in which the Hypothetical method is expected to work. And they point toward the construction of a model that collects ideas that belong together in a related account, rather than independent propositions that follow from each other. This reading is reinforced by the method's appearance in the *Meno* discussion and confirmed by the more technical explanation of the *Republic*.

As we recall, Socrates claims to have borrowed the method of Hypothesis from the geometers (an association echoed in the *Phaedo* [92d]) and his first illustration cements that connection. Having demonstrated the method with the boy from Meno's household, the larger challenge is to adopt it for more general, nongeometrical inquiries. Several things stand out as they proceed:

> Soc: Since we do not know what sort of thing [virtue] is, let's consider by adopting a hypothesis whether it is something acquired by teaching. Let's proceed as follows: Among the things belonging to the soul, what sort would virtue have to be if it is to be something not acquired by teaching, or not something acquired by teaching? First, if it is a different sort of thing than knowledge, or the same sort, is it acquired by teaching or not—or as we said just now, acquired by recollection? It makes no difference to us which name is used. Let's say acquired by teaching. Or isn't this, at least, clear to everyone, that a person is not taught anything except knowledge?
>
> Men: I think so.
>
> Soc: But if virtue is some sort of knowledge, it clearly would be acquired by teaching.
>
> Men: Of course.
>
> Soc: So, we finished that quickly. (*Meno* 87b–c)

This is the discussion that formed the bridge between this chapter and the last. Hypotheses respond to ignorance, testing possible ways forward. Here, they are introduced simply to see whether what follows from them is of value in addressing the issue in question. And, as we see, false routes are quickly identified. I will not pursue the elaborate investigation that ensues since my interest here is only to identify features of the method that inform (or conflict with) those in the *Phaedo* (see Robinson [1941] 1953, 115–16). Two things stand out. First, there is an insistence at *Meno* 87d that a sign of a good hypothesis is that it stands firm. When the two inquirers worry about the hypothesis that virtue is knowledge, Meno observes that it seemed fine a while ago, to which Socrates responds: "If it is going to be sound, it must seem right not just a moment ago, but also now and in the future" (*Meno* 89c). This reflects an earlier concern of the Socratic dialectic; one that the moving statements of the *Euthyphro*, for example, had emphasized. It anticipates the promotion of this feature of standing firm as that which distinguishes knowledge from correct belief, which will be introduced toward the end of the dialogue with the reappearance of those ambulatory statues of Daedalus (*Meno* 97d–e).

Second, of particular relevance to the debate that accompanies the *Phaedo* concerning the polysemy of *sumphonein*, is a remark Meno makes in response to one of Socrates's proposals: "That necessarily follows from what has been agreed" (*Meno* 87e). The language here is courtesy of G. M. A. Grube's Hackett translation (Plato 1997a). The text provides *anankē ek tōn hōmologemēnōn*, and we have already seen why commentators and translators are attracted to the power of *anankē* here. One disposed to see in Plato a concern for the power of entailment will find it confirmed in this apparent acknowledgment of deductive necessity. And, indeed, we can reconstruct the reasoning to express such insight (see Kahn 1996, 311). The question remains, though, whether this is a *Platonic* reading of the passage (Kahn doubts as much [1996, 331n30]) or whether we should adopt a weaker rendering of the line, with more emphasis on what coheres with the former agreement. This power of harmony or agreement is what we found suggested in the *Phaedo*, and it remains an equally if not more compelling reading.

This *Phaedo* account, illuminating the discussion of misology and deepening the understanding of what was first introduced in the *Meno*, provides what commentators call "the downward path" (Kahn 1996, 317; Robinson [1941] 1953). The contrasting use of hypotheses, and thus the development of what Plato has to say about them, involves an upward path, toward the unhypothetical. This is the crux of the account derived from the discussion of the Divided Line in Book VI of the *Republic*.

The Line, as we have seen, challenges Glaucon's grasp of philosophical ideas. He fares well in the lower half, dealing with what is visible, but he struggles with the shift to the intelligible realm. And it is there that hypotheses play a crucial role. As Socrates recounts, drawing on the practices of geometers and mathematicians:

> I think you know that students of geometry, calculation, and the like hypothesize the odd and the even, the various figures, the three kinds of angles, and other things akin to these in each of their methodical inquiries, regarding them as known. These they treat as hypotheses and do not think it necessary to give any account of them, either to themselves or to others, as if they were evident to everyone. And going from these first principles through the remaining steps, they arrive in full agreement at the point they set out to reach in their investigation. (*Rep.* 510c–d)

These hypotheses are not being tested as those of our earlier discussions were. They have passed such testing and are accepted as basic without need for support. This, in fact, Glaucon knows, so his knowledge is not restricted to things of the visible realm. Socrates continues, explaining that these practitioners make their discourses about visible things, while all the time thinking about the intelligible realities that they reflect—the square and the diagonal, for example. They use these images in pursuit of what can be seen by thought alone. This Glaucon also understands. And the account progresses, further upward: "Soc: This, then, is the kind of thing I said was intelligible. The soul is compelled to use hypotheses in the investigation of it, not traveling up to a first principle, since it cannot escape or get above its hypotheses, but using as images those very things of which images were made by the things below them, and which, by comparison to their images were thought to be clear and to be honoured as such" (*Rep.* 511a). This too Glaucon grasps, that the soul's investigation of the intelligible requires and depends upon the use of hypotheses and that they stand out in clarity against what lies below them. It is the next section that leaves hypotheses behind and relies on the power of dialectic. And this is where Glaucon's ability to follow fails him: "Also understand, then, that by the other subsection of the intelligible I mean what reason itself grasps by the power of dialectical discussion, treating its hypotheses, not as first principles, but as genuine hypotheses—underpinnings and stepping stones—in order to arrive at what is unhypothetical and the first principle of everything" (*Rep.* 511b). Having grasped *this*, the soul is able to turn and move back down, seeing the connections (the combinations) of all things, and, presumably, distinguishing them by division. We have moved naturally into the apparent use of another method, that of Collection and Division. But first, there is more to note here about hypothesis. The limits of the Method of Hypothesis mark the distinction between the two sections of the intelligible realm. While the knowledge of the first section—what, for a better term we will call "scientific knowledge"—depends on them; the dialectical knowledge of the upper section leaves them behind. In Book VII of the *Republic*, Plato reinforces this idea: "Dialectic is the only method of inquiry that, destroying the hypotheses, journeys to the first principle itself in order to be made secure" (*Rep.* 533c). This explains why the method disappears from the later accounts of Plato's dialectic.

The dialectician now emerges in possession of surer, firmer knowledge. Knowledge that can be communicated in an account. A dialectician is "able to grasp an account of the being of each thing," and failing this—"to give an account either to *himself* or to another"—there is no understanding (*Rep.* 534b). The refrain that began in the earlier examples of Socratic dialectic echoes here: if someone cannot give an account of what they know, they cannot be said to know. How this works remains unclear. As we saw in an earlier chapter, Socrates feels he has pushed Glaucon just about as far as he is capable of going, and so the latter's request to be told "in what way the power of dialectical discussion works, into what kinds it is divided, and what roads it follows" (*Rep.* 532a) remains unanswered, in part because "the power of dialectical discussion could reveal [its insights] only to someone experienced in the subjects we described" (*Rep.* 533a).

Collecting and Dividing

The dialectician is distinguished from the scientific practitioner in the lower section of the Line by a number of characteristics (see Reeve 1988, 72ff), but chief among these is that ability "to grasp an account of the being of each thing" (*Rep.* 534b), armed with which the return down the Line is conducted in terms of Forms and no longer reliant on any object of sense. It is a different way of seeing and, ostensibly, a different method than that which used hypotheses. It also may pave the way for Plato to solve problems that have perplexed him. Runciman (1962, 58) sees in the method of Collection and Division answers to the problem of error found in the *Theaetetus* and the problem of intercommunication between Forms in the *Parmenides*.

In his commentary on the *Philebus*, Hackforth remarks that the dialectical method we see practiced there is more one of Division than Collection and Division (Plato 1972, 26), leaving open the question of just how much this is a two-pronged method.[10] Indeed, as we anticipate the searches for the Sophist or Statesman in the respective later dialogues, we cannot fail to observe how reliant they are on the use of Division. But the correctness of this observation may be down to what is reflected in the lateness of the accounts in dialogues like the *Philebus*, where Glaucon may have found his answer to how the power of dialectical discussion works. The ability to divide assumes a grasp of unities, although this would suggest that the two parts operate separately and the participants in those late dialogues have achieved proficiency of the first (Collection) in order to practice the second (Division).[11] We will pursue this in chapter 12. Here, the interest is in exploring Collection and Division in combination and determining its role in Platonic dialectic, and I will retain the full name when mentioning the method.

Robinson describes them as "two parts of dialectic," one of which is "synthesis or generalization" and the other "division or classification" ([1941] 1953, 162). This fuels the view that by the upward and downward paths on the Line, Plato means the "method" of Collection and Division, as this is described elsewhere (*Phdr.* 265–66). Robinson believes such a view must be rejected, since it ascribes to Plato certain implausible beliefs or motives. He does not think that Plato would have viewed the Good (that pinnacle of the Line) as the *summum genus*, which the interpretation requires. Nor does he think collecting the genus in each case could make sense of "destroying the hypotheses." More importantly, while the notions of synthesis and division arise in the *Republic*, the terms that are used elsewhere do not.[12] At stake here is how much we expect one "part" of the larger dialectical method to map onto others. Appealing to the problem of the Good is essentially a debate stopper; there is little provided with which to move further. Once a genus has been satisfactorily achieved and the classification filled, there is no need for further hypothesizing. As the mind turns to division, it proceeds from an unhypothesized beginning.

---

10. Griswold (1986, 173) makes the same remark about Division and Collection in the *Phaedrus*.

11. Lloyd (1966) insists that Division is preceded in theory by Collection, but not always in practice (432).

12. In Book V (*Rep.* 454a) Socrates protests to Glaucon that those who practice eristics fall into contradiction because they focus on verbal opposition being unable "to consider the subject by dividing it into kinds."

The *Phaedrus* explicitly introduces the complementary moves of Collection and Division as related to each other, but the notions involved have been employed elsewhere. The *Cratylus*, for example, makes ample use of divisions (*Cra.* 424c; 425b). But these usages make no mention of dialectic.[13] The thrust of the account in the *Phaedrus* corrects this and inaugurates a general conception of dialectic that will serve Plato's purposes henceforth. The method of Hypothesis recedes into the silence of disuse. Whether it retains its potential for people at a particular stage of philosophical development remains possible, but for those like Phaedrus and the Socrates of the dialogue it has been superseded. The new focus matches Plato's metaphysical scheme of the One over the Many.

In chapter 6's examination of the development of rhetoric in the *Phaedrus*, I passed over the details of the account given of Collection and Division, noting only some aspects of its subsequent importance. This is the place to detail that account. Socrates is reviewing the importance of the second speech (the palinode), stressing certain features that, if grasped by art, would be of great value. There are two things assigned such value: "Soc.: For him whose sight comprehends things dispersed in many places to bring them into one idea, so that by dividing each thing, he makes clear what, on each occasion, he wishes to teach about. Just as the things said just now about love—what it is when divided—whether they were said well or badly, the speech was able through these things to say that which is distinct, at any rate, and itself in agreement with itself" (*Phdr.* 265d).[14] Beyond the process of bringing into one idea (Collection) and then dividing, what stands out here is the back reference to the concept they have been examining (love) and the test that the result be in agreement with itself.

Phaedrus then asks about the other thing of note, to which Socrates responds:

> Soc,: To be able, contrariwise, to cut apart forms, according to where the joints have naturally grown, and not to endeavour to shatter any part, in the manner of a bad butcher. But just as the two speeches, a little while ago, took the thought's folly as some one form in common, just as from one body the parts

---

13. Nor are the results of division particularly impressive in the *Cratylus* (Kahn 2013, 80).

14. James Nichols Jr. (Plato 1998b) renders ὁρίζω as "define," I have used "divide" to capture the process rather than the goal of the method.

have naturally grown double and of the same name (some called left, others right), so too the business of derangement, as the two speeches consider it one natural form in us, the one speech cut the part on the left, and cutting this further, did not leave off before it discovered among them a certain left-handed love, so named, which it reviled very much in accord with justice; the other speech, leading us toward the parts of madness on the right side, discovering something with the same name as that, a certain love that was in turn divine and, holding it out before us, praised it as the cause of the greatest goods for us. (*Phdr.* 265e–266b)

Strangely, Roochnik (2003) finds problems with what he calls the sparsity of the account here and complains that as a method it is out of synch with the way Socrates proceeds (134). But this both overlooks the context in which it has been introduced and ignores the explicit references in the above passages to the way the previous speeches have illustrated the method, dividing on one side and the other, with each speech pursuing the divisions further on each side. The dialectician proceeds like a butcher, the divisions are "natural" cuts at the joints. These natural cuts will be illustrated in the elaborate divisions of the *Sophist*, *Statesman*, and *Philebus*.

Furthermore, as I stressed in chapter 6, when Socrates insists that "a human being must understand that which is said in reference to a Form, that which, going from many perceptions, is gathered together into one by reasoning. And this is the recollection of those things that our soul saw once upon a time" (*Phdr.* 249b–c), he announces a methodical principle that will make possible the processes of division central to the later searches for definition. This collection into one through reasoning (*ek pollōn ion aisthēseon eis hen logismōi sunairoumenon*) is the primary accomplishment of the philosopher. In fact, this is a passage Roochnik overlooks in his critique, focusing rather on the more explicit introduction at 265d.[15]

Granted, we do not find here the complexity of application that awaits us in late dialogues, but (and again as Griswold observes [1986, 182–83]), Socrates's aim here is to provide a general description of a method, not a

---

15. Roochnik grounds his critical reading on that of Griswold (1986), but Griswold's principal complaint is that the description Socrates provides belies the complexity of what it is supposed to illustrate. Indeed, Griswold is able to provide divisions of both madness (179) and eros (181) based on the indications provided.

detailed account of his own practice in the speeches of the dialogue. This is indicated in Socrates's subsequent praise (and apparent recommendation) of the method he has described: "And I myself, for one, Phaedrus, am a lover of these dividings apart and bringing together, so that I may be capable of speaking and thinking" (*Phdr.* 266b).[16] Here, Plato introduces the word *diairesis* in his description of the tandem procedure along with *synagoge* for the first time in the dialogue. With hesitation, he calls those who can do this dialecticians, whose company the figure bearing his name will join in the *Philebus*.

Plato's "Best" Method

For Hugh Benson, "the methods of hypothesis introduced in the *Meno* and again in the *Phaedo* and the method of dialectic explicitly introduced in the *Republic* are versions of a single core method" (2009, 86). This might be a difficult thesis to sustain in light of some of the key differences we have explored. Robinson ([1941] 1953) insists that Plato's "ideal" method was "whatever seemed to him at the moment the most hopeful procedure" (70), with various candidates playing this role at different stages of his life. While there is a sense of correctness about this (the Hypothetical method, for example, plays no obvious role beyond the middle dialogues), it should also be noted that the "hopeful procedure" is understood in terms of a consistent target—the ultimate reality that can be known, and once known, can improve human affairs. The search for what is fixed and immovable, always constant in its truth, is the continuous concern. Leaving behind the frustrations of Daedalus's ambulatory statues, Plato enlists a set of methods more suited to this task than the limited power of Socratic dialectic. To this end the evolving method of hypothesis is directed ultimately toward the upward path of the intelligible realm to be resolved in the unhypothetical principles discovered there. To the degree that they may offer a "downward" path for discovering particular truths, this is refined in the method of Col-

---

16. Compare this last claim with the following remark in the *Parmenides*: "If someone, having an eye on all the difficulties we have just brought up and others of the same sort, won't allow that there are forms for things and won't mark off a form for each one, he won't have anywhere to turn his thought, since he does not allow that for each thing there is a character that is always the same. In this way he will destroy the power of *dialegesthai* [discourse; dialectic] entirely" (135b–c).

lection and Division where the language of the One over the Many will come into its own. These methods deserve the title of "dialectic" insofar as they share a common end and insofar as they meet the needs of people at different stages in their cognitive journeys.

Moreover, whether we are looking back at Socrates or ahead to Aristotle, dialectic centers on the practices of conversation, of "talking together" (*dialegesthai*), and in this sense, the Hypothetical method and Collection and Division stand out as the most advanced versions of cooperative inquiry. David Timmerman (1993) together with Edward Schiappa (Timmerman and Schiappa 2010) track the development of *dialegesthai* through dialogues like the *Protagoras* and *Gorgias* (2010, 21–26) but also identify passages corroborating Plato's usage in the *Dissoi Logoi* and Xenophon (23, 28–30). In distancing it from earlier Sophistic practice, Timmerman and Schiappa note of *dialegesthai* that sometimes Plato links it "with the method of division (*dihairesis*) and other times with the testing of hypotheses" (37). These two reflect the most advanced sense of talking together, far removed from the lighter conversational sense with which the term is also associated. But Plato's dialectic is not limited to these two methods; the rhetorician now accompanies the dialectician and so the methodological strategies may also include mythical discourse or the use of images and examples, depending on the audience.

The method of Example, for instance, that we earlier saw as playing a complementary role with other devices and serving the needs of specific participants in the dialogues, now finds a clear place in the dialectical toolbox. Examples, or paradigms, have their own important development: "[Socrates] builds up the concept of "paradigm" by defining it in contrast to *phantasmata* (phantasms) and *eidola* (shadow-images) while linking it closely to *tupoi* (types)," the latter serving as a synonym for either *paradeigma* or *eikones* (Allen 2010, 148). More than this, we have seen how closely the use of examples arises with the use of analogies or comparisons. This contributory method continues throughout, present in the *Republic* and central to the success of an investigation like that of the *Statesman*.

We should also pay attention to the difference between method and use. While we can see a method of hypothesis, it is more difficult to speak of a "method" of images, even though we found them to be an important strategy employed with growing facility by Socrates in order to further the educations of others. But insofar as images carry over into the use of comparisons (or analogy), a more coherent method takes its place alongside the others in the middle dialogues. In spite of the rarity of the term *analogia*,[17] analogies as we understand them are a pervasive "technique" of persuasion throughout Plato's work from the earliest dialogue to the *Laws* (Lloyd 1966, 402). This is one thesis advanced by Robinson with which we can agree. He devotes the penultimate chapter of his study[18] to the ways in which the method of hypothesis relies on image and analogy "in order to persuade us and also apparently in order to intuit the truth" (1941, 202, 204). We have reviewed the power of Plato's analogies, especially as they are used in the *Republic*, in an earlier discussion, drawing heavily on Llyod's seminal studies (1966; 2015). The ship's pilot or captain and the ruler of the state provide a lot of traction in the development of Plato's political reasoning. But this is just one noteworthy analogy among the many that Plato employs.

Analogy operates when the universal is absent. It "seems to be essentially an argument from a single case to a single case." And it depends on a particular kind of intuition, "to see into one thing by insight obtained on another" (Robinson [1941] 1953, 207).[19] This accomplishment is most impressive when it occurs on a larger scale, as with the insights that weaving provides into the operations of ruling a state in the *Statesman*. Example as explained in that dialogue effectively operates as analogy does on terms that are consistent with a more contemporary understanding of this type of reasoning.

This interweaving of strategies, if not methods, suggests that any search for a "best" or "ideal" method would be conducted in vain. The song that dialectic performs (*Rep.* 532a) is a medley, with a number of parts. Beyond the variety of competencies among those making use of the various methods, there are the contexts of use that may dictate the means employed. We see this in the activities of those operating more comfortably in the visible realm and struggling to move beyond it. What is clear is that those most proficient, who are able to use these methods on the way to achieving clear and stable definitions, are those Plato judges dialecticians. These stand apart

---

17. It occurs no more than a handful of times (most frequently three, in the *Timaeus*) and invariably is used to describe mathematical proportion (Robinson [1941] 1953, 209).

18. In the first edition (1941), it is the final chapter.

19. Robinson also notes places where Plato cautions against the use of analogy, and that he never really indicates how to determine when an analogy is good and when not. "There is," surmises Robinson, "no harmonization of these conflicting judgements" ([1941] 1953, 217).

from others in what they know and how they can communicate it. They are not the accomplished communicators of political persuasion for which rhetoric retains a necessary power. They belong to the more elite caste of Plato's preferred community. We will consider their nature and practices in the next chapter.

Chapter 12

The Dialectician

> [Dialectic] is the Method, or Discipline, that brings with it the power of pronouncing with final truth upon the nature and relation of things—what each is, how it differs from others, what common quality all have.
>
> —Plotinus (*Enneads* I, iii, 4)

The Candidates

Those who can collect and divide proficiently, says the Socrates of the *Phaedrus*, have a natural capacity to look to the one and the many and understand what is involved. He calls them dialecticians or experts in dialectic (266b–c). Jonathan Barnes (2007), in discussing Plotinian dialectic, observes that for the philosopher logic is but a tool, whereas dialectic is part of the individual's expertise (451).[1] It becomes appropriate, even necessary, for Plato to provide us with examples of such experts, and this he does in some of his later dialogues. The first thing that must strike us about the

---

1. This helps associate the philosopher with the dialectician. Bearing in mind Plato's insistence that a person performs one role well, seeing these two as distinct remains difficult. Aristides observed that while Plato seemed to designate his work as "philosophy," he used the word in two senses: often assigning it to "lovers of what is fine and lovers of learning, in a way close to the majority usage"; but also in a "restricted sense" to describe those who "deal in the Forms" (Aristides 2021, 553–55). In part II, we saw the popular usage employed at the close of the *Phaedrus*, even as the category of dialecticians emerged. And the philosophical education of Glaucon in the *Republic* involved dealing in the Forms, the domain of dialectic.

primary figures of these dialogues is that "Socrates," even Socrates$_M$, recedes into the background for some of the more powerful demonstrations. This could plunge us back into the Socratic problem if we were so inclined.[2] But the focus should remain on the task at hand, which is the nature of the late dialectic. Besides, Socrates's reappearance at the helm in the *Philebus* simply adds a further layer to that problem. What we have are several candidates to consider as bona fide dialecticians, with "Socrates" among them. Chief among these characters is the Eleatic visitor.

This visitor (*xenos*) from Elea, on whom history has conferred the even more enigmatic title "Stranger," is an addition to the company of the *Theaetetus* at the start of the *Sophist*.[3] Theodorus brings him along and introduces him by association rather than name. He is "from Elea, a member of the circle of Parmenides and Zeno, and a man very much a philosopher" (*Sph.* 216a).[4] Given a choice between a longer, uninterrupted discourse and a question and answer exchange, he chooses the latter (217c). In addition to the two Eleatic philosophers mentioned above it is wise to add a third name not mentioned, that of Melissus,[5] since he is associated with a clearer position on dialectic.

---

2. Rowe (2006) investigates the constancy of the Socratic character. Of the spokespersons in the later dialogues, he considers that "there is nothing in the actual processes of reflection exhibited by these speakers that marks them off from Socrates when he appears in the main role." And he notes that Socrates has announced himself in the *Phaedrus* a fan of the method of Collection and Division, the very method that unfolds in the *Sophist* and *Statesman* (167). For an alternative view see Corlett (2005, 25–73), who reviews the "mouthpiece" debate, including the case of the *Sophist*.

3. The *Sophist* begins with a reference back to the agreement to reconvene made between those who comprised the party of the *Theaetetus*. This indicates that we have a set of three related dialogues, since the *Statesman* continues the examination into the Sophist and Statesman (with the final investigation of the Philosopher not undertaken). The company of the *Theaetetus* includes the mathematicians Theaetetus and Theodorus, along with the Young Socrates (who will take over from Theaetetus as respondent to questions in the *Statesman*).

4. Christopher Gill observes that, while we cannot be sure of the philosophical character assigned to the Stranger, "the use of division as a means of systematic and detailed classification-cum-definition is confined to this figure in [the *Sophist* and *Statesman*]" (1996, 294).

5. What we know of Melissus tends to involve his doctrines rather than his methodology. Diogenes devotes one of his shortest entries to this Eleatic, identifying him as a pupil of Parmenides and ascribing to him a similar theory of being that is one, immovable and insusceptible to change. Aristotle's many references confirm this picture. In Hippocrates's *Nature of Man*, Melissus is implicitly linked to a tradition of debate when the author of

And the Stranger is an Eleatic who is quite happy to deviate from the orthodoxy (*Sph.* 241d, 2422c).[6] Taylor (1956) asserts confidently that the failure to name the Stranger (and the Athenian of the *Laws*) is an indication that they are "purely fictitious," and thus, with no historical position to uphold, they can "be used freely as simple mouthpieces for the views of their creator" (374).[7] But in the next sentence, he withdraws somewhat from concluding that this is Plato himself, prepared instead to allow that we have a representative position of the Academy. As we have seen earlier, this more measured claim can at least be supported by some of the existent evidence, like Epicrates's portrayal of Academy students. Whatever reasons Plato has for leaving this Eleatic unnamed, the association with the doctrine remains, and this expert in Division lends his expertise to finding the natural breaks in the whole of things that allows for distinctions to be made.

The advocate of the method in the *Philebus*, and the one who explains the nature of the method there, is, once again, Socrates. Stepping out from the shadows of the *Sophist* and *Statesman*, this Socrates shares the methodological facility witnessed in the discourse of the Stranger. Gill (1996) refers here to a "revived Socratic figure," justifying his appearance because he advocates for a Socratic-Platonic life of knowledge over pleasure (292). As we will see, he manages both the expert (Philebus) and the novice (Protarchus) in a display that recalls elements of the earlier Socrates.

Gonzalez (2000) finds the argument that the Stranger speaks for Plato implausible on several fronts. It's implausible that Plato should shift spokesperson from what amounts to one day to the next after the *Theaetetus* and implausible that Plato would abandon Socrates for an essential foreigner.

---

the text complains about the different accounts given because of the manner of debating used to establish knowledge: "Given the same debaters and the same audience, the same man never wins in the discussion three times in succession, but now one is victor, now another." The disputants end up confirming the discourse of Melissus by showing the difficulties that arise when Being is aligned with any particular element (Hippocrates 1959, *Nature of Man*, I, 1–35). There is a case to be made for seeing the arguments of Melissus and other Eleatics couched in the hypothetical statements that were favored in dialectical debates. For examples, "If Things were Many, they would have to be of the same kind as I say the One is. For if there is earth and water and air and fire . . . if these things exist . . ." (Melissus, reported in Freeman 1948, 30, 8, 2).

6. Kahn (2013) notes the ambivalence involved: "If everything were unchanging, there would be no life and no understanding"; yet if "everything were undergoing change, there would be nothing to know" (146–47).

7. See also Skemp's judgment in the introduction to Plato 1952 (24).

Socrates's trial sets the context of the dialogue, and what he says and what he does not say both "expose serious problems in what the Stranger says" (Gonzalez 2000, 162). Yet, a stronger case supports the plausibility of reading the Stranger as a practitioner of the dialectic that is espoused in the dialogue, and that is enough to take what he says both seriously and as reflective of Plato's position on the method.

Still, a puzzle remains. If the discussions of the preceding chapters have credence, Plato has evolved toward a refined dialectical method expressed in the use of Division, and presupposing Collection. Yet he has the method demonstrated first by a philosopher whose predilections are outside those of his own. And having marginalized Socrates during those dialogues, he sees fit to return him as a proficient dialectical practitioner in the *Philebus*. We need to hold this puzzle in our minds as we witness the performances of these dialecticians in the dialogues.

The *Sophist* and the *Statesman*

In part I, some attention was given to the *Sophist* in relation to its answer to the problem of false argument. And in part II, the *Statesman* was explored to determine the importance of rhetoric to the position developed there. Now, we can return to both dialogues to consider how the method of Division (and Collection) is introduced and demonstrated and the role it plays in the late dialectic.[8]

THE SOPHIST

The dialogue eases the reader into a familiarity with the dialectical method, setting the foundations for how to proceed both in discussion and in complexity of subject. Socrates (not Young Socrates, who is also present), opens with a puzzle: philosophers show up in all sorts of guises—sometimes as statesmen, sometimes as sophists. So are these three to be divided into separate classes and a name assigned to each (*Sph.* 217a)? The Stranger responds that they are separate but it is no easy task to distinguish them, although he is prepared to do so.

---

8. As with the *Philebus* below, my interest in these dialogues is with the nature of the method alone and not with the success or otherwise of any doctrine that Plato may (or may not) be espousing through the use of the method.

Then, it is a question of how to proceed. Socrates asks whether the Stranger prefers a long speech or the method of questions, observing that Parmenides had used the latter with him when he was young. For the Stranger, it will depend on the respondent. If the interlocutor is easily guided and not quarrelsome, then discussion is easier; otherwise, he would prefer to discourse alone. So, the method of questions and answers is adopted, with Theaetetus as the respondent.

Thus prepared, they begin the search for the Sophist, but not without testing the waters with a more accessible, smaller subject, before tackling what is larger. The lesser thing is taken as a pattern (*paradeigma*) for the larger (*Sph.* 218d). This essentially announces a role that paradigms or examples can play in the mature dialectic, a role that is given greater prominence in the *Statesman*. The simpler example they choose, one that is well known and small, is that of the angler.

The opening of the *Sophist* has thus provided us with important preliminaries before demonstrating the dialectic involved: a problem of distinguishing things that are closely associated; the possibility of exploring matters alone or in conversation with others; and the illustrative role that examples or simple patterns can play.

The dialogue will provide seven definitions of the Sophist using Division, and the preliminary search for the angler just happens to set some of the initial distinctions for these, indicating that its choice was not so arbitrary. The first division is between what is artful and artless. The angler is artful. Then the class of artful things is divided into arts that involve making (poetics) and those that are acquisitive. The angler is identified among the arts of acquisition. And so the divisions continue until we arrive at the appropriate place for the angler.

There are nine divisions, with the righthand class being the source of the next division: artless/artful; productive (poetic)/acquisitive; willing exchanges/coercions; open fighting/secret hunting; lifeless/living (animal hunting); pedestrian (land) animals/swimming (water) animals; feathered (fowling)/aqueous (fishing); fencing (enclosures)/striking; tridents/hooks; angling. This first demonstration of division is summarized at *Sph.* 221b–c, where the stress is laid on the fact that the Stranger and Theaetetus have arrived where they have on the basis of agreement between the two of them. Here, as in the decision to proceed with question-and-answer exchanges, we have vestiges of the earlier dialectic, now put to work as part of a more developed model.

As noted above, this simple exercise in Division forms the basis for what follows. In terms of this *paradeigma*, the Stranger proposes to find the Sophist (*Sph.* 221c). Both the angler and the Sophist are deemed to be hunters, so they return to the division of animal hunting and this time follow the division of land animals rather than those of water. The result (summarized at *Sph.* 223b) is satisfactory to Theaetetus but not to the Stranger for whom it lacks complexity. So, they return to another cut in the original example and begin this time from that of willing exchanges. The new division pursued here begins with exchanges not of willing gifts but of sales. The conclusion (a selling of learning) adds something to the inquiry, but the Stranger anticipates more, returning yet again to the original example and pursuing the different alternative in the open fighting or competition division, pursuing a track that begins with rivalry. This leads to the discovery of the Sophist as a purveyor of eristics, characterized by contradiction, disputation, and so forth (*Sph.* 226a). Further layers of this complex search are added, but it seems unnecessary to delineate them all. After a halt is called in the examination, the divisions are summarized at 231d–e. The final definition will recall divisions in the art of making and proceed to the infamous concluding "grasp" of the Sophist.

It is the dividing process that most rewards our attention and the way this is described as following a logical progression. Theaetetus happily submits himself to the guidance of the Stranger (*Sph.* 227d). Here, the novice recognizes the ability of the dialectician to identify unities, the genus in each case, as starting points. On one level, Division presupposes Collection. But there is also a sense in which a conception of the Sophist is being collected, drawn from the multiple definitions that they have produced. At one point, Theaetetus commends the Stranger for having discussed an extensive and complex species "and collected it all into one" (*Sph.* 234b).[9] This prefigures the final assault on the subject, which essentially investigates the various appearances of the Sophist, in the art of hunting, fighting, selling, and the like, which were subdivisions of the inquisitive art (*Sph.* 265a) and seeks an underlying, unifying definition. So, as much as the more prominent methodology on display involves the dividing or cutting of a genus, Collection would also appear to be involved in the practice of the dialectician, along with the use of appropriate examples.

The Stranger tells Theaetetus, "the method of argument is neither more nor less concerned with the art of medicine than that of sponging, but is indifferent if one benefits us little, the other greatly by its purifying.

---

9. Seth Benardete's translation (Benardete 1986).

It endeavours to understand what is related and what is not related in all arts, for the purpose of acquiring intelligence" (*Sph.* 227a–b). A similar remark will be expressed in the *Statesman* (285d). Moreover, the importance of Collection is reinforced in a passage where the Stranger explains the science of dialectic and the operations of the dialectician:

> Then he who is able to do this has a clear perception of one form or idea extending entirely through many individuals each of which lies apart, and of many forms differing from one another but included in one greater form, and again of one form evolved by the union of many wholes, and of many forms entirely apart and separate. This is the knowledge and ability to distinguish by classes how individual things can or cannot be associated with one another. (*Sph.* 253d–e)

This description explains first an ability to grasp the whole and recognize it in different individuals and then to grasp how one form might arise from the union of many wholes. The search for the Sophist, accumulating parts of the genus to grasp a greater whole, would appear to fit this part of the description.

Just as the definition of the angler acts as an introduction to the dialectical investigation of the Sophist, so the dialogue itself acts as an introduction to the developed dialectical method, with subsequent dialogues building on what is laid out here. The focus of investigation may be the Sophist, but the method itself, as the Stranger has just explained it, is indifferent to the details of any particular investigation. In addition, the power of the dialectician's discourse "is derived from the interweaving of the classes or ideas with one another" (*Sph.* 259e), a feature that reflects the developed theory of Forms that this dialogue introduces and that anticipates the analogy of the next dialogue.

The *Statesman*

In chapter 9's discussion of the *Statesman* the focus was on the features of dialectical method that were contributory and supplementary to the principal role played by Division without considering details involved in that role. Myth was used as a corrective to a path of division that had gone wrong, and the method of example played an important role in furthering the participants' understanding of the divisions, eventually promoting the analogy of weaving that will prove decisive in the final description of the Statesman. What we learned indirectly there about the method of Division was that it can go wrong. Here, we are interested in what more the dialogue reveals about the method.

The opening divisions of the *Statesman* are drawn from what was learned of the Sophist, just as the subsequent divisions of the *Sophist* devolved from aspects of the preliminary "simple" division of the angler. The Stranger and his new interlocutor—the Young Socrates—agree that, like the Sophist, the statesman will possess a kind of expert knowledge, and so they must first look within the forms of knowledge (*Stm.* 258b). This time, the first distinction separates applied sciences from those that are pure or theoretical, with the art they are pursuing assigned to the latter. They continue to make "natural" cuts up to, and even beyond, the point of error,[10] with the Younger Socrates exhorted to "share the work of dividing" (*Stm.* 261a).

Before the myth is introduced to play its corrective role, several aspects of the method are stressed by the Stranger, indicating that the dialogue, while ostensibly a major contribution to Plato's political thought, is equally, if not more, intended as a technical illustration of philosophical method. Later, at *Stm.* 285d, the Stranger will make this clear when he asks whether their goal was really the Statesman or to become "more skilled in dialectics about everything."[11] Here, at an earlier stage of the investigation, the instructions are integral to this goal. The Stranger explains:

> We must only divide where there is a real cleavage between specific forms. The section must always possess a specific form. It is splendid if one really can divide off the class sought for immediately from the rest—that is, if the structure of reality authorizes such immediate division. . . . But it is dangerous, Socrates, to chop reality up into small portions. It is always safer to go down the middle to make our cuts: the real cleavages among the forms are more likely to be found thus; and the

---

10. As noted in chapter 9, error enters when they divide according to rearing (the human herd) rather than tending (*Stm.* 261a). It takes them a few further steps before this becomes apparent and the myth is introduced to identify the nature of the error and then point the way to its correction.

11. Here, I adopt the Benardete (1984) translation. Alternatively, we can read "better dialecticians." Skemp's (Plato 1952a) "better philosophers" assumes that the two terms are synonyms, an assumption we would be unwise to make.

whole art of these definitions consists in finding these cleavages. (*Stm.* 262b–c)

An example of such an unwise cleavage comes in the case of dividing the class of humans into Greeks and Barbarians, a division natural for those living in that part of the world. The mistake lies in thinking that just because there is a common name describing a group, so that name must denote a natural class.

And again, before the myth, the Stranger recalls a principle from the *Sophist*, that no irrelevant distinction between what is low and what is exalted should distract them. "This method of discourse (argument) makes no more heed to the noble than the ignoble . . . but always goes on its own way to the most perfect truth" (*Stm.* 266d). The goal is clear, there should be no distractions from it.

After the myth has exposed their initial error (or two errors [274d–275a]), the search for the Statesman can resume. But as with the search for the Sophist, the new start involves a return to what had already been established: "We must go back again for reconsideration of one of our divisions. We said that there is a pre-directive art concerned with living creatures, and with these in herds rather than as individuals. . . . It was at a point in our tracking down of this art that we began to lose the scent" (*Stm.* 275c–d).[12] They quickly arrive at a definition that satisfies the younger Socrates ("tendance freely accepted by herds of free bipeds we call statesmanship" [276e]), but not the Stranger, who introduces the nature and method of example to assist them, observing, as noted before, "that a definition couched in words is a better description of a living creature than a drawing or any model of it can be—a better description, I mean, for those capable of following such a definition: for those who cannot do so the model or visible illustration is appropriate enough" (*Stm.* 277c). The concern here seems to be for a wider range of audience than those present, unless we suspect the younger Socrates of needing the help (he did, after all, think the search was complete). Why Plato raises the concern for audience accessibility at this point may seem unclear. But it is an interest that we saw active in the middle dialogues when the relative novices Glaucon and Adeimantus were being led toward insight. Now we have not just Young Socrates in that

---

12. It is a point worth observing how much the hunting metaphor (such as losing the scent) pervades translations of this search as it did in the *Sophist*. The Greek text would better support a reading of them having gone astray or missed their point.

role but also Theaetetus, resting from his part in the *Sophist* but still a very interested onlooker. Given the activities of the Academy against which we have seen these dialectical dialogues set, the concern for the philosophically astute but inexperienced students becomes less puzzling.[13]

Following the discussion of the method of example, the Stranger makes a move reminiscent of the opening of the *Sophist*, introducing weaving as "the smallest example (*paradeigma*)" with the same business as the political and so something that can be "set beside it" (*Stm.* 279a). After drawing on a myth to correct and focus the method of Division, that method now has a simple example brought in as an aid to advance it. The "dialectical method" has never appeared more like a repertoire of strategies than in this dialogue.

The concept of Weaving is subjected to the method of Division, and while the search for it is concluded at 283a, weaving will play a role throughout the remainder of the dialogue. But more pertinent to this discussion are the subsequent remarks made in the course of dividing the art of measurement that stress that the interlocutors' goal has been to understand the method of Division itself and not any particular application of it, a point repeated from the *Sophist*. Having determined as a goal that they should become better dialecticians, the Stranger proceeds, essentially advancing his earlier remark about descriptions in words being superior to visible illustrations:

> Likenesses which the senses can grasp are available in nature to those real existents which are in themselves easy to understand, so that when someone asks for an account of these existents one has no trouble at all—one can simply indicate the sensible likeness and dispense with any account in words. But to the highest and most important class of existents there are no corresponding visible resemblances, no work of nature clear for all to look upon. In these cases nothing visible can be pointed out to satisfy the inquiring mind: the instructor cannot cause the inquirer to perceive something with one or other of his senses and so make him really satisfied that he understands the thing under discussion. There we must train ourselves to give and understand a rational account (*logos*) of every existent thing. For the existents which have no visible embodiment, the existents which are of highest value and chief importance, are demonstrable only

---

13. See Kahn (2013, 147–48) for a discussion of the pedagogical role of dialectic in the late dialogues. I return to this below.

by reason (*logos*) and are not to be apprehended by any other means. All our present discussions have the aim of training us to apprehend this highest class of existents. (*Stm.* 285d–286a)

Yes, the search for the Statesman matters, and the dialogue makes an important contribution both to the plan set out at the start of the *Sophist* to define three crucial figures and to the development of the political philosophy of its author. But the larger value is the training in dialectical method, in order to know a thing through the kind of *rational* account for which earlier dialogues like the *Meno* and even the *Theaetetus* left us wanting. The method aims to disclose the nature of the Forms and thus is added to an evolved Platonic interest for which this has always been both a metaphysical and epistemological goal. A few lines later: "What we must value first and foremost, above all else, is the method itself, and this consists in ability to divide according to real Forms (*eidos*)" (*Stm.* 286d). As if to anticipate the kinds of impatience that some readers have expressed at the convoluted paths of dialectical inquiry in these later dialogues, the challenge is made that if people find "these discussions are long and circuitous," then the onus is on them to provide a more direct means to demonstrate real truth (*Stm.* 286e–287a). That said, they return to the other matter at hand and the final lengthy definition of the Statesman. No shorter, more direct path is suggested and, by implication, none is thought possible.

The characterization of the dialectician as one who is able to divide according to Forms recalls Socrates insisting on the importance of this point when addressing Glaucon (*Rep.* 454a). After the criticisms of the Parmenides, the theory of Forms undergoes some necessary revisions, especially in the account of the mixing of primary Forms in the Sophist. But it remains the metaphysical background for Plato's dialecticians and the language used by the Eleatic Stranger is reminiscent of the classical theory that preceded it and was the subject of the critique. Dividing according to Forms becomes the focal point of attention for the commentators, concerned to fathom precisely what is involved (Moravcsik 1973; Sayre 2006; Kahn 2013, Muniz and Rudebusch 2018). Moravcsik (168), for example, describes a crude version of the method that deals with Forms throughout, while at the other extreme Kenneth Sayre, rejecting this account (as does Moravcsik himself) because it falls short of descriptions in both the *Sophist* and *Statesman*, dismisses talk of Forms altogether, and replaces it with a discussion of classes and subclasses (2006, 213). After all, can a traditional Form be divided? As Parmenides famously challenged Socrates in the Parmenides, "being one and the same, it will be at the same time, as a whole, in things that are many and separate; and thus it would be separate from itself" (*Prm.* 131b).[14] The debate among these commentators pivots around whether what is divided amounts to intensions (like Forms) or extensions (Cohen 1973, 181). At issue is how to translate the terms eidos and genos in the Stranger's vocabulary. The precise details of the various positions in this debate fall outside of the present inquiry, concerned as we are with the method used and not what it is used to discover. Whether the method ultimately pursues definitions of Forms throughout or classes and subclasses, it remains the case that it is definitions that are at stake. Still, I believe the discussion of "kinds" in the *Philebus* sheds light on this debate.

The *Philebus*

This late dialogue sees the reappearance of Socrates, who Christopher Gill (1996) above called "the revived Socratic figure" (292).[15] He takes over the role that the Eleatic Stranger had performed in the other "late-dialectic" dialogues. And it is Socrates who discusses Philebus's thesis that the good is pleasure (in contrast with Socrates's view that the good is intelligence and involves things of the mind), not with Philebus himself (the expert) but with the young Protarchus (the novice).[16] The actual company consists of more than just these three, with Protarchus representing other unnamed young men who are present. I will return to the significance of this in the next section.

The importance of the method of Division is emphasized at the outset. Socrates discusses the problem of the one and the many, focusing on what he calls the real problem. There is a distracting tendency to discuss things

---

14. In chapter 7's discussion of Plato's use of silence, one response to this challenge was considered. The debate among commentators that emerges around these later dialogues takes the challenge at face value, however.

15. In chapter 9, I reviewed the debate around the date of the dialogue. Gosling in the notes to his translation (Plato 1975a) allowed that it was late (post-*Republic*) but hesitated to say much more because of the complexities involved. He observes, for example, that its relationship to the *Statesman* is uncertain (Plato 1975a, xx).

16. It is another measure of the evolution that the dialogues have undergone that the expert (who Socrates$_E$ loved to question) is moved to the sidelines and rendered largely ineffective. His silences at key moments might suggest another interesting reading of the dialogue.

that are generable or perishable. That is not what the debate of the one and the many is about. "For it is agreed that about a one of that sort, as we said just now, there is no need to waste time arguing. But when someone wishes to posit man, ox, beauty, or the good each as one, a burning interest in making divisions within this sort is a matter for controversy" (*Phil.* 15a).[17] The real questions about the one and the many are those that have resonated since the criticism of the *Parmenides*: Can there be such units in the strict sense? That is, how can each unit, while remaining unchanged and remaining one, but which is found in the plurality of perishable things, be scattered abroad and become many or "as itself while whole separated from itself, which seems impossible" (*Phil.* 15b)?[18] In pursuit of an answer, they must turn to the method.

Socrates explains how the answer is to apply dialectic (*Phil.* 15b–18e) and show how each (collected) unity has within itself a number of "kinds" that mediate between it and particulars. The philosopher (or dialectician) must know these intermediaries and their number.

Before proceeding to this, it is of value to note how Plato makes it clear that this method is *not* the Socratic method of earlier dialogues, where an interlocutor is led into contradiction (and refuted) in order to learn what they don't know. This is demonstrated by the presence of a brief elenctic exchange to illustrate the contrast (*Phil.* 21a–d). Socrates asks Protarchus whether he would care to live his whole life enjoying the greatest pleasures. On receiving an affirmative response, he proceeds to examine Protarchus's commitment to that statement until Protarchus experiences what many interlocutors had experienced before him: "Your argument has thrown me for the moment, Socrates, I have nothing to say (*Phil.* 21d).[19] On one level, this brief by-play could suggest that nothing really has changed, the old method is still being endorsed. But the contrast with all else that passes between Socrates and Protarchus is stark. And the passage serves no constructive role in the development of the dialogue. I suggest it is there simply to emphasize the contrast between the old Socratic method and what is now being employed.

---

17. Unless otherwise noted, I follow Gosling's (Plato 1975a) translation. Benardete (1991) translates ἑνάς (unit) as "henad" and notes that nowhere else in Plato is the term used for ideas.

18. This is a question that refers back to the debate of the commentators at the end of 12.2.2.

19. Hackforth's translation (Plato 1972) provides: "Has reduced me for the moment to complete speechlessness."

As introduced, the method of Dialectic is cloaked in myth. It is presented as a gift from the gods, comparable to the gift of fire given to Prometheus. Plato (as the actual originator of the method) in this sense is a Promethean figure. According to the gods' account:

> Since this is how things are constituted, we should always posit a single form in respect to every one and search for it, for we shall find one there—and if we are successful, then after the one we should look for two, if there are two, or otherwise for three or whatever the number is; each of these ones should be treated the same way, until one can see of the original not only that it is one, a plurality, and an infinite number, but also its precise quantity. But one should not attribute the character of indeterminate to the plurality until one can see the complete number between the indeterminate and the one. Then one can consign every one of them to the indeterminate with a clear conscience. As I said, this is the procedure for inquiring, learning, and teaching each other that the gods have handed on to us. (*Phil.* 16d–e)

There is a lot that could be analyzed here. Shorey (1933) judges it "one of the most frequently and gravely misinterpreted passages in the entire Platonic text" (268). But the main point is that the method, however we understand it, is not the dialectic of old. It is a new dialectic, inquiring into the nature of things. And while it still requires the combined efforts of several interlocutors working together to reach understanding, it is clearly no longer concerned with what those interlocutors believe or are committed to.

They take care to get their starting point right, drawing on earlier ideas to do so and addressing the distinction between the indeterminate (*apeiron*) and determinate. Essentially, it is both Division and Collection that is at stake, with the latter noted: "When one is forced to start with what is indeterminate, one should not immediately look to the unitary aspect, but again note some number embracing every plurality, and from all these end up at the one" (*Phil.* 18a–b). As Kahn (2013) notes, the discussion of the *apeiron* is expressed in terms of multitude and number, and there "is no mention of genus and species, of universals or particulars" (152). Between a unity and an unlimited plurality are a definite number of subdivisions. These, it seems, are the unities or ones. Socrates provides two illustrations of this structure, one involving the alphabet (*Phil.* 18b) and a shorter example of music (*Phil.* 56a).

The method of Division is then illustrated in various ways throughout the dialogue, exploring, for example, the pair Becoming and Being (*Phil.* 54a). But a division that should most interest us is that of Knowledge (*Phil.* 55c–59c) because this inquiry uncovers dialectic itself as part of the investigation. Here, the original division (*Phil.* 55d1–3) is between technical knowledge (production) and that concerned with education and culture. The first involves measuring (like in the art of carpentry), and the second involves guesswork (like in the art of music). Again, there are two types of arithmetic, one ordinary and the other philosophical (*Phil.* 56e). With respect to knowledge, then, there are two types, one purer than the other. This may also be the case for dialectic, since when Socrates says that no other art can be preferred to dialectic, Protarchus asks what identifies dialectic (*Phil.* 58a).[20] And this is also the point in the dialogue—discussed in chapter 9—where Protarchus appeals to Gorgias and his art of rhetoric.

Socrates will distinguish dialectic from rhetoric in both its character and domain: "[Dialectic would be] the one [branch of knowledge] that would understand at least every ability now being mentioned. In my view, at least, anyone who possesses the slightest intelligence will agree that the discipline concerned with the final truth, the real nature of things and unchanging reality is the most genuine (*alethes*) knowledge" (*Phil.* 58a).

It is in responding to Protarchus's appeal to Gorgias that Socrates stresses the distinction between what is expedient (rhetoric) and what is true (dialectic), no matter how little its power to benefit (*Phil.* 58c). On reflection, Protarchus has to agree: no other branch of knowledge has a firmer hold on truth. Subsequent to this, the dialogue achieves its goal: it explains pleasure and sets it in relation to the good. Pleasure is not the absolute good (nor is mind) because it is wanting in self-sufficiency and also in adequacy and perfection.

The inquiry in the *Philebus* differs from the searches in the *Sophist* and *Statesman* in that Socrates and Protarchus are not trying to define a particular concept; rather, they are interested in solving a philosophical puzzle about the best life and its nature. So, the *Philebus* is not populated with multiple

---

20. As Hackforth notes (Plato 1972, 119n2), the phrasing may imply two kinds, one with rigor and the other just conversation. This point recalls my discussion of *dialegesthai* in the last chapter, since this is the term used to describe dialectic here (57e).

divisions tracking a concept through its various associations. Nevertheless, as presented, the method reflects the efforts of the earlier dialogues, with a division in, say, knowledge, and the decision of which path to then pursue through further divisions.

Lessons in Method

Some commentators doubt the seriousness of Plato's treatment of Division in these dialogues. Paul Shorey (1933), for example, allows that "Plato may have been interested in seeing how far the method could be carried, and he may have regarded it as a useful, logical exercise for students," but, "in the *Sophist* and *Politicus* he is obviously playing with it" (247). Why? Well, in the *Sophist* Plato shows several definitions of the Sophist, and in the *Statesman* he needs to supplement the account by means of other methods.[21] Both of these points we have seen confirmed above. But neither indicates a lack of seriousness on Plato's part. Granted, there is humor in the Stranger's description that can be puzzling (Kahn 2013, 144). But, in fact, the earnestness of the discussions of the method itself indicates otherwise.

Earlier in this chapter, I pondered the nature of the dialectician and the candidates for this role served up in these dialogues—the Eleatic Stranger and a revised Socrates. Now, on reflection, the attention may have been on the wrong party in the dialogical exchanges. None of these exercises in dialectical method show investigations between seasoned dialecticians, something we might expect in serious studies of the subjects under consideration. Instead, we have in each case a mature dialectician leading a novice in a protreptic inquiry toward insight for that person and those accompanying them. We do not see the Eleatic Stranger working with Socrates or even Theodorus, and we do not see the Socrates of the *Philebus* working with Philebus. Instead, we have Theaetetus, Young Socrates, and Protarchus. These young men should be the focus of our attention, just as we considered the experiences of Glaucon and Adeimantus when exploring methods in the *Republic*.

If we read the dialectical lessons through the "eyes" of Theaetetus, Young Socrates, and Protarchus, as witnessed in their responses, we observe the

---

21. Shorey's tone of skepticism pervades his discussions of all the late dialogues in which Division plays a central role. Elsewhere (Shorey 1903), he identifies usages of the method in other, earlier dialogues for the "avoidance of eristic equivocation and the correction of hasty generalization or inarticulate empiricism" (51).

strangeness and power of the methodology from a very different perspective than if we focus only on the Eleatic Stranger and Socrates.

In the *Sophist*, Socrates advises the Stranger to choose Theaetetus as his interlocutor: "One of the young . . . or anyone of the rest" (*Sph.* 217d). The Stranger had asked for someone who would easily submit to guidance, and although Socrates claims that everyone would comply, it is still one of the younger members of those assembled that is put forward. Once chosen in this way, Theaetetus proves a formidable co-investigator. From early short and acquiescent answers that we are used to seeing from such interlocutors, as he gains experience in dividing, his responses increase in value, making real contributions to the search (*Sph.* 228e, 261a–b). He follows the divisions with such enthusiasm that he becomes perplexed by "the fact that [the Sophist] has come to light as so many" (*Sph.* 231b–c). But he is able to identify important features of the method ("You've spoken of a very extensive species and just about the most complex and collected it all into one" [*Sph.* 234b]). And he is able to enter into a sophisticated analysis of images and resemblance (*Sph.* 239d–240c), as well as understand the explanation of the basic Forms and how other Forms share in these primary kinds (*Sph.* 257a). He agrees with the cuts of division and asks for clarity about them when necessary, "Say once more at what point each of the two is divided" (*Sph.* 266b), to show that he is following the method as much as the search for the subject matter for which it is being used. And he understands this to the degree that eventually he is able to make cuts himself: "I understand better now, and I set down a pair of two species of making in a double way, a divine and human making according to the one cut, and, in turn, according to the other, one is of (the works) themselves, and one the offspring of certain similarities" (*Sph.* 266d). We might need reminding that this is Theaetetus speaking here. He has learned so well from the Stranger that he begins to sound like him.

The Young Socrates is Theaetetus's contemporary and fellow gymnast (*Stm.* 257c) who often works out with him (*Sph.* 218b) and who takes over the role as interlocutor in the *Statesman* in order to give his friend a rest. His early responses are hesitant, even though he has been witness to the previous exercise, and it needs to be stressed to him that any success they achieve is a joint success, based on their agreements (*Stm.* 258d). But he is the first one to begin to make mistakes. Becoming involved in the divisions earlier than had Theaetetus, he suggests making a cut between the nurture of men and the nurture of animals (*Stm.* 262a). But the Stranger corrects this: "We must beware lest we break off one small fragment of a class and then contrast it with the all important sections left behind. We must only divide where there is a real cleavage between specific forms" (*Stm.* 262b). This is where he advises that they go "down the middle" to make their cuts, and he introduces the false division between Greeks and Barbarians that was mentioned above. Younger Socrates is being allowed to make mistakes so that he can learn from them. And this lesson continues. Younger Socrates thinks they have reached their conclusion (*Stm.* 267c), only to be challenged: "Do you really think so, Socrates? Do you think our task as complete as you make out?" Here is identified the serious error that will require the introduction of the myth and an eventual return to an earlier stage in the divisions, one that Young Socrates had rushed over. It's to be noted that the error needs to be explained to him; he does not recognize it for himself, even when invited to do so (*Stm.* 274d).

The education of Young Socrates is richer in variety than what Theaetetus directly experienced (of course, indirectly he shares in what is transpiring); he is drawn into the examination of the myth and shares in the discussion of the method of example until he is satisfied in how it works (*Stm.* 278c). Still, he understands that their chief purpose is not so much to find the Statesman as to become better at using a method that can solve all such problems; his sight is correctly set on the general rather than the specific (*Stm.* 285d). This much he seems to learn. But he contributes less to the actual divisions after his initial error and is mainly reduced to asking question after question, with an occasional agreement. He is a different kind of interlocutor than was Theaetetus, less perceptive and, perhaps, less able. But his presence allows for further features of pedagogy to be inserted into the later dialogues.

Protarchus is invited to take up an argument from which Philebus has withdrawn. And he readily accepts to do so. But he is not actually alone. Early on he tells Socrates: "Can't you see, Socrates, that the whole crowd of us are young men?" (*Phil.* 16a). To which the reader might readily respond, "Who are these young men?" At *Phil.* 20a, these young men are thrown into confusion by Socrates's posing of questions that they "won't as yet be able to answer adequately." With subsequent allusions to those whom he represents (*Phil.* 23b, 28c, 67b), it becomes clear that Protarchus is spokesperson for a group of like-minded inquirers, and that, as is indicated at *Phil.* 67b, their concerns and agreements have been passed through him. The specter of the Academy looms large in these remarks.

In taking over Philebus's role, from the beginning Protarchus has a position to articulate and defend (*Phil.* 12d–13a), challenging Socrates when he disagrees (*Phil.* 20a). So, he is again an advance over Young Socrates and Theaetetus, having a greater stake in the ideas discussed. Socrates often finds himself on the defensive against a more aggressive and demanding interrogator. But when it comes to actual divisions, Socrates leads the way and Protarchus slips back into the role of asking simple questions, often of clarification. He makes little in the way of a contribution to the crucial division of knowledge until he counters Socrates's suggestion that knowledge would be the discipline that is concerned with the final truth and the real nature of things with Gorgias's art of persuasion as the preeminent knowledge (*Phil.* 58a). This may suggest something further about Protarchus's own background and how he would have been thinking about knowledge itself. But he is not hard to convince that it is Socrates who is right (*Phil.* 58e). Once he agrees to this, further agreements about the superiority of intelligence over pleasure naturally follow, setting up Protarchus's penultimate utterance, issued presumably on behalf of those he represents: "We are now all agreed, Socrates, on the truth of your position" (*Phil.* 67b).

In discussing the connections between unity and plurality in conceptual understanding, Charles Kahn, almost as an aside, echoes the observation made by Shorey about the method of Division: "In the *Sophist-Statesman* it is often difficult to see the philosophical implications of these intricate systems of dichotomy. We might compare these two displays of definition-by-division to examples in a logic textbook, interpreting them as pedagogical exercises designed to train the mind in reflection and analysis" (2013, 139). We would welcome further consideration of these apparent logical exercises for students from either Shorey or Kahn (Kahn does note the contemporary mockery of such examples that indicate a relationship to the practices of the Academy), but these suggestions are not pursued. Still, if we consider the late dialectical dialogues as pedagogical exercises reflective of the activity in the Academy a number of questions begin to receive answers. It is, for example, clearly of value to see firsthand how an inquiry can go wrong, as in the *Statesman*, and what strategies (like the use of myth) might be used to set it back on the right path. We might also be less puzzled at the introduction of humor, a device often useful in pedagogy. In the *Sophist*, for example, we see the Sophist described in ways that some find satirical: as a hunter of young men or a salesman of virtue. And in the *Statesman*, the Stranger is even more explicit in drawing attention to some of the comic images he conjures, like the description of human beings that "is another conclusion which we have reached by our divisions which is not without its interest for the comedians" (*Stm.* 266b–c). A mix of humor helps to dilute the rigor of the analyses and arguably provides for a more comfortable and accessible learning experience.

It is the pedagogical that runs as a theme through the discussions of this book, from the experiences of Cleinias in the *Euthydemus*, as he demonstrates a positive reaction to Socrates's hortatory argument, to the insights of Protarchus in the *Philebus*, as he grows in confidence in his exchanges with Socrates and his rebuffing of Philebus, with a collection of promising candidates in between. What a tutorial these young men make.[22]

Thus, Plato's dialectic has not shed all vestiges of its Socratic predecessor. The maieutic is apparent in these late pedagogical exercises. The examining (and refuting) of experts has been left aside after the *Republic*, as we saw. But the drawing of ideas out of young men, although modified in these late dialogues, has its roots in Socrates's midwifery. What we see here is how the young men both contribute to the ideas that are brought forward and to the testing of those ideas to see if they fit naturally in the declensions toward the concept of interest.

Christopher Gill's (2002; 1996) insistence on the constancy of dialogue itself in the dialogues now gains greater plausibility. What we witness in the use of the dialogue form throughout Plato's career is a constancy of interaction between minds in pursuit of the truth, whether that was through the *elenchus* of the early dialogues, which is abandoned in the middle period, or the pedagogy of the late dialogues as young men are coaxed toward acquiring the expertise that those interlocutors in the earlier Socratic dialogues failed to exhibit. Gill judges there to be two recurrent features of Platonic thought about dialectic: the first is that dialectic in the form of "philosophical dialogue conducted through systematic, one-to-one question and answer" is necessary for the pursuit of objective knowledge (2002, 149). This in turn makes specific demands in terms of the character and aptitude of those involved. The second general feature requires each philosophical problem to be situated correctly in relation to the principles of reality and the dialectical method (153), which gives emphasis to the integrity of each dialectical encounter.[23] Indeed, these features of interpersonal encounter seem

---

22. And there is no reason to limit the class to young men, given the openness of the Academy to female members, according, for example, to Philodemus in his *History of the Philosophers* (Philodemus VI, 26–27, in Kalligas et al. 2020). Badiou (2012), of course, captured this with the transformation of Adeimantus into a female (Amantha) in his "hyper-translation" of the *Republic*.

23. In 1996, Gill applies these features to the late dialogues in particular.

genuine constants in the dialogues and help to refocus our attention away from the dialectical method itself. Throughout our analyses, it is not just the topics of discussion or the methods alone—whether logical, rhetorical, or dialectical—that have mattered, but the personalities of those involved.

Dialectic itself, as promoted by the late Plato, cannot be restricted to the method of Collection and Division or to the pursuit of definitions. Indeed, defining does play a central role and successful definitions are the culminating achievement sought. But methodically, the dialectician relies on a set of devices and strategies in forming the dialectical method. Collection and Division are central components of this set, but we cannot deny important roles to hypotheses, myths, and examples. Nor should we lose sight of those who are adept at employing these dialectical strategies as they instruct those who are learning to acquire a similar facility.

References

Allen, Danielle S. 2010. *Why Plato Wrote*. London: Wiley-Blackwell.
Antiphon. 1997. *The Speeches*. Edited by Michael Gagarin. Cambridge: Cambridge University Press.
Aristides. 2017. *Orations*. Vol. 1. Edited and translated by Michael Trapp. Cambridge, MA: Harvard University Press.
———. 2021. *Orations*. Vol. 2. Edited and translated by Michael Trapp. Cambridge, MA: Harvard University Press.
Aristophanes. 1962. *The Complete Plays of Aristophanes*. Edited by Moses Hadas. New York: Bantam.
Aristotle. 1924. *Rhetoric*. Translated by W. Rhys Roberts. Oxford: Oxford University Press.
———. 1926. *The "Art" of Rhetoric*. Translated by John H. Freese. Cambridge, MA: Harvard University Press.
———. 1984. *The Complete Works of Aristotle: Revised Oxford Translation*. 2 vols. Edited by Jonathan Barnes. Princeton, NJ: Princeton University Press.
———. 1995. *On Sophistical Refutations*. Translated by E. S. Forster. Cambridge, MA: Harvard University Press.
———. 1997a. *Aristotle Selections*. Translated by Terrence Irwin and Gail Fine. Indianapolis, IN: Hackett Publishing.
———. 1997b. *Topics: Books I and VIII*. Translated with commentary by Robin Smith. Oxford: Clarendon Press.
———. 2007. *On Rhetoric: A Theory of Civic Discourse*. Translated by George A. Kennedy. 2nd edition. Oxford: Oxford University Press.
———. 2018a. *Rhetoric*. Translated with an introduction and notes by C. D. C. Reeve. Indianapolis, IN: Hackett Publishing.
———. 2018b. *The Art of Rhetoric*. Translated by R. Waterfield. Introduction and notes by H. Yunis. Oxford: Oxford University Press.
———. 2019. *Aristotle's Art of Rhetoric*. Translated with an interpretive essay by R. C. Bartlett. Chicago: University of Chicago Press.

Asmis, Elizabeth. 1986. "*Psychagogia* in Plato's *Phaedrus.*" *Illinois Classical Studies* 11 (1/2): 153–72.
Badiou, A. 2012. *Plato's "Republic": A Dialogue in Sixteen Chapters*. Translated by Susan Spitzer with an introduction by Kenneth Reinhard. New York: Columbia University Press.
Barnes, Jonathan. 2007. *Truth, etc.: Six Lectures in Ancient Logic*. Oxford: Clarendon Press.
Barney, R. 2001. *Names and Nature in Plato's "Cratylus."* New York: Routledge.
Benardete, Seth. 1986. *Plato's "Sophist": Part II of the Being of the Beautiful*. Chicago: University of Chicago Press.
Benjamin, James. 1997. "The Roots of Informal Logic in Plato." In *Historical Foundations of Informal Logic*, edited by D. Walton and A. Brinton, 25–35. Aldershot, UK: Ashgate Publishing.
Benson, Hugh H. 1990. "Misunderstanding the 'What-is-F-ness?' Question." *Archiv für Geschichte der Philosophie* 72, 125–42.
———. 2009. "Plato's Method of Dialectic." In *A Companion to Plato*, edited by Hugh Benson, 85–99. Oxford: Wiley-Blackwell.
Beversluis, J. 2000. *Cross-Examining Socrates: A Defense of the Interlocutors in Plato's Early Dialogues*. Cambridge: Cambridge University Press.
Black, E. 1958. "Plato's View of Rhetoric." *Quarterly Journal of Speech* XLIV (4): 361–74.
Blackburn, Simon. 2006. *Plato's "Republic": A Biography*. New York: Grove Press.
Bluck, R. S. 1957. "False Statement in the *Sophist.*" *Journal of Hellenic Studies* 77, 181–86.
Bocheński, Józef Maria. 1951. *Ancient Formal Logic: Studies in Logic and the Foundations of Mathematics*. Amsterdam: North-Holland Publishing.
Bonazzi, Mauro. 2020. *The Sophists*. Cambridge: Cambridge University Press.
Booth, Wayne C. 2004. "My Life with Rhetoric: From Neglect to Obsession." In *Rhetoric and Rhetorical Criticism*, edited by W. Jost and W. Olmstead, 494–504. Oxford: Blackwell Publishing.
Boys-Stones, George, and Christopher Rowe. 2013. *The Circle of Socrates: Readings in the First-Generation Socratics*. Indianapolis, IN: Hackett Publishing.
Brandwood, Leonard. 1990. *The Chronology of Plato's Dialogues*. Cambridge: Cambridge University Press.
———. 1992. "Stylometry and Chronology." In *The Cambridge Companion to Plato*, edited by Richard Kraut, 90–120. Cambridge: Cambridge University Press.
Brickhouse, Thomas C., and Nicholas D. Smith. 1989. *Socrates on Trial*. Princeton, NJ: Princeton University Press.
———. 1991. "Socrates' Elenctic Mission." *Oxford Studies in Ancient Philosophy* 9, 131–59.
Burger, Ronna. 1984. *The "Phaedo": A Platonic Labyrinth*. New Haven, CT: Yale University Press.

Burke, Kenneth. 1950. *A Rhetoric of Motives*. London: Prentice-Hall.
Burnyeat, Myles F. (1977) 1992. "Socratic Midwifery, Platonic Inspiration." *Bulletin of the Institute of Classical Studies* 24, 7–16. Reprinted in *Essays on the Philosophy of Socrates*, edited by Hugh H. Benson, 53–65. Oxford: Oxford University Press.
Burnyeat, Myles F., and Michael Frede. 2015. *The Pseudo-Platonic Seventh Letter*. Oxford: Oxford University Press.
Bussell, Frederick W. 1896. *The School of Plato: Its Origin, Development, and Revival under the Roman Empire*. London: Methuen and Co.
Calogero, Guido. 1957. "Gorgias and the Socratic Principle of *neomo sua sponte peccat*." *Journal of the Hellenic Society* 77, 12–17.
Cassin, Barbara. 2014. *Sophistical Practice: Toward a Consistent Relativism*. New York: Fordham University Press.
———. 2017. "Rhetoric and Sophistics." In *The Oxford Handbook of Rhetorical Studies*, edited by Michael J. MacDonald, 143–56. Oxford: Oxford University Press.
Castelnérac, Benoît, and Mathieu Marion. "Arguing for Inconsistency: Dialectical Games in the Academy." In *Acts of Knowledge: History, Philosophy and Logic*, edited by Giuseppe Primiero and Shahid Rahman, 37–76. London: College Publications, 2009.
Chance, T. 1992. *Plato's "Euthydemus": Analysis of What Is and Is Not Philosophy*. Berkeley: University of California Press.
Cicero. 1860. *De Oratore*. Translated by J. S. Watson. London: George Bell.
———. 1949. *On Invention; Best Kind of Orator; Topics*. Translated by H. M. Hubbell. Cambridge, MA: Harvard University Press.
———. 1954. *Rhetorica Ad Herennium*. Translated by Harry Caplan. Cambridge, MA: Harvard: Harvard University Press.
Clay, D. 2000. *Platonic Questions: Dialogues with the Silent Philosopher*. University Park: Pennsylvania State University Press.
Cohen, S. Marc. 1973. "Plato's Method of Division." In *Patterns in Plato's Thought*, edited by J. M. E. Moravcsik, 181–91. Dordrecht: Springer.
Cole, T. 1991. *The Origins of Rhetoric in Ancient Greece*. Baltimore, MD: University of John Hopkins Press.
Conley, Thomas M. 1990. *Rhetoric in the European Tradition*. Chicago: University of Chicago Press.
Consigny, Scott. 2001. *Gorgias: Sophist and Artist*. Columbia: University of South Carolina Press.
Cooper, John M. 1998. "Socrates and Plato in Plato's *Gorgias*." In *Reason and Emotion: Essays on Ancient Moral Psychology and Ethical Theory*, edited by John M. Cooper, 29–75. Princeton, NJ: Princeton University Press.
Cope, Edward M. 1877. *The Rhetoric of Aristotle with Commentary*. 3 vols. Cambridge: Cambridge University Press.

Corlett, J. Angelo. 2005. *Interpreting Plato's Dialogues*. Las Vegas, NV: Parmenides Publishing.

Cornford, F. M. 1957. *Plato and Parmenides*. New York: Liberal Arts Press.

Coulter, James A. 1979. "The Relation of the *Apology of Socrates* to Gorgias' *Defense of Palamedes* and Plato's Critique of Gorgianic Rhetoric." In *Plato: True and Sophistic Rhetoric*, edited by K. V. Erickson, 31–69. Amsterdam: Rodopi.

Crombie, I. M. 1963. *An Examination of Plato's Doctrines*. Vol. II. London: Routledge and Kegan Paul.

———. 1964. *Plato: The Midwife's Apprentice*. London: Routledge and Kegan Paul.

Crome, Keith. 2004. *Lyotard and Greek Thought: Sophistry*. New York: Palgrave Macmillan.

Crooks, James. 2000. "Writing Conversion: Notes on the Structure of the *Phaedo*." In *Retracing the Platonic Text*, edited by John Russon and John Sallis, 155–74. Evanston, IL: Northwestern University Press.

D'Angour, Armand. 2019. *Socrates in Love: The Making of a Philosopher*. London: Bloomsbury.

Dentith, Simon. 2000. *Parody*. New York: Routledge.

Deraj, I. 2013. "Xenophon's Representation of Socratic *dialegesthai*." *Electryone* 1, 28–38.

Diels, Hermann. 1903. *Die Fragmente der Vorsokratiker*. Berlin: Weidmannsche Verlagbuchhandlung. Translated by Kathleen Freeman in 1948 as *Ancilla to the Pre-Socratic Philosophers: A Complete Translation of the Fragments in Diels, Fragmente der Vorsokratiker*. 5th edition. Oxford: Harvard University Press.

Diels, Hermann, and Walter Kranz. 1952. *Die Fragmente der Vorsokratiker*. Berlin: Weidmannsche Verlagbuchhandlung. (Diels, Hermann, and Walter Franz. *The Older Sophists*. Edited by Rosamund Kent Sprague. Columbia: University of South Carolina Press, 1972.)

Dillon, John, and Tania Gergel. 2003. *The Greek Sophists*. Translated and with an introduction and notes by John Dillon and Tania Gergel. London: Penguin.

Laertius, Diogenes. 1853. *The Lives and Opinions of Eminent Philosophers*. Translated by C. D. Yonge. London: Henry G. Bohn.

Dorter, Kenneth. 1982. *Plato's "Phaedo": An Interpretation*. Toronto: University of Toronto Press.

Eades, T. 1996. "Plato, Rhetoric, and Silence." *Philosophy and Rhetoric* 29, 244–58.

Elders, Leo. 1968. "The *Topics* and the Platonic Theory of Principles of Being." In *Aristotle on Dialectic: The Topics*, edited by G. E. L. Owen, 126–37. Oxford: Clarendon Press.

Enos, Richard L. 1993. *Greek Rhetoric Before Aristotle*. Prospect Heights, IL: Waveland Press.

Fagan, P. 2013. *Plato and Tradition: The Poetic and Cultural Context of Philosophy*. Evanston, IL: Northwestern University Press.

Ferrari, G. R. F. 1987. *Listening to the Cicadas: A Study of Plato's "Phaedrus."* Cambridge: Cambridge University Press.
Field, G. C. 1930. *Plato and His Contemporaries.* London: Methuen and Co.
Flusser, Vilém. 2002. "Line and Surface." Translated by Erik Eisel. In *Writings*, edited by Andreas Ströhl, 21–34. Minneapolis: University of Minnesota Press.
Fossheim, Hallvard, Vigdis Songe-Møller, and Knot Ågotnes, eds. 2019. *Philosophy as Drama: Plato's Thinking Through Dialogue.* London: Bloomsbury.
Frank, Jill. 2018. *Poetic Justice: Rereading Plato's "Republic."* Chicago: University of Chicago Press.
Freeman, Kathleen. 1948. *Ancilla to the pre-Socratic Philosophers: A Complete Translation of the Fragments in Diels, Fragmente der Vorsokratiker.* Oxford: Harvard University Press.
Friedländer, Paul. 1945. "Review of Richard Robinson's *Plato's Early Dialectic*, 1st edition." *Classical Philology* 40 (4): 253–59.
———. 1958. *Plato: An Introduction.* New York: Harper and Row.
Futter, Dylan. 2014. "The Myth of Theseus in Plato's *Phaedo*." *Akroterion* 59, 98–103.
Gadamer, H.-G. 1980. *Dialogue and Dialectic: Eight Hermeneutical Studies on Plato.* Translated by P. C. Smith. New Haven, CT: Yale University Press.
Gagarin, Michael. 2002. *Antiphon the Athenian: Oratory, Law, and Justice in the Age of the Sophists.* Austin: University of Texas Press.
Gass, William H. 1985. *Habitations of the Word.* Ithaca, NY: Cornell University Press.
Gill, Christopher. 1996. "Dialectic and the Dialogue Form in Late Plato." In *Form and Argument in Late Plato*, edited by Christopher Gill and Mary Margaret McCabe, 283–311. Oxford: Oxford University Press.
———. 2002. "Dialectic and the Dialogue Form." In *New Perspectives on Plato, Modern and Ancient*, edited by Julia Annas and Christopher Rowe, 145–71. Cambridge, MA: Harvard University Press.
Gill, Mary Louise. 1996. *Parmenides.* Indianapolis, IN: Hackett Publishing.
Glucker, John. 2020. "Plato in the Academy: Some Cautious Reflections." In *Plato's Academy: Its Working and its History*, edited by Paul Kalligas et al., 89–107. Cambridge: Cambridge University Press.
Golden, James L, Goodwin F. Berquist, William E. Coleman, and J. Michael Sproule, eds. 2000. *The Rhetoric of Western Thought: From the Mediterranean World to the Global Setting.* 7th edition. Dubuque, IA: Kendall/Hunt Publishing.
Gonzalez, Francisco J. 1998. *Dialectic and Dialogue: Plato's Practice of Philosophical Inquiry.* Evanston, IL: Northwestern University Press.
———. 2000. "The Eleatic Stranger: His Master's Voice?" In *Who Speaks for Plato? Studies in Platonic Anonymity*, edited by Gerald A. Press, 161–81. Oxford: Rowman and Littlefield.
Graham, Daniel D. 1992. "Socrates and Plato." *Phronesis* 37 (2): 141–65.
Grassi, Ernesto. 1980. *Philosophy as Rhetoric: The Humanist Tradition.* Carbondale: Southern Illinois University Press.

Grimaldi, W. M. A. 1996. "How Do We Get from Corax-Tisias to Plato-Aristotle in Greek Rhetorical Theory?" In *Theory, Text, Context: Issues in Greek Rhetoric and Oratory*, edited by Christopher Lyle Johnstone, 19–43. Albany: State University of New York Press.

Griswold, C. L. 1988. "Plato's Metaphilosophy: Why Plato Wrote Dialogues." In *Platonic Writings, Platonic Readings*, edited by Charles L. Griswold Jr., 143–67. London: Routledge.

———. 1986. *Self-Knowledge in Plato's Phaedrus*. New Haven, CT: Yale University Press. Reprint 1996 with new preface and supplementary bibliography. University Park: Pennsylvania State University Press.

Grote, G. (1867) 2010. *Plato and the Other Companions of Socrates*. Vol. 1. Cambridge: Cambridge University Press.

Guthrie, W. K. C. 1978. *A History of Greek Philosophy*. Vol. 5. Cambridge: Cambridge University Press.

———. 1971. *The Sophists*. Cambridge: Cambridge University Press.

Hacking, I. 1973. "Proof and Eternal Truth: Descartes and Leibniz." In *Descartes: Philosophy, Mathematics and Physics*, edited by S. Gaukroger. Sussex, UK: Harvester Press.

Halliwell, Stephen. 2007. "The Life-and-Death Journey of the Soul: Interpreting the Myth of Er." In *Cambridge Companion to Plato's* Republic, edited by G. R. F. Ferrari, 445–73. Cambridge: Cambridge University Press.

Halliwell, Stephen. 1994. "Philosophy and Rhetoric." In *Persuasion: Greek Rhetoric in Action*, edited by Ian Worthington, 222–43. New York: Routledge.

Hamblin, Charles L. 1970. *Fallacies*. London: Methuen and Co.

Harris, John P. 2018. "Flies, Wasps, and Gadflies: The Role of Insect Similes in Homer, Aristophanes, and Plato." *Mouseion: Journal of the Classical Association of Canada* 15, 475–500.

Havelock, Eric A. 1957. *The Liberal Temper in Greek Politics*. London: Jonathan Cape.

———. 1963. *Preface to Plato*. New York: Grosset and Dunlap.

———. 1986. *The Muse Learns to Write: Reflections on the Orality and Literacy from Antiquity to the Present*. New Haven, CT: Yale University Press.

Heidlebaugh, Nola. 2001. *Judgment, Rhetoric, and the Problem of Incommensurability: Recalling Practical Wisdom*. Columbia: University of South Carolina Press.

Herrick, James A. 2001. *The History and Theory of Rhetoric: An Introduction*. Needham, MA: Allyn and Bacon.

Hippocrates. 1959. "Nature of Man." In *Hippocates*. Vol. IV. Translated by W. H. S. Jones. Loeb Classical Library. Cambridge, MA: Harvard University Press.

Hobbes, Angela. 2007. "Female Imagery in Plato." In *Plato's Symposium: Issues in Interpretation and Reception*, edited by D. Nails, J. Lesher, and F. Sheffield, 252–72. Hellenic Studies Series 22. Washington, DC: Center for Hellenic Studies.

Huby, P. 1997. "Aristotle and Informal Logic." In *Historical Foundations of Informal Logic*, edited by D. Walton and A. Brinton, 36–50. Aldershot, UK: Ashgate Publishing.

Hume, David. (1779) 1980. *Dialogues Concerning Natural Religion and Posthumous Essays*. Edited by Richard H. Popkin. Indianapolis, IN: Hackett Publishing.

Hutchinson, D. S. 1997. "Introduction to *Definitions*." In *Plato: Complete Works*, edited by John M. Cooper, 1677–78. Indianapolis, IN: Hackett Publishing.

Irani, Tushar. 2017. *Plato and the Value of Philosophy: The Art of Argument in the "Gorgias" and "Phaedrus."* Cambridge: Cambridge University Press.

Isocrates. 1929a. "Panathenaicus." In *Isocrates in Three Volumes*. Vol. II. Translated by George Norlin. Loeb Classical Library. Cambridge, MA: Harvard University Press.

———. 1929b. "Antidosis." In *Isocrates in Three Volumes*. Vol. II. Translated by George Norlin. Loeb Classical Library. Cambridge, MA: Harvard University Press.

Jarratt, Susan. 1991. *Rereading the Sophists: Classical Rhetoric Refigured*. Carbondale: Southern Illinois University Press.

Jebb, R. C. 2016. *Jebb's Isocrates*. Newly edited by E. Schiappa, D. M. Timmerman, and G. Lauren. Philadelphia, PA: Sophron Editor.

Johnson, David M., trans. 2003. *Socrates and Alcibiades: Plato Alcibiades* I, *Plato (?) Alcibiades* II, *Plato* Symposium *(212c–223b), Aeschines of Sphettus "Alcibiades."* Newburyport, MA: Focus Publishing.

Kahn, C. H. 1992. "Vlastos's Socrates." *Phronesis* 37 (2): 233–58.

———. 1996. *Plato and the Socratic Dialogue: The Philosophical Use of a Literary Form*. Cambridge: Cambridge University Press.

———. 2003. "Writing Philosophy: Prose and Poetry from Thales to Plato." In *Written Texts and the Rise of Literate Culture in Ancient Greece*, edited by Harvey Yunis, 139–61. Cambridge: Cambridge University Press.

———. 2009. "The Myth of the *Statesman*." In *Plato's Myths*, edited by Cataline Partenie, 149–66. Cambridge: Cambridge University Press.

———. 2013. *Plato and the Post-Socratic Dialogue: The Return to a Philosophy of Nature*. Cambridge: Cambridge University Press.

Kastely, James L. 1997. *Rethinking the Rhetorical Tradition: From Plato to Postmodernism*. New Haven, CT: Yale University Press.

———. 2015. *The Rhetoric of Plato's "Republic": Democracy and the Philosophical Problem of Persuasion*. Chicago: University of Chicago Press.

Kennedy, George. 1963. *The Art of Persuasion in Greece*. Princeton, NJ: Princeton University Press.

Kennedy, George A. 1999. *Classical Rhetoric and its Christian and Secular Tradition from Ancient to Modern Times*. 2nd edition. Chapel Hill: University of North Carolina Press.

Kerferd, G. B. 1955. "Review of Richard Robinson's *Plato's Earlier Dialectic*, 2nd edition." *The Classical Review* 5 (1): 50–52.
———. 1974. "Plato's Treatment of Callicles in the *Gorgias*." *Proceedings of the Cambridge Philological Society* 20 (200): 48–52.
———. 1981. *The Sophistic Movement*. Cambridge: Cambridge University Press.
Kinneavy, James L. 1994. "*Kairos*: A Neglected Concept in Classical Rhetoric." In *Landmark Essays in on Rhetorical Invention in Writing*, edited by Richard E. Young and Yameng Liu, 221–39. Mahwah, NJ: Lawrence Erlbaum Associates.
———. 2002. "*Kairos* in Classical and Modern Rhetorical Theory." In *Rhetoric and Kairos: Essays in History, Theory, and Praxis*, edited by Phillip Sipora and James S. Baumlin, 58–76. Albany: State University of New York Press.
Ledger, Gerard R. 1989. *Re-counting Plato: A Computer Analysis of Plato's Style*. Oxford: Oxford University Press.
Leroi, Armand Marie. 2014. *The Lagoon: How Aristotle Invented Science*. London: Penguin.
Levett, Brad. 2005. "Platonic Paraody in the *Gorgias*." *Phoenix* 59, 210–27.
Liddell, Henry George, and Robert Scott. (1843) 1968. *Greek-English Lexicon*. Oxford: Clarendon Press.
Lévystone, David. 2020. "Socrates' Versatile Rhetoric and the Soul of the Crowd." *Rhetorica* 38 (2): 135–55.
Lloyd, Geoffrey E. R. 1966. *Polarity and Analogy: Two Types of Argumentation in Early Greek Thought*. Cambridge: Cambridge University Press.
———. 1990. *Demystifying Mentalities*. Cambridge: Cambridge University Press.
———. 2015. *Analogical Investigations: Historical and Cross-cultural Perspectives on Human Reasoning*. Cambridge: Cambridge University Press.
———. 2018. *The Ambivalences of Rationality: Ancient and Modern Cross-Cultural Explorations*. Cambridge: Cambridge University Press.
Locke, John. (1689) 1996. *An Essay Concerning Human Understanding*. Edited by K. P. Winkler. Indianapolis, IN: Hackett Publishing.
Luria, Alexander. 1976. *Cognitive Development: Its Cultural and Social Foundations*. Translated by Martin Lopez-Morillas and Lynn Solotaroff. Cambridge, MA: Harvard University Press.
Lutoslawski, Wincenty. 1897. *The Origin and Growth of Plato's Logic, with an Account of Plato's Style and of the Chronology of His Writings*. London: Longmans, Green, and Co.
Luzzatto, Maria Tanja. 2020. "Did Gorgias Coin *Rhētorikē*? A Rereading of Plato's *Gorgias*." *Lexis* 38 (1): 183–224.
McAdon, Brad. 2004. "Reconsidering the Intention or Purpose of Aristotle's "Rhetoric." *Rhetoric Review* 23, 216–34.
McCabe, M. M. 1994. "Persistent Fallacies." In *Aristotelian Society Proceedings*, 73–79. Bristol, UK: Longdunn Press.
McCoy, Marina. 2008. *Plato and the Rhetoric of Philosophers and Sophists*. Cambridge: Cambridge University Press.

———. 2020. *Image and Argument in Plato's "Republic."* Albany: State University of New York Press.
McLuhan, Marshall. 1962. *The Gutenberg Galaxy: The Making of Typographic Man.* Toronto: University of Toronto Press.
McPherran, Mark L. 2009. "Platonic Religion." In *A Companion to Plato*, edited by Hugh Benson, 244–59. Oxford: Wiley-Blackwell.
McPherran, Mark L. 1996. *The Religion of Socrates*. University Park: Pennsylvania State University Press.
Magrini, J. M. 2017. *Reconceptualizing Plato's Socrates at the Limit of Education: A Socratic Curriculum Grounded in Finite Human Transcendence*. New York: Routledge.
Marion, Mathieu. 2021. "Plato's Dialogues: Dialectic, Orality and Character." In *Essays on Argumentation in Antiquity*, edited by Joseph A. Bjelde et al., 69–97. Dordrecht: Springer.
Mattéi, Jean-François. 1988. "The Theater of Myth in Plato." In *Platonic Writings, Platonic Readings*, edited by Charles L. Griswold Jr., 66–83. London: Routledge.
Milton, John. 1674. *Paradise Lost*. 2nd edition. London: S. Simmons.
Moore, Holly. 2021. "Does Plato have a Theory of Induction? *Epagôgê* and the Method of Collection 'Purified' of the Senses." In *Essays on Argumentation in Antiquity*, edited by Joseph A. Bjelde et al., 185–200. Dordrecht: Springer.
Moravcsik, Julius M. E. 1973. "Plato's Method of Division." In *Patterns in Plato's Thought*, edited by J. M. E. Moravcsik, 158–180. Dordrecht: Springer.
Morrow, Glenn R. 1953. "Plato's Conception of Persuasion." *Philosophical Review* 62 (2): 234–50.
Most, Glenn W. 1999. "From *Logos* to *Mythos*." In *From Myth to Reason? Studies in the Development of Greek Thought*, edited by R. Buxton, 25–47. Oxford: Oxford University Press.
Mueller, Ian. 1992. "Mathematical Method and Philosophical Truth." In *The Cambridge Companion to Plato*, edited by Richard Kraut, 170–199. Cambridge: Cambridge University Press.
Muniz, Fernando, and George Rudebusch. 2018. "Dividing Plato's Kinds." *Phronesis: A Journal of Ancient Philosophy* 63 (4): 392–407.
Murray, James Stuart. 2020. "Enchanted by the Search for Plato's Academy, 1955–1963." *Mouseion: Journal of the Classical Association of Canada* 17 (2): 213–39.
Nails, Debra. 2002. *The People of Plato: A Prosopography of Plato and Other Socratics*. Indianapolis, IN: Hackett Publishing.
———. 2009. "The Life of Plato of Athens." In *A Companion to Plato*, edited by Hugh H. Benson, 1–12. Oxford: Wiley/Blackwell.
Natali, C. 2013. *Aristotle: His Life and School*. Edited by D. S. Hutchinson. Princeton, NJ: Princeton University Press.
Nehamas, A. 1975. "Confusing Universals and Particulars in Plato's Early Dialogues." *Review of Metaphysics* 29, 287–306.

———. 1999. "Eristic, Antilogic, Sophistic, Dialectic: Plato's Demarcation of Philosophy from Sophistry." In *Virtues of Authenticity: Essays on Plato and Socrates*, edited by A. Nehamas, 108–122. Princeton, NJ: Princeton University Press.
Nightingale, Andrea. 1995. *Genres in Dialogue: Plato and the Construct of Philosophy*. Cambridge: Cambridge University Press.
———. 2004. *Spectacles of Truth in Classical Greek Philosophy: Theoria in its Cultural Context*. Cambridge: Cambridge University Press.
Notomi, N. 1999. *The Unity of Plato's "Sophist": Between the Sophist and the Philosopher*. Cambridge: Cambridge University Press.
Nye, A. 1990. *Words of Power*. New York: Routledge.
O'Grady, Patricia. 2008. "What is a Sophist?" In *The Sophists: An Introduction*, edited by P. O'Grady, 9–20. London: Gerald Duckworth.
Ong, Walter J. 1958. *Ramus: Method, and the Decay of Dialogue*. Chicago: University of Chicago Press.
———. 1982. *Orality and Literacy*. London: Methuen.
Owen, D. 2002. *Hume's Reason*. Oxford: Oxford University Press.
Pernot, Laurent. 2005. *Rhetoric in Antiquity*. Translated by W. E. Higgins. Washington, DC: Catholic University of America Press.
Philodemus. 2020. *History of the Philosophers*. Translated by Paul Kalligas and Voula Tsouna. In *Plato's Academy: Its Working and History*, edited by Paul Kallugas, Chloe Balla, Effie Baziotopoulou-Valavani, and Vassilis Karasmanis, 276–383. Cambridge: Cambridge University Press.
Philostratus. 1921. *Lives of the Sophists*. Translated by Wilmer C. Wright. Loeb Classical Library. Cambridge, MA: Harvard University Press.
Plato. 1914. *Euthyphro, Apology, Crito, Phaedo, Phaedrus*. Translated by H. N. Fowler. Loeb Classical Library. Cambridge, MA: Harvard University Press.
———. 1921. *Theaetetus*. Translated by H. N. Fowler. Loeb Classical Library. Cambridge, MA: Harvard University Press.
———. 1924. *Euthydemus*. Translated by W. R. M. Lamb. Loeb Classical Library. Cambridge, MA: Harvard University Press.
———. 1925a. *Philebus*. Translated by H. N. Fowler. Loeb Classical Library. Cambridge, MA: Harvard University Press.
———. 1925b. *Statesman*. Translated by H. N. Fowler. Loeb Classical Library. Cambridge, MA: Harvard University Press.
———. 1929. *Timaeus, Critias, Cleitophon, Menexenus, Epistles*. Translated by R. G. Bury. Loeb Classical Library. Cambridge, MA: Harvard University Press.
———. 1935. *Republic: Books VI–X*. Translated by Paul Shorey. Loeb Classical Library. Cambridge, MA: Harvard University Press.
———. 1942. *The Republic of Plato: A Version in Simplified English*. Translated by I. A. Richards. New York: W. W. Norton.
———. 1952a. *The Statesman*. Translated by J. B. Skemp. 2nd edition. Bristol: Bristol Classical Press.

———. 1952b. *Plato's Phaedrus*. Translated with introduction and commentary by R. Hackforth. Cambridge: Cambridge University Press.

———. 1953. *Apology*. In *Dialogues of Plato*. Translated by Benjamin Jowett. Oxford: Clarendon Press.

———. 1955. *Alcibiades I*. Translated by W. R. M. Lamb. Loeb Classical Library. Cambridge, MA: Harvard University Press.

———. 1959. *Gorgias: A Revised Text with Introduction and Commentary*. Translated and revised by E. R. Dodds. Oxford: Clarendon Press.

———. 1960. *Plato:* Gorgias. Translated by Walter Hamilton. London: Penguin Books.

———. 1961. *Euthydemus*. In *Plato: The Collected Dialogues*. Translated by W. H. D. Rouse, E. Hamilton, and H. Cairns. Princeton, NJ: Princeton University Press.

———. 1965. *Euthydemus*. Translated by R. Kent Sprague. New York: Bobbs-Merrill Co.

———. 1968. *The Republic of Plato*. Translated with a commentary by Allan Bloom. 2nd edition. New York: Basic Books.

———. 1972. *Plato's "Philebus."* Translated with a commentary by Reginald Hackforth. Cambridge: Cambridge University Press.

———. 1975a. *Plato: Philebus*. Translated with a commentary by J. C. B. Gosling. Oxford: Clarendon Press.

———. 1975b. *Plato: Phaedo*. Translated with a commentary by David Gallop. Oxford: Clarendon Press.

———. 1975c. *Phaedrus*. Translated with notes and introduction by A. Nehamas and R. Woodruff. Indianapolis, IN: Hackett Publishing.

———. 1984. *Plato's "Statesman": Part III of the Being of the Beautiful*. Translated with a commentary by Seth Benardete. Chicago: University of Chicago Press.

———. 1986. *Plato: Phaedrus*. Translated with a commentary by Christopher Rowe. Warminster, UK: Aris and Phillips.

———. 1989. *Symposium*. Translated by Alexander Nehamas and Paul Woodruff. Indianapolis, IN: Hackett Publishing.

———. 1991. *The Tragedy and Comedy of Life: Plato's "Philebus."* Translated with a commentary by Seth Benardete. Chicago: University of Chicago Press.

———. 1994. *Gorgias*. Translated with an introduction and notes by Robin Waterfield. Oxford: Oxford University Press.

———. 1997a. *Phaedo*. Translated by G. M. A. Grube. In *Plato: Complete Works*, edited by John M. Cooper. Indianapolis, IN: Hackett Publishing.

———. 1997b. *Theaetetus*. Translated by Myles F. Burnyeat. In *Plato: Complete Works*, edited by John M. Cooper. Indianapolis, IN: Hackett Publishing.

———. 1997c. *Laws*. Translated by Trevor Sanders. In *Plato: Complete Works*, edited by John M. Cooper. Indianapolis, IN: Hackett Publishing.

———. 1997d. *Sophist*. Translated by Nicholas P. White. In *Plato: Complete Works*, edited by John M. Cooper. Indianapolis, IN: Hackett Publishing.

———. 1997e. *Definitions*. Translated by Douglas Hutcinson. In *Plato: Complete Works*, edited by John M. Cooper. Indianapolis, IN: Hackett Publishing.

———. 1997f. *Parmenides*. Translated by Mary Louise Gill and Paul Ryan. In *Plato: Complete Works*, edited by John M. Cooper. Indianapolis, IN: Hackett Publishing.

———. 1998a. *Gorgias*. Translated by James H. Nichols Jr. Ithaca, NY: Cornell University Press.

———. 1998b. *Phaedrus*. Translated James H. Nichols Jr. Ithaca, NY: Cornell University Press.

———. 2004. *Republic*. Translated by C. D. C. Reeve. Indianapolis, IN: Hackett Publishing.

———. 2012a. *Meno*. Translated by C. D. C. Reeve. In *A Plato Reader: Eight Essential Dialogues*, edited by C. D. C. Reeve. Indianapolis, IN: Hackett Publishing.

———. 2012b. *Phaedo*. Translated by C. D. C. Reeve. In *A Plato Reader: Eight Essential Dialogues*, edited by C. D. C. Reeve. Indianapolis, IN: Hackett Publishing.

Plotinus. 1969. *The Enneads*. Translated by Stephen MacKenna. London: Faber and Faber Limited.

Poste, E. 1866. *Aristotle on Fallacies, or, the Sophistici Elenchi*. London: Macmillan and Co.

Poulakos, John. 1995. *Sophistical Rhetoric in Classical Greece*. Columbia: University of South Carolina Press.

Quintilian. 2015. *Institutes of Oratory*. Translated by John Selby Watson with revision by Curtis Dozier. CreateSpace Independent Publishing Platform.

Reeve, C. D. C. 1988. *Philosopher-Kings: The Argument of Plato's "Republic."* Princeton, NJ: Princeton University Press. Reissued 2006 by Hackett Publishing.

———. 2002. *The Trials of Socrates: Six Classic Texts*. Indianapolis, IN: Hackett Publishing.

Reeves, J. 2013. "Suspended Identification: *Atopos* and the Work of Public Memory." *Philosophy and Rhetoric* 46 (3): 306–27.

Richards, I. A. 1942. *How to Read a Page*. Boston: Beacon Press.

Ritter, Constantin. 1933. *The Essence of Plato's Philosophy*. London: George Allen and Unwin.

Robinson, R. (1941) 1953. *Plato's Earlier Dialectic*. Ithaca, NY: Cornell University Press. First edition published 1941; second edition published 1953.

———. 1942. "Plato's Consciousness of Fallacy." *Mind* LI (202): 97–114.

Robinson, T. M. 1984. *Contrasting Arguments: An Edition of the* Dissoi Logoi. Manchester, NH: Ayer Company Publishers.

Roochnik, David. 2003. *Beautiful City: The Dialectical Character of Plato's "Republic."* Ithaca, NY: Cornell University Press.

Rosen, S. 1995. *Plato's "Statesman": The Web of Politics*. New Haven, CT: Yale University Press.

Rosenstock, Bruce. 1997. "From Counter-rhetoric to *Askesis*: How the *Phaedo* Rewrites the *Gorgias*." In *The Rhetoric Canon*, edited by Brenda Schildgen, 83–105. Detroit, MI: Wayne State University Press.

Rossetti, Livio. 1989. "The Rhetoric of Socrates." *Philosophy and Rhetoric* 22 (4): 225–38.

Rowe, Christopher. 2006. "Socrates in Plato's Dialogues." In *A Companion to Socrates*, edited by Sara Ahbel-Rappe and Rachana Kamtekar, 159–70. Oxford: Wiley-Blackwell.

———. 2009. "Interpreting Plato." In *A Companion to Plato*, edited by Hugh H. Benson, 13–24. Oxford: Wiley-Blackwell.

Runciman, W. G. 1962. *Plato's Later Epistemology*. Cambridge: Cambridge University Press.

Russon, J., and J. Sallis, eds. 2000. *Retracing the Platonic Text*. Evanston, IL: Northwestern University Press.

Ryle, G. 1968. "Dialectic in the Academy." In *Aristotle on Dialectic: The Topics*, edited by G. E. L. Owen, 69–79. Oxford: Clarendon Press.

Ryle, Gilbert. 1966. *Plato's Progress*. Cambridge: Cambridge University Press.

Sachs, Joe, trans. 2009. *Plato "Gorgias" and Aristotle "Rhetoric."* Indianapolis, IN: Hackett Publishing.

Sansone, David. 2012. *Greek Drama and the Invention of Rhetoric*. Malden, MA: John Wiley and Sons.

Saxonhouse, Arlene W. 1978. "Comedy in Callipolis: Animal Imagery in the *Republic*." *American Political Science Review* 72, 888–901.

Sayre, Kenneth M. 2006. *Metaphysics and Method in Plato's "Statesman."* Cambridge: Cambridge University Press.

Schiappa, Edward. 1999. *The Beginnings of Rhetorical Theory in Classical Greece*. New Haven, CT: Yale University Press.

———. 2017. "The Development of Greek Rhetoric." In *The Oxford Handbook of Rhetorical Studies*, edited by Michael J. MacDonald, 33–42. Oxford: Oxford University Press.

———. 2022. "Plato or Gorgias? Considering the Origins of the Word *Rhētorikē* in the *Gorgias*." In *Gorgias/Gorgias: The Sicilian Orator and the Platonic Dialogue*, edited by S. Montgomery Ewegen and Coleen P. Zoller, 197–214. Siracusa, Sicily: Parnassos Press.

Schreiber, S. G. 2003. *Aristotle on False Reasoning: Language and the World in the "Sophistical Refutations."* Albany: State University of New York Press.

Schofield, Malcolm. 2006. *Plato: Political Philosophy*. Oxford: Oxford University Press.

Scott, Dominic. 2020. *Listening to Reason in Plato and Aristotle*. Oxford: Oxford University Press.

Scott, Gary Alan, ed. 2002. *Does Socrates Have a Method? Rethinking the "Elenchus" in Plato's Dialogues and Beyond*. University Park: Pennsylvania State University Press.

Seligman, Paul. 1974. *Being and Not-Being: An Introduction to Plato's "Sophist."* The Hague: Martinus Nijhoff.

Sesonske, Alexander. 1968. "To Make the Weaker Argument Defeat the Stronger." *Journal of the History of Philosophy* 6 (3): 217–31.

Shorey, Paul. 1903. *The Unity of Plato's Thought.* Chicago: University of Chicago Press.

———. 1933. *What Plato Said: A Résumé and Analysis of Plato's Writings with Synopses and Critical Comment.* Chicago: University of Chicago Press.

Sipora, P. 2002. "Introduction: The Ancient Concept of *Kairos.*" In *Rhetoric and Kairos: Essays in History, Theory, and Praxis,* edited by Phillip Sipora and James S. Baumlin, 1–22. Albany: State University of New York Press.

Slings, S. R. 1999. *Plato: Clitophon.* Cambridge Classical Texts. Cambridge: Cambridge University Press.

Smith, Nicholas D. 2004. "Did Plato Write *Alcibiades I*?" *Apeiron: A Journal for Ancient Philosophy and Science* 37 (2): 93–108.

Smith, P. C. 1998. *The Hermeneutics of Original Argument: Demonstration, Dialectic, Rhetoric.* Evanston, IL: Northwestern University Press.

Solmsen, Friedrich. 1968. "The Aristotelian Tradition in Ancient Rhetoric." In *Rhetorika: Schriften zur aristotelischen und hellenistischen Rhetorik,* edited by Rudolf Stark, 169–90. Hildesheim: Georg Olms Verlagbuchhandlung.

———. 1975. *Intellectual Experiments of the Greek Enlightenment.* Princeton, NJ: Princeton University Press.

Sprague, Rosamund Kent. 1962. *Plato's Use of Fallacy: A Study of the "Euthydemus" and Some Other Dialogues.* London: Routledge and Kegan Paul.

Strauss, Leo. 1964. *The City and Man.* Chicago: University of Chicago Press.

Talisse, Robert B. 2002. "Misunderstanding Socrates." *Arion* 9, 45–56.

Taplin, O. 1972. "Aeschylean Silences and Silences in Aeschylus." *Harvard Studies in Classical Philology* 76, 57–97.

Tarrant, H. 1988. "Midwifery and the Clouds." *Classical Quarterly* 38, 116–22.

———. 1993. *Thrasyllan Platonism.* Ithaca, NY: Cornell University Press.

———. 2000. *Plato's First Interpreters.* Ithaca, NY: Cornell University Press.

———. 2002. "*Elenchos* and *Exetasis*: Capturing the Purpose of Socratic Interrogation." In *Does Socrates Have a Method? Rethinking the Elenchus in Plato's Dialogues and Beyond,* edited by Gary Alan Scott, 61–77. University Park: Pennsylvania State University Press.

Tate, J. 1928. "'Imitation' in Plato's *Republic.*" *Classical Quarterly* 22 (1): 16–23.

Taylor, A. E. 1960. *Plato: The Man and His Work.* London: Methuen Press.

Tell, H. 2011. *Plato's Counterfeit Sophists.* Cambridge, MA: Center for Hellenic Studies.

Thompson, Roger, and James Kinneavy. 2000. "Kairos Revisited: An Interview with James Kinneavy." *Rhetoric Review* 19 (1/2, Autumn): 73–88.

Thompson, Wayne N. 1972. "The *Symposium*: A Neglected Source for Plato's Ideas on Rhetoric." *Southern Speech Communication Journal* 37 (3): 219–32.

Thucydides. 1910. *History of the Peloponnesian War*. Translated by Richard Crawley. New York: J. M. Dent & Sons.

Timmerman, David M. 1993. "Ancient Greek Origins of Argumentation Theory: Plato's Transformation of *Dialegesthai* to Dialectic." *Argumentation and Advocacy* 29 (3): 116–23.

Timmerman, David M., and Edward Schiappa. 2010. *Classical Greek Rhetorical Theory and the Disciplining of Discourse*. Cambridge: Cambridge University Press.

Tindale, Christopher W. 1999. *Acts of Arguing: A Rhetorical Model of Argument*. Albany: State University of New York Press.

———. 2007. *Fallacies and Argument Appraisal*. Cambridge: Cambridge University Press.

———. 2009. "Two-fold Arguments." In *Meaning, Content and Argument*, edited by J. Larrazabal and L. Zubeldia, 89–108. Bilbao: University of the Basque Country Press.

———. 2010. *Reason's Dark Champions: Constructive Strategies of Sophistic Argument*. Columbia: University of South Carolina Press.

———. 2021a. *The Anthropology of Argument: Cultural Foundations of Rhetoric and Reason*. New York: Routledge.

———. 2021b. "The Prospects for Rhetoric in the Late Plato." In *Essays on Argumentation in Antiquity*, edited by Joseph A. Bjelde et al., 173–83. Dordrecht: Springer.

Tomin, J. 1987. "Socratic Midwifery." *The Classical Quarterly* 37, 97–102.

Too, Yun Lee. 1995. *The Rhetoric of Identity in Isocrates: Text, Power, Pedagogy*. Cambridge: Cambridge University Press.

Tuominen, Miira. 2009. *The Ancient Commentators on Plato and Aristotle*. Berkeley: University of California Press.

Untersteiner, M. 1954. *The Sophists*. Translated by Kathleen Freeman. Oxford: Basil Blackwell.

Usher, Stephen. 2010. "Apostrophe in Greek Oratory." *Rhetorica: A Journal of the History of Rhetoric* 28 (4): 351–62.

Van Eemeren, Frans H., Bart Garssen, Erik C. W. Krabbe, A. Francisca Snoeck Henkemans, Bart Verheij, and Jean H. M. Wagemans, eds. 2014. *Handbook of Argumentation Theory*. Dordrecht: Springer Reference.

Vander Waerdt, Paul A., ed. 1994. *The Socratic Movement*. Ithaca, NY: Cornell University Press.

Versenyi, L. 1975. "Plato's Lysis." *Phronesis* 23, 185–98.

Vickers, Brian. 1988. *In Defence of Rhetoric*. Oxford: Clarendon Press.

Viidebaum, Laura. 2021. *Creating the Ancient Rhetorical Tradition*. Cambridge: Cambridge University Press.

Vlastos, G. 1983. "The Socratic Elenchus." *Oxford Studies in Ancient Philosophy* 1, 27–58.

———. 1991. *Socrates: Ironist and Moral Philosopher*. Cambridge: Cambridge University Press.

———. 1994. "The Demise of the Elenchus in the *Euthydemus*, *Lysis*, and *Hippias Major*." In *Socratic Studies*, edited by Myles Burnyeat, 29–33. Cambridge: Cambridge University Press.

Voegelin, Eric. 1966. *Plato*. Baton Rouge: Louisiana State University Press.

Walton, Douglas. 2006a. *Fundamentals of Critical Argumentation*. Cambridge: Cambridge University Press.

———. 2006b. *Character Evidence: An Abductive Theory*. Dordrecht: Springer.

Wardy, Robert. 1996. *The Birth of Rhetoric: Gorgias, Plato and Their Successors*. London: Routledge.

———. 2009. "The Philosophy of Rhetoric, and the Rhetoric of Philosophy." In *The Cambridge Companion to Ancient Rhetoric*, edited by Erik Gunderson, 43–58. Cambridge: Cambridge University Press.

Warman, M. S. 1983. "Plato and Persuasion." *Greece & Rome* 30 (1): 48–54.

Waterfield, Robin. 2009. "The Historical Socrates." *History Today* (Jan.): 24–29.

Wenzel, J. W. 2006. "Three Perspectives on Argument: Rhetoric, Dialectic, Logic." In *Perspectives on Argumentation: Essays in Honor of Wayne Brockriede*, edited by Robert Trapp and Janice Schuetz, 9–26. New York: International Debate Education Association.

White, Eric Charles. 1987. *Kaironomia: On the Will to Invent*. Ithaca, NY: Cornell University Press.

White, Michael J. 2009. "Plato and Mathematics." In *A Companion to Plato*, edited by Hugh Benson, 228–43. Oxford: Wiley-Blackwell.

White, Stephen. 1995. "Thrasymachus the Diplomat." *Classical Philology* 90, 307–27.

Woodruff, Paul. 1982. *Plato: Hippias Major*. Indianapolis, IN: Hackett Publishing.

Xenophon. 2013. *Memorabilia. Oeconomicus. Symposium. Apology*. Translated by O. J. Todd. Loeb Classical Library. Cambridge, MA: Harvard University Press.

Young, Charles M. 2009. "The Socratic Elenchus." In *A Companion to Plato*, edited by H. Benson, 55–69. Oxford: Blackwell Publishing.

Yunis, Harvey. 2007. "The Protreptic Rhetoric of the *Republic*." In *Cambridge Companion to Plato's* Republic, edited by G. R. F. Ferrari, 1–26. Cambridge: Cambridge University Press.

———. 2017. "Plato's Rhetoric in Theory and Practice." In *The Oxford Handbook of Rhetorical Studies*, edited by Michael J. MacDonald, 121–31. Oxford: Oxford University Press.

Zeller, Eduard. 1839. *Platonische Studien*. Tübingen: C. F. Osiander.

Zuckert, Catherine H. 2009. *Plato's Philosophers: The Coherence of the Dialogues*. Chicago: University of Chicago Press.

Index

Academy, 2, 10, 11, 27, 66, 68, 75, 87, 215, 223, 224n3, 225–26, 227n5, 234n7, 240, 243, 248, 273, 280, 288–89, 290n22
actions, as arguments, 7, 32, 33, 60, 103; and character, 60–62, 171, 253
Adeimantus, 35, 38, 95, 177, 186, 187, 189–90, 193–95, 198–99, 206, 213; education of, 195–96, 279, 286
Aeschines of Sphettus, 226, 237; *Alcibiades*, 40–41
Agathon, 133n19, 168
Ågotnes, Knot, 177
Alcibiades, 34n7, 36, 37, 39, 40–41, 50n4, 59, 96, 129, 136, 201
allegory of cave, 143, 150, 174, 182, 194, 197–98
Allen, Danielle S., 268
analogical reasoning, 208–209, 227; *see also* argument from analogy
analogy, 43, 69, 174–75, 192, 197, 205, 206n5, 208, 209, 210, 211, 213, 253, 268, 269, 277, 278; as a method, 203, 209
antilogoi, 36, 254, 258
Antiphon, 110, 159n6; *Tetralogies*, 17, 19, 145–46
Antisthenes, 226, 237n12; the *Ajax* 7, 89

aporia 56n9, 114, 120
argument from analogy, 16
argumentation: theory, Plato's place in, 1, 24; theories of, 2, 24
Aristides, 8, 48, 127, 155, 201, 271n1; *Reply to Plato*, 40, 41
Aristippus 226
Aristodemus, 168
Aristophanes, 168; *Clouds* 98, 99
Aristotle, 8n4, 9–10, 15, 16, 19, 20, 21, 77, 104, 110, 115, 150, 155, 169n15, 175, 227n5, 244, 251, 272n5; *atechnic* and *entechnic* distinction, 158; definition of rhetoric, 34n5, 167; dialectic, 82, 227, 244ff, 268; *ethos*, 61–62; *kairos*, 148; and Socrates, 23, 223, 235–37, 249; types of argument, 2
Aristotle's works, *Metaphysics*, 223, 229, 235–36; *Nicomachean Ethics*, 121, 137, 244, 245; *Parts of Animals*, 247n26; *Poetics*, 176; *Prior Analytics*, 246, 247, 248; *Rhetoric*, 3n1, 7, 11n5, 60, 97–98, 99, 116n2, 140, 146n15, 159, 179, 182, 220, 244, 246; *Sophistical Refutations*, 63–67, 72, 74, 85, 86; *Topics*, 72, 224n3, 245–46, 247, 248
Aristotelian orthodoxy, 2, 93

Asceticism, 252
Asmis, Elizabeth, 145n12
Aspasia, 96, 117
Athenian, the spokesperson of *Laws*, 217–18, 235, 273
atopos, 136, 150
audience, 58n11, 157, 164–67, 176, 191, 194–95, 197–200, 208, 209, 213, 216, 217, 279; jury as, 160–62; in *Phaedrus*, 141, 143, 147, 151, 152, 197; self as, 69, 94, 256

Badiou, Alain, 3–4, 199, 290n22
Barnes, Jonathan, 99, 271
Barney, Rachel, 27
Benjamin, James, 63n1
Benson, Hugh23n18, 230–31, 248, 252, 267
Bernardette, Seth, 80n16, 83, 204, 211n9, 215, 276n9, 278n11, 283n17
Beversluis, John, 182, 238n14
Black, Edward, 211
Blackburn, Simon, 124n12, 184
Bloom, Allan, 251
Bluck, R. S., 78
Bocheński, Józef Maria, 15
Bonazzi, Mauro, 112
Booth, Wayne, 157n3
Borges, Jorge Luis, 109
Boys-Stones, George, 7, 16n3, 89n1
Brandwood, Leonard, 156
Brickhouse, Thomas C., 53n6
Burger, Ronna, 180n1
Burke, Kenneth, 165
Burnyeat, Myles, 26, 40, 244n21, 255n5
Bury, R. G., 37n13, 116n4
Bussell, Frederick, 241n20

Calogero, Guido, 163
Callicles, identity of, 123, 130–31

Campbell, Lewis, 155
Cassin, Barbara, 84n23, 93, 148
Castelnérac, Benoît, 227n5, 244n22
Cebes, 22, 252–53, 257–58
Chance, T., 70
Charmides, 21n13, 23n17
Cicero, 8n4; *De Oratore*, 115; *Rhetorica Ad Herennium*, 115; *Topics*, 245n23
Clay, Diskin, 168
Cleinias, 28–34, 35, 38, 44, 58–59, 71–77, 79, 84, 169, 195, 202, 213, 290
Cleitophon, 34n7, 37
cognitive environment, 61, 200
Cohen, S. Marc, 282
collection and division, method of, 11, 16n2, 81, 121, 144, 199, 202–203, 207, 211–14, 217, 223, 227, 232–35, 247, 252, 263–66, 268, 272n2, 274, 276–77, 284, 291
Consigny, Scott, 116, 132, 215
Contexts, 2, 105, 149, 248, 259, 269
Conley, Tom, 111, 234
Cooper, John, 131n17
Cope, Edward M., 98
Corax, 146n15
Corlett, J. Angelo, 272n2
Cornford, F. M., 175n19
Coulter, James A., 163
Critias, 59
Crito, 31, 33–34, 56, 59, 71–72, 168, 207n8
Crombie, I. M., 43, 175
Crome, Keith, 92–93
Crooks, James, 180n1
Ctesippus, 31, 71–72, 77–78

D'Angour, Armand, 95–96
Daedalus, 56, 179–81, 243, 253, 261
deduction, 21n13, 65, 245–47, 251
definitions, study of, 11, 23, 81n17, 121, 126, 223–26, 230, 236, 242,

244, 247–48, 252, 258n9, 269, 282, 291
Dentith, Simon, 115n1
Deraj, I., 90
Descartes, Rene, 64
dialectic, as umbrella term, 10–11, 16n2, 267–69, 291; pedagogical purpose, 32, 38, 45, 198–99, 286–90; Platonic as distinct from Socratic, 2, 5, 60, 82n19, 114, 189, 192, 212, 226–27, 234–43, 283
dialegesthai, 1, 4n3, 10–11, 122, 230–32, 267–68, 285n20
dialogue form, 1, 9, 105, 157, 164, 176–77, 290
dialogue types, *see* Walton, Douglas
Diels, Hermann, 93
Dillon, John, 91
Dionysius of Halicarnassus, 185
Dionysodorus, 27–32, 54, 71–76, 79, 83, 86, 91, 168
Diotima, 38–39, 90, 95–96, 139, 141n7, 201
Disputation, 36n10, 66, 69, 122, 254, 276
Dissoi Logoi, see also *antilogoi*
divided line metaphor, 191, 197, 261
Division, *see* Collection and Division, method of
Dodds, Eric, 116, 121, 129–31
Dorter, Kenneth, 180n1
Dualism, 4, 252

Eades, T., 168
Eemeren, Frans H. van, 24
Elders, Leo, 246n25
Eleatic visitor, 80–83, 89, 178, 193n14, 203–207, 210–12, 225, 235, 272, 281–82, 286–87
elenchus, *see* Socratic argument
emotion, Plato's suspicions of, 10; role in argumentation, 160, 163

endoxa, 244–45
Enos, Richard, 17n4, 91, 131, 132
Epicrates, 135, 224, 226
epideictic speech, 17n4, 117, 129
eristic, 17n5, 17n6, 27, 31, 67, 72, 75, 79, 80, 85, 91, 93, 102, 264n12, 276; definition of, 70–71
Echecrates, 252
ethotic logic, defined, 6–7
ethos, 6–7, 60–62, 129, 252–54
Eucleides [Euclides], 16, 237n12
Eudoxus, mathematician, 240
Euripides, 110
Euthydemus, 27–35, 43, 71–73, 76–79, 83, 86, 91, 168
Euthyphro, 7, 23n16, 43–44, 49n2, 54–56, 58n11, 59, 180–81, 226, 253
evolutionary (versus creationist) view of human thought, 21n14, 101
example (paradigm), method of, 192n12, 203, 205–206, 206n6, 207–209, 213, 227, 268–69, 277, 279–80; definition of, 206

Fagan, Patricia, 96n7
Fallacy, 63ff; definition of, 66–67, 85; and sophistical refutations, 78, 80n13
Ferrari, G. R. F., 166
Ficino, Marsilio, 37n12
Field, G. C., 224, 240
Flusser, Vilém, 105
forensic rhetoric, 160, 163
formal logic, 15, 191
Forms, *see* Plato, his Forms
Forster, E. S., 67, 74
Fossheim, Hallvard, 177
Fowler, Harold N., 23n16, 41, 211, 235n8
Frank, Jill, 182n5
Frede, Michael, 244n21

Freeman, Kathleen, 93
Freese, John H., 98n9
Friedländer, Paul, 5, 188, 243–44
Futter, Dylan, 180n1

Gadamer, Hans-Georg, 86n27, 170–71
Gagarin, Michael, 159n6
Gallop, David, 259–60
Gass, William H., 93, 105
Geometry, 20, 240, 257, 262
Gergel, Tania, 91
Gill, Christopher, 172, 272n4, 273, 282, 290
Gill, Mary Louise, 174n18
Glaucon, 38, 150, 182, 186, 195, 213, 240, 244, 281; education of, 197–99, 261–63, 271n1, 279, 286
Glucker, John, 225n3
Golden, James L., 111n1, 113
Gonzalez, Francisco J., 75, 190n9, 273–74
Gorgias, historical figure, 17n4, 93, 110, 118, 119, 131–32, 135, 144, 215, 238; *Defense of Palamedes* 61–62, 146n14, 159–63; *Funeral Oration*, 116, 132; *Helen*, 99, 110, 157; *Olympic Speech*, 132; *On Not-Being*, 17, 109
Gosling, Justin, 214n12, 215, 282n15, 283n17
Graham, Daniel D., 236
Grassi, Ernesto, 111n1
Grimaldi, William, 70, 79
Griswold Jr., Charles, 136, 140, 176, 264n10, 266n15
Grote, G., 170
Grube, G. M. A., 69n7, 261
Guthrie, W. K. C., 18, 43n20, 170, 175

Hackforth, R., 136, 140, 166, 214, 215–16, 234–45, 263, 283n19, 285n20

Hacking, Ian, 64
Halliwell, Stephen, 111n1, 112, 119n7, 164, 165n11, 195n17, 198–200
Hamblin, Charles L., 64, 66
Harris, John P., 187
Havelock, Eric, 92, 100–101, 104, 230n2; and the oral state of mind, 137n3
Heidlebaugh, Nola, 17
Heracles, 253
Heraclitus, 42
Herrick, James, 111
Hesiod, 201
Hippias, 18, 70, 93–94, 138, 256
Hippocrates, companion of Socrates, 44
Hippocrates, physician, *Nature of Man*, 273n5
Hobbes, Angela, 39
Homer, 42, 151, 152m 181n3
hortatory argument, 6, 25–39, 44–47, 55, 57–58, 60, 71–72, 75, 90, 100, 112, 119, 141, 147, 169, 195, 203n3, 227, 290; distinguished from protreptic argument, 195n17
Hume, David on analogy, 208
Hutchinson, Douglas, 223
hypothesis, Method of, 230n3, 242–43, 249, 251–52, 257–61, 263, 265, 267–69

Images, 11, 157, 117, 190–98, 202, 208–209, 262, 268, 287, 289; of animals, 187; Socratic ambivalence towards, 190n1, 193
Indigenous knowledge, 12
informal logic, 63, 191
Iolaus, 253
Irani, Tushar, 105
Isocrates, 32, 92, 148, 152, 159, 164, 229; *Antidosis*, 149n18, 152n20; *Panathenaicus*, 124; *Panegyricus*, 109

Jarratt, Susan; 112
Jebb, R. C., 26n3, 152
Johnson, David, 96n7
justice, 37, 95, 120–30, 145, 150, 177, 179, 181, 183, 189, 213; and rhetoric, 9, 120–21, 132–33, 153, 164, 194n14, 200, 210–11, 218–19, 231

Kahn, Charles, 16, 21n13, 47, 61n18, 90, 195, 204, 226, 229, 235n9, 236–37, 239n19, 240, 249, 252, 252, 257, 261, 266n13, 273n6, 280n13, 281, 284, 286, 289
Kairos, 148–49
Kalligas, Paul, 290n22
Kastely, James, 114, 181, 186, 194, 201
Kennedy, George, 11n5, 92, 98–99, 111–12, 116, 129, 182n4
Kerferd, G. B., 5, 17, 43n20, 70, 91n4, 130n16
Kinneavy, James L., 148
Kranz, Walther, 93

Labyrinth, of statements, 1, 12, 44, 56–67, 59, 179, 181, 243, 253
Laches, 48–52, 54
Laertius, Diogenes, 17, 38n14, 140, 226
Lamb, W. R. M., 49n2, 96n8, 170n16
Leger, Gerard, 156
Leroi, Armand Marie, 247n26
Levett, Brad, 118n6, 158n4
Levett, M. J., 255n5
Lévystone, David, 96
Liddell, Henry, 47, 206n6
likelihoods (*eikoi*), as a type of evidence, 19, 98, 144n10, 146, 151, 162, 191
Lloyd, G. E. R., 165, 191–92, 206, 264n11, 269

Locke, John, 21–22
logos, in contrast with myth, 165; translated as "reason," 281; *see also* antilogoi
Luria, Alexander, 101
Lutoslawski, Wincenty, 15–16, 21n13, 65n4, 116, 155–56, 214n12, 239n19
Luzzatto, Maria Tanja, 118n6, 119n7
Lysias, 135–38, 141, 147, 148, 151–52, 233
Lysis, 59n12, 169–72

Magrini, J. M., 27
maieutic argument, 6, 12, 26, 38–41, 44–45, 47n1, 55, 57, 60, 90, 100, 119, 195, 203, 290
McAdon, Brad, 60n15
McCabe, Mary Margaret, 79, 85
McCoy, Marina, 114, 161n8, 163, 191n10, 194, 199
McLuhan, Marshall, 21, 158
McPherran, Mark, 241
Marion, Mathieu, 156n2, 227n5, 244
mathematical knowledge, 240–42
Mattéi, Jean-François, 167
Meletus, 53–54, 103–104, 159–61
Melian debate, 9, 124n11, 125, 127, 129, 182n5, 184, 186
Melissus, 272, 273n5
Melos, *see* Melian debate
Memory, 117, 136, 141, 144, 151; oral memory and writing, 167
Menexenus, 116n3, 117, 169–72
Meno, 58n11, 59, 133n19, 192, 226, 238–43, 261
Metaphor, 92, 199, 206; examples of, 26, 56, 77, 187, 197n18, 202, 279n12; of the midwife, 12, 25–27, 38–44, 290
Milton, John, *Paradise Lost*, 98n10
Minotaur, 179, 180n1

Misology, 49, 69, 253–54, 257, 261
Moravcsik, Julius M. E., 281
Morrow, Glenn R., 194
Most, Glenn W., 165n11
Mueller, Ian, 240
Muniz, Fernando, 281
Murray, James Stuart, 225n3
Myths, 92, 95, 128–29, 164–67, 192, 203, 291; of cicadas, 143, 166; of Er, 143, 182; eschatological, 128, 165; of Thamus and Theuth, 151, 166–67; and *logos*, 165

Nails, Debra, 70, 130n15
Natali, C., 169n15
Nehamas, Alexander, 23n18, 39n16, 136n2
Nicias, 48, 52
Nightingale, Andrea, 143, 182
nonliterate subjects, 21, 101n13
Notomi, N., 81
Nye, Andrea, 89

O'Grady, Patricia, 91n5
Odysseus, 161–63, 200
Ong, Walter, 8n4, 137
opposing arguments, *see* antilogoi
other*wise*, the, 12
Owen, David, 64

paralogism, *see* fallacy
Parmenides, 81–82, 172–76, 272, 275, 281
Pausanias, 180n
Peloponnesian war, 59, 124n11, 129
Pericles, 8, 123, 127, 128, 129–32, 147–48, 184, 232
Pernot, Laurent, 119n7, 201
personal experience, 55, 104
persuasion, 7, 27, 28–30, 35, 97, 101–102, 109–10, 114, 120, 167, 194, 211–12; Aristotelian, 167, 220; public, 95
Phaedo, 237n12, 252–53
Philodemus, *History of the Philosophers*, 15, 290n22
Philostratus, *Lives of the Sophists*, 131–32, 182
Pickard-Cambridge, Arthur, 20n12
Pindar, 135, 141
Plato, his Forms, theory of, 23, 68, 81–83, 140–42, 147, 172–75, 181, 198, 229, 241, 257–59, 263, 267n16, 271n1, 277, 281–82; as a theory of causation compared to a theory of mimesis or a theory of illumination, 252, 258n8; on writing, 105, 111, 136, 137n3, 166–67; religion 241–42
Platonic dialogues: chronology of, 16n1, 33, 38n15, 116, 155–56, 202n2, 214n12, 239n19, 272n3; *Alcibiades I*, 38n14, 96–97; *Alcibiades II*, 38n14; *Apology*, 7, 26, 43–44, 49, 53, 59–62, 86, 93, 97–104, 114, 117, 136, 156, 158–61, 163–64, 187, 238n16, 241; *Charmides*, 21n13, 23n17; *Cleitophon*, 37; *Cratylus*, 116, 225, 231, 265; *Crito*, 23n17, 56–57; *Definitions*, 11, 223, 225, 226n4, 258n9; *Euthydemus*, 27–33, 44, 48, 54n8, 58–59, 63n1, 64–65, 70–80, 82n1, 83–84, 86, 93, 116, 168, 195n17, 202, 207n8, 211–13, 239n19, 290; *Euthyphro*, 7, 23n17, 44, 49n2, 50n3, 54–56, 59, 179–81, 253, 261; *Gorgias*, 8–9, 92, 95, 111–12, 115, 118–33, 135, 136, 139, 144–45, 147–60, 153, 163–67, 177, 182, 184, 186, 202, 208, 211, 215–16, 218–20, 229, 231,

234, 239n19, 268; *Hippias Major [Greater]*, 23n17, 70, 94, 138, 256; *Hippias Minor [Lesser]*, 23n17, 94, 256n6; *Laches*, 23n17, 38n14, 47–55, 60, 211; *Laws*, 113, 155, 202, 204, 217–19, 269, 273; *Lysis*, 23n17, 38n14, 59n12, 169–72, 239n19; *Menexenus*, 27, 95, 115–17, 129, 147, 156, 158n5; *Meno*, 15, 23n17, 26, 50n3, 58n11, 59, 94, 116, 129, 133n19, 147n16, 163, 176, 192–93, 227, 237–43, 249, 251–52, 257, 259–61, 267, 281; *Parmenides*, 172–74, 176, 239n19, 263, 267n16, 283; *Phaedo*, 4, 22, 69–70, 92, 95, 104n16, 116n3, 165, 180n1, 191, 201n1, 227, 239n19, 241–42, 252–53, 256–57, 260–61, 267; *Phaedrus*, 9, 19, 21, 92, 98–99, 111–14, 116–17, 118n5, 119, 121, 132, 135–77, 182, 187–89, 195, 197, 200, 202–203, 205, 212, 217n16, 219–20, 231–34, 239n19, 241, 264n10, 265, 267, 271, 272n2; *Philebus*, 9, 27, 69n6, 111, 113, 133, 176, 202, 212n10, 213n11, 214–16, 219, 225, 234, 263–64, 266–67, 272–74, 282–86, 288, 290; *Protagoras*, 18n7, 23n17, 44, 94, 116, 129, 239n19, 268; *Republic*, 3, 4, 9–10, 12, 27, 32, 35–38, 49, 72, 92, 110, 114, 118, 120, 121, 124, 125, 129, 131, 132, 135n1, 143, 147, 148, 150, 155, 157, 165, 168, 177, 179–200, 201–202, 203, 205, 206, 208, 211, 212, 213, 214n12, 219, 220, 229, 230, 234, 235, 239n19, 240, 243, 248, 260, 261, 263, 264, 267, 268, 269, 271n1, 286, 290; *Statesman*, 9, 10, 111, 113, 114, 121, 132, 155, 167n13, 168, 172, 192,n12, 199, 202–209, 210, 212–14, 216, 219, 220, 225, 234, 235, 266, 268, 269, 272n2, 272n3, 272n4, 273–74, 275, 277–81, 282n15, 285–89; *Symposium*, 26, 36, 38, 44, 50n4, 90, 92, 104n16, 132, 139, 141n7, 163, 168, 170, 201, 239n19, 243; *Theages*, 38n14; *Theaetetus*, 16, 23n17, 26, 27, 38, 39–44, 60, 69, 80, 94, 95, 114, 135, 155, 174, 239n19, 255, 256, 263, 272, 273, 281; *Timaeus*, 155, 192, 202n2, 214, 269n17

Plotinus, *Enneads*, 271
Poetry, 110–11, 118, 181
Polemachus, 37, 135n1, 141, 182–83, 186
Polus, 94, 95, 118–25, 128, 131, 165, 231
Popper, Karl, 194n16
Poste, Edward, 67
Poulakos, John, 91
Prodicus, 93–94, 226
Protarchus, 213n11, 214–15, 225, 273, 282–89, 290
Protagoras, 17–18, 44, 80, 90, 92, 98, 110, 140, 144, 226; measure maxim, 41–42, 43n20, 94
protreptic argument, 6, 9, 25, 37, 195n17, 198, 212–13, 286

Quintilian, 8; *Institutio Oratoria*, 63

Ramus, Petr, 8n4
Rationality, model of, 85
recollection, theory of, 142, 241, 252, 254, 257–60, 266
Reeve, C. D. C., 23n16, 54n7, 57n10, 99, 181n3, 183n6, 238n15, 252n3, 263

Reeves, J., 150
refutations, *see* Socratic argument
relativism, epistemological, 94, 151
rhetoric, as aid to dialectic 114, 210–13, 216, 219–20; definitions, 11n5, 119–21, 126, 145, 150, 167, 200; dialogical, 176–77; *eikotic*, 142–45, 146, 149, 162, 182, 189; political, 126–27, 130, 133, 145n12; true, 127, 129, 142, 146–47
rhetorical, audience, 157; figures, 156–57; handbooks, 19, 100, 118, 144, 182; tradition, 19, 118, 135n1, 140, 148
rhetorical strategies, 9, 163, 176, 214; anticipation, 159–60, 162; apostrophe, 160, 162, 169; *praeteritio*, 103, 160–61, 163; ridicule, 159, 161–62; silence, 9, 157, 168–77, 188, 282n16; turning the tables, 159, 162
Rhys Roberts, W., 98, 111
Richards, I. A., 4
Ritter, Constantin, 15, 156
Robinson, Richard, 3–5, 15, 20–24, 47, 64, 65, 66n5, 68–69, 101, 192, 198n19, 208–209, 230, 231, 251, 252, 259–61, 264, 267, 269
Robinson, T. M., 18, 140
Roochnik, David, 186, 198n20, 266
Rosen, Stanley, 206n6
Rosenstock, Bruce, 112, 201n1
Ross, W. D., 247n27
Rossetti, Livio, 91
Rouse, W. H. D., 78
Rowe, Christopher, 7, 16n3, 89n1, 95, 136, 137n4, 157, 272n2
Rudebusch, George, 281
Runciman, W. G., 81n18, 83, 263
Ryan, Paul, 174n18
Ryle, Gilbert, 16n1, 18n7, 68, 215, 234n7, 238n14

Sachs, Joe, 90n2, 121n9
Sansone, David, 158–59, 163
Saunders, Trevor J., 217n15
Saxonhouse, Arlene, 187
Sayre, Kenneth, 281
Schiappa, Edward, 4n3, 10, 93, 119n7, 144, 226, 229, 230, 268
Schofield, Malcolm, 115n1, 116
Schreiber, S. G., 67
Scott, Dominic, 181n2
Scott, G. A., 47
Scott, Robert, 47, 206n6
self-deliberation, 69n6, 94, 97, 226, 255, 257
Seligman, Paul, 83
Sesonske, Alexander, 94, 100–104
Sextus Empiricus, 18n8
Shorey, Paul, 197, 198, 284, 286, 289
silence, *see* rhetorical strategies
simile, 40, 92, 179, 197
Simmias, 191, 252–53, 257
Simon the cobbler, 226
Sipora, P., 148, 149n18
Skemp, J. B., 202n2, 203, 204, 205, 210–11, 273n7, 278n11
Skeptics, school, 236
Slings, S. R., 37n12
Smith, Nicholas D., 53n6, 96, 97
Smith, Robin, 246, 248
Socrates, Socrates$_H$ and Socrates$_P$ distinction, 5; and mathematics 240, as mid-wife, 12, 25–27, 38–44; as non-teacher, 41, 55, 59, 238n16; Vlastos's distinction, 237–40
Socratic argument types, *elenchus*, 47–58; hortatory, 25–34; maieutic, 38–45; interior reasoning, 69–70
Socratic dialectic, 6, 24, 29n6, 34, 35, 54, 58, 62, 82n19, 89, 100, 172, 226, 231, 261, 263, 267; distinguished from Platonic dialectic, 60, 114, 212, 227, 234–43

Index | 317

Socratic method, 25, 26, 51, 113, 124, 159, 184, 190, 194, 208, 227, 234n7, 238n14, 242, 243, 283
Solmsen, Friedrich, 17, 19, 109–10, 220
Solon, 151, 152, 233
Songe-Møller, Vigdis, 177
sophism, *see* fallacy
Sophistic arguments, 31, 80n13, 102, 170; and fallacy, 77n12, 180; refutations, 65–67, 77, 78, 84–85, 100, 122
Sophists, 24, 37, 70, 91–95, 98; and humanism, 37–38, 188; threat of, 78–79, 84n23, 94
sophistry, definition of, 92, 93
Speusippus, 11, 223, 224
Sprague, Rosamund Kent, 28n1, 48n2, 65, 66n5, 74, 93, 99
Stavropoullos, Phoibos, 224n3
Stephanus, standard edition of Plato's works, 18n10, 230
Stoics, school, 236
Strauss, Leo, 186
Style, 33, 92, 109–10, 133, 144, 152n19, 155–58, 163; dialogical, 157, 164; imitative, 133n19, 163, 206
sumphonein, meaning in logical sequence, 4, 259, 261
syllogism, 15, 20–21, 22, 101n13, 236, 246

Talisse, Robert B., 235n9
Taplin, O., 168
Tarrant, Harold, 25n2, 40, 43, 44, 156n2, 239n17
Tate, J., 194n15
Taylor, A. E., 170, 273
Tell, Håkan, 91–92
Theodorus, 42, 44, 80, 272, 286
theoros, 143, 150, 161, 166, 180, 182

Theseus, 57, 180n1
Thompson, Roger, 148
Thompson, Wayne, 201n1
Thrasyllus, 156n2
Thrasymachus, 37, 95, 124, 131, 147, 168, 179–88, 189, 191, 193, 195, 198
Thucydides, *History of the Peloponnesian War*, 9, 124n11
Timmerman, David, 4n3, 10, 230, 268
Tindale, Christopher W., 12, 19n11, 61n17, 62n19, 66, 80n13, 86, 140n6, 161n8, 164n10, 202
Tisias, 98, 99, 144, 145, 146n15
Tomin, J., 40
Too, Yun Lee, 152n20
topos, 150, 245n3; see also *atopos*
Tuominen, Miira, 248
Translation, problems of, 3, 4, 93, 99

Usher, Stephen, 160

Vander Waerdt, Paul A., 90
Versenyi, L., 170
Vickers, Brian, 111, 112–13, 218, 234
Viidebaum, Laura, 135n1
virtue, seen in actions, 7–8, 49, 62, 103
Vlastos, Gregory, 5, 25n2, 33, 34, 355n9, 47, 192, 236, 237–42
Voegelin, Eric, 129

Walton, Douglas, 61n17; dialogue types, 11
Wardy, Robert, 111n1, 114, 118
Warman, M. S., 194
Waterfield, Robin, 5–6, 60n16, 99, 130n15
Wenzel, Joseph, 2
White, Nicholas P., 80n16, 82n20
White, Eric Charles, 149
White, Michael J., 240

White, Stephen, 182n5, 185–86
Woodruff, Paul, 39n16, 136n2, 256n7

Xenophon, 59n13, 90, 159, 161, 226, 237n12, 268; *Apology*, 161; *Memorabilia*, 25, 47, 190n9, 223–34, 241

Young, Charles, 47

Young Socrates, 80, 113, 203, 211–13, 225, 272, 274, 278–79, 286, 287–88, 289
Yunis, Henry, 179, 200

Zeller, Eduard, 116n2
Zeno, 16n1, 172, 272
Zuckert, Catherine H., 116n3, 117, 214n12, 239n19

www.ingramcontent.com/pod-product-compliance
Lightning Source LLC
Chambersburg PA
CBHW031705230426
43668CB00006B/117